Sensitive periods, language aptitude, and ultimate L2 attainment

Language Learning & Language Teaching (LL&LT)

The LL&LT monograph series publishes monographs, edited volumes and text books on applied and methodological issues in the field of language pedagogy. The focus of the series is on subjects such as classroom discourse and interaction; language diversity in educational settings; bilingual education; language testing and language assessment; teaching methods and teaching performance; learning trajectories in second language acquisition; and written language learning in educational settings.

For an overview of all books published in this series, please see
http://benjamins.com/catalog/lllt

Editors

Nina Spada
Ontario Institute for Studies in Education
University of Toronto

Nelleke Van Deusen-Scholl
Center for Language Study
Yale University

Volume 35

Sensitive periods, language aptitude, and ultimate L2 attainment
Edited by Gisela Granena and Mike Long

Sensitive periods, language aptitude, and ultimate L2 attainment

Edited by

Gisela Granena
Mike Long
University of Maryland

John Benjamins Publishing Company
Amsterdam / Philadelphia

The paper used in this publication meets the minimum requirements of
the American National Standard for Information Sciences – Permanence
of Paper for Printed Library Materials, ANSI z39.48-1984.

Library of Congress Cataloging-in-Publication Data

Sensitive periods, language aptitude, and ultimate L2 attainment / Edited by Gisela Granena,
         Mike Long.
      p.   cm. (Language Learning & Language Teaching, ISSN 1569-9471 ; v. 35)
Includes bibliographical references and index.
1. Second language acquisition. 2. Language awareness. 3. Communicative competence in
         children. I. Granena, Gisela. II. Long, Michael H.
P118.2.S465   2013
401'.93--dc23   2013000301
ISBN 978 90 272 1311 2   (Hb ; alk. paper)
ISBN 978 90 272 1312 9   (Pb ; alk. paper)
ISBN 978 90 272 7206 5   (Eb)

John Benjamins Publishing Co. · P.O. Box 36224 · 1020 ME Amsterdam · The Netherlands
John Benjamins North America · P.O. Box 27519 · Philadelphia PA 19118-0519 · USA

Table of contents

List of contributors

Niclas Abrahamsson
niclas.abrahamsson@biling.su.se
Stockholm University
Centre for Research on Bilingualism
Universitetsvägen 10C
10691 Stockholm
Sweden

Cylcia Bolibaugh
c_bolibaugh@alum.calberkeley.org
St. Mary's University College
Waldegrave Road
Twickenham
Middlesex TW14SX
United Kingdom

Emanuel Bylund
manne.bylund@biling.su.se
Stockholm University
Centre for Research on Bilingualism
Universitetsvägen 10C
10691 Stockholm
Sweden

Catherine J. Doughty
cdoughty@casl.umd.edu
Center for Advanced Study of Language
University of Maryland
Box 25
7005 52nd Avenue
College Park, MD 20742
USA

Fanny Forsberg Lundell
fanny.forsberg.lundell@fraita.su.se
Institutionen för franska
italienska och klassiska språk
Stockholms universitet
SE-106 91 Stockholm
Sweden

Pauline Foster
fosterp@smuc.ac.uk
St. Mary's University College
Waldegrave Road
Twickenham
Middlesex TW14SX
United Kingdom

Gisela Granena
ggranena@umd.edu
Program in Second Language
Acquisition
Jimenez Hall
University of Maryland
College Park, MD 20742
USA

Kenneth Hyltenstam
kenneth.hyltenstam@biling.su.se
Stockholm University
Centre for Research on Bilingualism
Universitetsvägen 10C
10691 Stockholm
Sweden

Scott R. Jackson
sjackson@casl.umd.edu
Center for Advanced Study
of Language
University of Maryland
Box 25
7005 52nd Avenue
College Park, MD 20742
USA

Judit Kormos
j.kormos@lancaster.ac.uk
Department of Linguistics
and English Language
Lancaster University
Lancaster LA1 4YL
United Kingdom

Michael H. Long
mlong5@umd.edu
Program in Second Language
Acquisition
Jimenez Hall
University of Maryland
College Park, MD 20742
USA

Maria Sandgren
maria.sandgren@psychology.su.se
Södertörns högskola
Institutionen för samhällsvetenskaper
Alfred Nobels allé 7
SE-141 89 Huddinge
Sweden

Katherine Spadaro
spadaro4@tpg.com.au
14 Ian St
Rose Bay NSW 2029
Australia

Medha Tare
mtare@casl.umd.edu
Center for Advanced Study of Language
University of Maryland
7005 52nd Avenue
College Park, MD 20742
USA

Karen Vatz
kvatz@casl.umd.edu
19 Pleasant St
Montpelier, VT 05602
USA

Introduction and overview

Gisela Granena & Mike Long
University of Maryland

Three decades of research on second language acquisition (SLA) have identified age of onset (AO), i.e. the age at which learners were first meaningfully exposed to the L2, as the variable that consistently accounts for the greatest proportion of variance (typically around 30%) in ultimate second language (L2) attainment. The second strongest predictor variable (typically accounting for 10%–20% of the variance), research has shown, is language aptitude. It is not surprising, therefore, that recent years have witnessed a surge of interest in the combination of age and aptitude as a powerful explanatory factor in SLA, and central to a viable SLA theory.

Research on maturational constraints on language learning has a long history, with well over 100 empirical studies published during the last 50 years (for review, see, e.g. DeKeyser 2012; Hyltenstam & Abrahamsson 2003; Long 1990, this volume; Meisel 2011; Montrul 2009). The inverse relationship between AO and achievement is one of the most widely attested and widely accepted findings in SLA. Some disagreement continues, however, as to the underlying causes of age differences; compare, e.g. Birdsong (2005) and Bongaerts (1999) arguing against maturational constraints, and DeKeyser and Larson-Hall (2005) and Meisel (2011) arguing in favor. Nevertheless, the preponderance of evidence points to the operation of a series of sensitive periods specific not just to linguistic domains (phonology, morphology and syntax, etc.), but to classes of linguistic features within domains (DeKeyser, Alfi-Shabtay & Ravid 2010; Granena 2012; Spadaro 1996, this volume). Supposed counter-evidence is generally the result of methodological problems with the studies concerned and/or faulty interpretation of findings (DeKeyser 2006; Long 2005, 2007b).

Researchers are gradually moving on from documenting sensitive period effects to studying alternative explanations for them. One idea, examined critically by Bylund et al. (this volume), is that first language (L1) entrenchment can explain the data. Another is that age differences are due to an age-related decline in the human capacity for implicit language learning, a decline that can be mitigated, but not overcome, by the influence of language aptitude. DeKeyser (2000) claims that high language aptitude is capable of supporting high, even near-native, levels of achievement, despite what he, like most contributors to this volume, takes to be biological barriers to genuine native-likeness in an L2.

Language aptitude has a lengthy track-record as a reliable predictor of *rate of instructed foreign language learning* (for review, see Dornyei & Skehan 2003; Granena 2012, this volume). The statistically significant correlations obtained in numerous studies have been between aptitude and speed of progress through the early stages of classroom language development. The strength of observed correlations has no doubt in part been due to the fact that the major standardized aptitude measures, such as the Modern Language Aptitude Test (MLAT) and the Language Aptitude Battery (LAB), load heavily on the same explicit and meta-linguistic abilities favored by traditional teaching approaches, with their emphasis on attention to linguistic code features rather than learning through communicative L2 use.

Also of interest to researchers, however, as well as to societies receiving ever larger numbers of immigrants who do not speak the receiving country's language(s), and to the immigrants themselves, is the relationship of aptitude to *ultimate attainment in naturalistic second language learning*, the primary focus of this book. Much SLA in this context will be implicit, not explicit, a function of years of natural exposure, meaning that different facets of aptitude can be expected to be relevant. Such considerations have led to a re-examination of language aptitude, once considered a unitary construct, with a view to identifying sub-components of greater or lesser importance in instructed and naturalistic settings (e.g. Bolibaugh & Foster this volume; DeKeyser & Koeth 2011; Dornyei 2005; Dornyei & Skehan 2003; Forsberg & Sandgren this volume; Granena 2012; Kormos this volume; Robinson 2002; Skehan 2002). It has also motivated some major recent studies of relationships among AO, aptitude and attrition (Bylund, Abrahamsson & Hyltenstam 2010), and of AO, language aptitude and L2 achievement in naturalistic settings (Abrahamsson & Hyltenstam 2008; DeKeyser 2000; Granena 2012; Granena & Long 2010, 2013).

The focus on ultimate levels of attainment, rather than rate of learning through the early stages, coupled with the rapidly increasing interest in many societies in producing learners with very high (professionally adequate) levels of L2 proficiency, has also stimulated research designed to produce new measures of language aptitude. For different reasons, the most significant new measures are the LLAMA (Meara 2005) and Hi-LAB, produced at the University of Maryland (Doughty et al. 2007). The LLAMA has several advantages, including its open access, availability in computer form, relatively short duration, and language independence, thus avoiding test takers' L1 literacy skills. Granena (this volume) reports a recently completed construct validation of this measure. Hi-LAB, as Doughty (this volume) explains, differs from its predecessors in two ways: it is designed to identify learners capable of achieving *advanced* levels of proficiency in foreign languages, especially in languages known to be particularly difficult to learn as a result of typological distance from the learners' L1. The Hi-LAB is informed by the past 40 years of research findings in cognitive science, as is visible in its departure from some of the constructs and kinds of measures employed in the older test batteries.

Given the long-standing research focus on relationships between AO and age of arrival in the target language community, aptitude is once again paired with age effects in the immigration studies, but this time as a predictor not just of rate of learning, but of ultimate L2 attainment. In this arena, the effects of each variable, AO and aptitude, and of both in combination, has fundamentally important implications for those concerned with SLA theory, but also with L1 maintenance, L1 attrition, language policy, and as discussed by Long (this volume), with the educational life chances of immigrants and ethnolinguistic minorities. In addition, as Vatz et al. (this volume) explain, matching students with measured language aptitudes of different kinds with appropriate instructional treatments, and avoiding inappropriate aptitude – treatment mismatches, shows considerable promise as a way of improving the effectiveness of classroom language learning and teaching.

Reflecting the history and state of the science, the book is divided into four sections. We start in **Section 1: Age differences and maturational constraints** with the most widely researched area to date. The findings of an inverse relationship between starting age and ultimate L2 attainment, and on sensitive periods for language acquisition, are robust, as Long sets out to show in Chapter 1, and as such, constitute a classic example of what the American philosopher of science Larry Laudan calls a 'problem' (Laudan 1977, 1996; Long 2007a), i.e. a salient, well attested, widely accepted, fact about the phenomenon of interest in need of explanation. The results for age effects were first established for phonology, morphology and syntax, but in recent years, have been extended to lexis and collocation. Studies in that domain are still scarce, however, making Spadaro's work, reported in Chapter 2, especially valuable. In the third chapter, Bylund, Abrahamsson and Hyltenstam consider the role of bilingualism as a potential alternative explanation for differences in ultimate attainment, concluding that explanatory roles for AO and the late starter's status as a bilingual need not be mutually exclusive.

The burgeoning interest in aptitude, inspired both by theoretical concerns and its classroom relevance, has led to increasing recent work on the construct, itself, and on the development of new measures. Both are the focus of **Section 2: Aptitude constructs and measures**. Of the newer instruments, the LLAMA (Meara 2005), a revised version of the Swansea LAT (Meara, Milton & Lorenzo-Dus 2003), has already figured in a number of SLA studies, despite not having been extensively standardized. In Chapter 4, Granena reports the results of an exploratory validation study that assessed the reliability of the LLAMA and explored its underlying structure. The results showed that internal consistency and stability in time were acceptable. A series of exploratory factor analyses further suggested that the test is measuring two different aptitude dimensions, analytic ability, a type of aptitude relevant for explicit language learning, and (sound) sequence learning ability, a type of aptitude relevant for implicit language learning. Examination of the components of language aptitude continues in Chapter 5, where Kormos examines connections among working memory, phonological short-term memory and language aptitude and describes how these cognitive abilities influence second language-learning processes, such as noticing, encoding in long-term memory, proceduralization and automatization. She also shows that some aptitude components can change as a result of intensive exposure to additional languages. In Chapter 6, Doughty describes the development, underlying constructs, and initial steps in the validation of a new measure of language aptitude, Hi-LAB, specifically designed to predict success at very advanced levels of L2 proficiency. Hi-LAB appears to be a direct, reliable measure, able to classify learners with known ultimate attainment levels correctly. The aptitude profiles that Hi-LAB generates have considerable diagnostic potential for tailoring L2 instruction.

The chapters in Section 1 established the robustness of findings on the timing and scope of age effects, the *explanandum*. Those in Section 2 considered recent work on a potential *explanans* for high-level achievement, apparent biological constraints notwithstanding, i.e. language aptitude, and recent work on its measurement. In **Section 3: Age, aptitude and ultimate attainment**, we turn to three empirical studies of the influence of aptitude in moderating age effects on high-level proficiency. Granena reports a study of long-term L2 achievement that showed an interaction between aptitude and GJT scores according to test modality. Bolibaugh and Foster find that differences in phonological short-term memory affect both rate and ultimate attainment in learning L2 collocations, conditioned as they are by both AO and learning context. Forsberg Lundell and Sandgren report a positive association between the phonetic memory/sound recognition dimension of aptitude, as measured by the LLAMA D, as well as certain social-psychological attributes, and high-level proficiency, also as measured by performance on a test of L2 collocations.

Finally, in **Section 4: Implications for educational policy and language teaching**, we consider the importance of work on age differences, language aptitude, and their interaction, in applied settings. Long argues that findings to date need to be brought to bear on such matters as the timing of foreign languages in schools and the provision of language instruction for immigrants cautiously, with explicit consideration of such matters as the status of the L1 and L2 as world languages, and of societal, familial and individual L2 aspirations and needs. Vatz, Tare, Jackson and Doughty provide a comprehensive, critical review of work to date on L2 aptitude-treatment-interaction (ATI) studies, with an emphasis on appropriate research design for future work in an area of considerable promise for improving the effectiveness of instructional programs for both learners and teachers.

Gisela Granena and Mike Long
University of Maryland
November, 2012

References

Abrahamsson, N., & Hyltenstam, K. (2008). The robustness of aptitude effects in near-native second language acquisition. *Studies in Second Language Acquisition, 30*, 481–509.

Birdsong, D. (2005). Interpreting age effects in second language acquisition. In J. Kroll, & A.M.B. de Groot (Eds.), *Handbook of bilingualism: Psycholinguistic approaches* (pp. 109–127). Oxford: OUP.

Bolibaugh, C., & Foster, P. (this volume). Memory-based aptitude for nativelike selection: The role of phonological short-term memory.

Bongaerts, T. (1999). Ultimate attainment in L2 pronunciation: The case of very advanced late L2 learners. In D. Birdsong (Ed.), *Second language acquisition and the critical period hypothesis* (pp. 133–159). Mahwah, NJ: Lawrence Erlbaum Associates.

Bylund, E., Abrahamsson, N., & Hyltenstam, K. (2010). The role of language aptitude in first language attrition: The case of prepubescent attriters. *Applied Linguistics, 31*, 443–464.

Bylund, E., Hyltenstam, K., & Abrahamsson, N. (this volume). Age of acquisition effects or effects of bilingualism in second language ultimate attainment?

DeKeyser, R.M. (2000). The robustness of critical period effects in second language acquisition. *Studies in Second Language Acquisition, 22*, 499–533.

DeKeyser, R. (2006). A critique of recent arguments against the critical period hypothesis. In C. Abello-Contesse, R. Chacón-Beltrán, M.D. López-Jiménez, & M.M. Torreblanca-López (Eds.), *Age in L2 acquisition and teaching* (pp. 49–58). Bern: Peter Lang.

DeKeyser, R.M. (2012). Age effects in second language learning. In S.M. Gass, & A. Mackey (Eds.), *The Routledge handbook of second language acquisition* (pp. 442–460). New York, NY: Routledge.

DeKeyser, R.M., Alfi-Shabtay, I., & Ravid, D. (2010). Cross-linguistic evidence for the nature of age-effects in second language acquisition. *Applied Psycholinguistics, 31*, 413–438.

DeKeyser, R.M., & Koeth, J. (2011). Cognitive aptitudes for second language learning. In E. Hinkel (Ed.), *Handbook of research in second language teaching and learning* (Vol. 2, pp. 395–406). London: Routledge.

DeKeyser, R.M., & Larson-Hall, J. (2005). What does the Critical Period really mean? In J.F. Kroll, & A.M.B. de Groot (Eds.), *Handbook of bilingualism: Psycholinguistic perspectives* (pp. 88–108). Oxford: OUP.

Dörnyei, Z. (2005). *The psychology of the language learner: Individual differences in second language acquisition*. Mahwah, NJ: Lawrence Erlbaum Associates.

Dörnyei, Z., & Skehan, P. (2003). Individual differences in second language learning. In C.J. Doughty, & M.H. Long (Eds.), *The handbook of second language acquisition* (pp. 589–630). Oxford: Blackwell.

Doughty, C.J. (this volume). Optimizing post-critical-period language learning.

Doughty, C., Bunting, M., Campbell, S., Bowles, A., & Haarmann, H. (2007). *Development of the high-level language aptitude battery*. Technical Report: Center for Advanced Study of Language. University of Maryland, College Park.

Forsberg, F., & Sandgren, M. (this volume). High-level proficiency in late L2 acquisition – Relationships between collocational production, language aptitude and personality.

Granena, G. (2012). *Age differences and cognitive aptitudes for implicit and explicit learning in ultimate L2 attainment*. Unpublished doctoral dissertation. University of Maryland.

Granena, G. (this volume, a). Cognitive aptitudes for second language learning and the LLAMA Language Aptitude Test.

Granena, G. (this volume, b). Reexamining the robustness of aptitude in second language acquisition.

Granena, G., & Long, M.H. (2010). Age of onset, length of residence, aptitude and ultimate L2 attainment in two linguistic domains. Paper presented at the 30th SLRF, College Park, MD: University of Maryland.

Granena, G., & Long, M.H. (2013). Age of onset, length of residence, language aptitude, and ultimate L2 attainment in three linguistic domains. *Second Language Research, 29*(1).

Hyltenstam, K., & Abrahamsson, N. (2003). Maturational constraints in SLA. In C.J. Doughty, & M.H. Long (Eds.), *The handbook of second language acquisition* (pp. 539–588). Oxford: Blackwell.

Kormos, J. (this volume). New conceptualizations of language aptitude in second language attainment.

Laudan, L. (1977). *Progress and its problems: Towards a theory of scientific growth*. Berkeley, CA: University of California Press.

Laudan L. (1996). A problem-solving approach to scientific progress. In L. Laudan (Ed.), *Beyond positivism and relativism. Theory, method, and evidence* (pp. 77–87). Boulder, CO: Westview.

Long, M.H. (1990). Maturational constraints on language development. *Studies in Second Language Acquisition, 12*, 251–285.

Long, M.H. (2005). Problems with supposed counter-evidence to the critical period hypothesis. *International Review of Applied Linguistics, 43*, 287–317.

Long, M.H. (2007a). Second language acquisition theories. In M.H. Long (Ed.), *Problems in SLA* (pp. 3–20). Mahwah, NJ: Lawrence Erlbaum Associates.

Long, M.H. (2007b). Age differences and the sensitive periods controversy in SLA. In M.H. Long (Ed.), *Problems in SLA* (pp. 43–74). Mahwah, NJ: Lawrence Erlbaum Associates.

Long, M.H. (this volume, a). Maturational constraints on child and adult SLA.

Long, M.H. (this volume, b). Some implications of research findings on sensitive periods in language learning for educational policy and practice.

Meara, P. (2005). *LLAMA language aptitude tests*. Swansea, UK: Lognostics.

Meara, P., Milton, J., & Lorenzo-Dus, N. (2003). *Swansea language aptitude tests (LAT) v.2.0*. Swansea, UK: Lognostics.

Meisel, J.M. (2011). *First and second language acquisition*. Cambridge: CUP.

Montrul, S. (2009). *Incomplete acquisition in bilingualism: Re-examining the age factor.* Amsterdam: John Benjamins.

Robinson, P. (2002). Individual differences in intelligence, aptitude and working memory during adult incidental second language learning: A replication and extension of Reber, Walkenfeld, and Hernstadt (1991). In P. Robinson (Ed.), *Individual differences and instructed language learning* (pp. 211–266). Amsterdam: John Benjamins.

Skehan, P. (2002). Theorizing and updating aptitude. In P. Robinson (Ed.), *Individual differences and instructed language learning* (pp. 69–93). Amsterdam: John Benjamins.

Spadaro, K. (1996). Maturational constraints on lexical acquisition in a second language. Unpublished doctoral dissertation. University of Western Australia.

Spadaro, K. (this volume). Maturational constraints on lexical acquisition in a second language.

Vatz, K., Tare, M., Jackson, S.R., & Doughty, C.J. (this volume). Aptitude-treatment interaction studies in second language acquisition: Findings and methodology.

PART I

Age differences and maturational constraints

Maturational constraints on child and adult SLA

Mike Long
University of Maryland

Claims for a biologically based schedule for language learning were first advanced 50 years ago. 100+ studies later, debates continue as to the existence, scope and timing of one or more sensitive periods for SLA. At least eight reasons can be identified for the lack of consensus, several of which appear to be without basis. They are discussed, along with ten more positive developments over the past decade, including research into the possibility that the very few learners who achieve near-native L2 abilities do so because of superior language learning aptitude(s).

1. Maturational constraints on language learning

The idea that language development is maturationally constrained, due to a loss of cerebral plasticity, was first suggested over 50 years ago by two Canadians, the neurologist Wilder Penfield and Roberts (1959). There followed Eric Lenneberg's (1967) postulation of a *critical period* (CP) for language acquisition closing at puberty, its effects most obvious in the accented L2 pronunciation of later starters. While initially framed by the Canadians within the context of first language acquisition (L1A) capacity, e.g. the prognosis at different ages for recovery from aphasia following brain injury, it was not long before research began to appear that was designed to test for age differences and CPs in second language acquisition (SLA) in normal populations. Since then, over 100 studies have appeared of relationships among age of first meaningful exposure to a foreign or second language, or age of onset (AO), various cognitive and environmental factors, and both rate of acquisition and ultimate level of L2 attainment.

Findings have been fairly consistent. There is now broad agreement that AO is the most reliable predictor of success in second language learning, but disagreement persists as to why. Lenneberg suggested that the loss of language-learning ability might be a function of lateralization, but it soon became apparent that this could not be the explanation, as research showed lateralization to be a process begun prenatally and complete by around age 5 (Hahn 1987; Krashen 1973).

The fact that the proposed explanation turned out to be wrong, it is worth noting, did not lead to rejection of the critical period idea, itself, and the lack of a clear biological explanation for maturational constraints today – or rather, the existence of rival explanations – should not, either. Scientists do not reject widely attested findings for lack of an explanation; identifying *problems* in Laudan's sense (e.g. Laudan 1996), and solving them, is a two-stage process.

2.   What is meant by a sensitive period for language development?

In most research on animal behavior, a *critical period* refers to a time of heightened sensitivity to environmental stimuli required to trigger some aspect of learning or development, including the *onset* (gradual increase), *peak* period, and *offset* (sharp decrease) of that sensitivity. In the case of human language learning, the child's sensitivity to subtle sound distinctions in natural languages is acute from birth, so there is no gradual onset; CPs for language start at 0. The years of peak sensitivity precede a period of gradual, not abrupt, decline, however – the offset – before closure of the CP, followed by a time from then until death in which the decline is slower and less noticeable, the flattening of the downward slope depending only partly on age, and more on other factors, such as amount of exposure, usually operationalized as length of residence (LOR), and the proportions of L1 and L2 use. The resulting shape is often referred to as a flattened, or stretched, Z (see Figure 1).

The term used in Figure 1 is sensitive period, not critical period. CPs in lower species are often very short, precisely specified, with little or no offset period

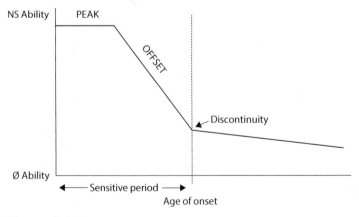

Figure 1. The stretched *Z*

before abrupt closure, and little or no variation at the level of individual animals. Stimulation, such as exposure to moving objects for imprinting in ducklings, or to light for the development of the visual cortex for vision in cats and flies, must often occur within periods measured in terms of hours or days, not years. However, even some of the clearest cases of CPs in the animal world, such as imprinting, are not *developmentally fixed*, i.e. genetically determined and impervious to environmental influence. (For definitions and detailed discussion, see Bornstein 1989). In contrast, sensitivity for language learning in humans exhibits residual plasticity after the period of peak sensitivity ends, and variability at the individual level. Individual differences (IDs) in such traits as language aptitude and intelligence, and differences in environmental conditions, including the linguistic environment for the language learner, can both vary far more than is the case for ducklings, fledgling zebra finches or de-winged walking flies. Contrary to the interpretation put on it by some critics, therefore, the absence of a sudden, *sharp*, almost vertical decline in ultimate L2 attainment for those who began exposure immediately after the period of peak sensitivity does not constitute counter-evidence to a proposed CP for SLA. For both these reasons, however – the gradual nature of the offset, and the degree of individual variation in human cognitive processes – it is preferable to think in terms of (multiple) *sensitive periods*, rather than critical periods, for SLA. *Sensitive period* (SP) is the term that will be used from here on, except when referring generically to "the CPH" (as if there were just one version) or quoting others who deal in *critical* periods.

By way of illustration, my own claim of a SP for L2 pronunciation has remained unchanged for over 20 years (see Long 1990: 280): native-like pronunciation of a second language or dialect is most likely (not guaranteed) for those with an AO between 0 and 6, still possible, but decreasingly likely, with an AO during the offset period from 6 to 12, and impossible for anyone with an AO later than 12. (Noticeable foreign accents in all but very early starters are so normal as no longer to cause surprise among SLA researchers, who instead are sometimes known to amuse themselves by identifying not just who is and who is not a NS, but the NNS's L1.) Beyond age 12, it seems that the degree of accentedness will depend on such factors as proportions of L1 and L2 exposure and use, motivation, and intensive training in pronunciation (Bongaerts 1999: 155), plus language aptitude, and so will only be indirectly and weakly related to increasing age, in the same way that other cognitive abilities tend to deteriorate over the life span, especially during a person's final years.

My claim of a SP for morphology and syntax has also remained unchanged: native-like morphology and syntax are most likely (not guaranteed) for those with an AO between 0 and 6, still possible, but decreasingly likely, with an AO during the slightly longer offset period from 6 to the mid-teens (15, plus or minus two), and impossible for anyone with an AO later than that. Beyond age 16 or 17, the degree of grammatical accentedness will, again, depend on such factors as the proportion of L1 and L2 exposure and use, language aptitude, motivation, and metalinguistic knowledge, and so will only be indirectly and weakly related to AO. To date, reviews show that despite occasional claims to the contrary, there have been no counter-examples to either claim that would stand up in court (see, e.g. DeKeyser & Larson-Hall 2005; Long 2005).

Full native-like L2 attainment, note, is claimed to be *possible* if sufficient exposure occurs during the SP – not guaranteed, as would be the case in L1A – precisely because of the heavier learning task the learner faces, in the form of two languages instead of one (see Meisel 2009, 2011). Thus, L2 learners exposed to the L2 during the SP who fail to achieve native-like abilities do not constitute counter-evidence to the hypothesized SPs for L2 pronunciation and grammar. The claim is not that everyone exposed before age X will achieve native-like abilities, but that no-one exposed after age X is capable of doing so. Thus, the SP claim for phonology can be falsified by unearthing a single subject first exposed to the L2 after age 12 able to perform with native-like pronunciation across an adequate sample of targeted and spontaneous L2 production, and that for morphology and syntax by a single subject first exposed after the mid-teens able to perform with native-like grammar on an adequate sample of off-line and, especially, on-line tasks. In my view, such abilities have yet to be documented in the SLA literature. The valuable series of studies by Bongaerts and colleagues (e.g. Bongaerts, Mennen & van der Slik 2000; Bongaerts, van Summeren, Planken & Schils 1997) has come closest to producing evidence of late starters capable of native-like pronunciation abilities. However, painstaking though they were, only the occasional subject among groups of exceptionally proficient learners screened into the studies was able to achieve native-like ratings, and then only on the basis of tiny, rehearsed speech samples from performance on tightly constrained tasks. I will return to the issue of ostensible counter-examples – individuals supposed to have achieved native-like abilities despite starting SLA after the close of a SP.

3.   Eight reasons for the lack of consensus on maturational constraints

After at least 100 studies over the past 40+ years, few, if any, researchers, including those who reject the notion of maturational constraints altogether, deny age of first meaningful L2 exposure, or AO, its status as the single most powerful predictor of ultimate L2 attainment. Agreement on maturational constraints, specifically SPs, as an *explanation* for age effects is a different matter. For key studies and reviews supportive of the existence of maturational constraints on SLA, see, e.g. Abrahamsson and Hyltenstam (2009), DeKeyser (2000, 2011, 2012), DeKeyser and Larson-Hall (2005), Granena and Long (2013), Hyltenstam and Abrahamsson (2003), Long (2005, 2007), Munnich and Landau (2010), Newport (2002). For studies and reviews recognizing the reality of age differences, but denying the existence of maturational constraints, see, e.g. Bialystok and Miller (1999), Birdsong (2005, 2006, 2009), Birdsong and Molis (2001), Herschensohn (2007), Muñoz and Singleton (2011), and Singleton (2005). At least eight reasons can be identified for the lack of consensus.

1. Alleged counter-evidence (a): Supposed lack of discontinuities in declining abilities

Statistically significant negative correlations are routinely obtained between AO and L2 proficiency in samples drawn from across the life-span, with AO typically accounting for about 30% of the variance in ultimate attainment in L2 grammar (e.g. Granena & Long 2010), and around 50% in pronunciation (e.g. Munro & Mann 2005). While evidence of age effects, such relationships are potentially problematic for SP claims. A recurring argument against the idea of maturational constraints (e.g. Birdsong 2005a; Birdsong & Molis 2001) is precisely that negative correlations in samples across the age range indicate steady and continuing declines with increasing age, rather than what is needed to substantiate claims for a SP, i.e. different degrees of decline, with *discontinuities* at specific ages, resulting in the so-called *flattened Z* or *flattened L* distributions depicted in Figure 1. If a SP closes at age X, the argument goes, there should be a steeper decline in ability during the offset period than the peak period, and little or no association between AO and ultimate attainment after X. Put another way, for a SP claim to go through, a *qualitative* difference must be shown in the strength of association between AO and ultimate attainment in the pre-X AO and post-X AO groups; the data should show a noticeable deterioration in achievement towards the end of the SP in question, not a monotonic decline across the full age range. Evidence consistent with a SP claim would be demonstrations of any or all of the following: achievement of nativelike abilities by some pre-SP, but no post-SP, starters, a lack of overlap between younger and older groups' scores, stronger inverse correlations between AO and ultimate attainment during the offset than after it, statistically significant differences between the long-term achievement of younger and older groups, or statistically significant differences between the older, but not the younger, groups' scores and those of NS controls. Evidence of *discontinuities* in the strength of the relationship between AO and ultimate attainment in younger and older groups is critically important.

Most findings of steady declines over the entire age span, with a *lack* of clear discontinuities in the rate of decline in abilities, come from studies that used self-report data from the US census (Bialystok & Hakuta 1999; Chiswick & Miller 2008; Hakuta, Bialystok & Wiley 2003; Munro & Mann 2005; Stevens 1999; Wiley, Bialystok & Hakuta 2005).[1] Chiswick and Miller, for example, conclude as follows:

> "A critical period, defined with reference to a discontinuity, that is, a *sharp*, statistically significant difference in English proficiency with respect to adjacent ages at migration, does not appear to exist for self-reported spoken English among immigrants in the USA." (2008:27, emphasis added)

Quite apart from the irrelevance, for reasons discussed earlier, of the 'sharpness' of the decline, it is surprising that some reviewers have attached such importance to the *census studies*. It is possible that they are overly impressed by the large n-sizes, sometimes in the millions, and forget issues of validity related to self-assessed abilities, especially linguistic abilities, as well as the maxim for data analyses of all kinds: junk in, junk out, however much junk it may be. There are at least seven problems with the *census studies*.

First, several reviewers (DeKeyser 2006:52–55; DeKeyser & Larson-Hall 2005; Long 2005; Stevens 2004) have commented on the notorious unreliability of self-assessed language proficiency in general, and in this context in particular. Ross (1998) reports an average correlation between actual proficiency and self-assessed abilities of about .5, meaning that shared variance is an unacceptably low 25%, with 75% of the data *noise*. Second, the widespread belief among the general population that younger is better for language learning, DeKeyser and Larson-Hall (2005:97–98) observed, is likely to be reflected in census responses, whereas there is no such widespread idea of a sharper decline in ability at one or more specific ages. Third, they pointed out, the five-point scale in the census that respondents must use to evaluate their use of English – "not at all," "not well," "well," "very well," and "speak only English" – is virtually guaranteed to produce misleading data. Many immigrants no longer use their L1, but the fact that they therefore check "speak only English" does not necessarily mean that they speak it better than bilinguals who report that they speak English "well" or "very well," yet that is what the scale implies. Fourth, DeKeyser (2006)

---

1.   An advantage for adults over children reported by Bialystok (1997) appears to have been due to inadequate LOR, i.e. opportunity for the children's long-term advantage to show itself. The anomalous finding by Birdsong and Molis (2001) of a statistically significant decline in GJT scores in their adult group – a stronger decline, even, than those in their child and adolescent starters – appears to have been largely due to a ceiling effect in the younger group. For detailed methodological critiques of the study, see DeKeyser (2006); DeKeyser and Larson-Hall (2005); Long (2005).

notes, when immigrants rate their own proficiency, they are naturally thinking in terms of general communicative ability, not underlying phonological, grammatical, or lexical ability, which is what "the CPH" speaks to. Fifth, if there are multiple sensitive periods, as some have proposed, or even differences within domains, a single self-rating makes little sense. Sixth, the census does not assess age at immigration/age on arrival (AoA) in the target language environment, meaning that researchers using census data to test some (usually unspecified) version of "the CPH" have to estimate AoA by subtracting LOR from respondents' age at the time they responded to the census. It is not possible to do that with any accuracy, given that the census does not ask for the exact year of immigration, but instead, has respondents check the relevant multi-year interval. For those with at least 10 years in the US (so sufficient LOR for ultimate attainment to be assessed), the intervals provided vary from five years ("1975 to 1979"), to ten ("1950 to 1959"), or more ("before 1950"). Seventh, I would add, the census does not ask about knowledge of English *before* immigration, or AO. DeKeyser (2006) concludes that neither the independent variable, AoA, nor the dependent variable, English proficiency, is measured with any precision. In sum, it is not clear that the census-data-based studies have any scientific standing as tests of "the CPH".

In any case, fortunately for those of the SP persuasion, there is ample evidence consistent with the existence of *qualitative* changes in the rate of decline necessary for a credible SP claim, although not, of course, of the *abrupt, sharp* decline often seen with lower animals. Detailed reviews are available in DeKeyser (2011, 2012), DeKeyser and Larson-Hall (2005), and Hyltenstam and Abrahamsson (2003). In long-term studies of grammatical attainment, when younger starters' oral grammaticality judgment test (GJT) scores are compared with those of older starters, the negative correlation between AO and proficiency is consistently stronger in the younger than in the older group (see Table 1):

Table 1. Relationship between AO/AoA and oral GJT scores

Study	Relationship AO/AoA-oral GJT scores
Johnson and Newport (1989)	−.77 across whole sample −.87 AoA below 16 −.16 AoA above 16
Flege et al. (1999)	−.71 for AO below 15 −.23 for AO above 15
DeKeyser (2000)	−.63 across whole sample −.26 for AoA below 16 −.04 for AoA above 16

(*Continued*)

Table 1. (Continued)

Study	Relationship AO/AoA-oral GJT scores
DeKeyser et al. (2010)	English −.17 for AO below 18 −.71 for AO above 18 Hebrew −.12 for AO below 18 −.51 for AO above 18
Granena and Long (2013)	−.09 for AO 3–6 −.43 for AO 7–15 −.17 for AO 16–29

The same patterns are observed with written GJT scores, e.g. −.54 across the whole sample, and −.73 for AoA below 15, in Johnson (1992).

A limitation of such results is that differences in the strength of correlations in and of themselves are insufficient to show qualitative changes in the slopes, although the strikingly different relative magnitude of the correlations in most studies suggests that statistically significant differences could have been found between them. Since SP claims entail predictions about changes in the slopes across the age range, as in the *flattened Z*, it is the slopes that need to be compared, using regression and beta coefficients (see Baayen 2008: 214–222). Researchers can use F-tests to decide whether a model incorporating breakpoints and two or more slopes fits the data better than a more parsimonious single-slope model, which would be all that was needed to reflect a decline closer to gradual and linear across the age range. Few studies have gone beyond simple correlation coefficients, but one that did was Granena and Long (2013). Multiple linear regression analyses showed that a regression model with two breakpoints provided a significantly better fit to the data than a model without breakpoints for each of the three language domains examined in the study: lexis and collocation ($F(2,61) = 3.423, p = .039, R^2$ change = .04), morpho-syntax ($F(2,61) = 3.191, p = .048, R^2$ change = .04), and phonology ($F(2,61) = 4.784, p = .012, R^2$ change = .05). The increase in variance that the more complex models accounted for was statistically significant, although only around 5%, probably due to the loss of degrees of freedom resulting from the additional parameters in the model, for which a larger sample size could compensate.

With oral and/or written *production* tests, depending on the kind of comparison, one again sees strong negative correlations between AoA and grammar scores, e.g. −.57 (Oyama 1978), and −.74 (Patkowski 1980), and statistically significantly poorer performance by adult starters than NS controls (Sorace 1993), often with no overlap between their scores (Coppieters 1987). An apparent counter-example

(Montrul & Slabakova 2003) probably found 22 of 64 subjects performing within the NS range because the data were obtained from an untimed written test of the kind conducive to the retrieval of explicit knowledge and unsuitable for assessing whether late L2 learners possess native-like, integrated, i.e. implicit, knowledge. Such tests may also interact with subject selection, especially when, as was the case, participants have been selected from among language instructors, professors, and college students in language programs.

The picture for phonology is similar, although the relevant age groups are different. The discontinuities occur earlier than those for grammar. Strong negative correlations are observed across the age-range between AO and global pronunciation (accentedness) ratings, e.g. $-.76$ (Patkowski 1980), $-.85$ (Yeni-Komshian, Flege & Liu 2000), and $-.77$ (Granena & Long 2010). Strong positive correlations are observed between AO and error rate, e.g. .69 (stories) and .83 (paragraph) (Oyama 1976), .81 (Thomson 1991), and .66, with subjects with AO < 6 all achieving native-like abilities (Tahta, Wood & Loewenthal 1981). AoA accounted for 60% of the variance in scores in Flege, Munro & MacKay (1995), with no native-like achievement by subjects with an AO above 16. When AO-defined groups are compared *within* studies, earlier starters always do better than later starters, and the AO – ultimate attainment relationship is stronger in the younger than older groups, e.g. $-.62$ for AoA below 12, and $-.50$ for AoA above 12 (Flege, Yeni-Komshian & Liu 1999). These are merely a sample of such findings of discontinuities in grammar and phonology. For additional examples, see DeKeyser (2011, 2012), and DeKeyser and Larson-Hall (2005). For different interpretations of several of these findings, see Birdsong (2005: 115–120).

The situation with lexis and collocations is less clear, mostly due to the scarcity of such research and the different ways variables have been defined and measured. The few studies to date suggest that vocabulary *size* is unrelated to AO, and, as in L1A, is largely a function of amount of exposure (LOR, etc.), IQ, and range of L2 use, as well as educational level and (professional) occupation (Mulder & Hulstijn 2011). There seem to be maturational constraints on sensitivity to priming (Silverberg & Samuel 2004), however, and on the acquisition of vocabulary, idioms and collocations (Abrahamsson & Hyltenstam 2009; Granena & Long 2013; Hyltenstam 1988, 1992; Lee 1998; Spadaro 1996, this volume). The evidence of a SP for these areas, with peak sensitivity from 0 to 6, and an offset ending somewhere between those for phonology and grammar, probably around age 9 or 10, is limited, but fairly consistent.

In one of the first studies of its kind, Hyltenstam (1992), subjects were 12 Swedish NS controls and 24 highly proficient 17- and 18-year-old bilinguals, half L1 speakers of Spanish, and half of Finnish, selected by their teachers as not readily identifiable as NNSs. 16 had started learning Swedish before age six, and eight after age 7. They completed oral retellings of four prepared texts and an unspeeded written composition based on an excerpt from a silent Charlie Chaplin film. The number of lexical errors in the two L1 groups was statistically significantly higher than in the Swedish control group, both in the oral and written data ($p < .025$), but there was no difference between the two L1 groups. 10 of the younger starters performed on a par with the NS controls; none of the later starters did. There were two main kinds of lexical errors: "close approximations" to target forms, sometimes involving frequent, as well as infrequent, words and phrases, and "contaminations," where two or more Swedish forms were combined to produce a non-existent one. There were 21 such errors in the control data, 59 in the L1 Finnish speaker corpus, and 70 in the L1 Spanish speaker corpus. Grammatical errors among the L2 groups were infrequent, but included quite basic points, such as gender agreement on definite and indefinite articles (*den* for *det*, and *ett* for *en*), choice of reflexive and non-reflexive pronouns, violation of the verb-second constraint in Swedish, and adverb placement. Such errors were rare in the NS data, and usually clearly performance slips. Hyltenstam argued that the differences between NS and NNS groups in the frequencies (not types) of lexical errors, especially lexical errors with high frequency lexical items, and both the frequency and type of grammatical errors, e.g. word order and verb tense forms, support the claim for SPs for areas other than phonology and grammar.

In a second major study, Spadaro (1996, this volume) also found clear evidence of age effects in the learning of L2 vocabulary and collocations. She concluded that her results were consistent with the operation of a sensitive period for lexical development, with a peak from birth to around age six, visible even in highly advanced learners like those she studied, and with syntagmatic and collocational links obtaining between words an important area for continuing research. Spadaro's findings were broadly replicated in a study by J. Lee (1998) of 15 monolingual NSs of "standard English" and 45 Korean L2 speakers of English.

In a study of the acquisition of Spanish phonology, morpho-syntax and lexis and collocations by 65 long-term Chinese residents in Spain whose AO ranged from 3–29, Granena and Long (2013) used six measures of participants' knowledge of lexical units and lexical phrases – idioms, set phrases and word constellations that are determined by language-specific sub-categorization rules and selection restrictions – modeled on those developed by Spadaro. They found that the decline in the lexical domain took place later than in the phonological domain, but before that in the grammatical domain. As shown by the significant negative correlation in the AO 7–15 group ($r = -.59$, $p = .001$), but non-significant correlation in the AO 3–6 group ($r = -.22$, $p = .361$), followed by a more gradual decline thereafter in the AO 16–29 group ($r = -.44$, $p = .066$), there was evidence of the clear discontinuities in the data, here around AOs 7 and 16, necessary for a SP claim to go through. While only very early starters in the AO 3–6 group were able to score within the NS range in pronunciation, two participants in the AO 7–15 group scored within the NS range in lexis and collocation, each with an AO of 9. The latest AOs at which there was evidence of native-like attainment were 5 in phonology, 9 in lexis and collocation, and 12 in morpho-syntax. These findings are consistent with the claimed existence of multiple SPs for different language domains (Long 1990; Meisel 2011; Schachter 1996; Seliger 1978), as shown by different AO-ultimate attainment functions.

Aptitude in the Granena and Long study was positively related to learners' L2 lexical and collocational abilities in the late (AO 16–29) group, but not to their command of morphology and syntax. The suggestion is that developing knowledge of vocabulary items and collocations are cases of item-based learning, as opposed to the predominantly rule-based learning of grammar, and as with native speakers, of a process that continues throughout the life-span. Since item-based learning is the kind for which the implicit learning capacity declines in adults (Hoyer & Lincourt 1998), a greater decline is predictable in the capacity for acquiring new lexis and collocations than morpho-syntax. It is noteworthy that Flege et al. (1999) also found that LOR predicted command of lexically based items, but not rules. Aptitude is compensating for AO effects in lexis and collocations, but not in morpho-syntax because, barring low frequency and otherwise perceptually non-salient grammatical examples, rule-learning is completed (or is unlikely to occur at all) within the shorter period (seemingly 2–5 years) for which LOR is relevant.

The supposed lack of discontinuities in declines in ultimate attainment, and the fact that declines continue (more slowly) beyond the close of supposed SPs, constitute two aspects of the first kind of putative counter-evidence to claims of maturational constraints on SLA, leading to the lack of consensus. In fact, as we have seen, the evidence for discontinuities is rather robust. The fact that gentler declines continue throughout the life-span is to be expected as a by-product of the normal aging process. Sherwood et al. (2011) have shown that homo sapiens differs from other primates in that gray matter in the human frontal lobe shrinks by an average of 14%, and gray matter in the hippocampus by an average of 13%, between the ages of 30 and 80, and white matter in the frontal lobe by about 24% during the same period. (Alzheimer's disease afflicts close to 50% of people in the USA over the age of 85.) The white matter shrinkage is especially severe between 70 and 80, and potentially very important for a decline in language-learning ability, as it is what supports connections between areas of the brain involved in the transmission of information during problem-solving and other complex tasks. Declines observed beyond the offset of various SPs are presumably a function of the general aging process, and again, not counter-evidence to the idea of maturational constraints.

2.   Alleged counter-evidence (b): Post-SP native-like attainment

The second type of alleged counter-evidence consists of cases of individuals who are claimed to have achieved native-like abilities despite having started too late to do so if SPs are real. DeKeyser (2006), DeKeyser and Larson-Hall (2005), and Long (2005) have pointed out that each case has a fairly straightforward alternative explanation, usually the result of methodological problems in the original studies. Also, while some studies have documented the achievement of very high levels of proficiency by late starters, the individuals concerned have all been near-native, not native-like, especially when subjected to close linguistic scrutiny (Abrahamsson & Hyltenstam 2009).

Two American women's Arabic abilities documented by Ioup et al. (1994) were very impressive, but as the original researchers reported, near-native, not native-like, in some areas. The performance of some late starters studied by White and Genesee (1996) on a written GJT and a written sentence-combining task did not correlate with AoA, and was statistically non-significantly different from that of a NS control group. However, the lack of correlation was unsurprising, given the lack of variability in the near-native scores. In addition, the two tasks employed were narrow measures of *language-like* behavior (far less than would be required to show genuinely native-like abilities), and AO in Montreal (where compulsory ESL usually begins at 9 or 10 and English is hard to avoid on the streets and in the mass media) is well below the often claimed closure of a sensitive period for grammar in the mid teens (see, e.g. DeKeyser 2000; Granena & Long 2010; Johnson & Newport 1989; Long 1990; Patkowski 1980).

In a very impressive, methodologically rigorous study (Van Boxtel 2005; Van Boxtel, Bongaerts & Coppen 2005), Van Boxtel tested 43 very advanced learners of L2 Dutch with a mean AoA of 23. She identified four – two speakers of German, one of French, and one of Turkish – with AoA in the Netherlands age 12 or later who could perform within the NS range on both a 20-sentence oral elicited imitation (EI) task and a 190-item, computer-delivered, unspeeded, sentence-preference test focusing on (phonologically non-salient, and occurring in non-salient, non-initial position) dummy subjects in Dutch. NS controls showed considerable inter- and intra-subject variation on both tasks. If dummy subjects produced by a NNS on the EI task were also produced by at least one NS, it was considered to fall within the NS range. With the preference task, NNSs were scored as either conforming or not conforming to the dominant (90% +) NS pattern. NSs outperformed all three

L2 groups on all nine categories of Dutch dummy subject constructions, with the German and Dutch subjects behaving quite similarly to, and the Turkish group quite differently from, the controls, apparently as a function of typological proximity to, or distance from, Dutch. (Turkish does not have dummy subjects at all.) At the individual level, subjects with z-scores greater than –1.96 were considered to fall outside the NS range. A total of four subjects – two with German L1, one with French L1, and one with Turkish L1 – performed within the NS range across all nine categories on both measures. Van Boxtel (p.c. 11/24/2011) reports their AO as 32 and 35 for the two German speakers, 14 for the French speaker, and 12 for the Turkish speaker.

While Van Boxtel et al. report their findings as counter-evidence to "the CPH," there are two, and possibly three, potential reasons to disagree. First, both measures involved language-like (small 'm'-monitored) behavior; the sentence-preference task was also unspeeded, and off-line. (There is no suggestion here that meta-linguistic knowledge could have been employed, as some of the rules are sufficiently complex to have eluded linguists to date.) Second, while 12 (puberty) is the age Van Boxtel et al. (2005: 376) assigned to the presumed closure of a critical period for L2 syntax (more evidence of the importance of specifying which version of "the CPH" is under test), it is earlier than my own and others' hypothesized closure of a SP for grammar in the mid-teens. Both the French and Turkish speaker would not constitute counter-examples to that (fairly standard) version of "the CPH." The performance of the two German participants clearly does constitute potential counter-evidence, however. The very close typological proximity and mutual intelligibility of German and Dutch might be assumed to render the results difficult to interpret, but Van Boxtel (p.c. 5/8/2012) points out that there are quite significant differences with respect to dummy subjects. Dutch has *0*, *er* and *het*, whereas German only has *0* and *es*, and no distinction like that in Dutch between *er* (there) and *het* (it) that Germans consequently have to learn. Also, German has *es* in combination with specific subjects, whereas Dutch does not. Third, showing native-like performance with a single syntactic construction, albeit with nine variants, would not warrant a conclusion that subjects had native-like syntax, i.e. were native-like across the board.

Care is needed here, however. It would be unwarranted and counter-productive for scientific progress for defenders of SPs to dismiss every finding of apparent native-like attainment by post-SP starters as inadequate counter-evidence on the grounds that other structures were not tested. Continuing too far down that path, a finding that an individual had been identified who was native-like on ten structures might eventually be dismissed on the grounds that if only an eleventh had been studied, he or she might have failed. Clearly, rational judgment is required. While one structure might not be considered sufficient, two or three might be. If the structure(s) concerned were absent or markedly different from those in the individual's L1, a result might be considered more decisive. If the structure(s) were complex (as was the case in Van Boxtel's study), a result would carry more weight, and so on.

Van Boxtel's results are striking, especially as the target dummy subject constructions are known to be very difficult for learners of Dutch, significantly different from French and Turkish, and to have to be learned implicitly because rarely taught. Van Boxtel reports (2005: 99) that the subjects who passed as NSs on one or both measures were typically highly educated individuals who had arrived in Holland in their early 20s, were in their 40s when tested, i.e. had considerable LOR, and had all "either studied a language or worked in an environment where language plays an important role," e.g. were translators, a language teacher, or a linguist. Exposure to massive input, alone, did not differentiate those who passed as NSs and those who did not. Van Boxtel et al. suggest (2005: 375) that the important background variables hinted at a role for general metalinguistic awareness, or language aptitude (Van Boxtel 2005: 126), although not aptitude used to obtain awareness of the dummy subject constructions, for participants' comments to Van Boxtel showed they lacked explicit knowledge of the (very complex) rules they applied.

Van Boxtel has raised another potentially very important point about a usually unstated corollary of defenses of SPs when findings like hers of near-native or native-like performance on a single structure are rejected as counter-evidence. She writes:

> "It seems to me that if we approach the CPH like that, we are drifting too far away from the biological concept. Please keep in mind the shape of the curve that a CPH normally has … There should be a flattening/plateau at a very low level. Late second language learners who are almost native-like or native-like, but not in every domain, do not fit that pattern. If we look at song birds for example, it is not the case that song birds who do not hear the song of their own species, start singing a song that is almost like the full song of their species, but only has one different tone or something. They will sing only a very basic song. I only know examples that are even more extreme (like vision in cats, imprinting in ducklings). It would be interesting if proponents of the CPH would come up with other examples from biology which show a pattern that resembles the one we found for L2 learning."   Van Boxtel (p.c. 10/21/2011)

These comments take us back to the earlier discussion of the importance of differentiating critical and sensitive periods. It is true that the capacity for human language learning does not decline suddenly and fatally, like various features of development in other animals. However, that does not in and of itself argue against the hypothesis that human language development is maturationally concerned. Rather, it speaks to the gradual nature of the offset in language learning capacity and to the importance of individual differences, such as language aptitude, of kinds not found in lower animals. Moreover, as Van Boxtel (p.c. 10/21/2011) also recognizes, opponents of sensitive periods need to explain how it is that, in the hypothesized absence of any biological schedule for language learning, all but the most severely intellectually impaired children achieve native-like abilities in the L1 provided simply that they are exposed to the language early enough.

In another narrowly focused study of late L2 attainment, this time of the intersection of morpho-syntax and pragmatics, Donaldson (2011) examined the grammatical accuracy and pragmatic appropriateness of left-dislocation to mark topic in French. Participants were 10 self-described very advanced speakers of English, resident in France for at least four years, screened into the study as the most accomplished in an initial pool of 20 volunteers. Donaldson reports (2011:411) that "native-like phonology was not a criterion," presumably indicating that some, at least, exhibited non-native-like accents. Age of first instruction (AOI) was between 10 and 14 in eight of 10 cases; AoA was 16 and 17 in two cases, and 20 or above in the other eight. This means that the only two subjects who constituted clear test cases for a claimed SP for grammar closing in the mid-teens were A1, with an AOI of 21 and AoA of 23, and A8, with an AOI of 16 and AoA of 21. The primary data base consisted of transcribed recordings of informal conversations between the subjects and long-standing conversational partners (friends, spouses, etc.) of their own choosing. That the recorded talk did indeed reflect informal colloquial French was ascertained by checking that items in a list of well-documented features of such French were present in the samples in appropriate quantities. This is a positive methodological innovation, as it means that one can assume that whatever abilities the subjects demonstrated were unmonitored samples of genuinely spontaneous speech. Subjects' intuitions regarding left-dislocation (LD) were assessed via two written felicity judgment tasks. In the first, they had to judge the naturalness of utterances using LD in short snatches of dialog; in the second, they had to indicate their preference for left- or right-dislocated responses in similar short exchanges.

Despite the fact that LD is relatively rare in English, a stylistically marked informal feature in French, and rarely taught, performance by the NNSs and NS controls was comparable on every measure. The two groups produced roughly equivalent numbers of LD tokens (473 by the NSs, 410 by the NNSs, in comparable overall quantities of talk), and roughly equivalent proportions of LDs encoding various grammatical categories (subjects, direct and indirect objects, etc.), and used the constructions appropriately and in the same ways as the NS controls.

The patterns were equivalent even in cases where English and French LD usage differ (brand new referents occur in LD in English, but not in French, and the opposite for evoked referents).The groups also performed equivalently (i.e. non-statistically significantly differently) on both tests of intuitions. In contrast to Sorace's findings for auxiliary selection in Italian (Sorace 1993) and for assigning anaphor for ambiguous subject pronouns (Sorace & Filiaci 2006), where near-native NNSs produced indeterminate judgments, the corpus data revealed no indeterminacy concerning discourse functions of French LD in Donaldson's subjects, and the two written tests showed their intuitions to be neither indeterminate nor divergent. Finally, the NNSs neither underused nor overused LD compared to the NS controls. Donaldson concludes that his subjects demonstrated native-like competence on LD, but he is careful to state (2011: 426) that "Finally, no claims are made about the near-natives' ability to pass as native speakers." This is appropriate, given (i) the relative ease of LD, (ii) the fact that this was the only structure examined, and as noted earlier, (iii) only two subjects had sufficiently late AOs and AoAs to make them relevant test cases.

Perhaps the most widely cited research of this type in recent years – ostensible counter-evidence to the operation of maturational constraints in *any* linguistic domain – is an unpublished Harvard doctoral dissertation by Marinova-Todd (2003). 12 post-adolescent learners – fully 40% of a sample of 30 – were reported to have been found capable of native-like performance in English, not just on one or two narrow, language-like tasks, but on a wide variety of tests of their phonological, lexical, grammatical, and sociolinguistic abilities. A potential death sentence for the idea of maturational constraints, this is clearly a study that warrants careful examination.

Marinova-Todd's work involved two groups. The first consisted of 30 native English-speaking controls, graduate students (mostly at Harvard) with a mean age at testing (AT) of 30. The second comprised 30 very advanced learners of English with a mean AT of 34, graduate students (also mostly at Harvard) from a variety of L1 backgrounds, who had been identified by English NSs as native-like speakers of English. They had a mean LOR of 10 years (range: 5–20), mean AO (usually, formal EFL instruction in their countries of origin) of 13 (range: 10–21), and mean age of arrival (AoA) in the USA of 22 (range: 16–31). (Note that without knowing anything about the study's findings, the fact that the average AO was 13, with a range of 10–21, means that the results for many subjects, whatever they might be, would be irrelevant as test cases for claims of SPs with closures beyond those ages.)

Marinova-Todd compared the two groups' performance on a broad range of tasks.

3.1   Phonology

1. After rehearsal, reading aloud a paragraph from a literary novel
2. Spontaneous speech, i.e. picture-guided retelling of a Frog Story (a task of which some might be wary as a means of eliciting a sample of truly spontaneous speech)

Three graduate students, "native speakers of standard American English" (sic) (2003: 62), rated one-minute excerpts from each task, using a five-point scale:

5 – sounds like a NS of standard American English
4 – sounds like a NS with a possible regional accent/dialect
3 – neither 2 nor 4
2 – sounds like a NNS with a minor accent
1 – sounds like a NNS with a heavier accent.

It should be noted that there is no such thing as standard *spoken* English, that *spontaneous speech* here referred to planned, picture-guided, oral production, and that three raters is a very small number on which to obtain a normal distribution. Intra-rater reliability was not reported. Overall agreement on the NS and NNS scores was .74. Inter-rater reliability on the NNS scores, alone, was very low ($r = .53$), meaning that 72% of the data on NNS ratings was noise.

3.2   Lexis

1. Receptive vocabulary size, measured by scores on the Revised Peabody Picture Vocabulary Test
2. Lexical diversity in participants' Frog stories

3.3   Morpho-syntax

1. Unspeeded written GJT (from White & Genesee 1996)
2. Unspeeded written Sentence Comprehension Test (SCT; from Dabrowska 1997)

3.4   Language use

1. Holistically analyzed narrative
2. Detailed analytic scoring of a pre-selected episode from the story
3. Unspeeded written discourse completion test (DCT, adapted from Blum-Kalka et al. 1989)

3.5   Background questionnaire

Items soliciting data on subjects' L1 and L2 use, AO, AoA, etc.

The results were as follows. At the group level, the NSs outperformed the NNSs statistically significantly on most variables, i.e. both measures of pronunciation, vocabulary size, and grammatical knowledge, and on narrative skill, but not on sentence comprehension, DCT scores for the appropriateness of request forms, or narrative skill judged holistically. Analyses of data at the individual level revealed that no NNSs had received a rating of 5 ("sounds like a NS of standard American English") on the reading-aloud task. Six received a rating of 4, which Marinova-Todd considered comparable:

> "None of the subjects in this study were judged to have definitely a native-like pronunciation on this [reading aloud] task, although six participants were judged to be native speakers with possible regional dialects, which is interpreted as a score within the native range." (2003:79)

Some researchers might reject ratings of 4, "native speaker with regional dialects," as evidence of native-like pronunciation, for this could easily constitute (i) an ambiguous category, and (ii) one that could allow, if not encourage, false positives through non-native accentedness being ascribed to regional variation by the three student raters, whose knowledge of regional accents is not reported. However, Marinova-Todd (p.c. 8/19/2011) argues that hers was a reasonable decision, given that some native speakers were also classified as 4.[2] Three NNSs were rated as 5 on the picture-guided story-retelling tasks.

Closer analysis at the individual level of the very best subjects' performance led Marinova-Todd to identify three females from Eastern Europe – one each from Hungary, Slovakia and Russia – all living with NS partners and rarely using their L1 any longer, whose scores across most tasks fell within the NS range, and in one case, that of the Russian female, within the NS range on all tasks. (However, even that individual's pronunciation had not received a 5 rating on the story-retelling task, it should be remembered.) Marinova-Todd reports that all three women were aged 25 or 26 when tested, had all arrived in the USA when aged 16 or older, had a LOR of 5–7 years, and had received an average of five years of formal instruction

---

2.   Marinova-Todd (p.c. 8/19/2011) reasons as follows. "It is possible that their non-native accent was considered regional dialect by the raters, but that is feasible, indicating that the non-native accent was weak enough, or unidentifiable, thus sounding more like a native-like variation, rather than a foreign accent. As you can tell, on most NNS the raters had no difficulty identifying their foreign accents, so the accent had to be very minor to not be perceived as such."

in English in their home countries. Thus, while AoA was in the late teens, since mean AO for the three was 13, AO in the case of either one or two of the three was earlier than 13, which disqualifies them, and the average being 13, possibly all three, as test cases for a claimed SP for grammar closing in the mid-teens. The three were possibly legitimate test cases for the claimed SP for phonology, the off-set of which is hypothesized to begin by age six for most people, and to close by age 12 for everyone, therefore, but probably not for grammar. In fact, given that English is a compulsory foreign language, starting in secondary school or even earlier, in all countries represented in the high-achieving samples, it is hard to see how subjects in the study constitute unambiguous test cases for almost any version of a CPH for grammar. It is unfortunate that background information at the individual level is not reported for participants in the study – information that would be necessary to evaluate claimed refutations of any version of a SPH.[3]

As noted, none of the three highest performers received a 5 rating on the basis of their elicited (reading aloud) speech samples, meaning that none had a perceptible "standard" accent, and so conformed to my own and most claims of a SP or CP for phonology. Where grammar was concerned, all three subjects performed within the NS range, but 'within the NS range' in this study was defined as any score falling within three standard deviations of the NS mean – a very liberal criterion with no apparent precedent in the literature.[4] Even then,

---

3. In response to a request for information on the AO for the three best speakers, and for the Russian female, in particular, Marinova-Todd (p.c. 8/19/2011) clarified as follows. "For my selection criteria, the NNS had to have been immersed in the L2 environment after the age of 16, and some had a minimal exposure to formal foreign language classes before that. I was not too concerned with foreign language instruction in school, we all know it is not very effective, particularly in terms of leading to nativelike performance on its own … According to my memory, the Russian speaker you are referring to had formal instruction in English in school before she came to the US, it was for half an hour twice a week and not through the whole period while she was in her home country."

4. The more conservative criterion of scores within two standard deviations of the NS mean has been used by Flege, Munro & Mackay (1995), Bongaerts, van Summeren, Planken & Schils (1997), and Van Boxtel (2005), among others. Responding to an email inquiry, Marinova-Todd justified use of the more generous criterion as follows:

> "The criterion for what scores qualified as native-like was based on whether the scores of the non-native speakers (NNS) fall within the range of the native speakers (NS). In my view, standard deviations in the NS's scores are irrelevant when considering degree of nativelikeness, since they are ALL native speakers (the bottom 5% of the distribution are not less native-like than the top!). Even though they vary a lot, they have all learned English as their native language, and this is part of why it is important to compare NNS to real NS." (Marinova-Todd, p.c. 8/11/2011)

two of the best three subjects failed to meet the criterion on the "spontaneous speech" task, and the third barely managed to meet it on the reading aloud task, falling just within the three SD range (see Figures 11 and 12, in Marinova-Todd 2003: 105–106). As noted, due to their AO, none was a clear test case for a claimed SP for grammar closing in the mid-teens. In addition, what was assessed on the unspeeded paper-and-pencil GJT, borrowed from the White & Genesee (1996) study, was off-line, language-like behavior. (RT data were collected, but not reported by Marinova-Todd.) Finally, the single sample item provided from the unspeeded Sentence Comprehension Test (SCT), along with the information about how questions were scored (2003: 169–170), makes some of the NNSs' strong performance in the morpho-syntactic domain (an average of their scores on the GJT and SCT) less surprising. While the sample (tough movement) sentence *Alison will be hard to get Tom to give a loan to* could well have been difficult to parse (RT scores would have been revealing here), the five questions on it, and their equivalents for all items in the SCT, were less challenging (correct answers in italics):

Q1 Who might give a loan to someone?   *Tom*
Q2 Who might be given a loan?   *Alison*
Q3 What will be hard?   *Getting Tom to give a loan to Alison*
Q4 [the strange] Who will find it hard to do something?   *Someone not mentioned in the sentence*
Q5 Do you think the sentence is grammatically correct?   *Yes*

The vocabulary size measure is largely irrelevant for any version of a CPH, for as Marinova-Todd herself recognizes (2003: 71), research has shown that vocabulary size is not constrained by age effects, is subject to large variation in both native and non-native populations, with size a function of literacy, especially type and quantity of reading, rather than language competence. The fact that these (and other NNS) participants' vocabulary scores fell within the typically wide NS range in the study is of little interest. The same could well be said of the DCT of request strategies, an unspeeded paper-and-pencil test, and of the picture-guided story retellings, where the scoring rubric shows that a subject's score was in large part a matter of logical sequencing, the amount of detailed information provided, and overall coherence, rather, again, than of linguistic competence.

In sum, Marinova-Todd's study should be seen for what it was, a valuable demonstration of the fact that, given sufficient time and opportunity, a tiny minority of NNSs are capable of achieving *near native* (not native-like) proficiency in a second language. Where maturational constraints are concerned, however, the study failed to unearth a single unambiguous counter-example to the version of the SP hypotheses that I and others have defended for the past 20+ years. Nevertheless, despite having yet to appear in a refereed journal, it continues to be cited as documenting a goodly number of *native-like* adult starters – supposedly as many as 40% of 30, i.e. 12, in some summaries – and as counter-evidence to the claim that post-SP starters cannot achieve native-like command of a L2 on a wide range of tasks.[5]

No-one denies that tiny numbers of learners can achieve native-like abilities on some tasks, especially off-line, language-like tasks, or with their control of some sounds, lexical items and collocations, or grammatical structures. What opponents of the idea of maturational constraints need to produce is a single case of a late starter who can perform like a NS across the board. If there really are no maturational constraints on adult SLA, it should be easy to find lots of them. Also, as noted earlier, if no biological schedule underlies human language acquisition, they need to explain how it is that all children exposed to a language before closure of hypothesized SPs succeed in achieving native abilities, despite sizable differences in IQ and exposure. Meanwhile, researchers seeking to unearth native-like late starters, whose L2 abilities would put a stop to talk of maturational constraints once and for all, should look carefully at the most sophisticated study in the area to date, Abrahamsson and Hyltenstam (2009), with its demonstration of the crucial importance of their construct, *scrutinized non-perceivable non-native attainment*. Abrahamsson and Hyltenstam found that out of a pool of 236 Spanish speakers of supposedly nativelike L2 Swedish who had volunteered for the study, including 41 who judges had rated as natives on the basis of a short recorded speech sample, none with an AoA above eight proceeded to score within the NS range on all 10 detailed measures of pronunciation, vocabulary and grammar. The rigorous methodological standards employed in the Stockholm study are those that future research on SP claims, for or against, must meet.

3.   Continuing confusion of rate and ultimate attainment

Another reason for the lack of consensus, confusion of rate and ultimate attainment, is easy to identify and deal with. There was some early confusion when short-term advantages for older children and adults were mistaken for evidence

---

5.   Birdsong (2005, p. 181), for example, states that "Three of Marinova-Todd's subjects performed within the range of native controls across all nine tasks. In some cases, these subjects performed above native means. In addition, six other subjects performed like natives on seven of the nine tasks." Fidler (2006, p. 403) reports that "[Marinova-Todd] found that 3 informants performed at or above native levels on all 9 tasks."

that adults were *better* learners than children (see, e.g. Snow & Hoefnagel-Hohle 1978).[6] Once short-term and long-term studies were differentiated (Krashen, Long & Scarcella 1979), however, it became clear that while adults and older children enjoyed an advantage for *rate* of acquisition in the early stages of morphological and syntactic development, younger children outperformed them in phonology in the long run, given continued access to the new language, and that both younger and older child starters outperformed adults in morphology and syntax in the long run.

The rate/ultimate attainment confusion persists in some quarters, nonetheless, occasionally because researchers purport to assess ultimate attainment in samples whose mean LOR is too short, e.g. presumably in Bialystok (1997), where LOR was not reported and adults found to outperform children, and 1–6 years in Bialystok and Miller (1999). Also, in studies of foreign language learning in schools, higher achievement by cohorts of children who begin a foreign language two or three years later (say, at age 11) than cohorts who begin foreign language study earlier (say, at age 8) is still sometimes mistaken for counter-evidence to the "younger is better" claim, and/or as justification for the later starting age (an issue discussed in detail in Chapter 11). It is forgotten that the total learning opportunity for either group (e.g. three hours a week × 40 weeks × six years = 720 hours) typically amounts to the equivalent 90 eight-hour days, or roughly just *three months* of naturalistic exposure by children learning their L1 – and in many foreign language classrooms, exposure to impoverished input at that. Three months is nowhere near a sufficient basis upon which to assess capacity for ultimate attainment, which in other areas of the SLA literature, such as that on (putative) fossilization, is typically assumed to require a minimum of *ten years* of full-time use. Studies that have compared the same groups of earlier and later starters over time have shown that short-term advantages for older learners disappear fairly quickly, with younger starters in naturalistic settings catching

---

6.   Hyltenstam and Abrahamsson (2001: 155–6) point out that the Snow and Hoefnagel-Hohle work suffered from a number of other methodological flaws, not least the fact that the tests employed were obviously far too difficult for the youngest children, ages 3–5. They included a translation task, a morphology test they could not complete, and a GJT on which they had a 100% error rate. The fact that they were outperformed on those measures by older children, including teenagers for whom the same tests, equally obviously, were too easy, does not justify Snow and Hoefnagel-Hohle's conclusion (1982: 108) that the "slowest [SLA] occurred in subjects aged 3 to 5 years" and their overall position that older is better in SLA, on the basis of which they subsequently recommend later starting ages for foreign language teaching in schools.

up in as little as ten months (Snow & Hoefnagel-Hohle 1977), and overtaking older starters in the long run in naturalistic settings (Jia & Fuse 2007).

4.   Varied claims and understandings of claims

A fourth source of confusion is to be found in the different claims made about ultimate attainment potential, e.g. as to the scope and timing of critical or sensitive periods, such that the same study can provide evidence consistent with one claim, but inconsistent with another (see Long 2005, for examples and discussion). It is not unusual for it to be declared that "the CPH" has been refuted because of a finding that only conflicts with one version of "the" hypothesis. Most confusion is caused by deniers of SPs who misrepresent predictions based on maturational constraints. For example, failure by some early starters to attain native-like proficiency is treated as if it were counter-evidence to SP claims. So, as we have seen, is achievement of native-like abilities of learners whose AO was *earlier* than the hypothesized closure of a SP. So is continued deterioration in ultimate L2 attainment across the life-span. And so, even, is differential performance on a test by speakers of different L1s.

5.   Conflation of maturational constraints and fossilization

A recent new source of potential confusion is visible in the conflation by some writers of maturational constraints and stabilization/fossilization (see, e.g. Fidler 2006; Han 2004; Han & Odlin 2005). Han (2004: 8–9), for example, states that at a macroscopic level, *fossilization research* aims to understand why children are more effective language learners than adults, *due to L1 transfer and the effects of maturational (i.e. critical period) constraints*:

> "L2 ultimate attainment has at least three facets: (1) cross-learner general failure; (2) inter-learner differential success/failure; and (3) intra-learner differential success/failure ... clearly, within the (sic) ultimate attainment, success and failure co-exist. Nevertheless, the three facets of ultimate attainment do exhibit fossilization in that they involve permanently arrested development of some sort."   (2004: 7–8, italics in the original)

Han invokes biological (critical period) constraints to support her claim that "L2 learners are *universally preconditioned* to fossilization" (2004: 44, italics in the original). The fact that maturational constraints have been shown to affect linguistic systems (phonology, morpho-syntax, etc.) at different ages is offered as evidence of fossilization at a local level (2004: 62).

It is worth reminding ourselves that (i) maturational constraints and stabilization/fossilization cannot be one and the same or share the same cause, and that (ii) if they were the same, there would be no need for two constructs. Table 2 summarizes some of the salient differences between them.

Table 2. Differences between maturational constraints and stabilization or fossilization

Maturational constraints	Stabilization/fossilization
Universal/affect whole population	Idiosyncratic/affect individuals
Age-related/dependent (affect everyone at the same age)	Age-independent (sub-systems can stabilize/fossilize at any age, including in children; Plann 1977)
Biological basis	Non-biological basis, e.g. input sensitivity × feature type (Long 2003)
Effects potentially mitigated (but not avoided) by some IDs, e.g. language aptitude	Probably affected by some IDs (e.g. input sensitivity)
Global effects (affect all linguistic sub-systems)	Local effects (affect some sub-systems, while others continue to develop)
Affect predictable classes of features (e.g. non-salient features)	Idiosyncratic (e.g. affects ESL negation, which is highly salient, in some learners, but not others)

6. Methodological issues

A variety of methodological issues add to the confusion. Since they have been illustrated and discussed in detail elsewhere (see, e.g. DeKeyser 2006; Long 2005, 2007), I will simply note the common problems with putative counter-evidence to one or more versions of "the CPH," without going through the original publications again. Studies interpreted by their authors as providing counter-evidence have suffered from one or more of the following flaws: (i) as indicated above, confusion of early rate of acquisition with capacity for ultimate attainment; (ii) inappropriate choice of subjects; (iii) inappropriate operationalization of AO and/or AoA; (iv) biasing of results through the use of leading instructions to raters of speech samples; (v) basing rater assessments of native-likeness through use of very limited and/or rehearsed speech samples and/or language-like behavior; (vi) use of markedly non-native samples that make near-native samples sound/look native to raters; (vii) use of unreliable or invalid measures; (viii) inappropriate L1 – L2 pairings; and (ix) faulty interpretation of statistical patterns.

7. Continued access to UG

In an interesting critical response to the paper (Long 2005) in which studies exhibiting each, and sometimes several, of the above methodological problems were identified, Rothman (2008) began by agreeing that whereas normal child language acquisition is "uniform with a virtual guarantee of success," typical adult language learning results in "various degrees of non-convergence and variability" (2008: 1063). He accepts that some of the methodological concerns are legitimate, but argues that they cannot account for an independent set of findings obtained by researchers working within a Chomskyian UG framework – findings that he considers refute "the CPH."

The structure of Rothman's argument is straightforward enough; it involves an assumption, followed by evidence inconsistent with a logical consequence of that assumption. He writes:

> "it is clear that a strict interpretation of the CPH (sic) universally entails a maturational decline/cessation for (sic) innate linguistic acquisition ability. Assuming a cognitive view of language, this means that (whatever) *implicit cognitive mechanisms – which I take to be Universal Grammar (UG)* (see Chomsky 2007 for a review of this position) – drive primary language acquisition become inaccessible to adult learners."   (Rothman 2008: 1064, emphasis added)

Rothman's assumption, it is important to note, is not simply of "a cognitive view of language," with which few SLA researchers would argue, but that support of any version of "the CPH" entails an account in terms of access, followed by loss of access, to innate linguistic knowledge. Many supporters of the idea of maturational constraints would dispute that. Rothman is very explicit on the matter:

> "Herein I conflate the terms implicit/explicit learning with domain-specific and domain-general acquisition ... I interpret claims of loss of implicit linguistic learning mechanisms as being essentially the same as loss of domain-specific acquisition abilities that would derive from a loss to (sic) UG ... And so, if the critical period (or sensitive periods) correlates to (sic) the (gradient) loss of accessibility to (sic) implicit linguistic mechanism (sic) (entirely or in part), then it is predicted that implicit acquisition can no longer take place as it does in the case of child language acquisition."   (2008: 1084, Footnote 1)

Given his (strong) assumption, Rothman argues (see, also, Coopmans 2006; Dekydspotter, Sprouse & Thyre 2000; Iverson 2010; Rothman & Iverson 2007, 2008; Slabakova 2006), that if adults can be shown to acquire grammatical knowledge (or in Slabakova's case, semantic knowledge) of an L2 attributed in L1A to the workings of UG, the same language acquisition capacity must still operate. This is unambiguously true, he claims, in the case of so-called poverty-of-the-stimulus (POS) knowledge, i.e. knowledge of grammatical properties of the target language, including their semantic entailments, learned despite an absence of evidence in the input that UGers claim is required for them to be learned. Therefore, any CP claim that ultimate adult L2 attainment is the result of an impaired capacity for implicit learning (equated with access to UG), forcing adults to try to learn languages differently, must be false. Rothman asks, rhetorically (2008: 1073), "how can adult L2 grammars, despite observable differences, be so good if language acquisition for adults is an entirely explicit, non-encapsulated process?" More specifically, how can adults learn POS knowledge that is not instantiated in the L1 and not learnable from positive evidence in the L2 input?

Rothman proceeds to enumerate examples of POS knowledge that some adult L2 learners have been shown to possess, including adult English learners' command of interpretative properties of Spanish grammatical aspect as a result of their acquiring the relevant morpho-syntactic features encoded in preterit and imperfect morphology. Slabakova and Montrul (2003) showed that English learners were more accurate with generic and specific subject restricted interpretations – supposedly regulated by innate knowledge of semantic universals – than with the imperfect and preterit's archetypal habitual and episodic meanings, even though only the second pair is explicitly taught. Adult learners, the argument goes, must have continued access to those semantic universals, which, therefore, constitutes counter-evidence to "the CPH." Rothman and Iverson (2007) have made the same argument with respect to a related POS semantic entailment successfully acquired by English learners of Portuguese. Song and Schwartz (2009) have done the same with English learners' acquisition of wh-constructions with negative polarity items in L2 Korean.

The problem with Rothman's argument is his equating implicit learning capacity with the working of innate linguistic knowledge (UG). If POS properties are indeed only acquired in L1A due to innate knowledge of linguistic universals, an explanation of uniformly successful L1A in terms of the workings of UG, and of non-native-like attainment in adult L2A as the result of loss of access to UG, would indeed be in trouble. But that is not the position held by many researchers with "a cognitive view of language," whose acceptance of some version of a CPH does not entail recognition of a role for UG in L1A, e.g. the general nativist position of O'Grady (1996), and an updated version of the Fundamental Difference Hypothesis (Bley-Vroman 2009). Both O'Grady and Bley-Vroman posit maturational constraints on SLA. Other supporters of (different) versions of the CPH do, indeed, explain poorer adult achievement in terms of loss of the capacity for implicit learning (see, e.g. De Keyser 2000; Paradis 2009; Ullman 2005), but their explanations have nothing to do with loss of access to UG, the operation of which they, like O'Grady and Bley-Vroman, do not recognise for L1A. Still others maintain that the capacity for implicit learning, especially the efficiency of instance learning, deteriorates with increasing age (Hoyer & Lincourt 1998), but is not lost, and in fact plays an important role in adult SLA (see, e.g. Granena & Long 2013; Long 2010; Rebuschat & Williams 2009; Williams 2009), and, again, do not invoke UG in their account of L1A.

As Rothman points out, acquiring POS features would be very hard to explain for those who claim all adult SLA is an 'entirely explicit, non-encapsulated process.' But not even proponents of skill-building models, such as DeKeyser (2007),

claim that. DeKeyser, for example, limits the role of explicit learning to the learning of simple grammar in a classroom setting by those with high aptitude. The
real challenge of the overwhelming findings of age differences and non-nativelike L2 attainment by adults is for those (e.g. Epstein, Flynn & Martohardjono
1996; Flynn & Manuel 1991; Flynn & Martohardjono 1995; Schwartz 1986; and
Rothman, himself) who hold that access to UG continues throughout the life-span.
If adult acquirers have the same capacity for language learning as young children,
how is one to explain the well documented, universal, at least partial, failure of
adult SLA? L1 transfer only goes so far.

8.   Conflicting explanations

As noted at the outset, the same level of consistency, and acceptance, of findings
on age differences in SLA cannot be found when it comes to explanations for
them, and especially, for claims of critical or sensitive periods. Disagreements
persist over the very existence of maturational constraints on SLA, as we have
seen, and to a lesser extent, even among those who share in some version of a
CPH, over the timing, scope and cause of any that do exist. It is also claimed that
factors correlated with age, such as the allegedly greater quality and quantity of
input children receive, or changed affective profiles, not AO itself, account for the
findings, but each of those arguments fails (Hyltenstam & Abrahamsson 2003;
Long 1990).

   Both quality and quantity of input can undoubtedly sometimes be problematic and contributing factors to low adult success. In a controlled laboratory study
of interaction during a block-building task, Scarcella and Higa (1982) found that
adult partners' input to seven younger children (aged 8.5–9.5) and seven adolescents (15.5–16.5) differed somewhat from that to seven adults (18–21). The adult
interlocutors created a more supportive atmosphere and carried more of the conversational load during negotiation for meaning with the younger children, provided somewhat shorter and grammatically less complex utterances, and checked
the children's comprehension more often. In extreme cases, poor immigrants may
live for years in an L1 linguistic ghetto and experience very little L2 input at all.
In many other cases, however, e.g. NNSs married to NSs of the target language
and living in the target language environment for decades, input is rich, varied
and unlimited, yet no such NNSs have been found who have achieved native-like
abilities, despite occasional claims to the contrary. LOR has typically been found
to be a relevant predictor only in short-term studies (for review, see DeKeyser &
Larson-Hall 2005: 96–97), e.g. after the first year in Snow & Hoefnagel-Hohle
(1978), and for the first five years, at most (Cummins 1981; Krashen et al. 1979;
Piske, MacKay & Flege 2001), usually to be uncorrelated with attainment at all
(e.g. DeKeyser 2000), or only once the effect of AO is removed (e.g. Oyama 1976),

and to explain 5% or less of the variance in ultimate attainment (Flege, Munro & Mackay 1995).

The same general pattern is observed with social-psychological factors, such as attitude and motivation. Any positive correlations between affective factors and ultimate attainment evaporate once the effect of AO is removed, but not vice versa. This is true for grammar (e.g. Jia 1998; Johnson & Newport 1989; Oyama 1978) and for phonology (e.g. Flege, Munro & Mackay 1995; Flege, Yeni-Komshian & Liu 1999; Purcell & Suter 1980; Thomson 1991).

L1 transfer does not account for the data, either. Transfer effects (e.g. Spanish L1 effects on ESL negation) are observed in subjects with the same L1, and apparently impede some learners, but not others, from going further. Learners from typologically different L1s show similar errors and error types in areas where their L1s differ. For example, Korean and Spanish spatial semantics are coded differently, but by the same English prepositions (*in, on,* and *over*); despite that, AO predicted accuracy for both Korean and Spanish learners of English equally, whereas neither L1 transfer nor LOR did so (Munnich & Landau 2010). Also, if L1 transfer is the problem, why are the same kinds of errors observed in late learners of the same language as L1 and as L2? Mayberry (1993) showed this for late learners of ASL as L1 (congenitally deaf children of hearing adults) and late learners of ASL as L2 (people who learned English as L1, and then lost their hearing, due to accidents.

4. Positive developments over the past decade, and future research programs

Despite the sources of confusion outlined above, there have been a number of positive developments in the field's understanding of the existence, scope, and timing of maturational constraints during the past two decades, each likely to influence future research programs in the area.

1. There is an emerging consensus as to the criteria a SP claim must meet, i.e. evidence of a clearly delineated peak period for acquisition, followed by a period of decline with increasing AO (the offset), interrupted by a discontinuity, followed by a flattening in the slope over the rest of the life-span – resulting in the *stretched Z* distribution (Birdsong 2005). Irrelevant criteria, such as a precipitous drop during the offset, are also becoming more widely recognized as such (DeKeyser & Larsen-Hall 2005, 2006; Long 2005).

2. A shift of focus has begun from global measures of overall performance in whole linguistic domains (phonology, morphology, semantics, etc.) to classes

of features within and across domains. An example, both within and across domains, is attention to non-salient features as those particularly susceptible to maturational constraints (DeKeyser 2011; DeKeyser, Alfi-Shabtay & Ravid 2010). Within a domain, e.g. morpho-syntax, some features, such as word order, subject-verb inversion, and do-support in yes-no questions, seem to be more robust and earlier acquired (DeKeyser & Larson-Hall 2005: 99), whereas others, including articles, plurals, and some subcategorization phenomena, seem more fragile and vulnerable to age effects, regardless of L1, and for both accuracy and RT.

3. Research exhibits increasing methodological sophistication, e.g. the careful screening of subjects into studies (Abrahamsson & Hyltenstam 2008), the use of scrutinized, rather than perceived, L2 performance (Abrahamsson & Hyltenstam 2009), and the measurement of native-likeness using linguistic features that exhibit minimal variability among NSs, but are hard for NNSs of a given L1, such as articles for Russians (DeKeyser et al. 2010).

4. Shorter peak periods of sensitivity are posited, especially, but not only, in phonology, where a number of researchers have found children with an AO earlier than six not to have attained native-like accents, despite lack of any apparent obstacle to their doing so (see, e.g. Flege, Munro & MacKay 1995; Granena & Long 2013; Hyltenstam 1992; Meisel 2009, 2011; Seliger 1978; Thompson 1991). Accentedness in young starters appears more likely in cases where learners have attained high proficiency in the L1 and/or continue to use that language in significant proportions of their everyday lives (Flege 1999; Flege, Frieda & Nozawa 1997; Yeni-Komshian, Flege & Liu 2000).

5. Use of bilingual controls in place of native speakers has been advocated, usually on one or both of two grounds. One is that the (alleged) ability of at least a few late-starters to achieve native-like ability in a L2 shows that the distinction between native and non-native speaker is illusory. That claim, however, implicitly assumes that native standards exist and are recognizable. Besides, as argued earlier, there have in fact been no such cases. Moreover, the psychological reality of the native/non-native distinction is shown by the consistently acceptable levels of inter- and intra-rater reliability among judges who are asked to distinguish NSs, not just from speakers with obviously non-native abilities, but from very advanced, near-native NNSs (see, e.g. Abrahamsson & Hyltenstam 2009), and/or to assess degree of foreign accent (e.g. Granena & Long 2013). They can do this reliably on the basis of quite small speech samples, despite the variability inherent in both NS speech and IL performance.

A second ground is that bilinguals are not just two monolinguals in the same person, the implication being that the bilingual's task is harder than that of the monolingual precisely because the language in which he or she is expected to perform like a NS is not his or her native language, and moreover, is competing with the influence of the L1. Studies have shown that ultimate L2 attainment even in some young child starters growing up in the L2 environment can differ from that of monolingual NSs of the language (for phonology, see, e.g. Flege, Frieda & Nozawa 1997; Piske, Mackay & Flege (2001); for lexical and grammatical "accents" in child starters, see, e.g. Abrahamsson & Hyltenstam 2009; Hyltenstam & Abrahamsson 2003). These findings have been used to argue that if some young children cannot attain native-like L2 norms for having to deal with two languages, then non-native-like attainment among adult starters may not be due to maturational constraints, but to the same problem – two languages into one individual won't go – making comparisons with monolingual NSs misguided (see, e.g. Muñoz & Singleton 2011). This argument misses the point that many child starters *do* achieve native-like L2 abilities, whereas *no* adult starters do. Comparisons between L2 speakers and monolingual NS controls are still relevant. The important thing is that they should not be the *only* comparisons. A safer, *additional* comparison for identifying age effects/maturational constraints is that between younger and older L2 starters. This has long been the case in studies of maturational constraints, which often involve three (or more) groups: younger starters, older starters, and NS controls. The fact is, much of the evidence for maturational constraints comes from comparisons of this latter kind, i.e. comparisons of two or more groups of bilinguals who share the same L1 and L2, but began the L2 at different ages.

6. Research has begun to appear that extends the scope of SP claims, and counter-claims, from phonology, morphology and syntax, to semantics, including lexical and collocational abilities, and from one CP to multiple SPs. Some scholars (e.g. Slabakova 2006) have purported to refute SP claims on that basis, while others have reported findings consistent with the existence of maturational constraints in the semantic domain, too. In their study of the acquisition of spatial prepositions by 30 Spanish and 30 Korean learners of English, Munnich and Landau (2010) found that AO, but neither LOR (range 5–30 years) nor L1, predicted learners' ability to judge the accuracy of spatial prepositional use (*in/on, over/under, above/below/under*) and to produce the prepositions themselves. AO was negatively correlated with accuracy across the AO range (–.82 for the Koreans, –.76 for Spanish speakers). With one minor modification, comparisons of three AO groups revealed the stretched Z. The correlations were as follows: for AO 0–8, production: $r = -0.14$, *n.s.*; judgment: $r = -0.26$, $p = .13$; for AO 8–13, production: $r = -0.26$, $p = .12$; judgment: $r = -0.37$, $p = .05$; and for AO 14–39, production: $r = -0.06$, *n.s.*;

judgment: $r = 0.49$, $p < .05$. The researchers attributed the unexpected positive correlation for AO and judgment in the oldest group to years of English in their home countries (a factor discounted by Marinova-Todd). AO remained a reliable predictor when LOR, attitudinal variables, and effects for proportion of L1 and L2 use in the first two years in the US were partialed out. Conversely, when AO was partialed out, there was no effect for LOR. (While maturational constraints on the acquisition of L2 semantics is well under way, as shown by research like this, studies of constraints on discourse and pragmatic abilities have been vanishingly few to date.)

7. Recognition has grown that AO or AoA can be cover terms for factors that tend to be related to age differences (e.g. Muñoz 2008a, b, 2011; Stevens 2004), but without negating the brute power of AO alone, or the possibility of maturational constraints.

8. New methods and sources of information, most obviously from neurolinguistic studies, have been adduced to supplement earlier exclusive reliance on behavioral data (Birdsong 2006; DeBot 2008, 2009; DeKeyser 2012: 13).

9. As in this chapter, a number of proposed counter-arguments to claims of maturational constraints have been shown to be unfounded. Eliminating such counter-arguments is important because it brings the field closer to a final understanding of the issue, much as knowing that, say, two of five roads do not lead to a desired destination brings the traveler closer to finding out which one (of the three remaining possibilities) does. Examples, some of which have been discussed here, some elsewhere (e.g. Long 2005, 2007), include the claim that a negative correlation with AO over the whole age range is counter-evidence; that different performance by two or more L1 groups on the same test is counter-evidence; that individual variation is counter-evidence; that (supposed) continued access to UG is counter-evidence; that collapse of a particular explanation for CPs (e.g. lateralization) is counter-evidence; that correlations between AO and other variables (affect, education, etc.) is counter-evidence; that the existence of small numbers of learners who can fool raters and "pass" as natives or who can score within the native speaker range on overly simple tests and/or on the basis of inadequate samples and/or language-like behavior is counter-evidence; that different results across tests of the same general domain, e.g. morphology and syntax, that in fact assess differentially sensitive sub-domains or (e.g. salient/non-salient) types of linguistic features in different studies is counter-evidence; and that self-assessed native-likeness, e.g. by respondents in census data and other surveys is counter-evidence.

10. While each of the above nine developments is important, perhaps most important of all is the increasing attention paid to a variety of potential

alternative *explanations* for age-related differences. They include general non-linguistic cognitive maturation, notably the *less is more* hypothesis (e.g. Cochran, McDonald & Parault 1999; Newport 1990, 2002), and related processing, rather than competence, explanations for non-native-like attainment (e.g. Hopp 2006; McDonald 2006). Another explanation, one with considerable traction, first proposed by DeKeyser (2000), is that maturational constraints are caused by a fundamental age-related shift from implicit to explicit learning. A corollary is that high language aptitude, especially aptitude for explicit learning, becomes increasingly important after the shift and will be present in any late starters who achieve near-native levels of L2 attainment.

The role of language aptitude has been the subject of four studies of ultimate attainment by long-term residents in L2 settings. Results to date have conflicted. DeKeyser (2000) and DeKeyser et al. (2010) reported statistically significant correlations between aptitude and ultimate grammatical attainment in older, but not younger, learners. Abrahamsson and Hyltenstam (2008), conversely, found an effect for aptitude in younger, but not older, learners, while agreeing with DeKeyser that language aptitude was probably important for near-native SLA by adult starters (and possibly with younger learners, too). Granena and Long (2013) suggested that the conflicting results of the first three studies were mostly due to methodological differences concerning sampling and sample sizes, as well as the aptitude tests, procedures and outcome measures employed. As hypothesized, they found no effect for aptitude in young starters (AO 3–15), but an effect in older learners (AO 16–29) in their mastery of lexis and collocations, consistent with a hypothesized deterioration in the capacity of older learners specifically for instance learning.

The relationship between starting age, language aptitude, and ultimate L2 attainment is clearly an issue deserving serious attention. Age effects are one of the most widely attested and widely accepted findings in SLA, with maturational constraints their likely cause. The role of language aptitude(s) is less clear, in part because the measurement of aptitude(s) is itself the subject of research. The appearance in recent years of new instruments for the purpose, such as the LLAMA and Hi-Lab, offers great potential for a new research program. Should certain dimensions of language aptitude turn out to be especially relevant for adult learners in classroom and/or naturalistic settings, the frequency of aptitude-treatment-interaction (ATI) studies is bound to increase, in turn offering the promise of more effective tailored instruction for adults with different aptitude profiles in an era when language teaching and learning are of ever greater importance.

References

Abrahamsson, N., & Hyltenstam, K. (2008). The robustness of aptitude effects in near-native second language acquisition. *Studies in Second Language Acquisition, 30*, 481–509.

Abrahamsson, N., & Hyltenstam, K. (2009). Age of onset and nativelikeness in a second language: Listener perception versus linguistic scrutiny. *Language Learning, 59*, 249–306.

Baayen, R.H. (2008). *Analyzing linguistic data. A practical introduction to statistics using R.* Cambridge: CUP.

Bialystok, E. (1997). The structure of age: In search of barriers to second language acquisition. *Second Language Research, 13*, 116–137.

Bialystok, E., & Hakuta, K. (1999). Confounded age: Linguistic and cognitive factors in age differences for second language acquisition. In D. Birdsong (Ed.), *Second language acquisition and the critical period hypothesis* (pp. 161–181). Mahwah, NJ: Lawrence Erlbaum Associates.

Bialystok, E., & Miller, B. (1999). The problem of age in second-language acquisition: Influences from language, structure, and task. *Bilingualism: Language and Cognition, 2*(2), 127–145.

Birdsong, D. (2005). Interpreting age effects in second language acquisition. In J. Kroll, & A.M.B. de Groot (Eds.), *Handbook of bilingualism: Psycholinguistic approaches* (pp. 109–127). Oxford: OUP.

Birdsong, D. (2006). Age and second language acquisition and processing: A selective overview. *Language Learning, 56*, 9–49.

Birdsong, D. (2009). Age and the end state of second language acquisition. In W.C. Ritchie, & T.K. Bhatia (Eds.), *The new handbook of second language acquisition*. Bingley: Emerald.

Birdsong, D., & Molis, M. (2001). On the evidence for maturational constraints in second-language acquisition. *Journal of Memory and Language, 44*, 235–249.

Bley-Vroman, R. (2009). The evolving context of the fundamental difference hypothesis. *Studies in Second Language Acquisition, 31*(2), 175–198.

Blum-Kalka, S., House, J., & Kasper, G. (1989). *Cross-cultural pragmatics: Requests and apologies.* Norwood, NJ: Ablex.

Bongaerts, T. (1999). Ultimate attainment in L2 pronunciation: The case of very advanced late L2 learners. In D. Birdsong (Ed.), *Second language acquisition and the critical period hypothesis* (pp. 133–159). Mahwah, NJ: Lawrence Erlbaum Associates.

Bongaerts, T., Mennen, S., & van der Slik, F. (2000). Authenticity of pronunciation in naturalistic second language acquisition. The case of very advanced learners of Dutch as a second language. *Studia Linguistica, 54*, 298–308.

Bongaerts, T., van Summeren, C., Planken, B., & Schils, E. (1997). Age and ultimate attainment in the pronunciation of a foreign language. *Studies in Second Language Acquisition, 19*(4), 447–465.

Bornstein, M. (1989). Sensitive periods in development: Structural characteristics and causal interpretations. *Psychological Bulletin, 105*, 179–197.

Chiswick, B.R., & Miller, P.W. (2008). A test of the critical period hypothesis for language learning. *Journal of Multilingual and Multicultural Development, 29*(1), 16–29.

Chomsky, N. (2007). Of minds and language. *Biolinguistics, 1*, 9–27.

Cochran, B.P., McDonald, J.L., & Parault, S.J. (1999). Too smart for their own good: The disadvantage of a superior processing capacity for adult language learners. *Journal of Memory and Language, 41*(1), 30–58.

Coopmans, P. (2006). L2 acquisition, age, and generativist reasoning. Commentary on Birdsong. *Language Learning, 56*(Supplement 1), 51–58.

Coppieters, R. (1987). Competence differences between native and near-native speakers. *Language, 63*, 544–573.

Cummins, J. (1981). Age on arrival and immigrant second language learning in Canada: A reassessment. *Applied Linguistics, 2*, 132–149.

de Bot, K. (2008). The imaging of what in the multilingual mind? *Second Language Research, 24*(1), 111–133.

de Bot, K. (2009). Multilingualism and aging. In W.C. Ritchie, & T.K. Bhatia (Eds.), *The new handbook of second language acquisition* (pp. 425–442). Bingley: Emerald.

Dekydspotter, L., Sprouse, R.A., & Thyre, R. (2000). The interpretation of quantification at a distance in English-French interlanguage: Domain specificity and second-language acquisition. *Language Acquisition, 8*, 265–320.

DeKeyser, R.M. (2000). The robustness of critical period effects in second language acquisition. *Studies in Second Language Acquisition, 22*, 499–533.

DeKeyser, R. (2006). A critique of recent arguments against the critical period hypothesis. In C. Abello-Contesse, R. Chacón-Beltrán, M.D. López-Jiménez, & M.M. Torreblanca-López (Eds.), *Age in L2 acquisition and teaching* (pp. 49–58). Bern: Peter Lang.

DeKeyser, R.M. (2007). Skill acquisition theory. In J. Williams, & B. VanPatten (Eds.), *Theories in second language acquisition: An introduction* (pp. 97–113). Mahwah, NJ: Lawrence Erlbaum Associates.

DeKeyser, R. (2011). Differential age effects within and across linguistic domains. Paper presented at the International Society for Bilingualism conference, Oslo, June 18.

DeKeyser, R.M. (2012). Age effects in second language learning. In S.M. Gass, & A. Mackey (Eds.), *The Routledge handbook of second language acquisition* (pp. 442–460). New York, NY: Routledge.

DeKeyser, R.M., Alfi-Shabtay, I., & Ravid, D. (2010). Cross-linguistic evidence for the nature of age-effects in second language acquisition. *Applied Psycholinguistics, 31*, 413–438.

DeKeyser, R., & Larson-Hall, J. (2005). What does the Critical Period really mean? In J.F. Kroll, & A.M.B. de Groot (Eds.), *Handbook of bilingualism: Psycholinguistic perspectives* (pp. 88–108). Oxford: OUP.

Dabrowska, E. (1997). *Cognitive semantics and the Polish dative.* Berlin: Mouton de Gruyter.

Donaldson, B. (2011). Left-dislocation in near-native French. *Studies in Second Language Acquisition, 33*(3), 399–432.

Epstein, S., Flynn, S., & Martohardjono, G. (1996). Explanation in theories of second language. *Behavior and Brain Sciences, 19*(4), 677–714.

Fidler, A. (2006). Reconceptualizing fossilization in second language acquisition: A review. *Second Language Research, 22*(3), 398–411.

Flege, J.E. (1999). Age of learning and second language speech. In D. Birdsong (Ed.), *Second language acquisition and the critical period hypothesis* (pp. 101–131). Mahwah, NJ: Lawrence Erlbaum Associates.

Flege, J.E., Frieda, A., & Nozawa, T. (1997). Amount of native-language (L1) use affects the pronunciation of an L2. *Journal of Phonetics, 25*, 169–186.

Flege, J.E., Munro, M., & Mackay, I. (1995). Factors affecting degree of perceived foreign accent in a second language. *Journal of the Acoustical Society of America, 97*, 3125–3134.

Flege, J.E., Yeni-Komshian, G., & Liu, H. (1999). Age constraints on second language acquisition. *Journal of Memory & Language, 41*, 78–104.

Flynn, S., & Manuel, S. (1991). Age dependent effects in language acquisition: An evaluation of 'Critical Period' hypotheses. In L. Eubank (Ed.), *Point/counterpoint: Universal Grammar in the second language* (pp. 118–145). Amsterdam: John Benjamins.

Flynn, S., & Martyohardjono, G. (1995). Is there an age factor for Universal Grammar? In D. Singleton, & Z. Lengyel (Eds.), *The age factor in second language acquisition: A critical look at the Critical Period Hypothesis* (pp. 135–153). Clevedon: Multilingual Matters.

Granena, G., & Long, M.H. (2010). Age of onset, length of residence, aptitude and ultimate L2 attainment in two linguistic domains. Paper presented at the 30th SLRF, College Park, MD: University of Maryland.

Granena, G., & Long, M.H. (2013). Age of onset, length of residence, language aptitude, and ultimate L2 attainment in three linguistic domains. *Second Language Research, 29*(1).

Hahn, W.K. (1987). Cerebral lateralization of function: From infancy through childhood. *Psychological Bulletin, 101*, 376–392.

Hakuta, K., Bialystok, E., & Wiley, E.W. (2003). Critical evidence: A test of the Critical Period Hypothesis for second-language acquisition. *Psychological Science, 14*(1), 31–38.

Han, Z.-H. (2004). *Fossilization in adult second language acquisition*. Clevedon: Multilingual Matters.

Han, Z.-H., & Odlin, T. (2005). *Studies of fossilization in second language acquisition*. Clevedon: Multilingual Matters.

Herschensohn, J. (2007). *Language development and age*. Cambridge: CUP.

Hopp, H. (2006). Syntactic features and reanalysis in near-native processing. *Second Language Research, 22*, 369–397.

Hoyer, W.J., & Lincourt, A.E. (1998). Ageing and the development of learning. In M.A. Stadler, & P.A. Frensch (Eds.), *Handbook of implicit learning* (pp. 445–470). Thousand Oaks, CA: Sage.

Hyltenstam, K. (1988). Lexical characteristics of near-native L2 learners of Swedish. *Journal of Multilingual and Multicultural Development, 9*, 67–84.

Hyltenstam, K. (1992). Non-native features of non-native speakers: On the ultimate attainment of childhood L2 learners. In R.J. Harris (Ed.), *Cognitive processing in bilinguals* (pp. 351–368). New York, NY: Elsevier.

Hyltenstam, K., & Abrahamsson, N. (2003). Maturational constraints in SLA. In C.J. Doughty, & M.H. Long (Eds.), *The handbook of second language acquisition* (pp. 539–588). Oxford: Blackwell.

Ioup, G., Boustagui, E., Tigi, M., & Moselle, M. (1994). Reexamining the Critical Period Hypothesis: A case study of successful adult SLA in a naturalistic environment. *Studies in Second Language Acquisition, 16*(1), 73–98.

Iverson, M. (2010). Informing the age-of-acquisition debate: L3 as a litmus test. *International Review of Applied Linguistics, 48*, 221–243.

Jia, G. (1998). *Beyond brain maturation: The critical period hypothesis in second language acquisition revisited*. Unpublished doctoral dissertation. New York University.

Jia, G., & Fuse, A. (2007). Acquisition of English grammatical morphology by native Mandarin-speaking children and adolescents: Age-related differences. *Journal of Speech, Language and Hearing Research, 50*, 1280–1299.

Johnson, J. (1992). Critical period effects in second language acquisition: The effect of written versus auditory materials on the assessment of grammatical competence. *Language Learning, 42*(2), 217–248.

Johnson, J.S., & Newport, E.L. (1989). Critical period effects in second language learning: The influence of maturational state on the acquisition of English as a second language. *Cognitive Psychology, 21*, 60–99.

Krashen, S.D. (1973). Lateralization, language learning, and the critical period: Some new evidence. *Language Learning, 23*(1), 63–74.

Krashen, S.D., Long, M.H., & Scarcella, R.C. (1979). Age, rate and eventual attainment in second language acquisition. *TESOL Quarterly, 9*, 573–582. Reprinted in S.D. Krashen, R.C. Scarcella, & M.H. Long (Eds.), *Child–adult differences in second language acquisition* (pp. 161–172). Rowley, MA: Newbury House, 1982.

Laudan, L. (1996). A problem-solving approach to scientific progress. In L. Laudan (Ed.), *Beyond positivism and relativism. Theory, method, and evidence* (pp. 77–87). Boulder, CO: Westview.

Lee, J. (1998). *Is there a sensitive period for second language collocational knowledge?* Unpublished master's thesis. University of Hawai'i, Honolulu.

Lenneberg, E.H. (1967). *Biological foundations of language*. New York, NY: Wiley.

Long, M.H. (1990). Maturational constraints on language development. *Studies in Second Language Acquisition, 12*, 251–285.

Long, M.H. (2003). Stabilization and fossilization in interlanguage development. In C.J. Doughty, & M.H. Long (Eds.), *Handbook of second language acquisition* (pp. 487–535). Oxford: Blackwell.

Long, M.H. (2005). Problems with supposed counter-evidence to the critical period hypothesis. *International Review of Applied Linguistics, 43*, 287–317.

Long, M.H. (2007). Age differences and the sensitive periods controversy in SLA. In M.H. Long (Ed.), *Problems in SLA* (pp. 43–74). Mahwah, NJ: Lawrence Erlbaum Associates.

Long, M.H. (2010). *Towards a cognitive-interactionist theory of instructed adult SLA*. Plenary address to the 30th Second Language Research Forum, October 14–17. College Park, MD: University of Maryland.

Marinova-Todd, S. (2003). *Comprehensive analysis of ultimate attainment in adult second language acquisition*. Unpublished doctoral dissertation. Harvard University.

Mayberry, R. (1993). First-language acquisition after childhood differs from second-language acquisition: The case of American Sign Language. *Journal of Speech and Hearing Research, 36*, 1258–1270.

McDonald, J.L. (2006). Beyond the critical period: Processing-based explanations for poor grammaticality judgment performance by late second language learners. *Journal of Memory and Language, 55*(3), 381–401.

Meisel, J.M. (2009). Second language acquisition in early childhood. *Zeitschrift für Sprachwissenschaft, 28*, 5–34.

Meisel, J.M. (2011). *First and second language acquisition*. Cambridge: CUP.

Montrul, S., & Slabakova, R. (2003). Competence similarities between native and near-native speakers: An investigation of the preterite/imperfect contrast in Spanish. *Studies in Second Language Acquisition, 25*(3), 351–398.

Mulder, K., & Hulstijn, J.H. (2011). Linguistic skills of adult native speakers as a function of age and level of education. *Applied Linguistics, 32*, 475–494.

Munnich, E., & Landau, B. (2010). Developmental decline in the acquisition of spatial language. *Language Learning and Development 6*(1), 32–59.

Muñoz, C. (2008a). Symmetries and asymmetries of age effects in naturalistic and instructed L2 learning. *Applied Linguistics, 29*(4), 578–596.

Muñoz, C. (2008b). Age-related differences in foreign language learning. Revisiting the empirical evidence. *International Review of Applied Linguistics in Language Teaching, 46*(3), 197–220.

Muñoz, C. (2011). Input in foreign language learning: More significant than starting age? *International Review of Applied Linguistics in Language Teaching, 49*(2), 113–133.

Muñoz, C., & Singleton, D. (2011). A critical review of age-related research on L2 ultimate attainment. *Language Teaching, 44*, 1–35.

Munro, M., & Mann, V. (2005). Age of immersion as a predictor of foreign accent. *Applied Psycholinguistics, 26*(3), 311–341.

Newport, E. (1990). Maturational constraints on language learning. *Cognitive Science, 14*, 11–28.

Newport, E.L. (2002). Critical periods in language development. In L. Nadel (Ed.), *Encyclopedia of cognitive science* (pp. 737–739). London: Macmillan/Nature Publishing Group.

O'Grady, W. (1996). Language acquisition without Universal Grammar: A general nativist proposal for L2 learning. *Second Language Research, 12*(4), 374–397.

Oyama, S. (1976). A sensitive period for the acquisition of a nonnative phonological system. *Journal of Psycholinguistic Research, 5*(3), 261–283.

Oyama, S. (1978). The sensitive period and comprehension of speech. *Working Papers on Bilingualism, 16*, 1–17.

Paradis, M. (2009). *Declarative and procedural determinants of second languages*. Amsterdam: John Benjamins.

Patkowski, M.S. (1980). The sensitive period for the acquisition of syntax in a second language. *Language Learning, 30*, 449–472.

Penfield, W., & Roberts, L. (1959). *Speech and brain-mechanisms*. Princeton, NJ: Princeton University Press.

Piske, T., MacKay, I., & Flege, J.E. (2001). Factors affecting degree of foreign accent in an L2: A review. *Journal of Phonetics, 29*, 191–215.

Plann, S. (1977). Acquiring a second language in an immersion situation. In H.D. Brown, C. Yorio, & R. Crymes (Eds.), *On TESOL '77* (pp. 213–223). Washington, DC: TESOL.

Purcell, E.T., & Suter, R.W. (1980). Predictors of pronunciation accuracy: A reexamination. *Language Learning, 30*(2), 271–287.

Rebuschat, P.E., & Williams, J. (2009). Implicit learning of word order. In N.A. Taatgen, & H. van Rijn (Eds.), *Proceedings of the 31th Annual Conference of the Cognitive Science Society* (pp. 425–430). Austin, TX: Cognitive Science Society.

Ross, S. (1998). Self assessment in second language testing: A meta-analysis and analysis of experiential factors. *Language Testing, 15*(1), 1–20.

Rothman, J. (2008). Why not all counter-evidence to the critical period hypothesis is equal or problematic: Implications for SLA. *Language and Linguistics Compass, 2*, 1063–1088.

Rothman, J., & Iverson, M. (2007). Input type and parameter resetting: Is naturalistic input necessary? *International Review of Applied Linguistics, 45*(4), 285–319.

Scarcella, R.C., & Higa, C.A. (1982). Input and age differences in second language acquisition. In S.D. Krashen, R. Scarcella, & M.H. Long (Eds.), *Child-adult differences in second language acquisition* (pp. 175–201). Rowley, MA: Newbury House.

Schachter, J. (1996). Maturation and universal grammar. In W.C. Ritchie, & T.K. Bhatia (Eds.), *Handbook of second language acquisition* (pp. 159–193). San Diego, CA: Academic Press.

Schwartz, B.D. (1986). The epistemological status of second language acquisition. *Second Language Research, 2*, 120–159.

Seliger, H.W. (1978). Implications of a multiple critical periods hypothesis for second language learning. In W.C. Ritchie (Ed.), *Second language acquisition research. Issues and implications* (pp. 11–19). New York, NY: Academic Press.

Sherwood, C.C., Gordon, A.D., Allen, J.S., Phillips, K.A., Erwin, J.M., Hof, P.R., & Hopkins, W.D. (2011). Aging of the cerebral cortex differs between humans and chimpanzees. *Proceedings of the National Academy of Sciences, 108*, 13029–13034.

Silverberg, S., & Samuel, A.G. (2004). The effect of age of second language acquisition on the representation and processing of second language words. *Journal of Memory and Language, 51*(3), 381–398.

Singleton, D. (2005). The Critical Period Hypothesis: A coat of many colours. *International Review of Applied Linguistics in Language Teaching, 43*(4), 269–285.

Slabakova, R. (2006). Is there a critical period for semantics? *Second Language Research, 22*(3), 302–338.

Slabakova, R., & Montrul, S. (2003). Genericity and aspecxt in L2 acquisition. *Language Acquisition, 11*, 165–196.

Snow, C., & Hoefnagel-Hohle, M. (1977). Age differences and the pronunciation of foreign sounds. *Language and Speech, 20*, 357–365.

Snow, C., & Hoefnagel-Hohle, M. (1978). The critical period for language acquisition: Evidence from second language learning. *Child Development, 49*, 1114–1128. Reprinted in S.D. Krashen, R. Scarcella, & M.H. Long (Eds.), *Child-adult differences in second language acquisition* (pp. 93–111). Rowley, MA: Newbury House.

Song, H.S., & Schwartz, B.D. (2009). Testing the fundamental difference hypothesis: L2 adult, L2 child, and L1 child comparisons in the acquisition of Korean wh-constructions with Negative Polarity Items. *Studies in Second Language Acquisition, 31*(2), 323–361.

Sorace, A. (1993). Near-nativeness. In C.J. Doughty, & M.H. Long (Eds.), *Handbook of second language acquisition* (pp. 130–151). New York, NY: Basil Blackwell.

Sorace, A., & Filiaci, F. (2006). Anaphora resolution in near-native speakers of Italian. *Second Language Research, 22*, 339–368.

Spadaro, K. (1996). Maturational constraints on lexical acquisition in a second language. Unpublished doctoral dissertation. University of Western Australia.

Spadaro, K. (this volume). Maturational constraints on lexical acquisition in a second language.

Stevens, G. (1999). Age at immigration and second language proficiency among foreign-born adults. *Language in Society, 28*, 555–578.

Stevens, G. (2004). Using census data to test the critical-period hypothesis for second-language acquisition. *Psychological Science, 15*, 215–216.

Tahta, S., Wood, M., & Loewenthal, K. (1981). Foreign accents: Factors relating to transfer of accent from the first language to a second language. *Language and Speech, 24*(3), 265–272.

Thompson, I. (1991). Foreign accents revisited: The English pronunciation of Russian immigrants. *Language Learning, 41*(2), 177–204.

Ullman, M.T. (2005). A cognitive neuroscience perspective on second language acquisition: The declarative/procedural model. In C. Sanz (Ed.), *Mind and context in adult second language acquisition* (pp. 141–178). Washington, DC: Georgetown University Press.

van Boxtel, S. (2005). *Can the late bird catch the worm? Ultimate attainment in L2 syntax.* Utrecht: LOT.

van Boxtel, S., Bongaerts, T., & Coppen, P.-A. (2005). Native-like attainment of dummy subjects in Dutch and the role of the L1. *International Review of Applied Linguistics, 43*, 355–380.

White, L., & Genesee, F. (1996). How native is near-native? The issue of ultimate attainment in adult second language acquisition. *Second Language Research, 12*(3), 233–265.

Wiley, E.W., Bialystok, E., & Hakuta, K. (2005). New approaches to using census data to test the Critical-Period Hypothesis for second-language acquisition. *Psychological Science, 16*(4), 341–343.

Williams, J.N. (2009). Implicit learning. In W.C. Ritchie, & T.K. Bhatia (Eds.), *The new handbook of second language acquisition* (pp. 319–353). Bingley: Emerald.

Yeni-Komshian, G., Flege, J.E., & Liu, S. (2000). Pronunciation proficiency in the first and second languages of Korean-English bilinguals. *Bilingualism: Language and Cognition, 3*(2), 131–149.

Maturational constraints on lexical acquisition in a second language

Katherine Spadaro

This study investigates the possibility of a sensitive period for the acquisition of lexical and collocational knowledge in a second language. The participants were ten adult native speakers of English and 38 very advanced adult non-native speakers with a range of ages of onset of learning. They performed a battery of tests, comprising a standard word-association test, an oral production task, and a range of written lexical tasks (developed for this study) focusing on the use of core vocabulary and multi-word units. The results are taken to support the existence of a sensitive period for lexical acquisition in a second language, and the overall tendency to similarity in scores obtained by NNSs with AOs of 7–12 and 13+ appears to indicate that this sensitive period closes around the age of six.

1. Introduction

Of all the personal and social variables which the second language learner brings to the learning process, the age of the learner is probably the most enduringly controversial (Long 2007). The adoption of any position whatsoever on this point is likely to have quite profound consequences for both theory and practice, as the issue bears directly or indirectly on such questions as the existence and continuing availability of a language learning mechanism, the possible alternative means by which languages might be acquired, the marked variation in outcome between typical processes of first and second language acquisition, the optimum timing of language-teaching efforts, and the degrees of success which such efforts might be reasonably expected to produce.

The lexicon is widely acknowledged to be of crucial importance in the language acquisition process; indeed, Clark (1993) makes the claim that "the lexicon is central in language, and central in the acquisition of language… (it) offers a unique window for the process of acquisition for language as a whole" (p. 1). Lexical knowledge is clearly indispensable for both productive and receptive communication, but acquiring such knowledge in a second language seems to be fraught with some difficulty (Cook 1988; Levelt 1989). The function of the internal lexicon involves the control of a staggering amount of information. The scale and complexity of this facility can be hinted at by the estimates which have been made of the number of lexical items controlled by a normal individual: although these estimates vary considerably, a typical claim is as follows: "Twelve-year-olds have a recognition vocabulary of about 135,000 words, Harvard freshmen know about 200,000 words, the typical thirty-year-old Ph.D. knows about 250,000 words" (Diller 1971:29, cited in Singleton 1989). The problems involved in defining the term *word*, together with the methodological issues involved in testing word knowledge (see Aitchison 2012, for a brief review), ensure that any such figures are controversial, but the enormity and intricacy of the mental lexicon remains beyond dispute.

One extremely significant feature of lexical use which must be taken into account in any research relating to the lexicon is the involvement at all levels of sequencing processes, labelled 'chunking' by Ellis (1995b). Words are first represented as phonological strings, and the acquisition process demands that the learner develop awareness and control of the language's permissible phonological sequences, syllabic structure, etc. Repeated sequences that are retained in short-term memory are then available to be consolidated in long-term memory and successfully acquired (Ellis 1995a).

The importance of sequencing is also evident at another level: that of collocation. Despite the transformational-generative emphasis on creativity and innovation in language use, most everyday examples of speech can be analysed as containing large numbers of prefabricated combinations (Pawley & Syder 1983). As Hanks (1987) has expressed it,

> the words of English simply do not, typically, combine and recombine freely and randomly… the distinction between the possible and the typical is of the greatest importance. It is possible, given a reasonably lively imagination, to use a particular word in any number of ways. But when we ask how the word is typically used… we can generally discover a relatively small number of distinct patterns (p. 87).

Thus, Sinclair (1991) argues for the use of two principles of interpretation to explain text. The *open choice* principle, which represents text as a series of slots to be filled by any one of a virtually unlimited range of words, restrained only by grammatical considerations (the principle on which linguistic grammars are normally constructed), needs to be supplemented by the *idiom principle*, which claims that the speaker has access to a large store of semi-constructed phrases. In a very similar vein, Carter lays emphasis on "the importance of viewing the lexicon of a language as a repository of potential for open and creative exploitation but also as a source of non-transacted, given, even stereotyped communication" (1987b: 133).

The extent to which everyday speech actually makes use of such combinations is indicated by the thousands of examples which have been analysed and presented in works such as the Oxford Dictionary of Current Idiomatic English (Cowie & Mackin 1975; Cowie, Mackin & McCaig 1983), the Oxford Dictionary of English Idioms (Ayto 2010) and the COBUILD corpus-based series of dictionaries published by Collins. Many such works are produced for the ESL market, and this reflects a wide-ranging consensus that multi-word units present particular problems for second language learners. Moon, for example, comments that "fixed expressions are the most difficult part of the vocabulary of a language for learners to acquire fully" (1992: 25). There is also some evidence that learners avoid using multi-word units, and particularly idioms (Irujo 1993; Yorio 1989; Dagut & Laufer 1985). This holds true even when the relevant idioms in the second language have direct native language equivalents (Kellerman 1977; Hulstijn & Marchena 1989). Given that idioms or fixed expressions appear to be both problematic for learners, and an intrinsic part of normal communication in English, the degree of control of such items by advanced non-native speakers (NNSs) appears to be an appropriate path by which to investigate lexical competence.

A second important feature of normal lexical use is the salience of *core vocabulary* (or *nuclear vocabulary* – Quirk 1982; Stubbs 1986): a relative label for that collection of frequently occurring lexical items in a language which are used to express simple and basic concepts: those words which are "more tightly integrated than others into the language system" (Carter 1987b: 35). Although a precise definition of what constitutes a core item is difficult to develop, quite strong support for the existence of such a concept can be taken from the fact that a certain set of words both occurs with greater frequency and demonstrates more functional versatility than others. The following eight main criteria for core vocabulary, most of which are derived from the results of informant-based testing, have been put forward by Carter (1987a, 1987b), suggesting that core items are:

1. More likely to substitute for other, more dispensable, words: in defining *guffaw*, *chuckle*, *giggle* or *snigger*, for example, *laugh* is normally used, whereas none of the other items would be used in defining *laugh*.
2. Likely to have a clear and universally recognised antonym: *laugh* is perceived as the opposite *of cry*, and *fat* as the opposite of *thin*, whereas the semantically-related but non-core *chuckle* and *podgy* have no clear antonyms.
3. Available to collocate with a much greater range of other words than non-core items. Thus a core word like *bright* can collocate with numerous other words (*bright sun, bright idea, bright colours, bright child*, etc.), whereas the less core *radiant* has a more limited range of partnerships (*radiant sun, *radiant idea, radiant colours, *radiant child*).

4. More likely to be capable of conveying a wide range of meanings than other words; thus the number of entries which lexicographers provide for a particular word provides a good starting-point for determining a word's coreness. Stubbs (1986) provides the example of *well*, which has been allocated 150 entries in the Collins English Dictionary.
5. Superordinate: core words tend to have a generic rather than specific quality, so *bed*, for example, is core, while *cot, bunk* and *four-poster* are not.
6. Used to label universals of human experience, such as bodily functions and natural physical phenomena, for example *sleep, eat, sun, earth, big* and *round*, although the precise semantic force carried by each term will frequently differ from language to language.
7. Likely to be used in preference to other alternatives in recounting and summarising narratives.
8. Likely to be perceived as neutral; located somewhere around the midpoint of the clines informal/formal; positive/negative; and strong/weak. *Thin*, for example, being placed at the mid-point of each, is perceived as less evaluative than *slim* or *skinny*, while *skinny* is rated as less formal than the other terms.

Studies such as those of Viberg (1993) appear to suggest that the use of core vocabulary is a domain in which the performance of NNSs appears to differ from that of native speakers (NSs). Viberg describes a study of verb use by 23 6-year-old immigrant children in Sweden, with a range of 13 first languages, all at an 'intermediary' level of proficiency. When the performance of the NNS children was compared to that of 12 NS controls, in recordings of free conversation, play and elicited retellings of video clips, the 10 most frequent verbs were used more by the NNSs (representing 61% of all verb use) than by the NSs (54% of all verb use). The relatively greater NNS emphasis on core verbs was reflected in both the statistics for frequency and in a much greater tendency for overextension in meaning, with one verb, for example, being used to mean *fly, rise* and *ride*. Viberg cites several other accounts of the importance of core verbs in lexical and syntactic L2 development, particularly in the earlier stages, including Sato (1988), Harley and King (1989), Dittmar (1984) and Klein and Perdue (1988), with similar accounts relating to L1 development in Clark (1978) and Bretherton and Beeghly (1982).

The notions of coreness and sequencing come together in a procedure which has been quite widely used to investigate lexical organisation in the less advanced L2 learner: word association experiments such as those of Meara (1978, 1982). Meara's tests were based on the Kent-Rosanoff list, which consists of 100 English words in frequent everyday use. The participant is presented with the entire list of stimulus words, asked to read them silently one by one, and to write the first word or phrase which each stimulus brings to mind. Given the speed of the test (it is normally completed within ten minutes) and the lack of any context whatsoever for the stimulus words, the responses provided are considered to be spontaneous and automatic. Because of this automaticity, together with the high level of predictability of response types, the process is regarded by many researchers as a useful tool for disclosing the nature of the links, semantic and phonological, that exist within the mental lexicon (Meara 2009). The particular advantage of the Kent-Rosanoff list is that it has been used extensively over several decades and in several languages by both psychologists and applied linguists, and so the standardised patterns of responses given by different populations are well-documented (Postman & Keppel 1970; Meara 1978, 1982; Soderman 1993).

The way in which word association tests are normally analysed is to divide responses into two main categories: the syntagmatic and the paradigmatic. Syntagmatic responses combine with the stimulus word to complete a word or a phrase: for example, *table* – cloth; *hold* – hands. Paradigmatic responses are normally of the same form class as the stimulus, often similar in meaning, and could be substituted for the stimulus in certain contexts: for example, *man* – woman; *tree* – bush. Normal adults have a marked preference for paradigmatic responses, as can be demonstrated by the first five words of the Kent-Rosanoff list together with their most common responses:

(1) *Table*   chair
(2) *Man*   woman
(3) *Soft*   hard
(4) *Black*   white
(5) *Hand*   foot

The specific responses shown above are highly predictable, and would be expected to occur in 70–80% of cases. Syntagmatic responses are given less frequently by adults, particularly when the stimulus words are common.

Studies as early as the 1960s demonstrated that with developing L1 competence, a shift in response type actually takes place (Brown & Berko 1960; Ervin 1961; Entwisle 1966, cited in Singleton 1993). Up to about the age of seven, children's responses tend to be syntagmatic rather than paradigmatic, and frequent 'clang' responses – i.e. those that are phonologically rather than semantically motivated – are also given. At approximately that age, a shift takes place and children begin to provide responses that are more in accordance with the adult preference for paradigmatic associations, while 'clang' responses become relatively rare.

In view of the fact that L1 development seemed to give rise to this regular and verifiable shift, the possibility of a similar process in L2 development was raised. Studies by Politzer (1978), Meara (1978) and Soderman (1993) specifically addressed this question. Meara's study, which is probably the best-known, examined the responses to a French version of the Kent-Rosanoff list of a group of 78 female students of French in a London secondary school. In comparing their associations with those of native French speakers, Meara came to the conclusion that, at least at this limited level of proficiency, the NNSs' semantic links were very unstable and loosely organised. Phonological factors, such as a random resemblance between an L1 word and an L2 word, could easily override semantic connections. His results thus seemed to corroborate the notion that the construction of an L2 lexical and semantic network bore significant similarities to the same process in L1. Soderman's study, which examined four groups of Swedish learners of English at different levels of proficiency, also tended to confirm that a shift from syntagmatic to paradigmatic associations with a concurrent decrease of 'clang' responses occurred in L2 development, as it did in L1. No previous studies appear to have used the word association technique to examine the lexical connections of extremely advanced learners or to compare their networks of association with those of NSs. Given the wealth of material available on norms of NS association, this test would seem to be a very suitable instrument for an investigation of what differences, if any, exist between NS and near-native NNS lexical systems.

2.   Method

2.1   Selection of NNS participants

"There is no value in studying obviously non-native-like individuals intensely in order to declare them non-native-like" (Long 1993:204). For this reason it was particularly important to involve participants who were genuinely advanced NNSs of English. Initial recruitment was carried out by two means: displaying posters in all areas of the University of Western Australia campus advertising for "people who learned English as a second language and now speak it really well", and approaching friends and other contacts who appeared to be potential participants. Later in the process of data collection, an advertisement was also placed in the campus staff newspaper asking for suitable volunteers. Of the 38 NNS individuals who finally participated, 14 were initially recruited through the posters, two through the newspaper advertisement, and the remaining 22 were contacted through friendship networks. Definitions of what constitutes a *native speaker* can be problematic (see Davies 1991), but for the purposes of this study a NNS was simply classified as one who regularly used another language or languages over a period of time before being first exposed to English. The length of this period of time varied according to the age of onset (AO) for English. Although some of the NNSs commenced learning English fairly early, none of them were exposed to the language in the first few years of life. Any potential participants who had had regular or significant exposure to English from birth were not included in the study.

Another desirable attribute for participation in the study was a substantial length of residence (LOR) in Australia or another English-speaking country, including full participation in that community through employment or study, in order to ascertain that adequate external conditions for the acquisition of English as the L2 had been met. Most of the participants met this criterion, although two who appeared to have almost native-like fluency but shorter LOR (two years and three years) were also included. Because most of the advertising and development of other contacts were done on the university campus, many participants were either members of the university community, staff or students, or their relatives or friends.

Individuals who responded to the public advertising were interviewed by phone. This conversation took the form of an explanation of the broad aims of the study and a discussion of the individual's linguistic background and experience with English. Some respondents were eliminated from the study at this point, as their levels of proficiency were evidently not native-like, indicating that self-report alone would have been an unsatisfactory basis for inclusion. The participants were not subjected to a formal test to qualify for inclusion, as the amount of input they were contributing to the study was already fairly formidable; it would also be difficult to find a standardized test which truly discriminated amongst participants at very advanced levels.

All participants completed a questionnaire giving information on relevant variables, such as age, gender, country of birth and L1. Although some of these could be measured without difficulty, others presented some complications. Age, being of crucial importance for this study, was given particular attention. AO represented the beginning of a serious and sustained process of language acquisition, usually as the result of either migration to an English-speaking community or commencement of a formal English language programme in primary or high school. LOR refers to the number of years the participants had spent in an English-speaking environment. This environment was in most cases Australia, although several individuals had spent some time in other English-speaking countries, and such periods of time were incorporated into this calculation. This variable is important because if a strong relationship existed between AO and LOR, such that those participants with earliest AO also had longest LOR, the influences of the two factors would be difficult to separate. Among these particular subjects, however, a good range of values for LOR seemed to exist, independent of AO values.

The NNS participants were divided into three categories, according to values for AO. Group 1 comprised those participants with an AO of 6 or younger ($n = 13$), Group 2 those whose AO ranged from 7–12 ($n = 15$), and Group 3 ($n = 10$) those with an AO of 13 or older. The ages of 6 and 12 were considered appropriate cut-off points, as evidence from earlier studies suggests that age six may be the approximate age for the closure of the period of peak sensitivity, and 12 the approximate age for closure of the offset period in other domains of language acquisition.

The control group of ten adult native English speakers were mainly contacted and recruited through friendship networks. Nine of the ten members of the group were born in Australia, and one was born in England but has lived in Australia for many years. English was the first language of all of the control participants, and although about half of the group had some knowledge of another language or languages, Australian English was the primary code used by all of them. The group was roughly matched with the NNS group on non-linguistic criteria. 84% of the NNSs (32 of the 38), and 80% of the NSs (8 of the 10), were tertiary educated. The gender balance was 61% (23/38) female, 39% (15/38) male in the NNS group, and 60% female, 40% male in the NS group. The NNS group, however, contained proportionately more language professionals than the NS group: 10 of the 38 NNSs were language professionals in some sense, including seven teachers of ESL and one applied linguist, compared to only two of the NSs (both applied linguists).

2.2   Test materials

The testing procedure was intended to focus as specifically as possible on those areas of lexical performance where NNSs might reasonably be expected to differ from NSs. Because the test population was expected to comprise extremely advanced NNSs, it was necessary to develop tests which would be sufficiently difficult to discriminate between the individuals and groups involved, if differences among them did exist. Another principle which was important in the development of materials was that successful performance on the tests should not depend on level of education or professional background of the participants: it was hoped that the tests would be such that any NS of Australian English with normal literacy levels would be able to complete them with a high level of success.

The battery of tests which was used in this study included the Kent-Rosanoff word association test, a written test consisting of seven tasks which were developed specifically for this study, and an oral production task (retelling of an excerpt from a video).

The tasks involved in the written test were as follows:

Task 1: Core Preference
The first task tested a possible preference on the part of even very advanced NNSs for core vocabulary. A series of twelve gap-fill sentences was constructed, with gaps which would normally be filled by a non-core word, but in which a core word would also be acceptable. Some examples are:

(1)   She agreed to _____ a kidney to save somebody's life
(2)   The drunk _____ over to the bus-stop
(3)   After being questioned, the butler _____ that he'd killed his employer

Although *give, walked* and *said* would be quite acceptable in the above examples, the non-core items *donate, staggered/stumbled/lurched*, and *confessed/admitted* would be equally or perhaps more probable.

Task 2: Word Discrimination
The second task required participants to distinguish between real English words and words which appeared plausible, conformed to English phonological rules, but had been devised for the purposes of the test. This task is similar to vocabulary tests designed by Meara (1992b), but differs in that the *counterfeit* words which appear in his tests are typically very short and simply constructed. In this task, however, the counterfeit words were actually created from English morphological segments which were recognisable to the participants from their appearance in other, familiar, words. Examples include:

(1)   *Kindwill*
(2)   *Nightbreak*
(3)   *Walkerby*
(4)   *Highbrained*

Twelve of those words were randomly mixed with twelve genuine words, also constructed of at least two separable morphological elements, and the participants were asked to circle those items which were "not real English words." It was expected that the ability to judge that a certain item, conforming to all the rules of English structure and with a fairly transparent probable meaning, is nonetheless definitely not part of the English lexicon, would require a very advanced knowledge of English on the part of the participant.

Task 3: Core Overextension
The third task, which also centred on core words, was partly derived from one described by Kellerman (1979, 1983). His studies indicated that Dutch learners of English tended to reject as unacceptable English sentences in which the most

abstract or metaphorical extended meanings of core words were used. For this task, a group of fifteen core words were selected on the basis of frequency and range of use. Four sentences were composed for each word, three of which represented commonly used senses of the word, and one which extended the sense of the word in a manner which is not normally acceptable. Participants were asked to identify by underlining the sentence which contained the odd use of the core word in question. The following are two sample items:

(1)   *draw*
      She drew some ice cream from the tub on the table.
      The old man was so weak he could hardly draw breath.
      A bus drew up to the terminal.
      The annual car rally always draws a large crowd.

(2)   *pass*
      Bessie passed a relaxing month in Provence.
      Twenty years have passed since they last saw each other.
      You've got the money you demanded – now pass the hostage.
      The whole class passed the weekly test.

As the above examples demonstrate, the task demands a fairly high level of knowledge of the potential meaning extensions and collocational possibilities of the core words selected. In the *draw* example, the participant must be aware (not necessarily at a conscious level) that only liquid materials taken from a source are normally said to be *drawn*; in the *pass* example, the participant must know that requests to pass items are normally restricted to inanimate objects.

Task 4: Multi-Word Unit Completion
Task 4, and the remaining tasks in the written test, examined participants' knowledge of multi-word units. According to studies such as that of Swinney and Cutler (1979), which found subjects had significantly faster reaction times to multi-word units than to matched-length control phrases, such units are stored and accessed as single lexical items. The fourth task provided participants with the first two words of 18 multi-word units, each consisting of three words, and required them to provide the final word to complete the phrase. Some examples of the phrases used for this task include:

(1)   *Aches and* _____
(2)   *Labour of* _____
(3)   *Tie the* _____

Given that the initial segments of a word or phrase seem to be the most salient in lexical storage and retrieval (Aitchison & Straf 1982) it was expected that participants who were familiar with these items would find their recall relatively easy.

Task 5: Multi-Word Unit Supply

The fifth task constituted a further and more challenging development of the previous one. Ten words which normally function only as part of a multi-word unit, with virtually no independent meaning, were provided, and the participants were asked to provide the entire phrase in which they usually occurred. The given words were not necessarily taken from the beginning of the phrases in question. Examples of these words include:

(1) *Gab*
(2) *Spick*
(3) *Kilter*
(4) *Beck*

Given this stimulus, participants were expected to provide the phrases *gift of the gab, spick and span, out of kilter* and *beck and call*. It was expected that this task would prove to be quite challenging for many of the participants.

Task 6: Multi-Word Unit Correction

Tasks 6 and 7 tested participants' knowledge of sentence-level multi-word units, or idioms. In the sixth task, the participants read 25 sentences, each of which was based on an idiom. One word in each idiom had been changed. Participants were told that one word was incorrect, asked to identify the incorrect word, and asked to supply the correct replacement word. Examples of this task are:

(1) *I'm afraid you're growling up the wrong tree*
(2) *The boss likes to throw his size around*
(3) *I didn't want to do it but he bent my arm*
(4) *The spy didn't remove his disguise until the coast was safe*

In each case, the incorrect substitute word retains some semantic connection with the correct word, so that the choice of the incorrect word should not be logically obvious to any participant who did not know the idiom. The supply of the correct word was of course possible only if the idiom was known.

Task 7: Multi-Word Unit Transformation

A degree of internal stability is a necessary feature of a lexical item, including those items which comprise more than one word. The seventh task tested the participants' awareness of the degree of *frozenness* (Cutler 1983; Moon 1992) of certain idioms: in other words, whether they can normally undergo transformations such as active/passive, declarative/interrogative or positive/negative, or changes in word order. In no case were normal rules of English syntax violated. Ten sentences which had been transformed in this way were randomly mixed with eight 'normal' sentences also containing multi-word units. The participants were told that each sentence was grammatically correct, but asked to identify the sentences which were "not expressed in the normal way… strange or unusual." Following are four examples of these abnormal sentences, followed by one unaltered sentence:

(1)   *Whose eye is she the apple of?*
(2)   *The bush was thoroughly beaten about by her*
(3)   *Dolores is the party's life and soul*
(4)   *The kids aren't pulling their weight with the housework*

This task, which formed the final part of the written test, was expected to examine whether the participants had internalised the multi-word units in question as internally stable single lexical entries, with varying capacities to undergo transformations.

Task 8: Oral Narrative
A further task, quite different in nature, was added to the battery of tests in order to provide the opportunity to examine stretches of free production by the participants. Each participant watched a short excerpt from a film which showed a dog amusing himself with some spectacularly destructive activities when left alone in a house. After watching the excerpt, the participants were asked to recall aloud as many as possible of the dog's actions, and these monologues were recorded for later transcription. The particular excerpt was chosen because it was memorable, entertaining, and also included actions which were fairly difficult to describe. These transcripts were used for a comparison of NS and NNS in regard to frequency of use of core and non-core vocabulary and of multi-word units; and also to determine whether expert raters could distinguish between NSs and NNSs solely on the basis of written transcripts of the spoken texts.

2.3   Coding data

The task of coding the word association tests was facilitated by the existence of a substantial and established literature on the subject. It was decided to adopt the system outlined in Soderman (1993), which was in turn partly derived from earlier work by Ervin (1961) and Lyons (1977), in deciding how to categorise each response. Each participant was given a score for the four categories *Paradigmatic*, *Syntagmatic*, *Clang* and *Other*, which combined to give a total of 100 response items.

Scoring the written test of lexical knowledge was, for most tasks, relatively straightforward, involving tallies of correct responses. Task 8 involved the most complex system of scoring. The monologues produced by the participants were transcribed by the researcher, organised in lines in accordance with the pauses made by the speakers, but without any attempt to impose sentence structure on the texts. Punctuation symbols were therefore omitted. The copies of the transcripts were then given to four raters, two of whom were applied linguists (university lecturers in applied linguistics), one a postgraduate student in applied linguistics, and the fourth an ESL teacher with over twenty years of experience teaching NNSs in English-medium schools in Africa and Australia. In order to help them understand what the speakers were attempting to describe, the raters were shown the video excerpt which had been viewed by the participants. The raters were asked to perform two tasks: to identify (by underlining) any words or phrases in the transcripts that they considered to be non-native-like choices, and to classify each transcript as having been produced by either a NS or a NNS.

Because of the high level of fluency of the participants, most of the texts contained few obvious syntactic or other grammatical errors. The raters were informed of the high level of proficiency of the speakers, and also reminded that repetitions, hesitations and disfluencies are normal features of NS as well as NNS speech. The first instruction given to the raters, to identify non-native-like choices, was left as open as possible, to allow for a wide range of impressions as to what those choices might involve. The second task built on the first, in that raters were expected to take the occurrence of non-native-like choices, together with a holistic impression of the entire text, to form a judgment as to whether the speaker belonged to the NS or NNS category. The raters were not told how many of the speakers belonged to each category, and all the transcripts were combined and presented in random order.

It was expected that the raters would have considerable difficulty in distinguishing between NNSs with early AO and NSs. If a sensitive period for lexical acquisition with consequences for ultimate attainment does indeed operate, then the judgments of expert raters would be expected to reflect a higher probability of assignment of NNS status as AO increased.

In order to investigate the possible preference of NNSs for core words further, the transcripts were also examined by the researcher to determine the number of non-core words used as a proportion of the total number of words spoken. Given that there is no canonical body of 'core words' to use as a reference point for such an analysis, it was decided to accept the 1,000 word *Little Language* list (Nation 1986) produced for both language teaching and research purposes at the Victoria University of Wellington, as a representative sample of items which could normally be considered *core*. For each transcript, the total number of words was calculated, and the number of non-core words was expressed as a percentage of the total.

2.4   Reliability and validity

As a measure of reliability, Cronbach's alpha was calculated for the overall test scores, and then separately for each of the seven tasks in the written test.

The minimum alpha obtained by this procedure was .6350 for Task 2 (Word Discrimination); maximum alpha was .9222 for Task 6 (MWU Correction). With an alpha of .8950 for the overall test scores, the level of reliability overall was considered acceptable. A Rasch analysis was also carried out on each section, and overall, the expected pattern of correct and incorrect responses was obtained. To ensure test validity, the selection of participants, development of test items and testing procedure were carefully controlled to eliminate extraneous variables as far as possible. The uniformly high scores obtained by the NS (as reported below) indicate that the test is measuring a particular construct – native-like lexical competence – which only the NS group as a whole appears to possess: in other words, the test has construct validity. f and q values were also plotted for each section of the test, and a reasonable spread of values for the two measures obtained, although slightly low q values and slightly high f values reflected the very high levels of proficiency of this particular group.

3.   Results

3.1   Word associations

As indicated in Table 1, the mean scores for Group 1 (AO 0–6), Group 3 (AO 13+) and the NS Group were similar. The scores obtained from Group 2 (AO 7–12) followed the same overall pattern, but with some apparent difference in the proportion of paradigmatic and syntagmatic responses. (As the test comprises 100 items, the raw scores are also percentages.)

Table 1. Means and standard deviations for response types

Group	Paradigmatic	Syntagmatic	Clang	Other
	M	*M*	*M*	*M*
NSs ($n = 10$)	54.3 (20.0)	42.2 (18.9)	0.2	3.3 (2.3)
AO 0–6 ($n = 1$)	53.3 (13.3)	40.4 (12.0)	0.4	5.7 (4.3)
AO 7–12 ($n = 15$)	65.7 (16.8)	28.1 (14.4)	0.9	5.3 (4.2)
AO 13+ ($n = 10$)	56.4 (20.2)	38.9 (19.2)	2.2	4.5 (2.6)

Note: Standard deviations appear between parentheses. Standard deviations for the *clang* category are not included as very few responses of this type were given.

These data were subjected to an analysis of variance, according to which the differences among groups were not statistically significant (F = 1.5356, p = .2186 for the paradigmatic scores; F = 2.3734, p = .0833 for the syntagmatic scores). The similarity of the results obtained here would suggest that the patterns of association between items in the internal lexicon of very advanced NNSs ultimately come to resemble those of NSs fairly closely.

3.2   Written test of lexical use

Those results obtained across all tasks for all four groups are presented in Table 2.

Table 2. Mean percentage scores and standard deviations for all tasks and all groups on written test

	Group NS (n = 10)	Group 1 (AO 0–6) (n = 13)	Group 2 (AO 7–12) (n = 15)	Group 3 (AO 13+) (n = 10)
	M	M	M	M
Task 1	88.6 (13.1)	86.3 (19.2)	75.2 (14.8)	77.8 (19.8)
Task 2	93.7 (06.0)	87.5 (10.6)	82.2 (09.8)	82.9 (13.4)
Task 3	99.3 (02.1)	90.3 (07.5)	85.8 (12.0)	84.0 (18.1)
Task 4	96.1 (05.3)	88.4 (12.3)	69.2 (21.2)	64.4 (25.4)
Task 5	89.0 (11.0)	60.8 (27.8)	51.3 (27.5)	50.0 (35.3)
Task 6	98.2 (02.0)	88.6 (18.8)	74.4 (23.8)	78.7 (17.3)
Task 7	95.6 (08.2)	88.4 (16.1)	77.4 (15.9)	73.9 (16.8)

Note: Standard deviations appear between parentheses.

As indicated in Table 2, interesting differences were found between the four groups tested. The mean overall NS scores were, on average, almost 10 percentage points higher than Group 1 (AO 0–6), which were in turn were over 10 percentage points higher than Groups 2 and 3 (AO 7–12 and 13+). The overall scores obtained for Groups 2 and 3 were very similar, suggesting no or little difference between the two groups. The mean scores obtained by the NSs were roughly equal across all task types, while all of the NNS groups found the phrase-level tasks substantially more difficult than the word-level tasks (see Figure 1 below).

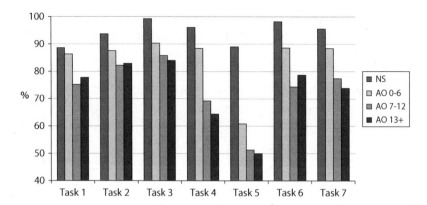

Figure 1. Means across seven tasks for all groups

The results are discussed separately for each task below, but an examination of the overall results gained across all word-level tasks shows a uniform tendency for the NSs to perform better, with Group 1 (AO 0–6) performing less well, but still substantially better than Groups 2 and 3 (AO 7–12 and 13+). There appears to be very little difference between the scores of the latter two groups.

In the four phrase-level tasks also, the NSs obtained the highest scores, with Group 1 (AO 0–6) performing better than the other NNSs. Groups 2 and 3 obtained very similar scores for the phrase-level tasks, and all tasks yielded a fairly similar distribution of scores, except for Task 5 (Multi-Word Unit Supply), which the participants appeared to find the most difficult.

The standard deviations obtained for these scores also showed noticeable differences between the NSs and NNSs, and between the three NNS groups. The overall tendency is for standard deviations from the mean to increase according to the AO of the participants. In each case, the NS group provided the most uniform set of responses, with the widest range of scores being obtained by Group 3 (AO 13+). This result is consistent with the everyday observation that, other things being equal, the process of language acquisition produces more predictable results for younger learners. The levels of ultimate attainment achieved by older learners, however, can vary quite markedly and cover a wide range of outcomes.

Task 1 scores
Task 1 (Core Preference), which measured preference for core vocabulary in sentence completion, contained 14 items. This task differed from the others included in the written test in that none of the items required one obligatory correct answer: participants had the choice of supplying one of many possible responses. Only non-core items were included in the scores, although of course other responses could not be regarded as *mistakes*. The scores obtained on this task were closer

together than on any other section of the written test, partly owing to the lower scores of the NS group. In testing for significance, a default setting of .05 for Scheffé tests was used (in results for this and all the other tasks described here); and there were no statistically significant differences between the NSs and NNSs, or between different NNS groups, in performance on this task.

Task 2 scores

Task 2 (Word Discrimination), which asked participants to discriminate between words and non-words, contained 24 items. The NS group obtained the highest scores on this task, followed by Group 1 (AO 0–6). Groups 2 and 3 (AO 7–12 and 13+) obtained lower scores, and their scores were very similar, although Group 2 scored slightly higher. The Scheffé test revealed a statistically significant difference between the NS group (mean 93.7) and the lowest scoring NNS Group, Group 2 (AO 7–12; mean 84.08), (effect size = 1.3).

Task 3 scores

Task 3 (Core Overextension), which required participants to identify inappropriate use of core vocabulary, contained 15 items. The scores indicate that all groups found Task 3 to be the easiest of the written tasks. This is probably a reflection of the fact that the task focuses on items which are in very frequent use, allowing participants to build up a substantial bank of knowledge about their range of meanings and possible contexts. Despite the overall higher scores, however, the Scheffé test revealed statistically significant differences between the NS Group (mean 99.3) and the NNS Groups 2 and 3 (means 85.2 and 84.9 respectively; effect size = 1.2).

Task 4 scores

Task 4 required participants to supply final words to complete 18 multi-word units. The participants among the NNS groups who did not know the final words in question were in general willing to guess, and some plausible though incorrect answers like *sticks and carrots* and *labour of birth* were supplied. Task 4 reflects the same overall pattern as the others, with NSs scoring highest, and scores descending according to rising AO. The Scheffé test indicated a statistically significant difference between the NSs (mean 96.1) and Groups 2 (AO 7–12) (mean 69.0) and 3 (AO 13+) (mean 65.1), but not between the NSs and Group 1 (AO 0–6) (mean 88.4). A statistically significant difference was also found within the NNS sample on this task: between Groups 1 and 3. This task, which yielded the highest F value of the seven ($F = 7.8269$), proved to be the best discriminator between groups, and the one with the largest effect size (effect size = 1.7).

Task 5 scores

Task 5 required participants to supply a complete multi-word unit and contained 10 items. It proved to be the most difficult for both the NSs and the NNSs in this study. Quite large differences can be seen between the scores obtained by the various groups. In this case, the largest and statistically significant difference is between the NSs (mean 89.0) and NNS Groups 2 (AO 7–12) (mean 50.7) and 3 (AO 13+) (mean 50.9), (effect size = 1.4). Group 1 (AO 0–6) received higher scores than the other NNS groups, with a mean of 60.8. The scores obtained on this task by Groups 2 and 3 are virtually indistinguishable.

Task 6 scores

Task 6 required participants to identify and correct the wrong element within a multi-word unit, and contained 25 items. From the responses given, it appears that those participants who were unfamiliar with a particular multi-word unit were often prepared to hazard a guess, although they did not necessarily select the appropriate word to replace. Item 13, for example, was *Vincent's father hauled him on the coals for denting the car*. In addition to numerous correct responses (*on* replaced by *over*), the following amendments were also suggested:

> Vincent's father dragged him on the coals for denting the car
> Vincent's father raked him on the coals for denting the car
> Vincent's father grilled him on the coals for denting the car
> Vincent's father held him on the coals for denting the car
> Vincent's father put him on the coals for denting the car
> Vincent's father hauled him through the coals for denting the car
> Vincent's father hauled him on the rocks for denting the car

These responses would appear to be motivated simply by guesswork. In other cases, participants were better able to identify the element to be changed, such as in item 9, "We want the party to be a surprise so keep it under your jumper." The correct response was to replace *jumper* with *hat*. All participants seemed to recognise the word to be changed, but the suggested replacements included *vest*, *bonnet, sleeve, collar, pyjamas, coat, belt* and, more idiosyncratically, *nose*. Whether those responses were motivated by some memory of having previously heard the expression, and a recollection that an item of clothing was involved, or simply by a shrewd sense that the replacement word should be similar to the incorrect word, is unknown. Some of the responses suggested here, of course, may be influenced by such expressions as *keeping something up one's sleeve, having something (e.g. experience) under one's belt* and *being hot under the collar*.

The NS group obtained almost perfect scores for Task 6. Group 1 (AO 0–6) scored lower than the NS, but higher than the other NNS groups. As in Task 2 (Word Discrimination), Group 3 (AO 13+) scored slightly higher than Group 2 (AO 7–12) (means of 79.0 and 73.9 respectively). The Scheffé test reveals a statistically significant difference between the NSs (mean 98.2) and the lowest-scoring group of NNSs (Group 2; mean 73.9), (effect size = 1.3).

Task 7 scores

Task 7, which asked participants to identify multi-word units which had undergone unacceptable transformations, contained 18 items. The NS group (mean 95.6) performed best on this task also, with Group 1 (AO 0–6) attaining the next highest mean score (88.4). According to the Scheffé test, the scores obtained by Groups 2 and 3 (AO 7–12 and 13+), with very similar means of 76.6 and 75.2, were significantly lower than those of the NS Group; (effect size = 1.4).

Overall, the means obtained for all seven written tasks reflect several tendencies. In each case the NS group obtained the highest scores. In each case the youngest learners (AO 0–6) constitute the next highest scoring group. In each case the lowest scores were obtained by the two groups of older learners (AO 7–12 and 13+), and in most tasks, those learners with AO 7–12 performed slightly better than those with AO 13+. In each task the scores obtained by the latter two groups were very similar, in some cases virtually indistinguishable. In all of the tasks, except Task 1 (Core Preference), statistically significant differences were found between the NSs and at least one of the NNS groups with later AO: in most cases, the NSs' scores were significantly different from those of both Group 2 (AO 7–12) and Group 3 (AO 13+). In no case were the NS scores found to be significantly different from those of the younger learners (AO 0–6). Task 4 (Multi-Word Unit Completion) proved to be the maximal discriminator, yielding significantly different results from within the NNS population, as well as between the NSs and NNSs. Overall, those tests which focused on lexical knowledge at phrase or multi-word unit level appeared to be the most reliable discriminators.

In order to account for the LOR variable, analyses of covariance were performed separately for each task, with LOR as the covariate. The only task in which LOR was a significant factor was Task 4 (Multi-Word Unit Completion), and these results are given in Table 3. However, the nature of that influence (on Task 4) was that differences between the AO-defined groups were found to be even greater when LOR was controlled than when it was not.

In summary, the results from these tasks suggest that the level of ultimate attainment of NNSs with regard to the lexicon is different from that of NSs. They

Table 3. Results of analysis of covariance for Task 4 (MWU Completion)

Source of variation	DF	Mean square	F	p value
Covariate: LOR	1	5829.143	24.402	.000
Main effects: AO Group	2	1526.075	6.389	.004
Residual	34	238.877		
Total	37	482.526		

also suggest that the levels of ultimate attainment are constrained by maturational factors, with younger learners (AO < 6) invariably performing better than older learners, and relatively little difference between the two groups with later AO. As the effect of AO remained strong even when the LOR variable was partialled out, it appears that increased exposure to the target lexicon does not have a significant influence upon learners' levels of attainment.

Task 8 scores (Oral Narrative)
The results gained for this task revealed some differences between the NS and NNS groups. In the first place, the NSs appeared to produce substantially longer stretches of text than the NNSs: the mean length of the narratives produced by all NNS groups was 244 words, whereas the mean length of narrative produced by the NSs was 320 words. However, this difference between NSs and NNSs with regard to performance of Task 8 proved not to be statistically significant when the data were subjected to an analysis of variance ($F = 1.5584$, $p = .2133$).

A particular focus of interest had been the use of core and non-core words by participants in producing spontaneous narrative text. However, all groups performed very similarly on this measure, with non-core words approximating 9–10% for all groups.

As previously described, the transcripts were submitted to four raters, all NS language professionals, who were asked to assign NS or NNS status to each transcript (see Table 4). Each transcript was then given a score from 0 to 4, depending on how many raters had classified it as having been produced by a NS.

Table 4. Participants assigned NS status by two or more raters

	Number in group	Number given NS status
Group NS	10	9
Group 1 (AO 0–6)	13	9
Group 2 (AO 7–12)	15	5
Group 3 (AO 13+)	10	5

These results can be seen as a reflection of the overall high level of proficiency of the NNS participants. On average, each participant was believed to be a NS by at least one of the four raters. As would be expected, the NS group received higher ratings, on average, with Group 1 (AO 0–6) receiving the next highest. After that point, however, the ratings did not decline as a function of AO, as Groups 2 and 3 (AO 7–12 and 13+) received very similar ratings.

3.3   General trends in use of core vocabulary

Three of the tasks performed by the participants focused on preference for, and use of, core vocabulary items. It appears that this group of advanced NNSs showed no significant preference for using core items. The results of Task 3 (Core Overextension), however, did indicate some difference between groups in regard to the kind of knowledge of core items which they possessed. It will be remembered that the words in question were all extremely frequent in English and generally regarded as simple; certainly all the participants would assert that they knew the meanings of *break, set, lead,* and the other words tested here. However, the results for the task indicated that many of the NNS participants did not have a clear sense of where the area of meaning of these items should end. Tasks 6 (Multi-Word Unit Correction) and 7 (Multi-Word Unit Transformation), although focusing on multi-word units as single entities, could also be perceived as testing participants' knowledge of the participation of core words in collocations and larger phrases: one of the criteria commonly put forward for *knowing* a word. The significantly lower scores obtained by the NNSs, particularly the older learners, on those tasks, is also suggestive of a difference in the nature of their knowledge of this vocabulary. In sum, those tasks which attempt to investigate the role of core items in the lexicon of NNSs indicate that they do not use such items with relatively more frequency than NSs – if anything, they prefer non-core items – but their knowledge of core items may in a sense be more limited or operate at a more superficial level than that of NSs; the NSs have a firmer sense of the semantic boundaries and the collocational possibilities of the core items.

3.4   General trends in use of multi-word units

The results described above indicate that NNSs differ quite markedly from NSs in the production of multi-word units. The NNSs in general scored significantly lower than the NSs on the relevant tasks, and there was a strong tendency for lower scores to occur with higher AO. In general, older learners who were given one element from a multi-word unit found it more difficult to supply the rest of that unit. They also found it more difficult both to identify and correct a wrong element within a multi-word unit, and to judge when a multi-word unit had undergone an inappropriate transformation. In sum, the NNSs, and particularly the older learners, appeared to have a considerably smaller repertoire of *memorized chunks* at their disposal. The inference to be drawn from these results is that they have not undergone the process of lexicalising familiar collocations to be comprehended or produced as wholes to the same degree as NSs.

4. Conclusions

As the literature review has suggested, there appears to be increasing evidence for the existence of maturational constraints, in some form, on the acquisition of first and subsequent languages. Despite the skepticism expressed by some within the discipline, a broader consideration of the prevalence of sensitive periods in non-human species, as well as their operation in the development of other human behaviours, make such a notion unsurprising. Indeed, given the highly predictable nature of the unfolding course of development undergone by most individuals in the early stages of childhood, the absence of a sensitive period (or series of sensitive periods) for language would be considerably more surprising. This study has attempted to investigate one of the linguistic domains in which a sensitive period might plausibly be expected to influence development, and has produced results consistent with the operation of such a sensitive period.

There are significant differences in ultimate attainment between NNSs and NSs with regard to the lexicon. Given the degree of success in acquiring and maintaining their second language which this elite NNS group has nonetheless been able to achieve, it could be suggested that the issue of sensitive periods is not really of particular importance. I would argue, however, that the issue remains extremely important, for a number of reasons. Firstly, there are many more unsuccessful learners than there are extremely successful ones, so the operation of sensitive periods in language acquisition has an ongoing impact on many more human beings than the relatively small coterie of high achievers. Secondly, some acknowledgement of the effects of sensitive periods could facilitate the injection of needed doses of realism into language learning programmes with regard to the levels that the majority of learners can be expected to attain, as well as to the periods of life where instruction and/or exposure is likely to produce the maximum benefit. And thirdly, continued investigation of the operation of sensitive periods provides an intriguing means of insight into the very processes of language acquisition, maintenance and decay in the brain, as well as a possible perspective from which some of the recently available neuroimaging data might be interpreted.

Given the above, there are numerous interesting possibilities for ongoing research. The total number of such language-related sensitive periods, the possibility and degree of overlap, and how they affect each other, are intriguing questions that are unlikely to be answered for some time. For each individual sensitive period that is identified, a range of detailed issues will require explanation, and Bornstein's list of relevant questions (1987) provides an excellent starting point for consideration of the timing, duration, mechanism and results that are involved.

The specific issue of the effect of maturational constraints on the lexicon has received less attention than their effect on either phonology or syntax. This being the case, there is considerable scope for future studies. As always when testing for small differences in competence between highly proficient individuals, whether NSs or NNSs, the focus of attention has to be on genuinely challenging items – in this case, the further reaches of the lexicon, at the limit of what might be labelled the participants' *comfort zone*. As shown by the present study, such challenging items need not include rarefied or obscure vocabulary (although that could be a legitimate focus of interest among some populations) – the role of core vocabulary, for example, is a topic which may well repay further attention. Studies which further test the possibility of a *fuzzier* sense of the semantic boundaries of core vocabulary on the part of some NNSs may be illuminating in this regard.

The results obtained in this study, together with the theoretical perspectives on the lexicon advanced by psychologists such as Ellis (1995a), indicate that the syntagmatic and collocational links that obtain between words is a particularly important feature of mature native-like linguistic competence. The possibilities for future research in this area are attractive. Given some incomplete stretches of text, for example, perhaps of a greater length than the sentence-level test items used here, how predictable are the types of responses with which NSs complete the texts? To what extent do the responses of highly proficient NNSs differ from them? What are the intuitions of NSs and NNSs about the predictability of such responses? Would they classify the same kinds of responses as obligatory in some contexts? Is there any relationship between AO and the level of confidence felt by NNSs in making such judgments?

The above questions represent only a few of the many possible lines of enquiry that remain to be pursued. With so much ground to be explored with regard to the (in some sense) simpler monolingual mental lexicon, the intricacies of the lexical networks of bilinguals and the timing involved in their construction can present a field of research so complicated as to be rather intimidating. Some reassurance can be drawn, however, from the fairly strong indications in this and previous studies of the existence of a relationship between the early lexical exposure experienced by individuals and their ultimate levels of attainment. If it is not yet possible to make confident assertions about the operation of a sensitive period for second language lexical development, the evidence is, at least, suggestive.

References

Aitchison, J., & Straf, M. (1982). Lexical storage and retrieval: A developing skill? In A. Cutler (Ed.), *Slips of the tongue and language production* (pp. 197–241). The Hague: Mouton.
Aitchison, J. (2012). *Words in the mind* (4th ed.). Oxford: Blackwell.
Ayto, J. (2010). *The Oxford Dictionary of English Idioms*. Oxford: OUP.

Bornstein, M. (1987). Sensitive periods in development: Definition, existence, utility and meaning. In M. Bornstein (Ed.), *Sensitive periods in development: Interdisciplinary perspectives* (pp. 3–17). Hillsdale, NJ: Lawrence Erlbaum Associates.

Bretherton, I., & Beeghly, M. (1982). Talking about internal states: The acquisition of an explicit theory of mind. *Developmental Psychology, 18*, 906–921.

Brown, R.W., & Berko, J. (1960). Word association and the acquisition of grammar. *Child Development, 31*, 1–14.

Carter, R. (1987a). Is there a core vocabulary? Some implications for language teaching. *Applied Linguistics, 8*(2), 178–193.

Carter, R. (1987b). *Vocabulary: Applied linguistic perspectives.* London: Allen & Unwin.

Clark, E. (1978). Discovering what words can do. In D. Farkas, W. Jacobsen, & K. Todrys (Eds.), *Papers from the parasession on the lexicon* (pp. 34–57). Chicago, IL: Chicago Linguistic Society.

Clark, E. (1993). *The lexicon in acquisition.* Cambridge: CUP.

Cook, V. (1988). *Chomsky's universal grammar.* Oxford: Blackwell.

Cowie, A. P., & Mackin, R. (1975). *Oxford dictionary of current idiomatic English. Vol.1: Verbs with prepositions and particles.* Oxford: Oxford University Press.

Cowie, A., Mackin, R., & McCaig, I. (1983). *Oxford dictionary of current idiomatic English* (2 volumes). Oxford: OUP.

Cutler, A. (1983). Lexical complexity and sentence processing. In G. Flores D'Arcais, & R. Jarvella (Eds.), *The process of language understanding* (pp. 43–79). New York: Wiley.

Dagut, M., & Laufer, B. (1985). Avoidance of phrasal verbs: A case for contrastive analysis. *Studies in Second Language Acquisition, 7*(1), 73–79.

Davies, A. (1991). *The native speaker in applied linguistics.* Edinburgh: EUP.

Diller, K. (1971). *Generative grammar, structual linguistics and language teaching.* Rowley, MA: Newbury House.

Dittmar, N. (1984). Semantic features of pidginized learner varieties of German. In R. Andersen (Ed.), *Second languages: A cross-linguistic perspective* (pp. 243–270). Rowley, MA: Newbury House.

Ellis, N. (1995a). Vocabulary acquisition: Psychological perspectives and pedagogical implications. *The Language Teacher, 19*(2), 12–16.

Ellis, N. (1995b). Seminar on the lexicon presented at the Department of ESL, University of Hawai'i, Spring 1995.

Entwisle, D.R. (1966). *Word associations of young children.* Baltimore, MD: John Hopkins University Press.

Ervin, S. (1961). Changes with age in the verbal determinants of word association. *American Journal of Psychology, 74*, 361–372.

Hanks, P. (1987). Definitions and explanations. In J.M. Sinclair (Ed.), *Looking up: An account of the COBUILD Project in lexical computing and the development of the Collins COBUILD English language dictionary* (pp. 116–136). London: Collins.

Harley, B., & King, M.L. (1989). Verb lexis in the written compositions of young L2 learners. *Studies in Second Language Acquisition, 11*(4), 415–439.

Hulstijn, J.H., & Marchena, E.M.T. (1989). How difficult are the phrasal verbs for Dutch learners of English? In M. Wintle, & P. Vincent (Eds.), *Modern Dutch studies: Essays in honour of Peter King* (pp. 48–59). London: The Athlone Press.

Irujo, S. (1993). Steering clear: Avoidance in the production of idioms. *International Review of Applied Linguistics in Language Teaching, 31*(3), 205–219.

Kellerman, E. (1977). Towards a characterization of the strategy of transfer in second language learning. *Interlanguage Studies Bulletin, 2*(1), 58–145.

Kellerman, E. (1979). Transfer and non-transfer: where we are now". *Studies in Second Language Acquisition, 2*, 37–57.

Kellerman, E. (1983). Now you see it, now you don't. In S. Gass, & L. Selinker (Eds.), *Language transfer in language learning* (pp. 112–134). Rowley, MA: Newbury.

Klein, W., & Perdue, C. (Eds.). (1988). *Utterance structure. Second language acquisition by adult immigrants. Final report. Vol. VI.* Strasbourg: ESF.

Levelt, W.J.M. (1989). *Speaking: From intention to articulation.* Cambridge, MA: The MIT Press.

Long, M. (1993). Second language acquisition as a function of age: Research findings and methodological issues. In K. Hyltenstam, & A. Viberg (Eds.), *Progression and regression in language-sociocultural, neuropsychological and linguistic perspectives* (pp. 196–221). Cambridge: CUP.

Long, M. (2007). *Problems in SLA.* Mahwah, NJ: Lawrence Erlbaum Associates.

Lyons, J. (1977). *Semantics (2 vols).* Cambridge: CUP.

Meara, P. (1978). Learners' word associations in French. *Interlanguage Studies Bulletin, 3,* 192–211.

Meara, P. (1982). Word associations in a foreign language: A report on the Birkbeck vocabulary project. *The Nottingham Linguistic Circular, 11*(2), 29–38.

Meara, P. (1992b). *EFL vocabulary tests.* Swansea: Swansea University College for Applied Language Studies.

Meara, P. (2009). *Connected words.* Amsterdam: John Benjamins.

Moon, R. (1992). Textual aspects of fixed expressions in learners' dictionaries. In P. Arnaud, & H. Bejoint (Eds.), *Vocabulary and applied linguistics* (pp. 13–27). London: Macmillan.

Nation, I.S.P. (Ed.). (1986). *Vocabulary lists: Words, affixes and stems* (Rev. ed.). Occasional Publication No. 12. Wellington: English Language Institute, Victoria University of Wellington.

Pawley, A., & Syder, F. (1983). Two puzzles for linguistic theory: Native like selection and native like fluency. In J. Richard, & R. Schmidt (Eds.), *Language and communication* (pp. 191–225). New York, NY: Longman.

Politzer, R. (1978). Errors of English speakers of German as perceived and evaluated by German natives. *Modern Language Journal, 62*, 253–261.

Postman, L., & Keppel, G. (1970). *Norms of word associations.* New York, NY: Academic Press.

Quirk, R. (1982). *Style and communication in the English language.* London: Edward Arnold.

Sato, C. (1988). Origins of complex syntax in interlanguage development. *Studies in Second Language Acquisition, 10*, 371–395.

Sinclair, J. (1991). *Corpus, concordance, collocation.* Oxford: OUP.

Singleton, D. (1989). *Language acquisition: The age factor.* Clevedon: Multilingual Matters.

Singleton, D. (1993). Exploring the mental lexicon. Paper presented at the 3rd annual meeting of the European Second Language Association (EUROSLA), Sofia.

Soderman, T. (1993). Word associations of foreign language learners and native speakers. In H. Ringbom (Ed.), *Near-native proficiency in English* (pp. 94–182). English Department Publications 2. Abo: Abo Akademi University.

Stubbs, M. (1986). *Educational linguistics.* Oxford: Blackwell.

Swinney, D., & Cutler, A. (1979). The access and processing of idiomatic expressions. *Journal of Verbal Learning and Verbal Behaviour, 18*, 523–534.

Viberg, A. (1993). Crosslinguistic perspectives on lexical and lexical progression. In K. Hyltenstam, & A. Viberg (Eds.), *Progression and regression in language – sociocultural, neuropsychological and linguistic perspectives* (pp. 340–385). Cambridge: CUP.

Yorio, C.A. (1989). Idiomaticity as an indicator of second language proficiency. In K. Hyltenstam, & L. K. Obler (Eds.), *Bilingualism across the life-span* (pp. 55–72). Cambridge: CUP.

Age of acquisition effects or effects of bilingualism in second language ultimate attainment?

Emanuel Bylund, Kenneth Hyltenstam & Niclas Abrahamsson
Centre for Research on Bilingualism, Stockholm University

One of the most robust findings in the field of SLA is the different rates of success with which children and adults achieve nativelike proficiency in a L2. Age-related differences have traditionally been explained in terms of the maturational state of the learner. Recently, however, a growing number of accounts hold that age effects in ultimate attainment are due to L1 entrenchment (e.g. Flege 1999; MacWhinney 2005; Ventureyra, Pallier & Yoo 2004). In this view, an increase in L1 proficiency leads to the progressive entrenchment of L1 representations, with the consequence that L2 acquisition becomes more difficult. Inherent in this interpretation is the assumption that the "less L1", the less it will interfere with the L2. In this paper, we analyse the theoretical underpinnings of the "L1 entrenchment accounts", and evaluate the existing evidence for and against such claims.

1. Introduction

Scientific disciplines are commonly characterised by recurring changes or transformations in the beliefs, values, standards, and methods that constitute exemplary ways of conducting research. The field of Second Language Acquisition (SLA) is not exempt from this trend. In the past two decades, SLA has experienced what has been labelled the "Social Turn (e.g. Block 2003). This is reflected in a growing number of studies emphasising the social and cultural context of second language (L2) learning. The significance of the Social Turn for SLA and the epis-temological diversity that has been the result have been – and still are – subject to fierce debate (see, e.g. Firth & Wagner 1997, 1998, 2007; Gregg 2004, 2006; Gregg, Long, Jordan & Beretta 1997; Lantolf 1996; Long 2007; Watson-Gegeo 2004).

In recent years, it has been suggested that the next *turn* in SLA will (or should) be the "Bilingual Turn" (Ortega 2010). In short, the notion of the Bilingual Turn is based on the assumption that there is a monolingual bias in SLA that is manifested in a disregard for L2 speakers' bilingualism along with the erroneous conception that the aim of the L2 learning enterprise is to behave monolingually in a new language. The Bilingual Turn, if taken, would instead entail giving full recognition to L2 speakers' bilingualism, by changing both the interpretative frames to which SLA researchers resort in describing and analysing L2 speakers' linguistic behaviour, as well as the methodology on which they rely to measure and compare the development of L2 proficiency.

Recognising L2 speakers as bilingual individuals who are qualitatively different from monolingual speakers could have potentially far-reaching consequences for the study of L2 ultimate attainment. This area of SLA has traditionally focused on the effects that age of acquisition has on the degree to which the endstate of L2 knowledge resembles that of a native speaker. The relationship between age of acquisition and L2 ultimate attainment was captured in the early days by Lenneberg (1967) in his Critical Period Hypothesis (hereinafter CPH), which posits that foreign accents are not easily overcome by post-pubescent learners. A great deal of empirical evidence has been gathered since the formulation of the CPH (for an overview, see Long this volume), and studies have not only corroborated Lenneberg's observation regarding age of acquisition effects on L2 phonetics, but they have also demonstrated age effects in other linguistic domains, such as syntax, morphology and lexis. Lenneberg's suggested cut-off point (i.e. puberty, or 12–13 years of age) for the critical period has also been subject to further empirical testing, with some studies supporting the age 12 (e.g. Abrahamsson 2012) and others proposing alternative termini, for example, age 6 (Johnson & Newport 1989) or age 18 (DeKeyser, Alfi-Shabtay & Ravid 2010), partially depending on the linguistic domain investigated. Despite some disagreement concerning the scope and timing of age effects, most CPH studies still adhere to the assumption that the low incidence of nativelike L2 ultimate attainment among (late) L2 learners is a result of the maturation of the cerebral areas subserving language.

However, if a "Bilingual Turn-perspective" on ultimate attainment were adopted, the *explanans* would change: focus would be shifted away from intrinsic neurological mechanisms of maturation and would instead be placed on the mutual influence that two (or more) co-existing linguistic systems exert on each other. It is, in other words, not the learner's age of acquisition that would explain the lack of adherence to native norms, but rather his/her bilingualism. In this view, the question of nativelike behaviour among L2 speakers is seen in a new light: because L2 speakers are bilingual, should they ever be expected to behave like native speakers of the target language (the assumption here being that the native speakers with whom they are being compared are monolingual)?

Although it might be early to talk about a Bilingual Turn in SLA, it is a fact that in recent years there has been an increase in the number of accounts advancing the idea that non-native behaviour in L2 speakers is first and foremost an effect of bilingualism. In the present chapter, we aim to scrutinize this claim. To do so, we will review the existing empirical evidence relevant to this discussion, and analyse the conceptual underpinnings of the arguments and interpretations of bilingualism effects.[1] Throughout the chapter, we will use the term *bilingualism effects* to refer to those instances of non-convergence with monolingual native speaker behaviour that occur as an effect of the speaker's knowledge of another language. It should be noted that, even though this definition applies to both the effects the L1 has on the L2, and the effects of the L2 on the L1, we will mostly be concerned with the former. The terms *L1* and *L2* will, as is customary, be used to refer to the order of acquisition of a given language. Although the concept of the native speaker is central to our discussion, the scope of the chapter is limited to a discussion of bilingualism effects in L2 ultimate attainment. This means that we will not engage in the controversy surrounding the native speaker concept (the reader is referred, e.g. to Davies 2003). In this chapter, the term *native speaker* will be used generally as a synonym for L1 speaker.

The chapter is organised in the following way: the subsequent section reviews the frameworks, arguments, and empirical findings that directly or indirectly address the question of bilingualism effects on ultimate attainment. After that, we critically discuss three aspects that are central to the bilingualism effects interpretation of L2 ultimate attainment. The chapter closes with some concluding remarks and suggestions for future research.

2. Review of the literature

2.1 Conceptual frameworks on bilingualism effects and supporting empirical research

The Multicompetence framework of V. Cook (e.g. 1992, 2002, 2003) is one of the most prominent accounts stressing the uniqueness of bi-/multilingual language

---

1. As we shall see, current conceptual and empirical studies that advance bilingualism effects on L2 ultimate attainment are by no means characterised by epistemological and ontological uniformity. We have nonetheless chosen to group them together, due to their common ground, which holds that the bilingualism of L2 speakers is the cause of their non-convergence with native speaker behaviour.

competence. In this framework, 'multicompetence' refers to the compound state of mind with two languages. The multicompetent mind of the L2 *user* (to use Cook's terminology) differs in several ways from the monocompetent mind of a monolingual: to begin with, his/her knowledge of the L2 is different from that of native speakers of the same language; second, his/her L1 knowledge is also different from that of monolingual speakers of that language; and third, his/her cognitive abilities (e.g. divergent thinking, executive control) are different from those of monolinguals (for an overview, see Bialystok 2009). Who, then, qualifies as an L2 user? Cook (2002) is fairly inclusive in this regard, positing that an L2 user is anybody who uses another language than his/her L1. It may be a singer performing an opera in a language that is not his/her first, a foreign professional carrying out all his/her work in a L2, or a child in an immigrant family who speaks a L2 at school and the L1 at home. Likewise, the L2 user's proficiency with the L2 may vary greatly, ranging from rudimentary skills barely enough to "ask for coffee at a restaurant" (Cook 2002: 3) to highly advanced mastery that allows for the person to write international best-sellers (e.g. Chinua Achebe or Joseph Conrad). While Cook (2002) acknowledges that it is yet to be settled whether native-like L2 ultimate attainment is possible, he also contends that there is no reason why L2 users should be expected to behave like native speakers or even be compared to this group, due to differences in the nature of their linguistic competencies (*native speaker* is here defined as a monolingual person who still speaks the language learnt in childhood, Cook 1999: 187).

Since Cook's original formulation of the Multicompetence framework the number of empirical studies demonstrating the effects of two co-existing grammars on language proficiency and cognition has steadily increased (although not all these studies necessarily label their findings as multicompetence). Of particular relevance for the purposes of the current chapter is the robust evidence that shows, first, that the languages of a bilingual L2 speaker are constantly activated, even in situations in which only one is needed to carry out the task at hand (e.g. word recognition and speech comprehension, see, e.g. van Assche, Duyck, Hartsuiker & Diependale 2009; Costa 2005; Marian & Spivey 2003), and second, that bilinguals have different conceptual representations than monolinguals (e.g. Ameel, Storms, Malt & Sloman 2005; Athanasopoulos 2007; Brown & Gullberg 2008; Bylund, Athanasopoulos & Oostendorp in press; Pavlenko & Malt 2011; for an overview, see Jarvis & Pavlenko 2008). Bylund (2011a, also 2011b) specifically set out to test whether the patterns of event conceptualization exhibited by L2 speakers were an effect of their bilingualism or a result of their age of acquisition. In these studies, event segmentation patterns elicited via a film-retelling task were studied in adult L1 Spanish-L2 Swedish bilinguals living in Sweden. These individuals, whose ages of L2 acquisition ranged from 1 to 19 years, used both the L1 and L2 on a daily basis. The results showed that the bilinguals' patterns of L2 event segmentation were significantly different from those of native Swedish speakers. The same was found for their L1 event segmentation patterns, which were different from native Spanish speakers' living in a Spanish-speaking country (in fact, no difference was found between the bilinguals' L1 and L2 segmentation strategies). Correlational analyses between event segmentation behaviour in the L2 and age of acquisition were run in order to see whether the variation among the bilinguals could be explained as a function of their differing acquisition onsets. The bilinguals were also divided into groups according to their acquisition age (prepubescent vs. postpubescent) with the intention of seeing whether a between-group comparison would yield visible age effects. However, neither approach produced statistically significant results. In other words, the bilinguals' L2 conceptual patterns could not be ascribed to their age of acquisition. In view of this finding and the fact that the bilinguals behaved similarly in the L1 and L2, Bylund suggested that the idiosyncratic segmentation patterns they produced should be ascribed to their knowledge and use of two languages.

Further compelling evidence of different conceptual representation among bilinguals is provided by Ameel et al.'s (2005) study of object categorization. In this investigation, simultaneous French-Dutch bilinguals were asked to name and match common household objects (different types of containers) in their two languages. A comparison with the naming and matching patterns of monolingual speakers of each language showed that the category boundaries between the groups differed, such that the bilinguals exhibited a pattern that to some extent could be characterised as a convergence of the two distinct monolingual patterns. Given the fact that the bilingual participants of Ameel et al. had acquired both languages from birth, it is clear that their idiosyncratic categorization patterns reflected bilingualism effects, as opposed to age of acquisition effects (for further evidence of conceptual and semantic crosslinguistic interaction in simultaneous and early bilinguals, see Ameel et al. 2009; Antón-Méndez & Gollan 2010; Gathercole & Moawad 2010).

Apart from the research mentioned above, there are some studies dealing specifically with phonetic knowledge in simultaneous adult bilinguals. One of these contributions is Sebastián-Gallés, Echeverría and Bosch's (2005) investigation of the perception of the Catalan /e/-/ɛ/ contrast in adult speakers of Catalan and Spanish who were either simultaneous or sequential bilinguals (with L2 acquisition onset around four years of age). The results of a series of word-discrimination experiments showed that sequential L1 Spanish-L2 Catalan bilinguals were outperformed by simultaneous bilinguals. Interestingly, however, simultaneous bilinguals were in turn outperformed by the L1 Catalan-L2 Spanish bilinguals in the study.

A second framework that models the relationship between L1 and L2 proficiency, and in particular the effects that the L1 exerts on ultimate attainment in L2 phonology and phonetics, is the Speech Learning Model. Developed by J. Flege and colleagues (e.g. Flege 1995, 1999), this model deals with the attainment of L2 pronunciation of consonants and vowels, and conceptualises the L1 as an element that may interfere with nativelike L2 mastery. Assuming that the phonic elements of the L1 and L2 exist in a common phonological space, the Speech Learning Model predicts that in the bilingual speaker, L1 and L2 phonetic categories may mutually influence each other. The extent to which the L1 influences L2 pronunciation depends on the strength of representation of L1 categories (in terms of developmental status), in the sense that the more strongly represented the L1 is, the more it will interfere with L2 pronunciation. Empirical evidence in support of these claims is presented by Flege and associates in a series of studies examining the relationship between L2 pronunciation ability and L1 use and proficiency. For example, Flege, Frieda and Nozawa (1997) investigated L2 pronunciation proficiency and L1 use in a group of adult L1 Italian – L2 English bilinguals who had started learning the L2 before puberty (on average, at the age of five). The results showed that those who used their L1 in an average of 30% of their daily interactions received significantly lower ratings on their L2 pronunciation than those who used their L1 in only 3% of their interactions. It is important to keep in mind, however, that this finding suggests a negative relationship between self-reported L1 *use* and L2 nativelikeness. It does not, in other words, provide a direct measure of the relationship between L1 and L2 proficiency, which would have constituted even stronger evidence of the hypothesis that L1 proficiency is a determinant for L2 nativelikeness.

Such evidence was, nevertheless, reported in a subsequent study on L1 Korean – L2 English bilinguals (Yeni-Komshian, Flege & Liu 2000), in which global pronunciation was assessed in both the L1 and L2. The results from this study effectively showed a significant negative correlation ($r = -.47$) between L1 and L2 pronunciation scores among those bilinguals whose L2 acquisition had begun before age 12, but not for those whose acquisition began beyond this point. Interestingly, though, one of the participant subgroups (with age of acquisition being 10–11 years) exhibited above average pronunciation in both the L1 and the L2. In interpreting the relationship between L2 ultimate attainment and the L1, Flege and associates claim that "the effects on foreign accent are due to the development of the native language phonetic system rather than to maturational constraints on L2 speech learning" (MacKay, Flege & Imai 2006: 157). However, they also present more ambivalent views, positing that L2 pronunciation skills are not "determined solely by an individual's state of neurological development at the time of first exposure to the L2" (Flege et al. 1997: 169). Moreover, as shown by

Yeni-Komshian et al. (2000), the Speech Learning Model holds that the interaction between L1 and L2 pronunciation proficiency first and foremost applies to learners who were immersed in the L2 environment before puberty (supposedly because young learners' L1 categories are not yet fully formed).

A third framework that concerns the effects of bilingualism on L2 ultimate attainment is the Competition Model (MacWhinney 1997, 2005; Hernández, Li & MacWhinney 2005; Li & Farkas 2002). In this model, the notions of competition, resonance, entrenchment, and parasitism are used to explain L1 and L2 acquisition. Competition occurs, for example, in a simultaneously bilingual child when two lexical items compete for the same referent. Thanks to experiential cues that the child has acquired in the acquisition process (e.g. one language is associated with the father, and the other with the mother), as well as language-internal resonance (when a language-specific form is activated, it has resonant effects and also keeps forms in the other language deactivated), the competition between the two lexical items is controlled and the appropriate form is produced. The situation is not the same for an L2 learner, because in this case the L1 representations are entrenched and the L2 forms are acquired as word associations dependent on L1 forms. The L2 forms may gain strength and their internal resonance may increase, but due to L1 entrenchment, they will always have an association with L1 forms. The L2 forms are, in other words, parasitic on the L1. Consequently, according to the Competition Model, repeated L1 use leads to entrenchment, with the consequence that L2 nativelikeness becomes increasingly more difficult as entrenchment proceeds. The Competition Model does not posit a certain age span during which the L1 entrenchment effect changes, but predicts that the ability to attain L2 nativelikeness declines gradually over the speaker's lifespan (MacWhinney 2005: 64).

The fourth and last framework that we will deal with here is the so-called Interference Hypothesis (Pallier et al. 2003; Ventureyra, Pallier & Yoo 2004), which originated from a series of studies on Korean adoptees living in France. In these studies, the adoptee participants had apparently lost their L1 Korean completely, as they were not able to discriminate between Korean and foreign languages, nor did they respond implicitly (as measured by fMRI) when exposed to Korean auditory material. Additionally, the observation was made that during the test sessions, the adoptees exhibited a command of French that in the ears of the test administrators seemed indistinguishable from that of native speakers. In view of these findings, Pallier and associates suggested that if the L1 is completely lost, the neural networks can "reset" (Ventureyra et al. 2004: 89), and, thus, a nativelike level of an L2 can be attained. The reason, then, why some early L2 learners who maintain their L1 (such as immigrant children) do not reach nativelike L2 proficiency is because their L1 "acts as a filter that distorts the way in which a second language can be acquired" (Pallier et al. 2003: 160). According to the Interference Hypothesis, the resetting of the L1 neural networks can only take place within the critical period (cf. Ventureyra et al. 2004). However, no systematic assessment of the L2 proficiency of the adoptee participants was carried out to bolster this claim (this was also recognised by Pallier and associates).

The accounts reviewed above constitute some of the most coherent conceptual frameworks of bilingualism effects on L2 ultimate attainment. As shown, these accounts differ to a certain extent in their content and the specificity of their predictions. The Multicompetence framework, for example, focuses on the intrinsic differences between bilingual L2 speakers and monolinguals. The suggestion that bilingual and monolingual language proficiencies should not be compared has parallels, for example, in Grosjean's (1989, 1998) work on bilingualism (cf. his famous statement, "the bilingual is not two monolinguals in one"), and certainly in Weinreich's (1953) observation that the two language systems of the bilingual individual exert mutual influence on one another. Even though the Multicompetence framework does not engage at length with the CPH debate, it still holds general relevance for the discussion and interpretation of age effects and the effects of bilingualism in L2 ultimate attainment. The Speech Learning Model, the Interference Hypothesis, and the Competition Model, on the other hand, do formulate explicit predictions regarding the relationship between L1 and L2 proficiency, as well as the timing of L1-L2 interacting proficiency levels (e.g. the first decade of life, before puberty, or gradually across the lifespan). These predictions share points with the communicating container metaphor, whereby a proficiency increase in one language is followed by a proficiency decrease in the other (see the Balance Theory of Bilingualism, Baker 2011). By extension, this line of argumentation also aligns with early behaviourist interpretations of the role of L1 proficiency for subsequent language learning. Dunkel (1948), for example, suggested that the success of the young L2 learner resides in his/her lack of "reflexes and habits which the adult has acquired" (p. 68) in the course of L1 acquisition (for further discussion of the behaviourist position, see Singleton & Ryan 2004).

The idea that a L2 speaker's bilingualism has an impact on his/her ultimate attainment does not, however, find support only among the authors of the above accounts. On the contrary, this idea is gaining greater currency among a number of SLA scholars. For example, in an extensive treatment of age effects in language acquisition, Herschensohn (2007) suggests that whereas *L1* acquisition is subject to a critical period, the "observed deficits in L2A [cquisition] are due not to a biological critical period, but to the excellence of the neural architecture of the first language" (p. 241). It is, in other words, the learner's L1 that interferes with the attainment of nativelike proficiency in the L2. This interpretation is supported by VanPatten and Benati, (2010: 26), who remark that the L1 is the apparent "culprit" accounting for the lack of success in nativelike L2 attainment. Likewise, in his recent reviews of age effects in L2 acquisition, Birdsong (2005, 2006, 2009) discusses the possibility that the documented decline in L2 ultimate attainment with increasing age of acquisition may in part be due to L1 entrenchment. He goes on to question the use of the monolingual native speaker as a benchmark against which L2 speakers' proficiency is typically measured. With reference to the documented reciprocal influence that the L1 and L2 exert on one another (see above), Birdsong (2009: 409) posits that the endstate of a L2 speaker's proficiency "cannot be expected to resemble, down to the most trivial detail, the language of a monolingual." A similar argument is presented by Muñoz and Singleton (2011: 5), who suggest that instead of comparing late L2 learners and native speakers, a more appropriate comparison "might be one between later L2 beginners and those who begin to acquire an L2 in early childhood." They later take this reasoning one step further, however, proposing native speaker behaviour as the "yardstick of L2 attainment for L2 acquirers beginning at *any* age may require some re-evaluation" (p. 6, emphasis in original). This line of reasoning is also found in de Leeuw (in press; see also de Leeuw, Mennen & Scobbie in press). In view of research on cognitive load in bilinguals (e.g. Bialystok 2009), de Leeuw suggests that the competition between the two languages of highly proficient bilinguals "prevents them from attaining monolingual proficiencies," and that this may "occur at any age of acquisition" (de Leeuw in press: 15). In the light of the findings on L1 attrition, de Leeuw (in press) and Birdsong (2009) remark that not all instances of non-nativeness exhibited by L2 speakers can be ascribed to age of acquisition, for the simple reason that non-native behaviour does not inherently reflect age of acquisition effects. An example of this is that non-convergence with native speakers in L1 attriters cannot logically be due to delayed acquisition onset, since these speakers acquired the L1 from birth. Rather, in these speakers, the instances of non-nativeness are due to L2 influence.

2.2   Counter-evidence to bilingualism effects on L2 ultimate attainment?

What kind of data would support the interpretation that L2 speakers' bilingualism does *not* necessarily result in non-nativelike L2 proficiency? Logically, one could present any finding demonstrating the attainment of L2 nativelike mastery by a bilingual L2 speaker as support for this interpretation. Adhering to this reasoning, one could then cite as supportive evidence the plentiful studies that have documented L2 nativelikeness among bilingual L2 speakers (e.g. Abrahamsson 2012; Abrahamsson & Hyltenstam 2008; Birdsong & Molis 2001; Johnson &

Newport 1989; Munro & Mann 2005). Even though this argument should not be taken lightly, we might want to allow for a little more complexity in the discussion. From the perspective of the Competition Model or the Speech Learning Model, it could be argued that a bilingual L2 speaker who has reached nativelike L2 proficiency has done so because he/she is not nativelike in the L1 (cf. the communicating container metaphor). In order to properly address this claim, proficiency data from both the L1 and L2 would have to be collected and compared. Unfortunately, this is a rare procedure in studies on L2 ultimate attainment. Against this background, Bylund, Abrahamsson and Hyltenstam (2012) set out to examine L1 and L2 knowledge in adult L1 Spanish-L2 Swedish bilinguals whose ages of acquisition ranged from 1 to 11 years (length of residence in L2 environment: 23.7 years). Two different proficiency tests were administered in each of the participants' languages on two different occasions: the first measured grammatical intuition (aural grammaticality judgement test), and the second, semantic and morphosyntactic inference (written cloze test). The bilingual participants' performance on these tests was compared to that of native speakers of the relevant language. The results from both tests showed that when compared at the group-level, the bilinguals scored significantly lower than the native speakers in both their L1 and L2. This finding would thus address the notion that bilingual language proficiency is intrinsically different from monolingual language proficiency. However, a closer inspection of individual scores by means of correlational analyses revealed a positive relationship between L1 and L2 proficiency, such that those who performed like native speakers in the one language, were likely to do so in the other language as well, and vice-versa. This behaviour was constant across both the cloze test and the grammaticality judgement test. In addition, Bylund et al. found that the bilingual participants' level of language aptitude was a reliable predictor of their nativelike/non-nativelike performance (i.e. those with higher aptitude levels were more likely to score within the native speaker range in both languages than those with lower levels). The variables of age of L2 acquisition and frequency of language use did not exert any documented effect on test performance.

Another valuable piece of information on the lack of bilingualism effects is offered by a handful of studies of ultimate attainment in simultaneous bilinguals. In a recent series of investigations, Kupisch and associates have examined proficiency with different morphosyntactic properties in adult simultaneous bilinguals. Kupisch (in press), for example, investigated the mastery of specific and generic subject nominals in Italian among German-Italian bilinguals (mean age: 27 years) who were born either in Germany or Italy and had grown up learning both languages from birth (one parent-one language). There was a correlation between country of birth and language dominance (as measured by cloze tests) in this study, in the sense that those who grew up in Italy were Italian-dominant and those who grew up in Germany were German-dominant. Results from two different judgement tests showed that whereas the German-dominant bilinguals exhibited diverging behaviour under certain test conditions, the Italian-dominant participants scored on par with Italian monolingual performance. This led Kupisch (in press: 19) to conclude that bilingualism per se does "not automatically lead to deviant grammars," but conditions of language input and use during childhood might do so. A similar finding is reported by Barton (2011), who, in a similar design, investigated proficiency with specifics and generics in French-German simultaneous adult bilinguals with different patterns of language dominance. In this study too, it was found that the bilinguals in their dominant language – and in some conditions also in their weaker language – exhibited scores similar to those of monolingual speakers of the relevant language.[2] However, under other conditions, deviant responses were registered in the participants' weaker language. Barton noted that the nature and extent of non-convergent forms in the weaker language was, among other things, related to the structural relationship between the weaker and the stronger language. Further evidence of nativelike command with other grammatical categories, such as gender, in the dominant language of simultaneous bilinguals is found in Bianchi (in press), Kupisch, Akpınar, and Stöhr (in press), and Stöhr, Akpınar, Bianchi and Kupisch (2012).

A third type of empirical finding that constitutes evidence against bilingualism effects in L2 ultimate attainment may be found in studies on international adoptees. This is a special group of L2 speakers, since they typically acquire the L2 as a primary socialization or home language (i.e. in the adoptive family), while at the same time losing their L1. This situation contrasts with that of immigrant children, who typically acquire the L2 outside the home environment and have continuous exposure to the L1. At present, however, the number of studies that examine L2 proficiency – and ultimate attainment in particular – among international adoptees in a systematic way is scant. An important contribution is Hene's (1993) investigation of L2 Swedish vocabulary comprehension among international adoptees. A matched group of native Swedish children was also included. The post-adoption period in this study was 6–10 years, and the age of arrival ranged from 3 months to 6 years. The chronological age of the participants at the time of the study was 10–12 years. None of the children had any *active command* of their L1, except in some cases where they claimed to remember one or two individual words (p. 16). Hene concluded that L2 proficiency in the participant

---

2.   It should, however, be noted that on some occasions, the scores of both the monolinguals and the bilinguals reached ceiling. It is unclear whether this means that both groups exhibited robust intuitions about the tested features or that the difficulty level of the test was too low.

group showed clear non-native features. Moreover, the findings were remarkable in the qualitative aspect of the divergences: when compared to a native control group, the adoptees showed a surprisingly low understanding of high-frequency words and phrases, such as *fortfarande* ('still'), or *i början av* ('in the beginning of'). It was also observed that those who were adopted before age two exhibited results similar to the Swedish native controls, whereas those who were adopted after that age did not.

Recent findings on international adoptees (IA) with a Chinese background acquiring French in Canada contribute to the picture that young adoptees do not behave linguistically like their native speaker peers (CTR) (Delcenserie, Genesee & Gauthier in press; Gauthier & Genesee 2011; Gauthier, Genesee & Kasparian 2012). In these studies, the IA and CTR groups were matched in terms of gender (all girls), age at testing, and SES. There were no statistically significant differences between the groups in terms of socio-emotional adjustment (as measured by Vineland Social-Emotional Early Childhood Scales), or intellectual ability (Brief IQ Screener Leiter-R). In Gauthier and Genesee (2011), a group of IA children with 13.5 months as their mean age of adoption was compared to a group of CTR children. The children were tested at an average age of 4;2 with a battery of language tests that assessed receptive and expressive language skills in vocabulary and grammar. In a follow-up at an average age of 5;5, additional tests for receptive and expressive language skills were used, including a Recalling Sentences Subtest and a Reformulated Language Subtest of the French version of the Clinical Evaluation of Language Fundamentals–Revised (CELF–R). The results of the first assessment revealed that the IA children lagged significantly behind in expressive vocabulary and general language abilities. At the assessment 16 months later, the gap between the IA children and the CTR children had not disappeared, as might have been expected, but, rather, had increased; the IA children now scored significantly lower than the CTR children not only on expressive vocabulary but also on receptive vocabulary, and furthermore, on expressive and receptive grammar. Thus, extended exposure had not resulted in closing the gap between the two groups.

In Delcenserie et al. (in press) 27 adoptees (with a mean age of adoption of 12.9 months), 12 of whom had participated in the Gauthier and Genesee study, were assessed when they were aged, on average, 7;10 years. The CTR children, as before, were matched for gender, age and SES. The IA children performed significantly lower than the CTR children on subtests of syntactic-semantic comprehension, expressive one-word picture vocabulary, word definitions and sentence recall. A substantial proportion of the IA children scored at least 1 SD below the mean of the CTR children (for example, 66.6% of the IA children in the recalling sentences test, 51.8% on the word definition test, and 50% on the expressive one-word picture vocabulary test). Nevertheless, the IA children performed at or above the norm for French-speaking children on all language tests, except on the recalling sentences test. In addition to this third reassessment of the IA children when they were nearly eight years old showing that three years of additional exposure apparently had no effect on closing the gap with the CTR children, a most interesting result of this study is that the sentence recall task posed the greatest challenge for the IA children. As the authors argue convincingly, successful performance on this test entails "the integration of syntactic and lexical knowledge of language from long-term memory along with phonological information that has to be retained in short-term memory" (p. 23). As the IA children performed within the age-expected norm ranges on all other language tests, albeit significantly below the performance of the CTR children, the conclusion is that the relevant factor lies in language processing problems related to limitations in verbal short-term memory. This interpretation is strengthened by the fact that the IA children had no corresponding problems with short-term memory components of non-verbal tests (in this case, the Wechler Non-Verbal IQ test): "unlike children with low working memory abilities who have difficulties with both verbal and visuospatial short-term memory [...] the IA children's difficulties were limited to the verbal domain" (p. 23). The hypothesis laid out by this research, then, is that a delay in exposure to a specific language has an effect on verbal short-term memory, which in turn has implications for further language development and language processing.

Gauthier et al. (2012) aimed at characterising the linguistic differences between the IA children and the CTR children in more detail. Therefore, this study examined proficiency with clitics, tense morphology, and vocabulary among both groups. It included twelve IA children and twelve CTR children, all drawn from the 24 participants of the Gauthier and Genesee study. The children were approximately four years old when investigated. Natural language samples from unstructured playtime between the children and the primary care-giver were recorded and transcribed for analysis. Data on lexical proficiency were collected by means of an expressive and a receptive vocabulary test. The analyses of the natural speech samples showed that the adoptee group had a higher error rate in its use of clitics than did the controls. The two groups, however, were equally proficient with tense morphology. With respect to lexical proficiency, it was found that whereas the adoptees and the controls obtained similar scores on the receptive vocabulary test, the controls outperformed the adoptees on the expressive counterpart.

Although the studies reviewed above provide valuable evidence of L2 acquisition by international adoptees, they do not directly address the issue of L2 ultimate attainment. As a consequence, it could be argued (although somewhat forcedly) that the non-convergences found in the adoptee's speech are but a sign of their lagging behind in the acquisitional process, and that if given enough time, they could eventually catch up with their native speaker peers. Preliminary observations on L2 ultimate attainment in international adoptees is found in an early investigation by Gardell (1979) on the situation of 177 internationally adopted individuals in Sweden. The age of arrival of the adoptees ranged from three months to 12 years (with more below six years of age), and at the time of the study, they were between 10 and 18 years old (equally distributed). Whereas some of the participants with higher ages of adoption could recall some individual words, or even fragments of a nursery rhyme, the remainder claimed to remember nothing of their L1. Gardell concluded that 43% of the participants showed diverging behaviour with Swedish language use when compared to their Swedish-born peers. The non-native features found in the adoptees included both syntactic and morphological errors, as well as "inexplicable gaps" in the understanding of "perfectly common, basic Swedish words" (p. 37). Gardell also pointed out that when the adoptees reached the senior level of elementary school and new demands were being placed on their command of Swedish, their non-convergent Swedish language knowledge became more salient (p. 38). The school performance of the participants was, nonetheless, good. Even though the report might be limited, in the sense that detailed linguistic observations are lacking, it suggests that L2 acquisition in adoptees does not automatically result in nativelike L2 knowledge.

A more systematic assessment of L2 ultimate attainment in adoptees is found in Hyltenstam, Bylund, Abrahamsson and Park (2009). In this study, a test battery that included 10 different measures of lexicon, syntax and phonology was used to measure L2 proficiency in speakers with either adoptee or immigrant backgrounds who had passed for native speakers in a listening experiment. The individuals in both groups were in their early thirties, and their age of L2 acquisition ranged from one to nine years. The participants with immigrant backgrounds used their L1 on a daily basis, whereas the adoptees claimed to have lost their receptive and productive L1 skills altogether. The results showed that the adoptee L2 speakers scored outside the native speaker range on several L2 measures, and more importantly, did so to the same extent as the immigrant L2 speakers.

To summarise, evidence that contradicts the argument that L2 speakers' bilingualism leads to non-nativelike L2 proficiency may be found in studies examining three different populations: simultaneous bilinguals, bilingual L2 speakers, and international adoptees who no longer have functional L1 knowledge. These populations are, in other words, the same as those investigated by the studies positing that there are bilingualism effects on L2 ultimate attainment. Although this may seem contradictory, it should be kept in mind that the studies differ in terms of scope and methodology. In the discussions below on communicative needs and domain-specificity, these conflicting findings should appear less contradictory.

3.   Discussion

Against the background laid out in the previous sections, we now move on to examine critically the assumptions, arguments and interpretations found in current conceptualisations of bilingualism effects. We will focus, in particular, on the following aspects: first, monolingualism and bilingualism as the norm among native speakers and L2 speakers, respectively; and second, bilingualism effects and the effects of different communicative contexts on language development. We will close this section with a brief discussion of domain specificity in bilingualism effects.

3.1   Assumptions about monolingualism among native controls and about bilingualism among L2 speakers

The terms *bilingual* and *monolingual* lie at the very heart of the discussion of bilingualism effects in L2 ultimate attainment. However, despite the centrality of these terms, it is rare to come across studies that actually define (and operationalize) them. Of the accounts reviewed above, the Multicompetence Framework seems to be the most specific with regards to terminology, as it defines a L2 user as anybody who uses a L2 (be it at a rudimentary or advanced proficiency level, and for a range of different purposes). By inference, a monolingual or *monocompetent* individual is, then, somebody whose mind is only inhabited by one language system, and that language system is the same as the one acquired from birth. The other frameworks, which focus primarily on the interference effects of the L1 on the L2, offer, to the best of our knowledge, no definitions of bilingualism or *monolingualism*. The same can be said for the numerous discussions of bilingualism effects in studies that do not necessarily subscribe to any of the reviewed frameworks. In fact, most of the current discussions of bilingualism effects seem to rely on *ad hoc* conceptualizations of these terms, whereby L2 speakers are considered bilingual according to the logic that L2 speakers must necessarily speak an L1, and the native speakers against which they are compared are considered monolingual because they are native speakers.

Thus, it is reasonable to ask in what sense native speakers are monolingual, and what it means to say that L2 speakers are bilingual. In this section, we will first attempt to problematize the use of the notions *monolingualism* and *bilingualism*. Subsequently, we will scrutinize the alleged monolingualism among native speakers, and then the alleged bilingualism among L2 speakers. Here, we will draw attention to the population of international adoptees, who are rarely treated in the discussion of bilingualism effects, and discuss the possible implications of the research findings on this group to date.

Starting with the question about monolingualism among native speakers, it seems as if many studies do not actually offer information about the linguistic background of their native speaker controls. In Johnson and Newport's (1989: 70) study, for example, the control group is simply described as "native speakers of English." In Yeni-Komshian et al. (2000: 134), the controls were Korean and English "monolinguals." In this case, it seems reasonable to assume that the (South) Korean controls, who were university students, had foreign language skills in English (this language is typically introduced in 3rd grade in South Korea). Likewise, the Swedish-speaking native controls in Abrahamsson and Hyltenstam (2008, 2009), Bylund et al. (2012), and Hyltenstam et al. (2009) had completed Swedish secondary education and had consequently had English as a subject since 3rd or 4th grade, and at least one additional foreign language (usually French, German, or Spanish) since 7th grade. The answer to the question of whether these native controls are monolingual or bilingual, then, ultimately depends on how we define the terms *monolingualism* and *bilingualism*. Should we adopt an incipient view of bilingualism, according to which anybody who is able to produce meaningful utterances in more than one language is considered bilingual, then it is quite possible that many of the native speakers against whom L2 speakers are compared could be called bilinguals (or multicompetent, for that matter) because of their knowledge of foreign languages. Should we adhere to a stricter (and admittedly, somewhat obsolete) view of bilingualism, according to which someone who has nativelike command of two languages is considered bilingual, then none of the native speaker controls, and only a small portion of L2 speakers, could be called bilingual.

In yet another view of bilingualism, a person is considered bilingual if he/she uses two (or more) languages in everyday life (e.g. Grosjean 2001). This definition, based on frequency of use (and function), seems to better capture the presupposed bilingualism and monolingualism among L2 speakers and native speakers, respectively, if we assume that L2 speakers actually use their L1 and that native speakers do not use any of the foreign language skills they might possess. In this regard, the native speaker controls could be characterized as "functional monolinguals" (de Leeuw in press). It does not seem, however, that a definition based on frequency of use, alone, is sufficient to separate monolinguals from bilinguals for the purposes of the present discussion. An attrition study by Köpke (2002) illustrates this problem. The study reports on the case of a German native speaker who had been living in an English-speaking country for decades, and used virtually no German at all, but was fluent in English. It turned out that the participant was reluctant to use German with the test administrator (who was a native speaker of German), even in the small-talk between the different language tests. Interestingly, however, the participant's German language skills were almost completely intact, as demonstrated by his performance on the tests. Should we adopt a definition of bilingualism that revolves around frequency of use, then this participant and people with similar backgrounds would not be considered bilingual, despite their proficiency with more than one language.

From this reasoning, it becomes clear that in order to specify the differences between native speaker controls' supposed monolingualism and L2 speakers' supposed bilingualism, it is necessary to take into account both language proficiency and frequency of use. As seen in the review above, both of these factors have a documented effect on bidirectional crosslinguistic influence (even among speakers with moderate levels of contact and proficiency). If taken into consideration, then, it is not inconceivable that many studies are actually comparing speakers with different degrees and types of bilingualism, as opposed to *monolingual native speakers* and *bilingual L2 speakers*.

Let us now turn to the issue of bilingualism among L2 speakers. The interpretation that L2 speakers do not attain nativelike proficiency because they are bilingual seems to rest on the tacit assumption that all L2 speakers retain their L1. This is probably a *common* situation for many L2 speakers: people may arrive in a new country with family members and learn the L2 outside the home while continuing to use the L1 at home. However, common does not mean universal. Some L2 speakers completely lose contact with the L1 the moment they leave their country of birth, and never use it again. The clearest and most dramatic example of such cases is found among international adoptees. This population is known to undergo drastic L1 attrition, often to the extent that they lose productive and receptive knowledge altogether (e.g. Isurin 2000; Pallier et al. 2003). Despite their unique characteristics, adoptee L2 speakers are very seldom mentioned in discussions of bilingualism effects on L2 ultimate attainment (an obvious exception being the Interference Hypothesis, where adoptee learners play a central role). The fact that the number of empirical studies of L2 proficiency in adoptees is low in comparison to the number of studies of L2 proficiency in *immigrant* L2 speakers can possibly have contributed to affording low visibility to adoptee L2 learners in the field of SLA. Another reason might be the confusing terminology sometimes used to describe the process by which an L2 becomes an individual's dominant language in terms of proficiency and use. De Bot and Weltens (1991), for example, discuss this phenomenon in terms of "mother tongue shift." Muñoz and Singleton (2011:7) refer to "cases where in functional terms the L2 *becomes* the L1" (emphasis in original). Similarly, de Geer (1992), with particular reference to international adoptees, characterises the L2 acquisition process of this group as the acquisition of a "second first language." Furthermore, the frequently referred to distinction between simultaneous and successive bilingualism using age three as a cut-off point between the two types (McLaughlin 1978) would imply that any language acquired before that age is a L1: "[b]oth languages are first languages" (p. 72). Although the authors may be aware of their somewhat unorthodox use of the terms *mother tongue* and *first language*, this terminology might lead to a general understanding that the language acquired by international adoptees upon arrival in the host country is not really an L2, and subsequently that these individuals are not actually L2 speakers.[3]

Whatever the reasons that underlie the lack of reference to internationally adopted L2 speakers in the debate of bilingualism effects, the consequence of this omission is that L2 speakers are by default constructed as bilingual (see, e.g. Ortega 2010). In a world where all L2 speakers are bilingual, it may seem appealing to ascribe non-adherence to native speaker behaviour to crosslinguistic influence. However, not all L2 speakers are bilingual (in the sense that they retain their L1). What effects does this observation then have on the interpretation of bilingualism effects in L2 ultimate attainment? Strictly speaking, the existence of functionally monolingual L2 speakers does nothing but falsify the claim that all L2 speakers are bilingual, that is to say, the observation itself does not automatically overthrow the bilingualism effects interpretation. In order for an argument to be advanced in support of, or in opposition to, this interpretation, we need data on the linguistic behaviour of monolingual L2 speakers. If it were found that this group behaved like native speakers of the target language, it would considerably strengthen the interpretation that L2 speakers who retain their L1 diverge from native speaker behaviour because of their bilingualism. The available empirical evidence on L2 proficiency in international adoptees, however, points in the opposite direction. The studies reviewed in the previous section demonstrate that the L2 proficiency of this group does not converge with that of native speakers. As such, these findings seriously weaken an interpretation of L2 non-nativelikeness based on bilingualism effects. A more

---

3.   A third possible reason why adoptees are seldom mentioned in this debate might be related to political correctness. That the pre-adoption conditions of some children are inhumane (see below) probably contributes to an awareness that adoptees might hold vulnerable positions. To then claim that these individuals are monolingual L2 speakers might, in some views, be seen as linguicism. We believe, however, that it would be a great disservice not to recognise adoptees as L2 speakers, since we would then ignore the possibility that this group may be in as much need of L2 educational support as, for example, bilingual immigrant L2 speakers.

convincing interpretation seems to be that international adoptees do not attain nativelike proficiency in the L2 because, similar to bilingual L2 speakers, they are not exposed to this language from birth.

A number of counter-arguments to this reasoning could, nonetheless, be conceived. For example, it could be argued that international adoptees have not completely lost their L1. Instead, it is only inaccessible to them, and they are therefore to some extent still bilingual. As a result of their latent bilingualism, they cannot be expected to possess nativelike L2 proficiency. This argument is, however, inconsistent in the way it conceptualises the relationship between bilingualism and bilingualism effects. It may very well be the case that international adoptees have not completely lost their L1. In fact, several recent studies seem to suggest that some degree of L1 reactivation is possible, especially in the area of phonetics (Hyltenstam et al. 2009; Oh, Au & Jun 2010; Singh, Liederman, Mierzejewski & Barnes 2011). However, the critical question is whether initially inaccessible L1 remnants might influence L2 attainment to such an extent as to produce an outcome that is different from native speaker knowledge. Moreover, if international adoptees who have not retained their L1 perform at the same level as L2 speakers who, in contrast, have retained their L1 (which was found in Hyltenstam et al. 2009), there seems to be no correlation between degree of L1 retention and degree of L2 proficiency. Put more generally, this argument assumes that any degree of bilingualism will produce an equal degree of non-nativelikeness. In view of the existing evidence, we hold this to be unlikely.

The relevance that non-nativelikeness among adoptees has for the bilingualism effects discussion could also be questioned by taking into consideration the L1 development that characterises this population. Unlike bilingual L2 speakers, international adoptees experience a disruption in L1 development as L1 input suddenly ceases. This, it has been suggested, could put adoptees in a vulnerable position, because the neural-cognitive substrates that subserve language learning are disrupted. According to this reasoning, infants adopted around 12 months of age would be at disadvantage when acquiring their L2 (Gauthier et al. 2012: 305). Following this logic, it would then seem as if children who are adopted at older ages, and consequently have a more developed L1, should be at a more advantageous position when acquiring the L2. However, the available, but scarce, evidence on this matter runs counter to that interpretation. Findings from Hyltenstam et al. (2009) and Hene (1993) suggest that L2 speakers adopted at younger ages outperform those adopted at higher ages.

Another circumstance that could cast doubt on the significance of non-nativelike L2 proficiency among adoptees relates to the pre-adoption conditions. Studies of national and international adoptees have shown that the circumstances under which some children are brought up prior to adoption are conducive to social deprivation. One of the clearest and most frequently studied cases of this is that of Romanian orphans in the 1980s and 1990s, who, according to reports, often spent 20 hours a day unattended in cribs from as early as the first month of life. Follow-up post-adoption studies have demonstrated that the early global deprivation suffered by this population is later in life commonly manifested in cognitive impairment and poor mental health (e.g. Chugani, Behen, Muzik, Juhász, Nagi & Chugani 2001; Glennen & Masters 2002; Rutter 1998). Fortunately, however, such conditions are not common in the upbringing of all adoptees, as many spend their first year(s) in life in orphanages with high child-to-caregiver ratios, or with foster (or even biological) families. Research suggests that the better the pre-adoption conditions are, the greater the chances for normal development. For example, in a study of foreign-born adoptees living in Sweden, Cederblad, Höök, Irhammar and Mercke (1999) examined the relationship between mental health (e.g. attention problems, anxiety, depression, and aggressive behaviour), age of adoption, and pre-adoption conditions. They found that with the exception of a slightly higher obsessive compulsive behaviour index among the adoptees, this group did not differ from a non-adopted Sweden-born control group in terms of mental health. It was also documented that pre-adoption conditions could predict emotional attachment problems, in the sense that those adoptees who had spent longer in orphanages were more prone to experience such problems. Taken together, these findings suggest that the pre-adoption situation plays an important role in the child's subsequent cognitive and emotional development.

The findings on the impact of socially deprived pre-adoption rearing environments on an individual's subsequent development are potentially important for the interpretation of the non-nativelike proficiency exhibited by adoptees, as they show that this group may be at a cognitive disadvantage when compared to other groups of L2 speakers. This does not mean, however, that these findings automatically invalidate the explanation that international adoptees display non-nativelike behaviour because they are L2 speakers. There are two reasons for this: first, not all adoptees suffer from early social deprivation; and second, the precise way language development is influenced by the type of cognitive impairment found in this group is yet to be ferreted out. The findings do, however, show with great clarity that SLA scholars should not only be careful in their selection of adoptee participants, but preferably also control for their cognitive and emotional maturity. The studies by Gauthier and associates (e.g. Delcenserie in press) are exemplary in this regard, as they empirically assess a number of different cognitive and emotional variables in the adoptee participants.

To summarise, in this section, we have pointed out that, in order to make a robust argument that L2 speakers' L2 proficiency is different from that of native speakers because the former are bilingual and the latter are monolingual, it is first necessary to define what is meant by the terms *monolingualism* and *bilingualism*. Second, we have questioned the assumption that L2 speakers are bilingual by default, and have drawn attention to the importance of studying ultimate attainment in L2 speakers who have not retained their L1.

3.2   Bilingualism effects or different communicative contexts

As the literature review showed, certain views of bilingualism effects on L2 ultimate attainment conceive of L1 and L2 proficiencies as communicating containers, in the sense that an increase in the one leads to a decrease in the other. Perhaps the most compelling evidence in support of this interpretation to date is Yeni-Komshian et al.'s (2000) finding on negatively correlated L1 and L2 pronunciation proficiencies in L1 Korean – L2 English bilinguals living in the U.S. In interpreting this result it should be kept in mind, however, that a correlation between two events does not imply that these events are causally related. Although this observation may seem like a truism, it has important implications for the interpretation of negative correlations between L1 and L2 proficiencies. If it is recognised that inverse L1–L2 proficiency levels do not necessarily reflect a causal relationship, explanations for this phenomenon can be sought elsewhere. In this section, we will focus on the effects that the communicative context of the bilingual individual exerts on his/her language development. In doing so, we will explore the limits of the interpretation that the mechanisms underlying bilingual language development to a great extent relate to the individual's communicative context.

The notion of communicative context of a given language can be broadly understood as a set of variables related to the characteristics of input (e.g. frequency, quality, and variation) and social presence (i.e. the extent to which speakers of the language are represented in different age groups/peers). Decades of research on bilingualism have provided robust evidence that communicative context plays a crucial role for an individual's development of language proficiency. The field of language attrition provides convincing findings in this regard, showing that the degree to which acquired linguistic knowledge is retained largely depends on the degree of contact that the speaker maintains with the language. This phenomenon is particularly salient in children, who may undergo severe L1 loss if removed from the L1 communicative context (cf. the case of international adoptees; for L2 attrition, see Olshtain 1989). It is, however, not necessary to go to extreme cases of attrition to illustrate the importance of the communicative context. The growing field of heritage language acquisition has shown that bilingual development may be affected by shifts in dominance between two different communicative contexts. Here, the typical case is that the child spends the first years of life in a home environment, in which the L1 (minority language) is dominant, and has limited contact with the L2 (majority language). As the child grows older, the communicative context of the L2 expands, while at the same time, the L1 context stays the same or even diminishes. The result is commonly that the child eventually develops higher proficiency in the L2 than in the L1.

Concrete data on such a shift of language dominance is provided by Kohnert, Bates and Hernández (1999) in a cross-sectional study of lexical acquisition by Spanish heritage speakers in the US. The L2 English acquisition of these individuals began around the first school year, and their age at the time of testing ranged between five and 22 years. The results from a picture-naming task showed that the child participants, who had the least experience with English and the highest exposure to Spanish, were both faster and more accurate in Spanish than in English. The oldest participants, on the other hand, whose exposure to English was the highest and longest, obtained higher scores in English than in Spanish. Further insight on shift in language dominance is provided in a longitudinal study by Jia and Aaronson (2003). In this study, L1 Mandarin Chinese children and teenagers were investigated as they were in the process of developing their English L2 skills, with a specific focus on how language proficiency changes as a function of patterns of use and preference. The results showed that over a period of three years, the youngest children (age 5–9), who upon arrival spoke little or no English, experienced a switch to English in terms of language dominance and preference (English morphosyntactic proficiency was empirically assessed while Mandarin overall proficiency indices were calculated based on parental reports). This switch could in part be explained by taking into account the children's communicative contexts, that is, the social interactions with native English-speaking peers and the generally rich L2 environment in which they were immersed. The young teenagers (age 12–16), in contrast, did not display such language dominance shift. The authors ascribed this behaviour to the communicative contexts of the teenagers (fewer English native peers, and a less rich L2 environment).

In view of these findings, it seems well-founded to suggest that inverse proficiency levels in bilingual speakers need not be evidence of causation. Rather, the fact that different communicative contexts are conducive to different types of proficiency development can produce negative *correlations* between proficiency levels.[4]

---

4.   This possibility is also mentioned by Yeni-Komshian et al. (2000).

So far, this discussion has mainly concerned the "communicating container" view of bilingual proficiency. The points made concerning the impact of communicative context presented until now are, however, also relevant to the bilingualism effects discussion on a more general level. The finding that the linguistic environment shapes bilingual proficiency, for example, has implications for general statements about bilingual speakers being different from monolingual speakers. This is neatly illustrated in the studies by Kupisch and associates (e.g. Kupisch in press), in which it was found that simultaneous bilinguals performed like monolinguals in their stronger language, but not in their weaker language. As is typically the case with simultaneous bilinguals, the stronger language of the participants was also the majority community language (i.e. German in Germany or Italian in Italy). There was, in other words, a correlation between language dominance and communicative context. Even though correlation does not imply causation, as pointed out above, the accumulated evidence suggests that there are strong reasons to maintain that this correlation indeed reflects a causal relationship. Another important piece of information on the role of communicative context is provided by Thordardottir's (2012) study of lexical proficiency in simultaneously French-English bilingual children in Montreal. In this study, it was documented that those children who had equal amounts of exposure to both languages (as measured by parental reports) exhibited receptive vocabulary skills that were comparable to those of monolingual children.[5] Children who, in contrast, had unequal degrees of contact with the two languages exhibited stronger lexical skills in the language in which they had received most exposure. This study thus provides robust evidence concerning the impact of communicative context in the process of bilingual acquisition.

If we accept the reasoning that a correlation between communicative context and language proficiency implies causation, the following interpretation can be made: the simultaneous bilingual is more likely to behave like a monolingual speaker of X if the communicative context of language X is rich (i.e. high frequency, variation, and quality of input, and high social presence), than if it is poor. Trivial as this statement may seem, it confers great importance to communicative context as an explanation for bilingual proficiency, and suggests bilinguals are not necessarily different from monolinguals because of

---

5.   Interestingly, there was an asymmetry in the impact of exposure on different modalities of vocabulary knowledge, such that the development of productive vocabulary skills comparable to monolingual levels was dependent on higher exposure than the development of receptive skills.

their bilingualism, but rather, because of the context in which they acquired their languages.

We do, however, wish to stress that even though communicative context undeniably plays a crucial role in language development, there are reasons to believe that this factor should be applied and interpreted with care. First of all, it is important that the interpretation of communicative contexts does not turn into too powerful an explanation. That is to say, as a counter-argument to bilingualism effects on language proficiency, it could always be claimed that the reason why a given bilingual individual has not attained nativelike proficiency in the investigated language is because his/her past and present communicative context of that language was not optimal. Considering the intrinsic difficulties in backtracking and measuring every aspect of language contact across an individual's lifespan, it would be methodologically very challenging to falsify such a claim. Second, there may actually be individual differences in the way bilingual speakers respond to communicative contexts. For example, it seems to be the case that some bilinguals are less dependent than others on a rich communicative context in order to develop and retain linguistic knowledge. Evidence of this was reported in Bylund et al.'s (2010) investigation of incomplete L1 acquisition and attrition in L1 Spanish – L2 Swedish adult bilinguals living in Sweden. In this study, it was found that at the group level, the bilinguals were outperformed in their L1 by Chilean Spanish-speaking controls on a grammaticality judgement test. However, an inspection of individual results revealed that a considerable portion (60%) of the bilinguals scored within the native speaker range. More importantly, it was found that test performance was intimately connected to language aptitude such that those bilinguals who had higher levels of aptitude were more likely to exhibit nativelike performance than those with lower levels. Put more generally, this finding shows that even in cases where the communicative context is that of a minority language, cognitive factors such as language aptitude may allow bilingual speakers to attain a mastery comparable to that of native speakers in a majority language setting.

The third and final reason concerns the fact that the function of communicative context for language development does not seem to apply equally across the age span. Evidence for this may be found in L1 attrition research, in which it has been demonstrated that shifts in communicative context affect the linguistic knowledge of children to a much greater extent than that of adults. Whereas children are dependent of continuous contact with the L1 in order to retain their proficiency in this language, adults cope much better with reductions in L1 contact and undergo attrition to a much lesser degree (Bylund 2009; Montrul 2008; Schmid 2011). Further evidence in support of the timing of communicative context effects on language proficiency may be found in SLA studies. If it were the case that an optimal communicative context was automatically conducive to nativelike proficiency, it could be expected that virtually every learner who is immersed in such a context would develop L2 skills indistinguishable from those of native speakers. As is well known, however, this is not the case. Lardiere (2007), for example, examined L2 proficiency in an adult L2 learner who had been living in the L2 setting for over two decades, using the L2 on a daily basis both privately and professionally. Although fully functional in her L2, this speaker displayed non-native inflectional morphology (among other things). International adoptees constitute another case in point. Being immersed in a communicative context that does not differ from that of native speakers, one would expect this group of L2 speakers to exhibit native-like mastery of the L2. Contrary to this expectation, however, research findings suggest that the extent to which adoptee L2 speakers resemble native speakers is governed by their age of acquisition. In sum, the explanatory potential of the factor of communicative context seems to vary as a function of the age of the bilingual.

In this section, we have sought to draw attention to the role that the communicative context plays in bilingual language development with the intention of illustrating that non-convergence with native speaker behaviour found among bilingual speakers is not necessarily an effect of their bilingualism. To conclude the discussion, we posit that not all instances of divergence from native speaker behaviour exhibited in the bilingual speaker can be ascribed to the co-existence of two (or more) languages in one mind, since bilingual speakers immersed in a rich communicative context have been shown to be more likely to exhibit nativelike behaviour than are bilingual speakers who acquired the same language in a context that is less rich. The extent to which the communicative context has an impact on the attainment of nativelike language proficiency is, however, ultimately related to individual differences and age.

3.3   Differential effects as a function of linguistic domain

The last point to be treated in the discussion relates to the question of whether some linguistic domains or elements are more susceptible to bilingualism effects than others. This possibility is intuitively appealing, as it finds parallels in research findings on the selective nature of language development. First, studies of language attrition show unequivocally that different domains of the language system are differentially affected in the attrition process. More specifically, it seems as if the lexicon is the most vulnerable domain, whereas phonology is the most stable. Selective vulnerability within domains has also been attested, for example, morphological features that are rich in semantic content (so-called *interpretable* features) are more susceptible to attrition than features with low semantic content (*uninterpretable features*) (Sorace 2004). Similar evidence of selectivity in language development is provided by SLA studies of ultimate attainment. These suggest that different linguistic domains may be subject to different sensitive periods (*multiple sensitive periods*), such that the time window during which nativelike mastery can be achieved varies among domains and even for elements within domains. Whereas the optimal window for attainment of nativelike pronunciation seems to close early in life, morphology and syntax may be acquired to nativelike level up until the mid-teens (see, however, Meisel 2011) (for further discussion, see Long 2007).

In view of these findings, it is reasonable to assume that to the extent that there are bilingualism effects, they do not apply equally across the board. However, the general scarcity of empirical studies focusing particularly on bilingualism effects makes it difficult to formulate specific predictions as to their selectivity. This problem is exacerbated by the fact that the studies carried out to date exhibit great variation in terms of scope and foci. Some preliminary observations may, nonetheless, be made on the basis of the available findings. It is noteworthy that a great number of studies of semantic and conceptual competence find support for bilingualism effects on ultimate attainment, in both simultaneous bilinguals and L2 speakers. A number of theoretical frameworks highlight the notion that the languages of the bilingual overlap at the conceptual level (e.g. de Bot 1992; Francis 2004; Paradis 2004; this is also discussed in Cook's Multicompetence framework). The extent of the overlap is determined in part by the linguistic trajectory of the bilingual and in part by crosslinguistic differences between the two languages (Jarvis & Pavlenko 2008). Taken together, the empirical findings and theoretical work on semantic-conceptual interaction in speakers of more than one language seem to make this domain a strong candidate for bilingualism effects. There are, however, exceptions to this pattern, showing that the age of acquisition of a L2 speaker may still influence the extent to which his/her attainment of conceptual patterns resembles that of native speakers (e.g. Boroditsky 2001). The exceptions are important, nonetheless, in as much as they illustrate the complexity that surrounds the phenomenon of bilingualism effects. To say that a given domain is subject to bilingualism effects while another one is not would, of course, be an oversimplification. It is quite possible that bilingualism effects may in fact be found in virtually every linguistic domain. Rather, the issue at stake concerns the extent to which such effects are found, as well as the internal linguistic conditions that increase or decrease the likelihood of their occurrence (as opposed to external conditions, e.g. communicative context).

The notion that there is selectivity in the way two co-existing language systems may or may not influence one another is potentially of tremendous importance to the emerging debate on bilingualism effects in L2 ultimate attainment. Claims along the lines that the bilingualism of L2 speakers has as a consequence that their target language proficiency will always be different from that of native speakers seem to conceive of bilingualism effects as a phenomenon that strikes indiscriminately across an individual's linguistic repertoire. However, if the notion of selectivity is recognised, it has the potential of steering the debate towards more specific questions, such as which linguistic behaviours are affected, to what extent, by the co-existence of two languages in one mind.

4. Conclusions

In this chapter, we set out to analyse the emerging view that non-native behaviour in L2 speakers is an effect of bilingualism, as opposed to an effect of age of acquisition. After reviewing the empirical evidence relevant to this notion, we discussed and analysed the conceptual underpinnings of the arguments and interpretations of bilingualism effects with a particular focus on assumptions about monolingualism and bilingualism in native speakers and L2 speakers, respectively, and the effects of communicative context on bilingual proficiency. In our discussion, we have presented the related issues and problems in a somewhat dichotomous way, in order to illustrate different stances and interpretations, put them in relation to one another, and explore their underlying assumptions.

We wish to underscore, however, that a fruitful approach for future research on this issue consists of recognising that bilingualism effects on L2 ultimate attainment are not an either-or phenomenon. Three different aspects illustrate this: the first relates to the generalizability of bilingualism effects across different linguistic domains. As discussed above, it is conceivable that different domains and different components within domains are differentially affected by two co-existing language systems, such that some are more susceptible to bilingualism effects than others. Although this may seem obvious, the implication of this statement is that a single piece of evidence of bilingualism effects (or lack thereof) must be interpreted in context, and will never suffice to overthrow one interpretation or the other. The second issue concerns the mechanisms underlying idiosyncratic linguistic behaviour among bilinguals when compared to monolinguals. In our discussion, we underscored the fact that different proficiencies among bilingual speakers need not be an effect of crosslinguistic influence, but can also be the consequence of the communicative contexts in which the language proficiencies developed. It is, in other words, not a given that two co-existing language systems automatically lead to linguistic behaviour that is different from that of monolingual speakers.

The third issue – and perhaps the most important one for the current discussion – is that bilingualism effects and effects of age of acquisition are not necessarily mutually exclusive. This is neatly illustrated in the study by Sebastián-Gallés et al. (2005)

of the perception of minimal pairs in Catalan. Here it was found that even though the simultaneous Catalan-Spanish bilinguals were outperformed by sequential L1 Catalan-L2 Spanish bilinguals, they were, nonetheless, more proficient than sequential L1 Spanish-L2 Catalan bilinguals. This finding thereby shows a two-way distinction, in the sense that L1 speakers who are monolingual from birth may be different from L1 speakers who are bilingual from birth, who in turn may be different from L2 speakers. On a more general level, this suggests that an explanation of non-native behaviour based on bilingualism effects does not necessarily have to be invoked at the expense of age of acquisition effects.

Apart from recognising the potential and limits of bilingualism effects as an explanation for non-nativelike ultimate attainment among L2 speakers, future empirical research into this issue will also benefit from taking some methodological considerations into account. The first relates to the proficiency and use of different languages in both L2 speakers and native speaker controls. As seen in the discussion above, the terms bilingualism and monolingualism often remain undefined in the emerging debate on bilingualism effects. One way of getting around this problem, obviously, is to collect data on knowledge and frequency of use of additional languages among native speakers, and on the knowledge and frequency of use of the L1 (and additional languages) among L2 speakers. Empirical data on the supposed monolingualism and bilingualism among native speakers and L2 speakers, respectively, are a prerequisite for evaluating the argument that L2 speakers' L2 proficiency is different from that of native speakers because the former are bilingual and the latter monolingual.

The second point concerns the procedures for carrying out quantitative analyses of simultaneous bilinguals and bilingual L2 speakers. In several studies, the L1 and L2 behaviour of these groups is analysed in group-wise comparisons with native speaker control groups. Even though comparisons at a group-level are informative for a range of different purposes, they also involve the risk of contributing to an unwarranted picture of bilingual proficiency as inherently non-convergent with that of native speakers. This is illustrated in Bylund et al. (2012), where it was found that although the bilingual L2 speakers as a group performed significantly lower than the native speaker control groups, individual analyses revealed that around half the participants exhibited scores within the native range in both their languages (and vice-versa). This finding suggests a rather complex picture of bilingual proficiency, in which the extent to which bilinguals behave like monolinguals is related to individual differences (e.g. language aptitude) and communicative context.

In light of some of the empirical findings reviewed in this chapter, it seems clear that in some instances, non-native ultimate attainment may be an effect of the knowledge and use of more than one language. However, in view of the discussion above, it must also be recognised that the extent and nature of bilingualism effects on ultimate attainment are far from straightforward. In order to avoid the question of bilingualism effects turning into an ideological debate, the field is in need of empirical data stemming from studies that rely on solid methodological and conceptual frameworks.

References

Abrahamsson, N. (2012). Age of onset and ultimate attainment of L2 phonetic and grammatical intuition. *Studies in Second Language Acquisition, 34,* 187–214.

Abrahamsson, N., & Hyltenstam, K. (2008). The robustness of aptitude effects in near-native second language acquisition. *Studies in Second Language Acquisition, 30,* 489–509.

Abrahamsson, N., & Hyltenstam, K. (2009). Age of onset and nativelikeness in a second language: Listener perception versus linguistic scrutiny. *Language Learning, 59,* 249–306.

Ameel, E., Storms, G., Malt, B., & Sloman, S. (2005). How bilinguals solve the naming problem. *Journal of Memory and Language, 53,* 60–80.

Ameel, E., Malt, B., Storms, G., & van Assche, F. (2009). Semantic convergence in the bilingual lexicon. *Journal of Memory and Language, 60,* 270–290.

Antón-Méndez, I., & Gollan, T. (2010). Not just semantics: Strong frequency and weak cognate effects on semantic association in bilinguals. *Memory and Cognition, 38,* 723–739.

van Assche, E., Duyck, W., Hartsuiker, R., & Diependaele, K. (2009). Does bilingualism change native-language reading? Cognate effects in a sentence context. *Psychological Science, 20,* 923–927.

Athanasopoulos, P. (2007). Interaction between grammatical categories and cognition in bilinguals: The role of proficiency, cultural immersion, and language of instruction. *Language and Cognitive Processes, 22,* 689–699.

Baker, C. (2011). *Foundations of bilingual education and bilingualism* (5th ed.). Bristol: Multilingual Matters.

Barton, D. (2011). Cross-linguistic influence in adult early bilinguals: Generic noun phrases in German and French. *Arbeiten zur Mehrsprachigkeit, 96,* 26.

Bialystok, E. (2009). Bilingualism: The good, the bad, and the indifferent. *Bilingualism: Language and Cognition, 12,* 3–11.

Bianchi, G. (in press). Gender in Italian-German Bilinguals: A comparison with L2 learners of Italian. *Bilingualism: Language and Cognition.*

Birdsong, D. (2005). Nativelikeness and non-nativelikeness in L2A research. *International Review of Applied Linguistics, 43,* 319–328.

Birdsong, D. (2006). Age and second language acquisition and processing: A selective overview. *Language Learning, 56,* 9–49.

Birdsong, D. (2009). Age and the end state of second language acquisition. In W.C. Ritchie, & T.K. Bhatia (Eds.), *The new handbook of second language acquisition* (pp. 401–424). Bingley: Emerald.

Birdsong, D., & Molis, M. (2001). On the evidence for maturational constraints in second-language acquisition. *Journal of Memory and Language, 44,* 235–249.

de Bot, K. (1992). A bilingual production model: Levelt's speaking model adapted. *Applied Linguistics, 13,* 1–24.

de Bot, K., & Weltens, B. (1991). Regression, recapitulation, and language loss. In H. Seliger, & R. Vago (Eds.), *First language attrition* (pp. 31–52). Cambridge: CUP.

Block, D. (2003). *The social turn in second language acquisition*. Washington, DC: Georgetown University Press.

Boroditsky, L. (2001). Does language shape thought? Mandarin and English speakers' conceptions of time. *Cognitive Psychology, 43*, 1–22.

Brown, A., & Gullberg, M. (2008). Bidirectional crosslinguistic influence in L1-L2 encoding of manner in speech and gesture: A study of Japanese speakers of English. *Studies in Second Language Acquisition, 30*, 225–251.

Bylund, E. (2009). Maturational constraints and first language attrition. *Language Learning, 59*(3), 687–715.

Bylund, E. (2011a). Ultimate attainment of event construal patterns in speakers of L2 Swedish. *Vigo International Journal of Applied Linguistics, 8*, 29–53.

Bylund, E. (2011b). Segmentation and temporal structuring of events in early Spanish-Swedish bilinguals. *International Journal of Bilingualism, 15*, 8–54.

Bylund, E., Abrahamsson, N., & Hyltenstam, K. (2010). The role of language aptitude in first language attrition: The case of prepubescent attriters. *Applied Linguistics, 31*, 443–464.

Bylund, E., Abrahamsson, N., & Hyltenstam, K. (2012). Does first language maintenance hamper nativelikeness in a second language? A study of ultimate attainment in early bilinguals. *Studies in Second Language Acquisition, 34*, 215–241.

Bylund, E., Athanasopoulos, P., & Oostendorp, M. (in press). Motion event cognition and grammatical aspect. Evidence from Afrikaans. *Linguistics*.

Cederblad, M., Höök, B., Irhammar, M., & Mercke, A.-M. (1999). Mental health in international adoptees as teenagers and young adults. An epidemiological study. *Journal of Child Psychology and Psychiatry, 40*, 1239–1248.

Chugani, H., Behen, M., Muzik, O., Juhasz, C., Nagy, F., & Chugani, D. (2001). Local brain functional activity following early deprivation: A study of postinstitutionalized Romanian orphans. *Neuroimage, 14*, 1290–1301.

Cook, V. (1992). Evidence for multicompetence. *Language Learning, 42*, 557–591.

Cook, V. (1999). Going beyond the native speaker in language teaching. *TESOL Quarterly, 33*, 185–209.

Cook, V. (2002). Background to the L2 user. In V. Cook (Ed.), *Portraits of the L2 user* (pp. 1–28). Clevedon: Multilingual Matters.

Cook, V. (2003). The changing L1 in the L2 user's mind. In V. Cook (Ed.), *Effects of the second language on the first*. Clevedon: Multilingual Matters.

Costa, A. (2005). Lexical access in bilingual production. In J. Kroll, & A.M.B. de Groot (Eds.), *Handbook of bilingualism: Psycholinguistic approaches* (pp. 308–325). Oxford: OUP.

Davies, A. (2003). *The native speaker: Myth and reality*. Clevedon: Multilingual Matters.

DeKeyser, R.M., Alfi-Shabtay, I., & Ravid, D. (2010). Cross-linguistic evidence for the nature of age-effects in second language acquisition. *Applied Psycholinguistics, 31*, 413–438.

Delcenserie, A., Genesee, F., & Gauthier, K. (in press). Language abilities of internationally adopted children from China during the early school years: Evidence for early age effects? *Applied Psycholinguistics*.

Dunkel, H. (1948). *Second language learning*. Boston, MA: Ginn & Company.

Firth, A., & Wagner, J. (1997). On discourse, communication, and (some) fundamental concepts in SLA research. *The Modern Language Journal, 81*, 285–300.

Firth, A., & Wagner, J. (1998). SLA property: No trespassing! *The Modern Language Journal, 82*, 91–94.

Firth, A., & Wagner, J. (2007). Second/foreign language learning as a social accomplishment: Elaborations on a reconceptualized SLA. *Modern Language Journal, 91*/Focus Issue, 800–819.

Flege, J. (1995). Second language speech learning: Theory, findings, and problems. In W. Strange (Ed.), *Speech perception and linguistic experience: Issues in cross-language research* (pp. 233–277). Timonium, MD: York Press.

Flege, J. (1999). Age of learning and second language speech. In D. Birdsong (Ed.), *Second language acquisition and the critical period hypothesis* (pp. 101–132). Mahwah, NJ: Lawrence Erlbaum Associates.

Flege, J., Frieda, E., & Nozawa, T. (1997). Amount of native-language (L1) use affects the pronunciation of an L2. *Journal of Phonetics, 25*, 169–186.

Francis, N. (2004). The components of bilingual proficiency. *International Journal of Bilingualism, 8*, 167–189.

Gathercole, V., & Moawad, R. (2010). Semantic interaction in early and late bilinguals: Not all words are created equal. *Bilingualism: Language and Cognition, 13*, 385–408.

Gardell, I. (1979). *A Swedish study on intercountry adoptions: A report from Allmänna Barnhuset.* Stockholm: Allmänna Barnhuset.

Gauthier, K., & Genesee, F. (2011). Language development in internationally adopted children: A special case of early second language learning. *Child Development, 82*, 887–901.

Gauthier, K., Genesee, F., & Kasparian, K. (2012). Acquisition of complement clitics and tense morphology in internationally adopted children acquiring French. *Bilingualism: Language and Cognition, 15*, 304–319.

de Geer, B. (1992). *Internationally adopted children in communication: A developmental study.* Unpublished doctoral dissertation, Lund University, Sweden.

Glennen, S., & Masters, G. (2002). Typical and atypical language development in infants and toddlers adopted from Eastern Europe. *American Journal of Speech–Language Pathology, 11*, 417–433.

Gregg, K. (2004). A theory for every occasion. Postmodernism and SLA. *Second Language Research, 16*, 383–399.

Gregg, K. (2006). Taking a social turn for the worse. The language socialization paradigm for second language acquisition. *Second Language Research, 22*, 413–442.

Gregg, K., Long, M., Jordan, G., & Beretta, A. (1997). Rationality and its discontents in SLA. *Applied Linguistics, 18*, 538–558.

Grosjean, F. (1989). Neurolinguists, beware! The bilingual is not two monolinguals in one person. *Brain and Language, 36*, 3–15.

Grosjean, F. (1998). Studying bilinguals: Methodological and conceptual issues. *Bilingualism: Language and Cognition, 1*, 131–149.

Grosjean, F. (2001). The bilingual's language modes. In J. Nicol (Ed.), *One mind, two languages: Bilingual language processing* (pp. 1–22). Oxford: Blackwell.

Hene, B. (1993). *Utlandsadopterade barns och svenska barns ordförståelse: En jämförelse mellan barn i åldern 10–12 år.* (SPRINS-gruppen 41). Sweden: Gothenburg University.

Hernández, A., Li, P., & MacWhinney, B. (2005). The emergence of competing modules in bilingualism. *Trends in Cognitive Sciences, 9*, 220–225.

Herschensohn, J. (2007). *Language development and age.* Cambridge: CUP.

Hyltenstam, K., Bylund, E., Abrahamsson, N., & Park, H.-S. (2009). Dominant language replacement: The case of international adoptees. *Bilingualism: Language and Cognition, 12*, 121–140.

Isurin, L. (2000). Deserted islands or a child's first language forgetting. *Bilingualism: Language and Cognition, 3*, 151–166.

Jarvis, S., & Pavlenko, A. (2008). *Crosslinguistic influence in language and cognition*. London: Routledge.

Jia, G., & Aaronson, D. (2003). A longitudinal study of Chinese children and adolescents learning English in the United States. *Applied Psycholinguistics, 24*, 131–161.

Johnson, J., & Newport, E. (1989). Critical period effects in second language learning: The influence of maturational state on the acquisition of English as a second language. *Cognitive Psychology, 21*, 60–99.

Kohnert, K.J., Bates, E., & Hernandez, A.E. (1999). Balancing bilinguals: Lexical-semantic production and cognitive processing in children learning Spanish and English. *Journal of Speech, Language, and Hearing Research, 42*, 1400–1413.

Köpke, B. (2002). Activation thresholds and non-pathological L1 attrition. In F. Fabbro (Ed.), *Advances in the Neurolinguistics of Bilingualism. Essays in Honor of Michel Paradis* (pp. 119–142). Undine: Forum.

Kupisch, T. (in press). Generic subjects in the Italian of early German-Italian bilinguals and German learners of Italian as a second language. *Bilingualism: Language and Cognition*.

Kupisch, T., Akpınar, D., & Stöhr, A. (in press). Gender assignment and gender agreement in adult bilingual and L2-speakers of French. *Linguistic Approaches to Bilingualism*.

Lantolf, J. (1996). SLA theory building: "Letting all the flowers bloom!" *Language Learning, 46*, 713–749.

Lardiere, D. (2007). *Ultimate attainment in second language acquisition. A case study*. Mahwah, NJ: Lawrence Erlbaum Associates.

de Leeuw, E. (in press). Reassessing maturational constraints through evidence of L1 attrition in the domain of phonetics. In E. Thomas, & I. Mennen (Eds.), *Unravelling bilingualism: A cross-disciplinary perspective*. Clevedon: Multilingual Matters.

de Leeuw, E., Mennen, I., & Scobbie, J.M. (in press). Dynamic systems, maturational constraints, and phonetic attrition. *International Journal of Bilingualism*.

Lenneberg, E.H. (1967). *Biological foundations of language*. New York, NY: Wiley.

Li, P., & Farkas, I. (2002). A self-organizing connectionist model of bilingual processing. In R. Heredia, & J. Altarriba (Eds.), *Bilingual sentence processing* (pp. 59–85). Amsterdam: Elsevier.

Long, M. (2007). *Problems in SLA*. Mahwah, NJ: Lawrence Erlbaum Associates.

MacKay, I., Flege, J., & Imai, S. (2006). Evaluating the effects of chronological age and sentence duration on degree of perceived foreign accent. *Applied Psycholinguistics, 27*, 157–183.

MacWhinney, B. (1997). Second language acquisition and the Competition Model. In J. Kroll, & A.M.B. de Groot (Eds.), *Tutorials in bilingualism* (pp. 113–140). Mahwah, NJ: Lawrence Erlbaum Associates.

MacWhinney, B. (2005). A unified model of language acquisition. In J. Kroll, & A.M.B. de Groot (Eds.), *Handbook of bilingualism: Psycholinguistic approaches* (pp. 49–67). Oxford: OUP.

McLaughlin, B (1978). *Second language acquisition in childhood*. Hillsdale, NJ: Erlbaum.

Marian, V., & Spivey, M. (2003). Competing activation in bilingual language processing: Within- and between-language competition. *Bilingualism: Language and Cognition, 6*, 97–115.

Meisel, J.M. (2011). *First and second language acquisition: Parallels and differences*. Cambridge: CUP.

Montrul, S. (2008). *Incomplete acquisition in bilingualism: Re-examining the age factor*. Amsterdam: John Benjamins.

Munro, M., & Mann, V. (2005). Age of immersion as a predictor of foreign accent. *Applied Psycholinguistics, 26*, 311–341.

Muñoz, C., & Singleton, D. (2011). A critical review of age-related research on ultimate attainment. *Language Teaching, 44*, 1–35.

Oh, J., Au, T., & Jun, S.-A. (2010). Early childhood language memory in the speech perception of international adoptees. *Journal of Child Language, 37*, 1123–1132.

Olshtain, E. (1989). Is second language attrition the reversal of second language acquisition? *Studies in Second Language Acquisition, 11*, 151–165.

Ortega, L. (2010). The bilingual turn in SLA. Plenary delivered at the Annual Conference of the American Association for Applied Linguistics. Atlanta, GA, March 6–9 2010.

Pallier, C., Dehaene, S., Poline, J.-B., LeBihan, D., Argenti, A.-M., Dupoux, E., & Mehler, J. (2003). Brain imaging of language plasticity in adopted adults: Can a second language replace the first? *Cerebral Cortex, 13*, 155–161.

Paradis, M. (2004). *A neurolinguistic theory of bilingualism*. Amsterdam: John Benjamins.

Pavlenko, A., & Malt, B. (2011). Kitchen Russian: Cross-linguistic differences and first language object naming by Russian-English bilinguals. *Bilingualism: Language and Cognition, 14*, 19–45.

Rutter, M. (1998). Developmental catch-up, and deficit, following adoption after severe global early privation. English and Romanian Adoptees (ERA) Study Team. *Journal of Child Psychology and Psychiatry, 39*, 465–476.

Schmid, M.S. (2011). *Language attrition*. Cambridge: CUP.

Sebastián-Gallés, N., Echeverría, S., & Bosch, L. (2005). The influence of initial exposure on lexical representation: Comparing early and simultaneous bilinguals. *Journal of Memory and Language, 52*, 240–255.

Singh, L., Liederman, J., Mierzejewski, R., & Barnes, J. (2011). Rapid reacquisition of native phoneme contrasts after disuse: you do not always lose what you do not use. *Developmental Science, 14*, 949–959.

Singleton, D., & Ryan, L. (2004). *Language acquisition: The age factor*. Clevedon: Multilingual Matters.

Sorace, A. (2004). Native language attrition and developmental instability at the syntax-discourse interface: Data, interpretations and methods. *Bilingualism: Language and Cognition, 7*, 143–145.

Stöhr, A., Akpınar, D., Bianchi, G., & Kupisch, T. (2012). Gender marking in Italian-German heritage speakers and L2-learners of German. In K. Braunmueller, & C. Gabriel (Eds.), *Multilingual individuals, multilingual societies*. Amsterdam: John Benjamins.

Thordardottir, E. (2012). The relationship between bilingual exposure and vocabulary development. *International Journal of Bilingualism, 15*, 426–445.

VanPatten, B., & Benati, A. (2010). *Key terms in second language acquisition*. London: Continuum.

Watson-Gegeo, K. (2004). Mind, language, and epistemology: Toward a language socialization paradigm for SLA. *The Modern Language Journal, 88*, 331–350.

Weinreich, U. (1953). *Languages in contact*. New York, NY: Linguistic Circle of New York.

VanPatten, B., & Benati, A. (2010). *Key terms in second language acquisition*. London: Continuum.

Ventureyra, V., Pallier, C., & Yoo, H. (2004). The loss of first language phonetic perception in adopted Koreans. *Journal of Neurolinguistics, 17*, 79–91.

Yeni-Komshian, G., Flege, J., & Liu, S. (2000). Pronunciation proficiency in the first and second languages of Korean-English bilinguals. *Bilingualism: Language and Cognition, 3*, 131–149.

PART II

Aptitude constructs and measures

Cognitive aptitudes for second language learning and the LLAMA Language Aptitude Test*

Gisela Granena
University of Maryland

The LLAMA Language Aptitude Tests (Meara 2005) are a set of exploratory tests designed to assess aptitude for second language (L2) learning. In its current or earlier version (i.e. the LLAMA or LAT), this battery of four subtests has been used in an increasing number of studies in the second language acquisition field. However, as indicated by Meara, it has not been extensively standardized. This chapter reports on the results of an exploratory validation study that assessed the reliability of the test and explored its underlying structure with a sample of 186 participants. The results showed that internal consistency and stability in time were acceptable. A series of exploratory factor analyses further suggested that the test is measuring two different aptitude dimensions.

1. Introduction

In 2002, Skehan observed that research on language aptitude had "languished" over the previous three decades (p. 69). Ten years later, in 2012, he pointed out that aptitude was revitalized and changing "from a marginal position to one where it is center-stage" (p. 381). Indeed, the second language acquisition (SLA) field has witnessed a renewed interest in the study of language aptitude, spurred by developments in areas of cognitive psychology, such as working memory and attention control, as well as by developments in understanding how second languages are learned and in language teaching methodology (Long & Doughty 2009).

These recent advances have reinforced a componential view of language aptitude (Robinson 2007; Skehan 1986) and its conceptualization as a combination of cognitive and perceptual abilities (i.e. aptitudes) (Carroll 1981; Doughty,

* This material is based upon work supported by the National Science Foundation under Grant # 1124126.

Campbell, Mislevy, Bunting, Bowles & Koeth 2010), which may be differentially important according to such factors as type of second language (L2) task, acquisition stage, instructional treatment, learning context (formal vs. informal), language domain (phonology, grammar, lexis and collocation), language aspect (e.g. salient vs. non-salient), and time (short-term vs. long-term differences in acquisition).

The renewed interest in aptitude has also highlighted the need for aptitude measures that are easy to administer, preferably computer based, and widely available to SLA researchers. Some well-known aptitude batteries are available, but commercially so (MLAT; Carroll & Sapon 1959, PLAB; Pimsleur 1966), others are easily accessible, but in paper-and-pencil formats (CANAL-F; Grigorenko, Sternberg & Ehrman 2000), while others have restricted accessibility as a result of their development in a military context. A recent development that does not suffer from any of these limitations is the LLAMA aptitude test (Meara 2005), a revised version of the Swansea LAT (Meara, Milton & Lorenzo-Dus 2003). Probably for this reason, it has been increasingly used in a number of research studies (Abrahamsson & Hyltenstam 2008; Bylund, Abrahamsson & Hyltenstam 2010; Cherciov 2011; Forsberg & Sandgren this volume; Granena & Long 2013; Granena 2012; Granena this volume; Serrano & Llanes 2012; Smeds 2012; Yalcin 2012; Yilmaz 2013). These studies provide an invaluable source of data to calibrate the tests by comparing results across a variety of learning environments and learner populations. Despite the increasing popularity of the LLAMA, the test has not been extensively standardized, as warned in the LLAMA manual, which further discourages its use in high-stakes situations, where accuracy and reliability are at a premium.

The results reported in this chapter are from an exploratory validation study of the LLAMA that aimed at assessing the reliability of the test and exploring its underlying structure. After a detailed description of the measure, an overview is provided of the research studies that have used it, and of their findings. Then, the results of the reliability analyses and exploratory factor analyses are presented. This leads to a discussion of the type of aptitude measured by the LLAMA and the implications for SLA research.

2. The LLAMA aptitude test

The LLAMA is a computer-based aptitude test battery that is available for free downloads (www.lognostics.co.uk/tools/llama/index.htm). It grew out of a series of projects carried out by students of English Language and Linguistics at the University of Wales, Swansea, and, as cautioned by Meara (2005), the tests are exploratory and should be avoided in high-stakes situations. The battery is user-friendly and requires approximately 25 minutes to administer. Each subtest is individually and automatically scored. Although largely based on the MLAT, the LLAMA tests are described as being language-independent, unlike the MLAT. They rely on picture stimuli and verbal materials adapted from a British-Columbian indigenous language and a Central-American language. This is an innovative feature with respect to its earlier version, the LAT, which included materials loosely based on Polish and Turkish that made stimuli more familiar to test-takers who spoke Hungarian or Azeri. Language independence is also a highly desirable methodological feature for cognitive measures, in order to avoid confounds that may arise in L1- or L2-based cognitive tests, such as those related to language background, proficiency level, literacy skills and language dominance in bilingual L2 learners. Language independence also minimizes the use of long-term memory strategies, which aid remembering of verbal stimuli through meaningful connections. Finally, it facilitates test administration to speakers of any L1 without the need for translations that may threaten the validity and reliability of the test, as well as comparisons of findings cross-linguistically.

The LLAMA includes four sub-tests: LLAMA B, a test of vocabulary learning, LLAMA D, a test of sound recognition that requires previously heard sound sequences to be identified in new sequences, LLAMA E, a test of sound-symbol associations, and LLAMA F, a test of grammatical inferencing. With the exception of sound recognition (LLAMA D), the sub-tests include default study phases that last between two and five minutes. Testing phases are untimed. The score for each of the LLAMA sub-tests ranges between 0 and 100 (LLAMA B, E, and F) and between 0 and 75 (LLAMA D). Feedback is provided after each response in the form of an acoustic signal.

2.1 LLAMA B: Vocabulary learning

LLAMA B (see Figure 1) is a test that measures the ability to learn new words. According to the LLAMA manual, it is loosely based on the original vocabulary learning subtask of Carroll and Sapon (1959), the paired-associates test. The words to be learned, 20 in total, are presented visually and are real words taken from a Central-American language. Each of them is assigned to a target image. Test-takers have to learn as many words as possible by associating each of them with a target image. There is a timed study phase (two minutes by default) in which test-takers click on the different images displayed on the screen. The name of each object is

Figure 1. LLAMA B

shown in the centre of the panel. In the testing phase, the program displays the name of an object and test-takers have to identify the correct image on the screen.

2.2 LLAMA D: Sound recognition

LLAMA D (see Figure 2) is described as a new task that does not appear in the work of Carroll and Sapon (1959) and that measures the ability to recognize patterns in spoken language. According to Meara (2005), this ability should help learners recognize the small morphological variations that many languages use to signal grammatical features. The test is loosely based on work by Service (Service 1992; Service & Kohonen 1995) and on Speciale, N. Ellis and Bywater (2004). Test-takers listen to a string of 10 sound sequences that are computer-generated and based on the names of objects in a British-Columbian Indian language. There is

Figure 2. LLAMA D

no time to study, and the sound sequences are only played once. Then, test-takers complete a recognition test where they have to discriminate between old and novel items (see Footnote 1 for an explanation of the distinction between recollection and familiarity in episodic memory retrieval).

2.3   LLAMA E: Sound-symbol association

LLAMA E (see Figure 3) measures the ability to form novel sound-symbol associations (phonemic coding ability). Similar to the MLAT phonetic script subtest, it requires test-takers to work out relationships between sounds (i.e. recorded syllables), 24 in total, and a written representation of those sounds in an unfamiliar alphabet. There is a timed study phase (two minutes by default) in which test-takers click on the different symbols displayed and try to learn the corresponding sound association. They then hear a combination of two syllables and have to decide its symbol correspondence by clicking on the right button.

Figure 3. LLAMA E

2.4   LLAMA F: Grammatical inferencing

LLAMA F (see Figure 4) is measures of the ability to infer or induce the rules of an unknown language (i.e. explicit inductive learning ability). Test-takers see a set of pictures and sentences describing the pictures, 20 in total, and try to work out the grammatical rules that operate in the language. There is a timed study phase (five minutes by default) in which test-takers click on a series of small buttons displayed on the screen. For each button, a picture and a sentence describing the picture are displayed. In the testing phase, the program shows a picture and two sentences, one grammatical and one ungrammatical, and test-takers click on the one they consider correct.

Figure 4. LLAMA F

3.   The LLAMA aptitude test in SLA research: An overview

The LLAMA, or its earlier version, the Swansea LAT, has been used in a number
of studies in the SLA literature, mostly in studies of ultimate L2 attainment by very
advanced speakers in naturalistic contexts (Abrahamsson & Hyltenstam 2008;
Forsberg & Sandgren this volume; Granena 2012 this volume; Granena & Long
2013), but also in studies of L1 attrition (Bylund et al. 2010; Cherciov 2011), study
abroad (Serrano & Llanes 2012), and instructed SLA (Yalcin 2012; Yilmaz 2013),
and even in studies with visually impaired L2 learners (Smeds 2012).

In studies of ultimate attainment by very advanced L2 speakers, relationships
between LLAMA scores and L2 attainment have been reported in different language domains: morphosyntax, lexis and collocations, and pronunciation. In the
morphosyntactic domain, Abrahamsson and Hyltenstam (2008) found a significant positive correlation between aptitude as measured by the LAT test and the
combined scores of two grammaticality judgment test (GJT) modalities (written
and auditory), both characterized by very long, syntactically complex sentences, in
a group of early L2 learners who started learning the new language before age 12.
In addition, the four late L2 learners who were able to score within native-speaker
range on the GJT, and who had also passed as native speakers in a stringent screening process, were all above average in terms of aptitude. Granena (2012) also found
significant correlations between average LLAMA scores and morphosyntactic
attainment, but only in L2 measures that focused participants' attention on language forms, especially if they allowed time to reflect on language correctness and
structure. Like Abrahamsson and Hyltenstam (2008), Granena (2012) reported
significant correlations in both early L2 learners (ages of onset between three

and six) and adult L2 learners. However, LLAMA scores did not correlate with an auditory (online) GJT (Granena this volume; Granena & Long 2013) or with a word-monitoring task tapping automatic use of L2 knowledge (Granena 2012). The exception was the LLAMA D subtest (sound recognition), which predicted L2 learners' grammatical sensitivity to gender, number and person agreement in Spanish in the word-monitoring task in Granena (2012).

As for lexis and collocations, two studies (Forsberg & Sandgren this volume, and Granena & Long 2013) found significant relationships between the LLAMA and L2 attainment in the area of collocations by highly advanced adult L2 learners, all long-term residents in an L2-speaking country. Interestingly, in both studies, LLAMA D (sound recognition) was the subtest that yielded the strongest relationship with collocation knowledge. Finally, one study (Granena & Long 2013) found a significant positive correlation between average scores on the LLAMA and adult L2 learners' pronunciation ratings on a controlled reading-aloud task.

Regarding studies of L1 attrition, Bylund et al. (2010) reported a positive correlation between average LAT scores and GJT performance, as a measure of L1 proficiency, among early attriters who had started acquiring the L2 before age 12 and who were in a situation of reduced L1 contact. Cherciov (2011) also investigated L1 attrition, but did not find any relationships between L1 maintenance and the LLAMA. Unlike Bylund et al. (2010), participants in Cherciov (2011) were not early, but late (or post-pubescent) attriters, and the outcome measures used (a C-test, a verbal fluency task, and a spontaneous production task) did not include a GJT.

As for study abroad research, Serrano and Llanes (2012) examined the effects of different learning contexts (either classroom instruction or a combination of immersion and instruction) and vocabulary learning skills, as measured by LLAMA B, on language gains on two tasks: a written GJT with a correction component and a lexical test of formulaic sequences. The study found that the effect of learning context was not significant, but that learners with higher LLAMA B scores had greater pre-to-post gain scores on the written GJT than on the formulaic test in all contexts, as well as greater gain scores than learners with lower LLAMA B scores on the two tasks.

In the area of instructed SLA, Yalcin (2012) and Yilmaz (2013) investigated aptitude in relation to form-focused instruction (FFI), a proactive teaching approach, and corrective feedback, respectively. Yalcin (2012) found a significant interaction between average LLAMA scores and time (pretest–posttest) on a written GJT, but no relationship between aptitude and scores on an oral performance task. The effect of aptitude was greater for the structure considered difficult in the study (the English passive) than for the structure considered easy (the past progressive). In Yilmaz (2013), results showed a strong, statistically significant relationship between posttest performance and grammatical inferencing (LLAMA F) under the explicit feedback condition (i.e. explicit correction), but not under the implicit feedback condition (i.e. recasts). Explicit feedback was more effective than implicit feedback in the study, but only among L2 learners with high LLAMA F scores.

Finally, the only study carried out with visually impaired L2 learners (Smeds 2012) found that visual status was a significant factor determining test scores on LLAMA D (sound recognition). Early and late visually impaired L2 learners obtained significantly higher scores on LLAMA D than sighted, and sighted but blindfolded, participants. The learners in the early group, most of whom had become visually impaired before age five, also performed descriptively better than late L2 learners who had become visually impaired after age 18. Interestingly, there were no differences between any of the groups regarding episodic memory, a type of declarative (explicit) memory for past events.[1]

Taken together, the results of these 11 studies indicate that consistent correlations are obtained between language aptitude as measured by the LLAMA and L2 outcome measures in different learning contexts (immersion and instructed) and studies (experimental, quasi-experimental, and ex-post facto). A recurrent pattern across the studies is the fact that the LLAMA correlated with L2 measures that call for the use of analytic, metalinguistic abilities and with L2 learning under explicit instructional treatments or feedback conditions. No studies showed a significant relationship between the LLAMA and L2 measures that required automatic use of L2 knowledge (e.g. a word-monitoring task or spontaneous oral production tasks), except for LLAMA D, the sound recognition subtest. This aptitude component was related to degree of sensitivity to agreement violations and to lexical and collocation knowledge, a type of knowledge that relies on item-based learning

---

1.   It is important to distinguish conscious recollection, which is closer to what is meant by episodic memory, from familiarity, recognition based on the sensation that an item has been seen before without explicitly remembering any detailed contextual information. It has been argued that episodic recollection and feelings of familiarity may have different neuro-anatomic correlates (Baddeley, Vargha-Khadem & Mishkin 2001). The relatively preserved recognition as opposed to recall performance of some amnesics may reflect the fact that such a procedure relies less on slow, controlled search processes and more on fast, automatic processes. It has been further speculated that the same processes that support preserved performance on implicit tests in amnesics may be responsible for familiarity-based recognition judgments (Mandler 1980). In fact, familiarity, but not recollection, has been found to be significantly correlated with conceptual priming in healthy individuals (Wang & Yonelinas 2012). Finally, while recollection processes are impaired by aging, familiarity shows minimal or no age-related decline (e.g. Bastin & Van der Linden 2003).

(Hoyer & Lincourt 1998), among highly advanced L2 learners. In addition, the aptitude measured by LLAMA D was shown to undergo special development in the visually impaired, even well into adulthood, a type of development that was not observed in declarative types of memory.

4. The LLAMA aptitude test: An exploratory validation study

The research overview shows that the LLAMA tests have been used in several SLA studies. The results obtained provide an invaluable source of data with which to calibrate the tests and cross-validate the measure. However, as Meara points out, the LLAMA has not been extensively standardized, which is why it should not be used in high-stakes situations. Standardization, which involves administering the test to a large sample from a variety of ages and socioeconomic and racial backgrounds, in order to establish a basis for meaningful comparison, was beyond the scope of the study to be reported here. This study did not seek to create norms for the LLAMA, but was rather an exploratory validation study with two main goals, (1) to assess the reliability of the LLAMA in terms of its internal consistency and stability in time, and (2) to explore the underlying structure of the test by means of exploratory factor analyses.

4.1   Participants

A total of 186 participants from three different L1 backgrounds (Chinese, Spanish, and English) were included in the study. There were 107 females (57.5%) and 79 males (42.5%). Participants' age at time of testing was 25 years on average ($SD = 5.29$) and ranged from 18 to 39. Maximum age at testing was set at 40 in order to avoid possible confounds with normal cognitive aging.

4.2   Instruments and procedure

All participants completed the four LLAMA subtests in a random order, and their performance was audio-recorded.[2] Each subtest was automatically scored by the

---

2.   In order to compute reliability for a test such as the LLAMA, which does not provide itemized data, researchers should audio-record participants' performance during the test. To the best of my knowledge, no published study has provided a reliability index for the test yet. The belief that reliability cannot be computed may be a major drawback for using the measure, given the increasing demand for reliability information in scientific journals. The solution I propose is to (1) administer the items in every subtest in the same order to the sample of participants (in other words, randomize tests, but do not randomize items),

program. As noted earlier, LLAMA B, E and F have a maximum score of 100, and LLAMA D a maximum of 75. In addition, 110 of the 186 participants also completed a general intelligence test (GAMA) and a probabilistic serial reaction time (SRT) task, while the other 76 participants were administered a working memory (WM) test (the Operation Span), a short-term memory (STM) test (the Letter Span), a processing speed test (the Digit-Symbol Correspondence) and a test of attention control (the Simon task).

4.3   GAMA

The general ability measure for adults (GAMA) is a non-verbal measure of general intelligence. It is self-administered (booklets were used), timed (25 minutes), and includes 66 multiple-choice items that require the application of reasoning and logic to solve visual problems involving abstract designs, shapes, and colors.

4.4   Probabilistic SRT task

The probabilistic SRT task is a measure of implicit sequence-learning ability. Unlike other paradigms for studying implicit learning (e.g. Artificial Grammar learning tasks), learning is measured online during the training phase. Originally developed by Nissen and Bullemer (1987), the SRT task used in the present study was a probabilistic version created using the same stimuli as Kaufman, DeYoung, Gray, Jiménez, Brown and Mackintosh (2010). Participants saw a visual cue (an asterisk) appear at one of four prescribed locations on a computer screen. Their task was to press a key corresponding to the location of the asterisk as fast and accurately as possible. No instructions to memorize the series or look for underlying rules were provided.

Unknown to the participants, the asterisks played out a sequence of 12 positions that followed a probabilistic order. In every task block, trials were congruent with the target sequence 85% of the time and intermixed with an alternate sequence 15% of the time. The two sequences used exclusively differed in the second-order conditional information they conveyed. Reed and Johnson gave the sequences of three locations the name of *second order conditionals* (SOCs) (as distinct from first-order probabilities, where the location of an item is unambiguously predicted by the preceding item with a probability of 1.0). In second-order conditionals, at least two previous locations are needed to predict

(2) audio-record performance to have a record of the feedback given to each participant in the form of an acoustic signal, (3) transcribe *dings* and *beeps* into the binary code (1 and 0) needed to compute internal consistency.

the next location in the sequence. The target sequence chosen (Sequence A) was 1-2-1-4-3-2-4-1-3-4-2-3, while the alternate sequence (Sequence B) was 3-2-3-4-1-2-4-3-1-4-2-1. Transitions in one sequence respect the second-order conditionals of the other sequence, but lead to different predictions.

Participants completed eight training blocks of 120 trials each (960 in total) in approximately 20 minutes. There was a break after every block. Degree of learning was quantified as the average difference in reaction time between correct responses to congruent and incongruent trials (incongruent RT – congruent RT). After the training phase, participants completed a recognition test that assessed the extent to which they explicitly discriminated between 24 old and novel three-element sequences on a six-point Likert scale and the extent to which explicit recognition was associated with speed of response. The only difference between old and new sequences was second-order conditional information (e.g. transition 3–4 was followed by location 2 in Sequence A and by location 1 in Sequence B). Recognition scores were computed as the difference between the mean judgment for old sequences minus the mean judgment for new sequences, and priming scores were computed as the difference between the mean reaction time elicited by the third element of old sequences minus the mean reaction time elicited by the third element of new sequences. Evidence of a dissociation between explicit recognition and implicit priming (i.e. poor recognition, but faster reaction times, for segments of the old sequences) is considered evidence of implicit learning during the training task (Shanks & Johnstone 1999).

4.5   Operation span (OSPAN) test

WM capacity was measured by means of the OSPAN test (Unsworth, Heitz, Schrock & Engle 2005), a test that requires solving simple arithmetic operations as quickly as possible and recalling 15 randomly distributed sets of letters, ranging from three to seven, in correct serial order. Phonologically distinct letters (i.e. B, F, H, J, L, M, Q, R, X) served as stimuli (Kane, Hambrick, Tuholski, Wilhelm, Payne & Engle 2004). Each letter remained on-screen for 800 milliseconds, and participants were given nine seconds to type in the set of letters in the correct serial order at recall. The test was administered individually, and an 85 % accuracy criterion was established for the secondary (arithmetic) task. Participants were instructed to say each operation-letter string aloud, in order to attenuate rehearsal. The OSPAN test is the latest by Engle and his associates. It is a verbal task that tries to overcome previous limitations of word selection by having letters recalled instead of words (i.e. word knowledge and frequency, language proficiency and long-term memory strategies).

The test was scored following a partial credit scoring method with equal weighting (Conway, Kane, Bunting, Hambrick, Wilhem & Engle 2005). This method gives credit to partly correct recalled sets, as long as elements are in correct serial position. Equal weighting was applied to the partial credit scoring method by scoring each item as a proportion of correctly recalled elements. These proportions were, then, averaged. Kane et al. (2004) showed an advantage for this type of scoring method in terms of the internal consistency of the test.

4.6   Letter span test

STM capacity (i.e. storage capacity) was measured by means of a visual letter span test. In this test, letter sequences (two to eight letters each) were presented visually at a rate of one per second. When prompted, participants were given nine seconds to recall the letters in the exact sequence by typing them in. There were three sets for each letter sequence (i.e. three sets of two-letter sequences each, three sets of three-letter sequences, etc.). Like the OSPAN, the letter span was also scored following a partial credit scoring method with equal weighting.

4.7   Digit-symbol correspondence test

The digit-symbol task is a non-verbal test of information-processing speed. It is a subtest of the Wechsler Adult Intelligence Scales that measures the ability to link symbols with numbers in 90 seconds. It requires eye-hand coordination, visual scanning, symbolic translation, and motor speed, as well as learning skill. The test consists of nine symbols and each symbol represents a number from 1 to 9. Participants were given a grid with 4×25 series containing the digits 1 to 9 in random order (100 digits in total). Following a practice trial and with the key available, participants were asked to write the symbol corresponding to each digit.

The score was the number of squares filled in correctly in 90 seconds. An intelligent person usually begins with the first digit and supplies the proper symbol for it at each place it occurs in the test. Then, s/he begins with the second digit and so on. Those of average intelligence more frequently try to supply the proper symbol for each different digit in order as they appear in the test.

4.8   Simon task

The Simon task (Simon & Rudell 1967) is a non-verbal task of attention control. Participants have to attend to the color of a stimulus while ignoring its spatial location. A colored square (red or blue) is presented on either side of a fixation point and is associated with a keyboard response aligned with the presentation location. Red squares are associated with a key on the right and blue squares with a key on the left. On congruent trials, stimuli appear on the same side as their associated key press. On incongruent trials, they appear on the opposite side. The test consisted of 36 trials presented in a randomized order: nine congruent and nine incongruent with each of the two colors.

Attention control was measured as the reaction time difference between incongruent and congruent items (i.e. incongruent minus congruent stimuli or Simon effect). A smaller Simon effect shows greater attention control. The sign of the variable was reversed, so that a larger Simon effect indicated greater attention control.

4.9   Data analysis

Two measures of test reliability were employed: internal consistency and test-retest reliability. Internal consistency, or the degree to which the results on the tests were consistent across items, was assessed by means of Cronbach's alpha. Test-retest reliability, or the degree to which the results on the tests were stable over time, was assessed by means of a correlation of test scores on two different occasions over a two-year time period. The reliability analysis also included comparisons of test scores across L1s (Spanish, Chinese, English) and gender.

With regard to validity, a principal components analysis (PCA) with Varimax rotation, an exploratory factor analytic technique, was used to explore the underlying structure of the test, specifically whether the LLAMA was measuring a single general factor or multiple independent dimensions.

4.10   Results

4.10.1   Reliability

The average scores on each of the LLAMA subtests for the entire set of participants ($N = 186$) were 52.72 ($SD = 19.80$) on LLAMA B, 30.27 ($SD = 15.72$) on LLAMA D, 74.70 ($SD = 23.87$) on LLAMA E, and 56.67 ($SD = 24.09$) on LLAMA F. The average score on the test overall, computed as the raw average of the four subtests, was 53.67 ($SD = 14.19$). Scores were all normally distributed, according to Kolmogorov-Smirnov (K–S) tests ($p > .05$).

A series of one-way analyses of variance (ANOVAs) revealed no significant differences between the three L1 groups (Chinese, Spanish, and English) on either the overall LLAMA test score ($F(2,183) = .903$, $p = .407$) or subtest scores: LLAMA B ($F(2,183) = 2.882$, $p = .059$), LLAMA D ($F(2,183) = 2.207$, $p = .113$), LLAMA E ($F(2,183) = .104$, $p = .901$), or LLAMA F ($F(2,183) = .319$, $p = .727$).

There were no significant differences between male and female participants on the test overall ($t(184) = -.156$, $p = .876$) or on any of the subtests, either, according to independent-samples t-tests: LLAMA B ($t(184) = -1.196$, $p = .233$), LLAMA D ($t(184) = .365$, $p = .716$), LLAMA E ($t(184) = -.167$, $p = .868$), or LLAMA F ($t(184) = .328$, $p = .744$).

Internal consistency was estimated for a subsample of 74 participants. This was the number of participants from whom audio recordings could be obtained (see Endnote 2). Table 1 displays the Cronbach's alpha coefficients for each of the LLAMA subtests and for the entire test battery. The internal consistency of the battery ($k = 90$) was acceptable ($\alpha = .77$). The internal consistency of each of the subtests, was, however, lower, ranging from .60 to .76. The criteria for acceptable alpha coefficients have ranged from .80 to .90, down to .60 to .70 (Nunnally 1968; Nunnally & Bernstein 1994). Typically, .60 to .80 indicates acceptable reliability, .80 or higher means good reliability, and the coefficients greater than .95 may indicate redundancy in the items. Aron, Aron and Coups (2005) suggest that the widely-accepted cut-off in the social sciences is .70, with some researchers using .75 to .80, and others being as lenient as .60. An internal consistency that is lower than .70 indicates that the standard error of measurement (i.e. a measure of response stability) is over half (0.55) a standard deviation.

Table 1. Internal consistency: Cronbach's alpha

Test	α
Overall LLAMA ($k = 90$)	.77
LLAMA B ($k = 20$)	.76
LLAMA D ($k = 30$)	.64
LLAMA E ($k = 20$)	.63
LLAMA F ($k = 20$)	.60

Stability over time was estimated for a subsample of 20 participants. The same participants were measured twice with a time interval of two years, in 2009 and 2011. The correlations between test scores on the two testing occasions were all moderate, or moderately strong, and statistically significant, indicating that high scores at Time 1 were paired with high scores at Time 2 (see Table 2). Note that the magnitude of the correlations in test-retest estimates of reliability depend in part by how much time elapses between the two measurement occasions. In general, the longer the interval, the lower the correlation tends to be, because the factors that contribute to error are less similar.

Table 2. Test retest: Pearson correlations

Test	r
Overall LLAMA ($k = 90$)	.64**
LLAMA B ($k = 20$)	.53*
LLAMA D ($k = 30$)	.60**
LLAMA E ($k = 20$)	.61**
LLAMA F ($k = 20$)	.56**

*$p < .05$.
**$p < .01$.

4.10.2   Validity: An exploratory approach

A series of exploratory PCAs with Varimax rotation were conducted, in order to establish independent factors on the basis of factor loadings. The first PCA was performed on the four LLAMA subtest scores for the 186 participants. The Kaiser-Meyer-Olkin (KMO) measure of sampling adequacy was .661. Conventionally, values that are higher than .600 suggest that the partial correlations between the variables are adequate for the analysis. Barlett's test of sphericity was significant ($p < .001$), indicating significant relationships among variables. The analysis revealed a first component with an eigenvalue greater than 1.0^3 ($\lambda = 1.81$), which accounted for 45.15% of the total variance, and a second factor with an eigenvalue approaching 1.0 ($\lambda = .91$), which accounted for 22.82% of additional variance. According to the rotated solution, three subtests loaded on the first component with loadings greater than .4:[4] LLAMA B ($\lambda = .74$), LLAMA E ($\lambda = .67$), and LLAMA F ($\lambda = .82$). LLAMA D, on the other hand, loaded strongly on the second component ($\lambda = .97$) and weakly on the first ($\lambda = .09$) (see Table 3).

The same pattern of loadings was obtained via a non-orthogonal type of rotation (Oblimin). LLAMA B, D, E, and F received loadings of .74, .21, .70, and .81, respectively, on the first component, and loadings of .15, .98, .35, and .04 on the second component. The analysis with Oblimin rotation, which allows components to be interrelated, further showed that the correlation between the two components

---

3.   Different criteria have been suggested for retaining factors. According to the more liberal Jolliffe criterion, factors with eigenvalues $\geq .7$ should be kept, whereas according to the more conservative Kaiser criterion, only factors with eigenvalues ≥ 1.0 explain a substantial enough amount of variation to be retained.

4.   Factor loadings with absolute values greater than .3 or .4 are usually judged to be substantial or "significant."

Table 3. Loadings for exploratory principal component analysis
(with Varimax rotation)

	Component 1	Component 2
LLAMA B	.739	.083
LLAMA D	.092	.975
LLAMA E	.671	.298
LLAMA F	.817	−.037

Table 4. Correlation matrix for the four LLAMA subtests

	LLAMA B	LLAMA D	LLAMA E	LLAMA F
LLAMA B	–	.18*	.30**	.38**
LLAMA D		–	.22**	.12
LLAMA E			–	.37**
LLAMA F				–

*$p < .05$.
**$p < .01$.

was .21. This weak correlation was also reflected in the correlation patterns between the subtests (see Table 4). The subtests that were more strongly related were LLAMA B, E, and F, whereas LLAMA D was correlating weakly with LLAMA B and E, and non-significantly with LLAMA F.

The second PCA was performed on the battery of eight cognitive tests that a subsample of 76 participants completed, which included the four LLAMA subtests, plus tests of WM, STM, processing speed, and attention control. The tests of sampling adequacy were all met. The KMO value was .674, and Barlett's test was significant ($p < .001$). The analysis revealed three factors with eigenvalues greater than 1.0 that accounted for 60.56% of the total variance. The first component ($\lambda = 2.32$) accounted for 29.01% of the variance, while the second and third components accounted for 16.83% and 14.72% additional variance, respectively. According to the rotated solution, three variables loaded on the first component with values greater than .4: WM ($\lambda = .88$), STM ($\lambda = .79$), and processing speed ($\lambda = .52$). Three variables also loaded on the second component with values greater than .4: LLAMA B ($\lambda = .65$), LLAMA E ($\lambda = .74$), and LLAMA F ($\lambda = .79$). Finally, two variables loaded on the third component: LLAMA D ($\lambda = .68$) and attention control, with a negative loading, ($\lambda = -.79$). Table 5 displays the loadings on each component.

Table 5. Loadings for exploratory principal component analysis (with Varimax rotation)

	Component 1	Component 2	Component 3
Working Memory	.882	−.014	−.038
LLAMA B	.127	.645	.106
LLAMA D	.345	.105	.679
LLAMA E	.124	.742	−.142
LLAMA F	.039	.791	.017
Processing Speed	.520	.223	−.198
Attention Control	.280	.098	−.793
Short-term Memory	.791	.171	.289

The last PCA was performed on the battery of six tests that a subsample of 110 participants completed, which included the four LLAMA subtests, plus the general intelligence test (GAMA) and the probabilistic serial reaction time task. The tests of sampling adequacy were all met. The KMO value was greater than .600 (.712), and Bartlett's test of sphericity was significant ($p < .05$). The analysis, conducted with Varimax rotation, yielded two principal components with eigenvalues greater than 1.0 that explained 57.34% of the total variance. The first component had an eigenvalue of 2.304 and accounted for 38.41% of the variance. The second component had an eigenvalue of 1.136 and accounted for an additional 18.94% of the variance. The rotated component matrix showed that four tests loaded on the first component with loadings greater than .4: GAMA, LLAMA F, LLAMA B, and LLAMA E. On the other hand, two tests loaded more strongly on the second component: the probabilistic SRT task and LLAMA D. The same pattern of results was obtained via a non-orthogonal rotation (Oblimin), which yielded a correlation of −.07 between the two components (see Table 6 for the distribution of loadings).

Table 6. Loadings for exploratory principal component analysis (with Varimax rotation)

	Component 1	Component 2
LLAMA B	.720	.048
LLAMA D	.316	.660
LLAMA E	.655	.290
LLAMA F	.749	−.026
GAMA	.788	−.117
SRT Task	.244	.784

4.11   Discussion

This study sought to estimate the reliability of the LLAMA aptitude test and explore its underlying structure. Regarding test reliability, two different indexes measuring internal consistency and stability over time showed that each of the four LLAMA subtests had acceptable reliability. The reliability of the test overall increased from acceptable to good, an expected result, given the increase in the number of items and, therefore, available information. Its internal consistency approached .80, meeting the widely-accepted social science cut-off of .70 (Nunnally & Bernstein 1994), although its test-retest reliability was below .70 ($r = .64$, $p = .002$). This could have been due to the long interval between the two test administrations (two years), since with increasing time intervals, test-retest coefficients tend to decrease. Overall, the moderate and significant correlations obtained suggest that the LLAMA has stable test-retest reliability over a two-year time period. This result also shows that aptitude is a fairly stable trait, as claimed by Carroll (1993).

In addition, analyses comparing LLAMA test scores across L1 group (Chinese, Spanish, and English) and gender revealed no significant differences in any of the analyses. The fact that speakers of three typologically different languages had comparable scores provides some support for the language-independence feature of the test. This was one of the improvements of the LLAMA over its earlier version, the LAT, which included materials based on Polish and Turkish that were familiar to speakers of some L1s. The fact that males and females also scored comparably indicates no differences in level of language aptitude across genders.

With respect to the underlying structure of the test, the results of a series of exploratory PCAs converged on solutions which showed that LLAMA D, the sound recognition subtest, loaded separately from the other three subtests. According to this result, the LLAMA aptitude test measures two different aptitude dimensions. The pattern of correlations between all pairs of subtests further confirmed the weak relationship between LLAMA D and the other subtests, which, on the other hand, were more strongly and significantly interrelated. This result is in line with the existence of individually unique aptitude profiles (Robinson 2001 2002; Skehan 1998, 2002). The fact that LLAMA D did not correlate, or correlated weakly, with the other subtests means that scores on LLAMA D and on LLAMA B, E, and F varied separately. That is, when the magnitude of one was high, the magnitudes of the others were sometimes high, sometimes low. Therefore, there could be participants with high LLAMA D scores, but low scores on the other subtests, and vice-versa. This uncorrelated variation could be used to look at aptitude abilities through a componential approach by identifying individual aptitude profiles, for example L2 learners with strong sound sequence learning ability, but low grammatical inferencing skills, and vice-versa – a situation with obvious potential for aptitude-treatment interaction (ATI) studies (see Vatz et al. this volume).

LLAMA B, E, and F have in common the fact that they include a study phase that gives test-takers time to study and rehearse testing materials, as well as opportunities to use strategies and problem-solving techniques. Rote learning and explicit associative learning play a role in the three subtests, as well as analytical ability, since the three subtests involve working out relations in datasets. Two, LLAMA E and F, explicitly instruct those taking the test to "work out the relationship" and "work out the grammatical rules," respectively. LLAMA B asks them to learn the names of objects, but test-takers can also work out relationships between objects and names as a strategy. These are cognitive abilities that involve explicit cognitive and memory processes. In fact, the subtest that consistently received the strongest loading in the analyses that were conducted, meaning that it was the subtest that correlated the strongest with the underlying component, was LLAMA F. In this subtest, test-takers are given time to infer or induce the rules governing a set of language materials presented visually. Although the test does not involve verbalization of grammatical rules, test-takers are instructed to search for rules intentionally; therefore, the test is primarily measuring (explicit) inductive language learning ability. This is an ability that, according to Skehan (1989), should not be separated from grammatical sensitivity. In fact, he reconceptualized inductive language-learning ability and grammatical sensitivity as language analytic ability (Skehan 1998). Meara (2005: 18) further points out that LLAMA F (based on the earlier LAT C) is "particularly good at identifying outstanding analytical linguists." The manual explicitly recommends this subtest if the researcher's main purpose "is to identify really good analytical linguists".

While LLAMA F requires test-takers to work out the grammar of an unknown language by means of pictures and short written sentences, LLAMA D measures their ability to discriminate short stretches of spoken language by analogy. As pointed out by Meara (2005: 8), LLAMA D "owes something to Speciale (Speciale, N. Ellis & Bywater 2004)" who "suggest that a key skill in language ability is your ability to recognize patterns, particularly patterns in spoken language." Speciale et al.'s (2004) work is based on a strand of cognitive psychology that investigates the implicit induction of phonological sequences (e.g. Saffran, Newport, Aslin, Tunick & Barrueco 1997; Saffran, Johnson, Aslin & Newport 1999). In addition, LLAMA D is the only subtest that does not include a study phase, and therefore, does not allow time to rehearse, which minimizes problem-solving and strategy use. Unlike the other subtests, it does not call for the use of analytical abilities. Participants are exposed to a set of instances, one after the other, which are consistent with the phonetic patterns of a British-Columbian Indian language, but they are not asked to work out rules or relations. These learning conditions are closer to implicit induction (i.e. exposure to a set of instances or memorization of a set of exemplars) than explicit induction (i.e. figuring out rules and relations). LLAMA D could, therefore, be measuring a cognitive ability involving more implicit cognitive processes than LLAMA B, E, and F (Granena 2012).

The PCA performed on the LLAMA subtests, the GAMA, and probabilistic SRT task would lend support to this interpretation, since LLAMA D loaded on the same component as the SRT task, considered to be a measure of implicit learning (Kaufman et al. 2010), while LLAMA B, E, and F loaded together with general intelligence, a construct that, as measured by currently available intelligence tests, is biased towards explicit processes that are attention-driven (Woltz 2003). In fact, several studies have found that intellectual quotient (IQ) measures correlate with artificial grammar learning under intentional learning conditions (e.g. Gebauer & Mackintosh 2007), but not under more incidental learning conditions, a type of learning that shares with implicit learning the fact that it is "unintentional and uncontrolled" (Reber & Allen 2000: 238). IQ does not correlate, either, with implicit cognitive processes, as measured by probabilistic SRT tasks (e.g. Kaufman et al. 2010), or implicit memory measures of priming (e.g. Woltz 1990, 1999). In a replication and extension of Reber, Walkenfeld and Hernstadt (1991), Robinson (2002) found a correlation between explicit learning and IQ, as measured by a short form of the Wechsler Adult Intelligence Scale (WAIS-R), but no correlation under an incidental learning condition, which involved meaning-based processing. Findings also showed a significant negative correlation between IQ and implicit artificial grammar learning ($r = -.34$, $p < .05$), which Robinson explained as indicating participants' adoption of an explicit code-breaking set towards the implicit learning task, a strategy that had more negative effects for those participants with higher IQ scores and who are better at explicit learning.

The PCA performed on the LLAMA subtests and the WM, STM, processing speed, and attention control tests further showed that the aptitude dimension measured by LLAMA B, E, and F is different from memory (as measured by the OSPAN and a visual letter span) and processing speed. LLAMA D received a stronger loading from the memory component than the other three LLAMA subtests, but the strongest loading it received was from the component where attention control also loaded the strongest. While LLAMA D received a positive loading, indicating a positive correlation with the underlying component, attention control received a negative loading, indicating a negative correlation with the component. If LLAMA D taps an underlying cognitive ability that is relevant for implicit learning, as hypothesized, this result would mean that a high ability to maintain task goals and avoid capture by irrelevant stimuli and/or processes is detrimental to implicit learning, which takes place largely without drawing from the central executive. Further research should investigate this relationship to further validate the construct underlying LLAMA D.

As part of the construct validation process, the relationship between a measure and relevant criterion variables is also assessed. Research studies that have used it indicate that consistent correlations are obtained between the LLAMA as an omnibus measure of language aptitude and language development. Specifically, significant relationships were reported with L2 learning under explicit instructional treatments or feedback conditions and/or with L2 measures that call for the use of analytic, metalinguistic abilities. No study showed a significant relationship between the LLAMA and implicit treatments or L2 measures that require automatic use of L2 knowledge (e.g. spontaneous oral production tasks). This may indicate a positive association between the LLAMA and conditions that induce learners to process language explicitly.

In addition to explicit cognitive processes, however, individuals differ in other domains of cognitive ability. Although little research exists, studies have suggested that cognitive aptitudes for implicit learning may be relevant for complex cognition (e.g. Woltz 2003), for example, implicit cognitive processes such as those tapped by probabilistic serial reaction time tasks or measures of priming (Kaufman et al. 2010; Woltz 1990, 1999). This has led some researchers to conceptualize implicit learning as an *ability*, "the ability to automatically and implicitly detect complex and noisy regularities in the environment" (Kaufman et al. 2010: 321). This ability is characterized by automatic, associative, and unintentional learning processes that place minimal demands on attention. Contrary to Reber (1993), who views individual differences in implicit cognition as minimal, these researchers claim that implicit learning is a cognitive ability with meaningful individual differences that can explain learner differences in complex forms of learning (Pretz, Totz & Kaufman 2010).

One of the subtests in the LLAMA that was suggested as a measure tapping a cognitive aptitude relevant for implicit language learning and processing is LLAMA D, the sound recognition subtest. This subtest was related to degree of sensitivity to agreement violations on a task requiring automatic use of L2 knowledge and to lexical and collocation knowledge, a type of knowledge that relies on item-based learning, among highly advanced L2 learners (Forsberg & Sandgren this volume; Granena 2012; Granena & Long 2013). In addition, the aptitude measured by LLAMA D was shown to undergo special development in the visually impaired, even well into adulthood, a type of development that was not observed in declarative (explicit) types of memory.

Based on the differences between the four LLAMA subtests and the results of the PCAs, the two aptitude dimensions that the LLAMA aptitude test was found to measure were interpreted as explicit language aptitude (ELA) and implicit language aptitude (ILA). ELA taps cognitive aptitudes that are more relevant for explicit language learning and processing, such as language analytical ability, whereas ILA taps cognitive aptitudes more relevant for implicit language learning, such as sequence learning ability.

4.12   Conclusions and directions for further research

This chapter reported on the results of an exploratory validation study that assessed the reliability of the LLAMA aptitude test (Meara 2005) and explored its underlying structure. The results showed that internal consistency and stability over time were acceptable, and that test scores were independent of participants' L1 and gender. A series of exploratory factor analyses further suggested that the test is measuring two different aptitude dimensions, which were interpreted as analytic ability, a type of aptitude relevant for explicit language learning, and (sound) sequence learning ability, a type of aptitude relevant for implicit language learning.

It was argued that the domain of implicit cognitive processes is a fruitful area for investigating cognitive aptitudes that can explain variation in language development beyond initial rate of success in traditional language classes at high levels of functional L2 ability. Individual differences in implicit cognitive processes may also be relevant in accounting for variation in the learning outcomes of child L2 learners who started learning early enough to acquire language without awareness, but late enough to be affected by age of onset.

It was further argued that LLAMA D is a test that may be tapping implicit language aptitude. This claim, however, should not be overstated. Given the exploratory nature of the test, the use of additional measures of implicit cognitive processes is highly recommended. The domain of implicit cognition is, after all, a broad domain that includes phenomena known in the literature under terms such as *implicit memory, implicit learning, procedural skill learning,* and *priming* (Woltz 2003). Further research is clearly needed that investigates potential relationships between individual differences in these different implicit processes and language acquisition.

References

Abrahamsson, N., & Hyltenstam, K. (2008). The robustness of aptitude effects in near-native second language acquisition. *Studies in Second Language Acquisition, 30,* 481–509.

Aron, A., Aron, E.N., & Coups, E.J. (2005). *Statistics for the behavioral and social sciences: A brief course* (3rd ed.). Upper Saddle River, NJ: Pearson Education.

Baddeley, A., Vargha-Khadem, F., & Mishkin, M. (2001). Preserved recognition in a case of developmental amnesia: Implications for the acquisition of semantic memory? *Journal of Cognitive Neuroscience, 13,* 357–369.

Bastin, C., & van der Linden, M. (2003). The contribution of recollection and familiarity to recognition memory: A study of the effects of test format and aging. *Neuropsychology, 17*, 14–24.

Bylund, E., Abrahamsson, N., & Hyltenstam, K. (2010). The role of language aptitude in first language attrition: The case of pre-pubescent attriters. *Applied Linguistics, 31*, 443–464.

Carroll, J.B. (1981). Twenty-five years of research in foreign language aptitude. In K. Diller (Ed.), *Individual differences and universals in language learning aptitude* (pp. 83–118). Rowley, MA: Newbury House.

Carroll, J.B. (1993). *Human cognitive abilities: A survey of factor-analytic studies.* Cambridge: CUP.

Carroll, J.B., & Sapon, S. (1959). *Modern language aptitude test: Form A.* New York, NY: Psychological Corporation.

Cherciov, M. (2011). *Between attrition and acquisition: The dynamics between two languages in adult migrants.* Unpublished doctoral dissertation. University of Toronto.

Conway, A.R.A., Kane, M.J., Bunting, M.F., Hambrick, D.Z., Wilhem, O., & Engle, R.W. (2005). Working memory span tasks: A methodological review and user's guide. *Psychonomic Bulletin & Review, 12*(5), 769–786.

Doughty, C.J., Campbell, S.G., Mislevy, M.A., Bunting, M.F., Bowles, A.R., & Koeth, J.T. (2010). Predicting near-native ability: The factor structure and reliability of Hi-LAB. In M.T. Prior, Y. Watanabe, & S. Lee (Eds.), *Selected Proceedings of the 2008. Second Language Research Forum* (pp. 10–31). Somerville, MA: Cascadilla Proceedings Project.

Forsberg, F., & Sandgren, M. (this volume). High-level proficiency in late L2 acquisition. Relationships between collocational production, language aptitude and personality.

Gebauer, G.F., & Mackintosh, N.J. (2007). Psychometric intelligence dissociates implicit and explicit learning. *Journal of Experimental Psychology: Learning, Memory, and Cognition, 33*(1), 34–54.

Granena, G. (2012). *Age differences and cognitive aptitudes for implicit and explicit learning in ultimate L2 attainment.* Unpublished doctoral dissertation. University of Maryland.

Granena, G., & Long, M.H. (2013). Age of onset, length of residence, language aptitude, and ultimate L2 attainment in three linguistic domains. *Second Language Research, 29*(1).

Grigorenko, E.L., Sternberg, R.J., & Ehrman, M.E. (2000). A theory based approach to the measurement of foreign language learning ability: The Canal- F theory and test. *The Modern Language Journal, 84*, 390–405.

Hoyer, W.J., & Lincourt, A. (1998). Aging and the development of learning. In M.A. Stadler & P.A. Frensch (Eds.), *Handbook of implicit learning* (pp. 445–470). Thousand Oaks, CA: Sage.

Kane, M.J., Hambrick, D.Z., Tuholski, S.W., Wilhelm, O., Payne, T.W., & Engle, R.W. (2004). The domain generality of working-memory capacity: A latent-variable approach to verbal and spatial memory span and reasoning. *Journal of Experimental Psychology: General, 133*, 189–217.

Kaufman, S.B., DeYoung, C.G., Gray, J.R., Jimenez, L., Brown, J., & Mackintosh, N. (2010). Implicit learning as an ability. *Cognition, 116*, 321–340.

Long, M.H., & Doughty, C.J. (2009). *Handbook of language teaching.* Oxford: Blackwell.

Mandler, G. (1980). Recognizing: The judgment of previous occurrence. *Psychological Review, 87*(3), 252–271.

Meara, P. (2005). *LLAMA language aptitude tests.* Swansea, UK: Lognostics.

Meara, P., Milton, J., & Lorenzo-Dus, N. (2003). *Swansea language aptitude tests (LAT) v.2.0.* Swansea, UK: Lognostics.

Nissen, M.J., & Bullemer, P. (1987). Attentional requirements of learning: evidence from performance measures. *Cognitive Psychology, 19*, 1–32.

Nunnally, J.C. (1968). *Psychometric theory*. New York, NY: McGraw-Hill.

Nunnally, J.C., & Bernstein, I.H. (1994). *Psychometric theory* (3rd ed.). New York, NY: McGraw-Hill, Inc.

Pimsleur, P. (1966). *Pimsleur language aptitude battery (PLAB)*. New York, NY: The Psychological Corporation.

Pretz, J.E., Totz, K.S., & Kaufman, S.B. (2010). The effects of mood, cognitive style, and cognitive ability on implicit learning. *Learning and Individual Differences, 20*, 215–219.

Reber, A.S. (1993). *Implicit learning and tacit knowledge: An essay on the cognitive unconscious*. Oxford: OUP.

Reber, A.S., & Allen, R. (2000). Individual differences in implicit learning: Implications for the evolution of consciousness. In R.G. Kunzendork, & B. Wallace (Eds.), *Individual differences in conscious experiences* (pp. 228–247). Philadelphia: John Benjamin.

Reber, A.S., Walkenfeld, F.F., & Hernstadt, R. (1991). Implicit and explicit learning: Individual differences and IQ. *Journal of Experimental Psychology: Learning, Memory and Cognition, 17*, 888–896.

Robinson, P. (2001). Individual differences, cognitive abilities, aptitude complexes, and learning conditions in SLA. *Second Language Research, 17*, 368–392.

Robinson, P. (2002). Individual differences in intelligence, aptitude and working memory during adult incidental second language learning: A replication and extension of Reber, Walkenfeld, and Hernstadt (1991). In P. Robinson (Ed.), *Individual differences and instructed language learning* (pp. 211–266). Amsterdam: John Benjamins.

Robinson, P. (2007). Aptitudes, abilities, contexts and practice. In R.M. DeKeyser (Ed.), *Practice in second language learning: Perspectives from applied linguistics and cognitive psychology* (pp. 256–286). Cambridge: CUP.

Saffran, J.R., Newport, E.L., Aslin, R.N., Tunick, R.A., & Barrueco, S. (1997). Incidental language learning: Listening (and learning) out of the corner of your ear. *Psychological Science, 8*, 101–105.

Saffran, J.R., Johnson, E.K., Aslin, R.N., & Newport, E.L. (1999). Statistical learning of tone sequences by human infants and adults. *Cognition, 70*, 27–52.

Serrano, R., & Llanes, À. (2012). Examining L2 gains in three learning contexts: Study abroad, summer camp and intensive English courses. Paper presented at the *Asociación Española de Lingüística Aplicada (AESLA)* 30th Conference, Universitat de Lleida, Lleida, Spain.

Service, E. (1992). Phonology, working memory and foreign language learning. *Quarterly Journal of Experimental Psychology, 45*, 21–50.

Service, E., & Kohonen, V. (1995). Is the relation between phonological memory and foreign language learning accounted for by vocabulary acquisition? *Applied Psycholinguistics, 16*, 155–172.

Shanks, D.R., & Johnstone, T. (1999). Evaluating the relationship between explicit and implicit knowledge in a sequential reaction time task. *Journal of Experimental Psychology: Learning, Memory, and Cognition, 25*, 1435–1451.

Simon, J.R., & Rudell, A.P. (1967). Auditory S–R compatibility: The effect of an irrelevant cue on information processing. *Journal of Applied Psychology, 51*, 300–304.

Skehan, P. (1986). Cluster analysis and the identification of learner types. In V. Cook (Ed.), *Experimental approaches to second language acquisition* (pp. 81–94). Oxford: Pergamon.

Skehan, P. (1989). *Individual differences in second language learning*. London: Arnold.

Skehan, P. (1998). *A cognitive approach to learning language*. Oxford: OUP.

Skehan, P. (2002). Theorizing and updating aptitude. In P. Robinson (Ed.), *Individual differences and instructed language learning* (pp. 69–93). Amsterdam: John Benjamins.

Smeds, H. (2012). Perceptual compensation in blind second language learners. Paper presented at the *Nordic Conference on Bilingualism*, University of Copenhagen, Denmark.

Speciale, G., Ellis, N.C., & Bywater, T. (2004). Phonological sequence learning and short-term store capacity determine second language vocabulary acquisition. *Applied Psycholinguistics, 25*, 293–321.

Unsworth, N., Heitz, R.P., Schrock, J.C., & Engle, R.W. (2005). An automated version of the operation span task. *Behavior Research Methods, 37*, 498–505.

Yalcin, S. (2012). *Individual differences and the learning of two grammatical features with Turkish learners of English.* Unpublished doctoral dissertation. University of Toronto.

Yilmaz, Y. (2013). The role of working memory capacity and language analytic ability in the effectiveness of explicit correction and recasts. *Applied Linguistics, 34*(2).

Wang, W.C., & Yonelinas, A.P. (2012). Familiarity is related to conceptual implicit memory: An examination of individual differences. *Psychonomic Bulletin & Review, 19*(6), 1154–1164.

Woltz, D.J. (1990). Repetition of semantic comparisons: Temporary and persistent priming effects. *Journal of Experimental Psychology: Learning, Memory, and Cognition, 16*, 392–403.

Woltz, D.J. (1999). Individual differences in priming: The roles of implicit facilitation from prior processing. In P.L. Ackerman, P.C. Kyllonen, & R.D. Roberts (Eds.), *Learning and individual differences: Process, trait, and content determinants* (pp. 135–156). Washington, DC: American Psychological Association.

Woltz, D.J. (2003). Implicit cognitive processes as aptitudes for learning. *Educational Psychologist, 38*, 95–104.

New conceptualizations of language aptitude in second language attainment

Judit Kormos
Lancaster University

This chapter discusses the link between working memory, phonological short-term memory and language aptitude and describes how these cognitive abilities influence second language-learning processes. I provide a critical review of the definitions and constructs of aptitude and elaborate on how phonological short-term and working memory and components of language aptitude might influence processes of language learning, such as noticing, encoding in long-term memory, proceduralization and automatization, and aid second language processing and production. The chapter also considers the stability of cognitive variables in the course of language learning and presents evidence that certain components of language aptitude are prone to change with intensive exposure to second/third languages.

1. Introduction

Research in the field of second language acquisition (SLA) has long been concerned with the question of why students show such great variation in their language-learning success. Studies in this area have concluded that individual differences (IDs) are the most important predictors of achievement in a second language (L2) (Dörnyei 2005). Therefore, it is widely acknowledged that IDs have to be taken into consideration, both in theoretical accounts of SLA and in practical pedagogical decision-making. Researchers often point to the necessity of making further advances towards uncovering how certain IDs affect and underlie important language-learning processes (Dörnyei 2005; Kormos & Sáfár 2008; Robinson 2005).

The individual factors that influence language learning have been widely researched in the past thirty years (for a recent overview see Dörnyei 2005). The variables in which language learners differ are generally subdivided into affective, cognitive and personality-related individual differences (Gardner 1985). With some overlaps, motivation, language-learning anxiety and self-confidence are generally listed among affective factors, whereas personality-related differences comprise traits, such as openness to experience, conscientiousness, extraversion, agreeableness and emotional stability (Costa & McCrae 1992). The cognitive factors that are held to be important predictors of success in language learning are intelligence (Skehan 1986), foreign language aptitude (Carroll 1981; Carroll & Sapon 1959), working memory capacity and phonological short-term memory capacity (for an overview see Juffs & Harrington 2011). The roles of intelligence and foreign language aptitude in second language acquisition have been extensively researched, and in the past ten years a number of studies have been conducted on how working memory capacity and phonological short-term memory influence language learning.

In this paper I first provide a critical review of the definitions and constructs of aptitude. This is followed by a discussion of the inter-relationship of traditional aptitude components, on the one hand, and working memory and phonological short-term memory, on the other. Next, I elaborate on the role of aptitude, working memory and phonological short-term memory in language-learning processes and present evidence for the dynamic nature of aptitude components. The paper concludes with a summary of the role of aptitude complexes in ultimate attainment.

2. Definitions and constructs of aptitude

In order to elucidate the construct of language-learning aptitude, it is worth examining the meaning of the term 'aptitude' itself and summarizing current views on the role of aptitude in skilled performance in the field of educational psychology. As Snow (1992) points out, aptitude has several meanings, including readiness, suitability, susceptibility and proneness for learning in particular situations. He also highlights the fact that aptitude is not a constant and innate intellectual capacity; rather, it is a conglomerate of individual characteristics that interact dynamically with the situation in which learning takes place. From this view of aptitude, it follows that different sets of abilities can enhance learning under various learning conditions.

The most important cognitive components of aptitude in educational psychology include crystallized intelligence, on the one hand, which is a construct consisting of verbal abilities, such as comprehension and fluency, and domain specific knowledge and fluid intelligence (Cattell 1957), on the other; the latter is usually seen as comprising abstract reasoning skills and short-term-memory-related skills (Horn & Knoll 1997). Additional proposed aptitude constructs include learning strategies, self-regulatory capacity, motivational orientation and certain personality traits, such as openness to experience, extraversion and conscientiousness (Ackerman 2003; Snow 1992). In a series of research projects, Ackerman and colleagues found that crystallized intelligence plays a more important role in learning among adults than children (Ackerman 1996), and that it can also explain learning outcomes in self-study settings and in less constrained learning environments better than fluid intelligence (Ackerman & Beier 2006). This pattern of findings was replicated both in the case of tasks that required the acquisition of explicit declarative knowledge and those aiming to assess the learning of complex new skills (Ackerman 2007). Ackerman (2007:237) concluded that "what one already knows is a more important determinant of the knowledge one acquires than working memory." Snow (1992:28), however, made more detailed claims concerning the interaction of aptitude complexes and learning settings and tasks when he argued that unstructured learning situations are more favourable for "able, independent, mastery-oriented and flexible" individuals, whereas highly structured learning contexts are more suitable for "less able, less independent, less mastery-oriented learners" (ibid.).

Early conceptualizations of foreign language aptitude were conceived in line with the traditional meanings of the construct of aptitude and aimed to describe students' readiness to learn another language in instructed foreign language settings. In line with this, traditional definitions of language aptitude, such as the one provided by Carroll (1981), focused on the role of cognitive abilities when predicting the rate of progress learners are likely to make, rather than final language-learning outcomes. Nevertheless, once aptitude tests had become widely available to the research community, a large number of studies were conducted to investigate the link between aptitude components and attainment in proficiency at a particular point of time (e.g. Ehrman & Oxford 1995; Grigorenko et al. 2000; Kiss & Nikolov 2005). Thus the meaning of the term 'aptitude' started to shift from readiness to learn to capacity to acquire another language. Furthermore, in the second language context, the construct of aptitude has prevailingly been associated with the cognitive characteristics of the individual, with the exception of Pimsleur's Language Aptitude Battery (PLAB) (Pimsleur 1966), which includes a measure of motivation, as well.

A longstanding issue in the field of SLA is the lack of a clear definition of what one means by language-learning aptitude, and this derives from the fact that most developers of language aptitude tests have followed the empirically based psychometric approach to test development. For example, Carroll and Sapon (1959) administered a variety of tests that seemed likely to predict language learning success on about 5,000 students. Based on the results, they selected the tasks that best differentiated between successful and unsuccessful language learners but did not correlate highly with each other (Carroll & Sapon 1959). These components of language aptitude included: (i) phonetic coding ability, i.e. the "ability to identify distinct sounds, to form associations between those sounds and symbols representing them, and to retain these associations"; (ii) grammatical sensitivity, i.e. the ability "to recognize the grammatical functions of words (or other linguistic entities) in sentence structures"; (iii) rote learning ability, defined as "the ability to learn associations between sounds and meanings rapidly and efficiently, and to retain these associations"; and (iv) inductive learning ability, which is "the ability to infer or induce the rules governing a set of language materials, given sample language materials that permit such inferences" (Carroll 1981:105).

Such a pragmatic, assessment-based and atheoretical approach is not without precedent in research into cognitive abilities; in fact, this is the approach most commonly adopted in the development of intelligence tests. Instruments devised in this manner may have appropriate psychometric qualities (by definition, in fact, since their development was based on measures of validity and reliability). Moreover, such instruments may be used to define the construct in question by using complex statistical analyses to extract underlying factors. This was also the approach followed by Carroll when defining components of language aptitude. However, from a theoretical point of view, the process may be criticized for producing a construct which is, in fact, nothing more or less than what the test measures. This is a common critique of tests of intelligence and, according to Dörnyei (2005:35), "the tacit understanding in the L2 research community has been that language aptitude is what language aptitude tests measure."

In response to criticisms of the traditional construct of aptitude, Robinson (2001) proposed a theoretically motivated model of aptitude, in which cognitive resources and abilities are combined into aptitude complexes. In Robinson's model, primary abilities include pattern recognition, speed of processing in phonological working memory, and grammatical sensitivity. These general cognitive abilities which, with the exception of phonological memory, are based on the traditional construct of aptitude, help the so-called second-order abilities. The latter abilities are specific to language learning and include noticing the gap, memory for contingent speech, deep semantic processing, memory for contingent text, and metalinguistic rule rehearsal. This view, in which aptitude is a complex construct consisting of several cognitive characteristics, has also been recently endorsed by DeKeyser and Koeth (2011).

3.   Aptitude, working memory and phonological short-term memory

A number of researchers have argued that working memory capacity might be a cognitive ability that is just as important in language learning as the traditional concept of foreign language aptitude. Sawyer and Ranta (2001:340) pointed out that "working memory capacity may be the key to elaborating the concept of language aptitude itself and to clarifying its relationship with the second language acquisition (SLA) process". Miyake and Friedman (1998) proposed the "working memory as language aptitude" hypothesis, claiming that working memory may be the central component of language aptitude.

In order to explain the link between aptitude and working memory, it is important to describe the construct of working memory and its constituents. The first important issue to consider with regard to the conceptualization of working memory is the relationship between working memory and long-term memory, which is a repository of all the knowledge and skills that an individual has acquired throughout his/her lifespan. In this long-standing debate, there are two opposing views. According to Baddeley and Loggie (1999), working memory is a processing module which is separate from, but interacts with, long-term memory, whereas other researchers perceive working memory as the relevant activated component of long-term memory (e.g. Cowan 1995, 1999; Engle et al. 1999). Although these two standpoints differ greatly, they both agree that long-term memory representations, in other words, previous knowledge and expertise, play an important role in the mental operations carried out in working memory.

The most widely accepted conceptualization of short-term memory today is the working memory model developed by Baddeley and Hitch (1974; Baddeley 1986). While previous theories of memory systems focused on the storage function of memory, the new model, as its name suggests, adapted a more dynamic approach. This conceptualization of working memory combines storage with the processing and manipulation of information; thus, in this view, working memory plays a far greater role in cognitive activities, such as comprehension, reasoning and learning, than was previously supposed (Baddeley 2003).

The working memory model proposed by Baddeley (2003) comprises a multi-component memory system consisting of the central executive, which coordinates two modality-specific subsystems, the phonological loop and the visuo-spatial sketchpad. Later, a fourth component was added to the model – the episodic buffer; this uses multi-dimensional coding, integrates information to form episodes, and is in communication with long-term memory (Baddeley 2000). The visuo-spatial sketchpad works with visual and spatial information, while the phonological loop is specialized for the manipulation and retention of speech.

The central executive has several functions, including attentional control, directing the flow of information through the system, and planning (Gathercole 1999). The architecture of the central executive in cognitive operations has been further elaborated and is now seen to play an important role in three processes of attention control (for review see Miyake et al. 2000). First, the central executive is assumed to assist individuals shift between tasks they need to carry out in parallel or consecutively (Monsell 1996), which is called the "task switching" function of attention. Second, the updating and monitoring function of attention control helps people select, revise and review information which is relevant to successful completion of the task (Morris & Jones 1990). For example, while driving, one needs to manipulate relevant information about traffic signs, road conditions and other vehicles on the road in working memory dynamically, in order to arrive safely at one's destination. Finally, the central executive also has an inhibitory function that hinders automatic responses when they are not relevant or useful to a particular task. To stay with my previous example, when one is driving on a route, part of which is a daily routine but which then continues on to a less-frequently driven road, conscious attention is needed to inhibit taking conventional turns and making sure we follow the relevant new route.

Another widely researched component of working memory is the phonological loop. This subsystem consists of a phonological store, which holds information for a few seconds, and an articulatory rehearsal process, which refreshes decaying information, amongst other functions. The rehearsal process is analogous to sub-vocal speech and takes place in real time, resulting in a limited span of immediate memory (after a certain number of items, the first one will fade before it can be rehearsed). Phonological loop capacity is often measured by tasks involving immediate serial recall of numbers (digit span) or words (Baddeley 2003).

In a number of research projects, working memory was found to show strong correlations with general aptitude complexes, with the strongest link being between working memory and fluid intelligence (e.g. Daneman & Carpenter 1980; Engle et al. 1999). In its original conceptualization, fluid intelligence included short-term memory ability (Cattell 1957), but Unsworth and Engle (2007) proposed that both aptitude complexes and working memory are determined by the individual's ability to control his/her attention. In this respect, working memory constitutes an important component of aptitude complexes in general educational psychology.

In the field of second language acquisition, Robinson (2005) discussed how general working memory and phonological short-term capacity can be seen as important components of aptitude complexes, in addition to some other traditional components of aptitude, such as inductive ability. Robinson (2002) also tested the link between working memory and foreign language aptitude. He found that working memory, as measured by a reading span test, had a moderately strong correlation with language aptitude scores. In another research project, Sáfár and Kormos (2008) found a moderately strong relationship between the backward digit span score and total aptitude score, with the two tests sharing approximately 13% of the variance, indicating that these two constructs are related but only partially overlap. The level of correlation established in Sáfár and Kormos's (2008) study closely approximated Robinson's (2002) results, despite the fact that the two studies used different tests of working memory capacity. With regard to the correlation between the different components of aptitude and working memory capacity, the only significant relationship that emerged in Sáfár and Kormos' (2008) research was between working memory scores and the inductive ability test. This indicates that the ability to maintain and manipulate verbal information in working memory might be related to the efficiency with which students can induce linguistic rules from the input in a language unknown to them, as measured by this component of the aptitude test. These findings lend support to the most recent arguments of DeKeyser and Koeth (2011:397) that "various aspects of working memory are important for all forms of language learning and processing, and must therefore be represented in any aptitude test."

Sáfár and Kormos (2008) also examined the link between aptitude test scores and phonological short-term memory capacity, which was assessed using a non-word repetition task. They found no significant correlation between phonological short-term memory capacity and aptitude components and the total aptitude test score, which might suggest that the storage capacity for verbal material in itself, without a processing and attention regulating function, is a cognitive ability distinct from traditional aptitude constructs. This assumption can also be supported by findings from educational psychology that have shown that short-term memory exhibits weaker links with aptitude complexes than working memory capacity (Daneman & Carpenter 1980; Engle et al. 1999).

4. Aptitude in L1 and L2, and its role in ultimate attainment

From the foregoing discussion of the cognitive constituents of aptitude complexes, it is apparent that the abilities that assist L2 learning greatly overlap with the cognitive factors that underlie knowledge and skill learning in any domain. Therefore, a logical question to ask is whether a separate concept, such as *language learning aptitude*, exists at all and whether the cognitive abilities that influence L2 learning processes are the same that affect L1 acquisition. If one endorses a multi-componential view of aptitude, consisting of a set of basic cognitive characteristics, and a view that from a cognitive perspective second language learning is no different from any other kind of learning, there might not be a need for a separate construct of language learning aptitude. There are, however, certain underlying cognitive abilities that are specifically related to language acquisition. Research into specific learning differences, such as dyslexia, has convincingly shown that the reasons for the difficulties students with learning differences experience in their L1 are related to the differential functioning of phonological short-term memory, working memory and phonological perception abilities (for a recent review, see Snowling 2008). This latter construct is very similar to the construct of phonological sensitivity in Carroll's conceptualization of aptitude.

At the core of the individual difference variables that can potentially influence the success of second language acquisition, we can find basic cognitive capacities that are also necessary in order to acquire one's mother tongue and L1 literacy skills successfully. Memory for verbal material, which is primarily associated with phonological short-term memory, helps us remember words in our first language, as well as in a second language. Phonological short-term memory aids in the decoding of sequences of sounds and associating them with words and their meanings, which is essential when learning to read and spell in both L1 and L2. Verbal reasoning skills are related to grammatical sensitivity and inductive language learning ability, both of which play an important role in the acquisition of syntax and morphology by helping students to discover rules and regularities of the language. Working memory resources assist in regulating attention to relevant linguistic features, maintaining chunks of language in memory for further processing and inhibiting irrelevant stimuli and automatic response patterns, such as L1 words and phrases when speaking in the L2. These similarities between the cognitive capacities necessary for the acquisition of one's L1 and L1 literacy skills, on the one hand, and outcomes in learning an L2, on the other, led Sparks and Ganshow (1993) to formulate their Linguistic Coding Differences Hypothesis, which claims that the underlying reasons for lack of success in L2 acquisition are highly similar to the causes of learning difficulties in L1.

If we consider that L1 skills provide an important foundation for L2 learning (Dufva & Voeten 1999; Skehan 1986; Spolsky 1989), it can be seen that in addition to a direct effect, the cognitive components of aptitude also influence ultimate L2 attainment indirectly through the mediation of L1 skills (see Figure 1). It is also worth revisiting Ackerman's (2007) conclusion that crystallized intelligence, which mainly comprises previous subject-matter knowledge, is a more important pre-determinant of learning outcomes in naturalistic learning situations than fluid intelligence (i.e. working memory capacity and verbal reasoning skills). This shows that there is an additive effect of cognitive abilities as they contribute to initial states of knowledge, in our case to L1 skills, and the initial level of L2 competence from which development should proceed.

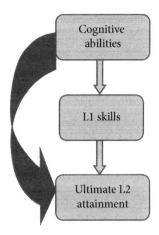

Figure 1. The direct and indirect role of cognitive abilities in ultimate L2 attainment

5.   Aptitude and language learning processes

Another important question when defining aptitude is how we describe the processes of second language learning. From a cognitive perspective, learning another language may involve the acquisition of declarative knowledge, such as the meanings of words, and that of skills (procedural knowledge and its automatic application), such as assembling a sentence fluently by using syntactic building procedures. Alternatively, acquisition can be considered to take place implicitly through non-conscious, associative and unintentional learning, and by means of explicit learning, which can be characterized as a conscious, deliberate and reflective process (for a more detailed discussion of the differences between explicit and implicit learning mechanisms in SLA see Hulstijn (2003)). In the latter case, implicit knowledge of simple grammar, such as English plural -s, may subsequently be raised to the level of declarative knowledge. For a long time the mainstream position in educational and cognitive psychology was that explicit learning mechanisms were greatly influenced by individual learner differences, such as crystallized and fluid intelligence, the latter including executive functioning and working memory (e.g. Reber 1993). In contrast, as implicit learning was seen to be an automatic associative process, individual learner factors were assumed to play a minimal role in it (e.g. Feldman et al. 1995; Reber et al. 1991). However, these assumptions have recently been challenged by explorations into the role of attention in implicit learning. A number of studies have found that in order for implicit learning to take place, selective attention to the relevant aspect of the input stimulus is necessary, and only after the input stimulus is selectively attended to will automatic and unintentional learning mechanisms be operational (Jiménez & Méndez 1999; Jiang & Chun 2001). Therefore individual learner characteristics that cause variation in selective attention can be assumed to influence the outcomes of implicit learning processes. In a study examining the factors accounting for differential outcomes in an implicit learning task, Kaufman et al. (2010) found that, among cognitive variables, processing speed and scores on a verbal reasoning test were the best predictors of performance, and that openness and intuition also strongly correlated with the results of the implicit learning experiment.

As mentioned earlier, the traditional Carrollian concept of aptitude was originally developed to account for learning outcomes in classroom settings where second language acquisition processes were predominantly explicit. The relevance of the Carollian concept of language aptitude in the communicative classroom, where most learning is assumed to take place implicitly, was first questioned by Krashen (1981). Since then the role of aptitude in various language-learning settings and under different learning conditions has been explored by a number of studies. Reves (1983, cited in Skehan 2002), who investigated Arabic learners studying English in a classroom setting and acquiring Hebrew in the target language environment, showed that aptitude plays a role in predicting success in both situations. Skehan (1989) also argued that aptitude might in fact be more important in naturalistic SLA than in an instructional setting. Harley and Hart (1997) found that for young immersion learners, aptitude had little power in predicting competence in L2, but for older ones, for whom accuracy and academic language proficiency were a more focal point of instruction than for younger students, aptitude correlated highly with most proficiency measures. Horwitz (1987) and Ehrman and Oxford (1995), investigating older age groups primarily taught with communicative methods, also found that certain sub-tests of language aptitude were related to L2 performance. Although correlational analyses in Ranta's (2002) research suggested that language analytic ability plays a relatively insignificant role in communicative classrooms, the cluster analysis in her study also revealed links between L1 metalinguistic awareness and L2 performance measures among some groups of language learners. Additionally, Robinson (1997, 2002), De Graaff (1997) and Williams (1999) found that language aptitude and working memory capacity correlated with learning outcomes under both explicit and implicit learning conditions.

Skehan (2002) also suggested that certain components of the traditional construct of aptitude, such as grammatical sensitivity and inductive ability, might assist L2 learning in naturalistic contexts, where learners have few opportunities to acquire L2 linguistic rules through explicit explanation. Research evidence on the role of aptitude among naturalistic language learners has been mixed. On the one hand, DeKeyser (2000) and DeKeyser et al. (2010) found no link between ultimate morphosyntactic attainment in the case of L2 users who were child acquirers of the target language. On the other hand, Abrahamsson and Hyltenstam's (2008) study demonstrated a significant relationship between aptitude and ultimate attainment among early acquirers. In contrast, most studies have found a significant link between ultimate attainment and aptitude among older L2 speakers whose age of arrival into the target language country was over 12 years (e.g. DeKeyser 2000; DeKeyser et al. 2010; Abrahamsson & Hyltenstam 2008), with the exception of Granena and Long's research (2010, 2013), where no such relationship could be established. The contradictory findings are most probably due to the fact that different studies used different measures of language aptitude (e.g. DeKeyser (2000) only administered one component of the aptitude test), and that in all of these studies, the composite of aptitude scores was correlated with linguistic measures.

As argued above, language-learning aptitude is not a unitary construct, but rather a conglomerate of different abilities that can assist in the different stages and processes of language learning. Therefore, in order to elucidate the role of cognitive factors in language learning, it is necessary to define which components of aptitude assist in particular phases of language learning.

In order for learning to take place, L2 speakers must first attend to the input and notice relevant stimuli (Robinson 1995; Schmidt 1990), in which process the ability to control attention can be supposed to be the most important cognitive factor. As described above, and also emphasized by Kane and Engle (2003), an important function of working memory is to regulate attention; therefore, working memory capacity can be expected to play an important role in assisting L2 learners to notice relevant linguistic input. This is supported by studies investigating the role of working memory capacity in learners' uptake of interactional feedback (see, e.g. Mackey et al. 2002; Mackey & Sachs 2012; Révész 2012). L2 learners also need to be able to process and understand the input before noticing can take place. Working memory capacity, which assists in maintaining and manipulating information in short-term memory, can be assumed to affect the efficiency of input processing. Currently, evidence for the role of working memory in input processing has mainly been studied in the field of sentence processing, and evidence for the role of working memory in affecting sentence comprehension has been mixed (for a review, see Juffs & Harrington 2011). Further cognitive factors that might influence input processing are phonological short-term memory resources, which might determine the length of the linguistic chunks L2 learners can hold in memory, phonological sensitivity, which assists in differentiating sounds

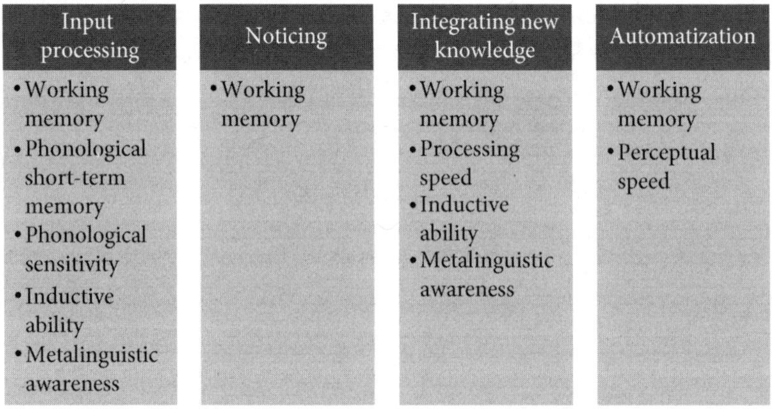

Input processing	Noticing	Integrating new knowledge	Automatization
• Working memory • Phonological short-term memory • Phonological sensitivity • Inductive ability • Metalinguistic awareness	• Working memory	• Working memory • Processing speed • Inductive ability • Metalinguistic awareness	• Working memory • Perceptual speed

Figure 2. The role of cognitive individual difference factors in language-learning processes

and decoding words, and inductive ability and metalinguistic awareness, which facilitate syntactic analysis of the input (see Figure 2).

It can be assumed that regardless of the level of intention and consciousness involved in learning, input-processing mechanisms are similar, and, therefore, that the same cognitive factors play a role during this stage. The next phase of learning, the integration of new knowledge, can vary greatly, however, depending on whether learning is primarily associative and implicit or explicit and conscious. Kaufman et al. (2010) demonstrated that in an implicit learning task, processing speed and scores on a verbal reasoning test were related to performance outcomes. This might indicate that general cognitive processing speed, and possibly inductive language-learning ability, which is the component of language learning aptitude that bears the strongest resemblance to verbal reasoning, might play a role in implicit L2 learning processes. The aptitude components that might assist in the conscious integration of new linguistic knowledge into the L2 system can be assumed to include inductive ability and metalinguistic awareness, as they help learners revise their L2 system and compare new linguistic information gained with the help of their existing knowledge. Working memory capacity, as a key cognitive characteristic responsible for regulating attention when manipulating several pieces of information, might also play an important role at this stage.

The final phase of language learning considered here is the process of automatization, in the course of which, acquired knowledge becomes proceduralized and, as a next step, turns into automatic processes (see, e.g. Anderson's (1995) ACT* theory). For implicit learning, which involves the acquisition of skills as chunks, automatization processes are also relevant. In a series of research projects,

Ackermann (1987) showed that at this stage of skill learning, the most important cognitive ability that can facilitate automatization is perceptual speed. Further studies (e.g. Ramsey et al. 2004; Ruthruff et al. 2006) also demonstrated that working memory resources can aid in the automatization of knowledge. Therefore, in second language acquisition, we can assume that working memory capacity and perceptual speed will also play a role in determining the success with which L2 skills are automatized.

To summarize, it is apparent that several of the components of the original construct of aptitude, as defined by Carroll, might be relevant for the underlying cognitive abilities that promote language-learning success and ultimate attainment in naturalistic learning settings. Inductive learning ability and grammatical sensitivity might help learners notice linguistic patterns in communicative input and help them to integrate these into their L2 system. Phonetic coding ability might play an important role in the acquisition of the phonological and orthographic system of the L2 and in L2 reading, in which one of the key abilities is phonological awareness (for a recent review, see Grabe 2009). Furthermore, metalinguistic awareness and deductive ability might facilitate second language writing processes (see, e.g. Kormos & Trebits 2012).

Phonological short-term memory is also a significant factor in L2 learning, both in instructed and in naturalistic contexts. Service and her colleagues (Service 1992; Service & Kohonen 1995) found that the ability to repeat English-sounding pseudo-words was a good predictor of English language-learning success among Finnish primary school pupils during the first three years of training. Papagno and Vallar (1995) showed that phonological short-term memory and word-learning ability are related among adults, as well. In a study with university students, Speciale et al. (2004) also found that both phonological sequence learning and phonological short-term memory capacity contributed to the success of vocabulary learning. Phonological short-term memory not only aids the acquisition of L2 words, but also the learning of syntactic structures. Ellis (1996) argued that learning sequences of different linguistic units (such as phonemes, morphemes, words and grammatical structures) is an important aspect of second language acquisition. As phonological short-term memory is responsible for remembering sequential information, the successful acquisition of syntax might also be influenced by short-term memory capacity. Furthermore, O'Brien et al.'s (2006) study demonstrated that there is a link between phonological memory and oral production skills in another language. Phonological short-term memory capacity was also found to correlate with L2 writing test scores in Kormos and Sáfár's (2008) study, and Adams and Guillot's (2008) research revealed the existence of links between spelling performance among bilingual writers and phonological short-term memory capacity.

With regard to working memory capacity, Harrington and Sawyer (1992) found that L2 reading span scores showed a strong correlation with performance in the grammar and reading and vocabulary sections of the TOEFL exam. Miyake and Friedman (1998) obtained evidence for the causal role of working memory in certain aspects of second language proficiency (e.g. syntactic comprehension) using path analysis. Kormos and Sáfár found that L2 learners' performance in a working memory test (backward digit span) strongly correlated with overall language proficiency test scores, as well as with achievement in three of the major skills, reading, listening and speaking, and in a Use of English test. These three skills require learners to hold verbal material in working memory, as well as to carry out other cognitive processes simultaneously. In the case of speaking, L2 learners have to store bits of their message already processed in memory while planning or linguistically encoding the next segment of their utterance (see Kormos 2006). While reading and listening, students also have to maintain processed bits of a text in memory, as well as read or listen to the next part simultaneously; otherwise, they will not be able to understand the text as a whole. The relatively strong relationship between performance in the Use of English test and working memory scores in Kormos and Sáfár's (2008) study might be explained by assuming that working memory affects the acquisition of syntactic and vocabulary knowledge, also through its attention-regulating function. As argued by Schmidt (1990), attention is at the core of noticing and encoding both new pieces of information, as well as regularities in long-term memory, which constitutes the basic mechanism responsible for learning words and the rules of grammar in L2.

6. The stability of language learning aptitude

One of the basic assumptions behind the concept of language aptitude is that it is a relatively stable characteristic, an endowment that is not modified by training or affected by previous experience (Skehan 1998). However, not all researchers agree with this view. McLaughlin (1990: 173) claims that "aptitude should not be viewed as a static personality trait; novices can become experts with experience." Grigorenko et al. (2000: 401) assert that "language aptitude is a form of developing expertise rather than an entity fixed at birth." Recently Dörnyei (2010) put forward a similar argument about the dynamic nature of language-learning aptitude. He proposed that aptitude can be affected by a range of internal and external learner factors and that, similar to motivation, aptitude is not a stable individual characteristic but, rather, a complex dynamic system.

Research evidence concerning the stability of language aptitude is ambiguous. In an early study, Politzer and Weiss (1969, cited by Skehan 1989) attempted to improve achievement in language aptitude measures by training, but they could not provide convincing evidence that this was possible. Sawyer (1992) did not observe any correlation between previous language learning experience and aptitude among students taking part in short intensive language courses. Harley and Hart (1997) did not find higher levels of aptitude among early immersion students having 12 years of exposure to a foreign language compared to late immersion students with only four years of exposure. Other studies, however, provide evidence for the effect of experience on language aptitude. A study conducted by Eisenstein (1980) showed that both bilinguals and students with previous training in foreign languages showed higher levels of aptitude than students without previous language-learning experience. She also found that polylinguals tended to outperform bilinguals, and that bilinguals who received formal education in a second language had an advantage over those who did not, although these differences were not statistically significant. In an experimental study, Sparks, Ganshow, Fluharty and Little (1995) reported that instruction in Latin resulted in an increase in language aptitude scores in the case of both learning-disabled and non-learning-disabled high school students.

Sáfár and Kormos (2008) conducted a quasi-experimental study in which they administered the standardized Hungarian language aptitude test to two groups of learners, both at the beginning and at the end of an academic year. One of the groups participated in an intensive language-learning programme with fifteen hours of English language instruction per week, whereas the control group only received four hours of instruction per week in English. They found that the change in overall aptitude scores between the two testing occasions was significantly higher among the students participating in the intensive language-learning programme than among the control group. The results also showed that students in the intensive language-learning programme improved in the tests of phonological sensitivity and metalinguistic awareness to a significantly greater extent than the participants in the control group. They called attention to the fact that research in the field of specific learning differences has shown that phonological sensitivity can be developed with the help of specialized teaching (Nijakowska 2010), and that it appears that intensive language learning without considerable explicit training in phonological sensitivity can also contribute to the enhancement of students' ability to recognize and memorize different sounds. They also pointed out that because, in instructed SLA, it is highly important to understand the grammatical function of lexical items, it is understandable that metalinguistic awareness develops as a result of intensive second language instruction.

Although language-learning aptitude might seem to be a relatively stable individual characteristic when compared with other factors, such as motivational orientation and action control mechanisms, there seems to be some converging evidence that certain components of aptitude, such as phonological sensitivity and metalinguistic awareness, might improve in the course of language learning. If this improvement is considered together with the cognitive advantages of bi- and multilingualism (e.g. Bialystok & Majumder 1998), it is apparent that previous language-learning experience and knowledge of other languages might be an important determinant of ultimate attainment, both directly and indirectly, through the mediation of aptitude constructs.

7. Redefining aptitude in ultimate attainment

In order to advance our understanding of language-learning aptitude, it is also necessary to address the question of how language is defined, and this question is especially pertinent for describing the role of aptitude in ultimate attainment. In most conceptualizations of aptitude, language is seen to consist of phonological, orthographic, morphological, syntactic and semantic systems (see, e.g. the Modern Language Aptitude Test (MLAT) (Carroll & Sapon 1959) or the Canal F theory by Grigorenko et al. (2000)). Instruments developed to measure language aptitude, such as the Modern Language Aptitude Test (MLAT) (Carroll & Sapon 1959) and Pimsleur's Language Aptitude Battery (PLAB) (Pimsleur 1966), test language learners on the above-mentioned four components.

However, even the models of L2 competence applied in language testing and the theories of communicative competence in the 1980s and 1990s highlight the fact that discourse competence, i.e. the knowledge and ability to combine sentences and utterances to form meaningful texts of different types, as well as sociolinguistic competence, which is the ability to use language appropriately in a given social context, should also be part of language competence (see Bachman & Palmer 1996, or Canale & Swain 1980, for a more detailed discussion of these components). Furthermore, language is an interpersonal communication tool, and as such, it is intricately related to culture, ethnicity, identity and self-perception. The ability to participate in communities of discourse and the inter-related nature of language and identity are particularly relevant in contexts where a second language is acquired outside the classroom and is used as a means of everyday interaction. In these settings, ultimate attainment needs to be seen not only as the acquisition of linguistic abilities, but also as a process of opening up access and participation in a variety of discourse communities. If, however, aptitude is conceived of as a conglomerate of cognitive abilities alone, we will not be able to explain a wide range of factors contributing to ultimate attainment.

In order to account for success in the acquisition of a wider range of second language-related abilities and skills, it might be useful to consider broadening the predominantly cognitive concept of language-learning aptitude, which even today is often based on Carollian conceptualization. Non-cognitive components of aptitude complexes traditionally consist of students' relatively stable affective and conative (motivational) characteristics, such as personality traits, self-regulation skills and motivational orientation. As mentioned above, Snow (1992) included learning strategies, self-regulatory functions and motivational orientation in aptitude complexes. Similarly, Ackerman (2003) argued that in addition to cognitive abilities, achievement motivation and volition and action control, which are components of self-regulatory learning behaviour, aptitude constructs should also be considered. Furthermore, in a series of research projects, the positive role of two components of the Big Five model of personality traits (Costa & McCrae 1992), openness to experience and impulsivity, in implicit learning was also shown (for a review, see Kaufman et al. 2010). Achievement motivation, volition control and openness to experience might be important factors in determining how actively second language users engage in language-learning processes in natural settings. One might even argue that the extent to which learners create opportunities for themselves and exploit opportunities inherent in naturalistic learning settings to receive input, engage in interaction and produce output is, in all likelihood, better predicted by affective and conative components of aptitude than by learners' cognitive characteristics.

In this chapter, I have described the cognitive characteristics that might affect how students attend to input, process it, and then integrate it into their existing language system. I have also explained the role of working memory capacity and other aptitude components in implicit learning and in learning from interactional feedback. However, as pointed out above, the affective and conative characteristics of L2 learners might be more significant contributors to ultimate attainment than cognitive factors. Furthermore, even though aptitude complexes are relatively stable characteristics of individuals, they can also be affected by previous language-learning experience and can interact dynamically with affective, motivational and social factors. Various types of aptitude complexes also assist learners to different degrees in the diversity of learning situations. Therefore, although cognitive characteristics can in themselves contribute to the ultimate success of L2 learning, it is likely to be more important that L2 learners combine their different characteristics in ways that will assist them in the given learning task (Dörnyei 2005).

References

Abrahamsson, N., & Hyltenstam, K. (2008). The robustness of aptitude effects in near-native second language acquisition. *Studies in Second Language Acquisition, 30*, 481–509.

Ackerman, P.L. (1987). Individual differences in skill learning: An integration of psychometric and information processing perspectives. *Psychological Bulletin, 102*, 3–27.

Ackerman, P.L. (1996). A theory of adult intellectual development: Process, personality, interests, and knowledge. *Intelligence, 22,* 229–259.

Ackerman, P.L. (2003). Aptitude complexes and trait complexes. *Educational Psychologist, 38,* 85–93.

Ackerman, P.L. (2007). New developments in understanding skilled performance. *Current Directions in Psychological Research, 16,* 235–239.

Ackerman, P.L., & Beier, M.E. (2006). Determinants of domain knowledge and independent study learning in an adult sample. *Journal of Educational Psychology, 98,* 366–381.

Adams, A.-M., & Guillot, K. (2008). Working memory and writing in bilingual students. *International Journal of Applied Linguistics, 156,* 13–28.

Anderson, J.R. (1995). *Learning and memory. An integrated approach.* New York, NY: Wiley.

Bachman, L., & Palmer, A. (1996). *Language testing in practice.* Oxford: OUP.

Baddeley, A.D. (1986). *Working memory.* Oxford: OUP.

Baddeley, A.D. (2000). The episodic buffer: A new component of working memory? *Trends in Cognitive Sciences, 4*(11), 417–423.

Baddeley, A.D. (2003). Working memory: looking back and looking forward. *Nature Reviews Neuroscience, 4,* 829–839.

Baddeley, A.D., & Hitch, G.J. (1974). Working memory. In G.A. Bower (Ed.), *Recent advances in learning and motivation,* Vol. 8 (pp. 47–90). New York, NY: Academic Press.

Baddeley, A.D., & Logie, R.H. (1999). Working memory: The multiple component model. In A. Miyake & P. Shah (Eds.), *Models of working memory: Mechanisms of active maintenance and executive control* (pp. 28–61). Cambridge: CUP.

Bialystok, E., & Majumder, S. (1998). The relationship between bilingualism and the development of cognitive processes in problem solving. *Applied Pyscholinguistics, 19,* 69–85.

Canale, M., & Swain, M. (1980). Theoretical bases of communicative approaches to second language teaching and testing. *Applied Linguistics, 1,* 1–47.

Carroll, J.B. (1981). Twenty-five years of research on foreign language aptitude. In K.C. Diller (Ed.), *Individual differences and univerals in language learning aptitude* (pp. 119–154). Rowley, MA: Newbury House.

Carroll, J.B., & Sapon, S.M. (1959). *The modern language aptitude test.* San Antonio, TX: Psychological Corporation.

Cattell, R.B. (1957). *Personality and motivation structure and measurement.* Yonkers, NY: World Book.

Costa, P.T., & McCrae, R.R. (1992). *NEO-PI-R. Professional manual.* Odessa, FL: Psychological Assessment Resources.

Cowan, N. (1995). *Attention and memory.* Oxford: OUP.

Cowan, N. (1999). An embedded-process model of working memory. In A. Miyake & P. Shah (Eds.), *Models of working memory: Mechanisms of active maintenance and executive control* (pp. 62–101). Cambridge: CUP.

Daneman, M., & Carpenter, P.A. (1980). Individual differences in working memory and reading. *Journal of Verbal Learning and Verbal Behaviour, 19,* 450–466.

de Graaff, R. (1997). The eXperanto experiment: Effects of explicit instruction on second language acquisition. *Studies in Second Language Acquisition, 19,* 249–276.

DeKeyser, R.M. (2000). The robustness of critical period effects in second language acquisition. *Studies in Second Language Acquisition, 22,* 499–533.

DeKeyser, R.M., Alfi-Shabtay, I., & Ravid, D. (2010). Cross-linguistic evidence for the nature of age-effects in second language acquisition. *Applied Psycholinguistics, 31,* 413–438.

DeKeyser, R., & Koeth, J. (2011). Cognitive aptitudes for L2 learning. In E. Hinkel (Ed.), *Handbook of research in second language teaching and learning*, Volume II (pp. 395–406). New York, NY: Routledge.

Dörnyei, Z. (2005). *The psychology of the language learner: Individual differences in second language acquisition.* Mahwah, NJ: Lawrence Erlbaum Associates.

Dörnyei, Z. (2010). The relationship between language aptitude and language learning motivation: Individual differences from a dynamic systems perspective. In E. Macaro (Ed.), *Continuum companion to second language acquisition* (pp. 247–267). London: Continuum.

Dufva, M., & Voeten M. (1999). Native language literacy and phonological memory as prerequisites for learning English as a foreign language. *Applied Psycholinguistics, 20,* 329–348.

Ehrman, M.E., & Oxford, R.L. (1995). Cognition plus: Correlates of language learning success. *Modern Language Journal, 79,* 67–89.

Eisenstein, M. (1980). Childhood bilingualism and adult language learning aptitude. *International Review of Applied Psychology, 29,* 159–174.

Ellis, N. (1996). Sequencing in SLA: Phonological memory, chunking and points of order. *Studies in Second Language Acquisition, 18,* 91–126.

Engle, R.W., Kane, M.J., & Tuholski, S.W. (1999). Individual differences in working memory capacity and what they tell us about controlled attention, general fluid intelligence, and functions of the prefrontal cortex. In A. Miyake & P. Shah (Eds.), *Models of working memory* (pp. 102–134). Cambridge: CUP.

Feldman, J., Kerr, B., & Streissguth, A.P. (1995). Correlational analyses of procedural and declarative learning performance. *Intelligence, 20,* 87–114.

Gardner, R.C. (1985). *Social psychology and second language learning: The role of attitudes and motivation.* London: Edward Arnold.

Gathercole, S.E. (1999). Cognitive approaches to the development of short-term memory. *Trends in Cognitive Sciences, 3,* 410–419.

Granena, G., & Long, M.H. (2010). Age of onset, length of residence, aptitude and ultimate attainment in two linguistic domains. Paper presented at the 30th Second Language Research Forum, University of Maryland, College Park.

Granena, G., & Long, M.H. (2013). Age of onset, length of residence, language aptitude, and ultimate L2 attainment in three linguistic domains. *Second Language Research, 29*(1).

Grigorenko, E.L., Sternberg, R.J., & Ehrman, M.E. (2000). A theory based approach to the measurement of foreign language learning ability: The Canal-F theory and test. *Modern Language Journal, 84,* 390–405.

Grabe, W. (2009). *Reading in a second language. Moving from theory to practice.* Cambridge: CUP.

Harley, B., & Hart, D. (1997). Language aptitude and second language proficiency in classroom learners of different starting ages. *Studies in Second Language Acquisition, 19,* 379–400.

Harrington, M., & Sawyer, M. (1992). L2 working memory capacity and L2 reading skills. *Studies in Second Language Acquisition, 14,* 25–38.

Horn, J.L., & Knoll, J. (1997). Human cognitive capabilities: Gf–Gc theory. In D.P. Flanagan, J.L. Genshaft, & P.L. Harrison (Eds.), *Contemporary intellectual assessment: Theories, tests, and issues* (pp. 53–91). New York, NY: Guilford Press.

Horwitz, E. (1987). Linguistic and communicative competence: Reassessing foreign language aptitude. In B. VanPatten, T.R. Dvorak, & J.F. Lee (Eds.), *Foreign language learning: A research perspective* (pp. 146–157). Rowley, MA: Newbury House.

Hulstijn, J. (2003). Incidental and intentional learning. In C. Doughty, & M. H. Long (Eds.), *The handbook of second language acquisition* (pp. 349–381). Malden, MA: Blackwell.

Juffs, A. & Harrington, M.W. (2011). Aspects of working memory in L2 Learning. *Language Teaching: Reviews and Studies, 42,* 137–166.

Jiang, Y., & Chun, M.M. (2001). Selective attention modulates implicit learning. The *Quarterly Journal of Experimental Psychology, 54A,* 1105–1124.

Jiménez, L., & Méndez, C. (1999). Which attention is needed for implicit sequence learning? *Journal of Experimental Psychology: Learning, Memory, and Cognition, 25,* 236–259.

Kane, M.J., & Engle, R.W. (2003). Working memory capacity and the control of attention: The contributions of goal neglect, response competition, and task set to Stroop interference. *Journal of Experimental Psychology: General, 132,* 47–70.

Kaufman, S.B., DeYoung, C.G., Gray, J.R., Jiménez, L., Brown, J., & Mackintosh, N.J. (2010). Implicit learning as an ability. *Cognition, 116,* 321–340.

Kiss, C., & Nikolov, M. (2005). Developing, piloting, and validating an instrument to measure young learners' aptitude. *Language Learning, 55,* 99–150.

Kormos, J. (2006). *Speech production and second language acquisition.* Mahwah, NJ: Lawrence Erlbaum Associates.

Kormos, J., & Sáfár, A. (2008). Phonological short term-memory, working memory and foreign language performance in intensive language learning. *Bilingualism: Language and Cognition, 11,* 261–271.

Kormos, J., & Trebits, A. (2012). The role of task complexity, modality and aptitude in narrative task performance. *Language Learning, 62*(2), 439–472.

Krashen, S.D. (1981). Aptitude and attitude in relation to second language acquisition and learning. In K.C. Diller (Ed.), *Individual differences and universals in language learning aptitude* (pp. 155–175). Rowley, MA: Newbury House.

Mackey, A., Philp, J., Egi, T., Fujii, A., & Tatsumi, T. (2002). Individual differences in working memory, noticing of interactional feedback, and L2 development. In P. Robinson (Ed.), *Individual differences and instructed language learning* (pp. 181–209). Amsterdam: John Benjamins.

Mackey, A., & Sachs, R. (2012). Older learners in SLA research: A first look at working memory, feedback, and L2 development. *Language Learning, 62*(3), 704–740.

McLaughlin, B. (1990). The relationship between first and second languages: Language proficiency and language aptitude. In B. Harley, P. Allen, J. Cummins, & M. Swain (Eds.), *The development of second language proficiency* (pp. 158–178). New York: CUP.

Miyake, A., & Friedman, N.P. (1998). Individual differences in second language proficiency: Working memory as language aptitude. In A.F. Healy & L.E. Bourne (Eds.), *Foreign language learning: Psycholinguistic studies on training and retention* (pp. 339–364). Mahwah, NJ: Lawrence Erlbaum Associates.

Miyake, A., Friedman, N.P., Emerson, M.J., Witzki, A.H., Howerter, A., & Wager, T.D. (2000). The unity and diversity of executive functions and their contributions to complex "frontal lobe" tasks: A latent variable analysis. *Cognitive Psychology, 41,* 49–100.

Monsell, S. (1996). Control of mental processes. In V. Bruce (Ed.), *Unsolved mysteries of the mind: Tutorial essays in cognition* (pp. 93–148). Mahwah, NJ: Lawrence Erlbaum Associates.

Morris, N., & Jones, D.M. (1990). Memory updating in working memory: The role of the central executive. *British Journal of Psychology, 81,* 111–121.

Nijakowska, J. (2010). *Dyslexia in the foreign language classroom.* Bristol: Multilingual Matters.

O'Brien, I., Segalowitz, N., Collentine, J., & Freed, B. (2006). Phonological memory and lexical narrative, and grammatical skills in second language oral production by adult learners. *Applied Psycholinguistics, 27*, 377–402.

Papagno, C., & Vallar, G. (1995). Verbal short-term memory and vocabulary learning in polyglots. *Quarterly Journal of Experimental Psychology, 48A*(1), 98–107.

Pimsleur, P. (1966). *Pimsleur language aptitude battery.* New York, NY: Harcourt Brace Jovanovich.

Politzer, R., & Weiss, L. (1969). *An experiment in improving achievement in foreign language learning through learning of selected skills associated with language aptitude.* Stanford University. (ERIC Document Reproduction Service, ED 046261).

Ranta, L. (2002). The role of learners' language analytic ability in the communicative classroom. In P. Robinson (Ed.), *Individual differences and instructed language learning* (pp. 159–180). Amsterdam: John Benjamins.

Ramsey, N.F., Jansma, J.M., Jager, G., Van Raalten, T., & Kahn, R.S. (2004). Neurophysiological factors in human information processing capacity. *Brain, 127*, 517–525.

Reber, A.S. (1993). *Implicit learning and tacit knowledge: An essay on the cognitive unconscious.* Oxford: Clarendon Press.

Reber, A.S., Walkenfeld, F.F., & Hernstadt, R. (1991). Implicit and explicit learning: Individual differences and IQ. *Journal of Experimental Psychology: Learning, Memory, and Cognition, 17*, 888–896.

Reves, T. (1983). What makes a good language learner? Unpublished doctoral dissertation. Hebrew University.

Révész, A. (2012). Working memory and the observed effectiveness of recasts on different L2 outcome measures. Language Learning, *62*(1), 93–132.

Robinson, P. (1995). Attention, memory and the 'noticing' hypothesis. *Language Learning, 45*, 283–331.

Robinson, P. (1997). Individual differences and the fundamental similarity of implicit and explicit adult second language learning. *Language Learning, 47*, 45–99.

Robinson, P. (2001). Individual differences. Cognitive abilities, aptitude complexes and learning conditions in second language acquisition. *Second Language Research, 17*, 368–392.

Robinson, P. (2002). Effects of individual differences in intelligence, aptitude and working memory on adult incidental SLA: A replication and extension of Reber, Walkenfeld and Hernstadt, 1991. In P. Robinson (Ed.), *Individual differences and instructed language learning* (pp. 211–266). Amsterdam: John Benjamins.

Robinson, P. (2005). Aptitude and second language acquisition. *Annual Review of Applied Linguistics, 25*, 45–73.

Ruthruff, E., Van Selst, M., Johnston, J.C., & Remington, R. (2006). How does practice reduce dual-task performance: Structural limitation or strategic postponement? *Pyschological Research, 70*, 125–142.

Sáfár, A., & Kormos, J. (2008). Revisiting problems with foreign language aptitude. *International Review of Applied Linguistics in Language Teaching, 46*, 113–136.

Sawyer, M. (1992). Language aptitude and language experience: Are they related? *The Language Programs of the International University of Japan Working Papers, 3*, 27–45.

Sawyer, M., & Ranta, L. (2001). Aptitude, individual differences, and instructional design. In P. Robinson (Ed.), *Cognition and second language instruction* (pp. 319–353). Cambridge: CUP.

Schmidt, R. (1990). The role of consciousness in second language learning. *Applied Linguistics, 11*, 129–158.

Service, E. (1992). Phonology, working memory and foreign language learning. *Quarterly Journal of Experimental Psychology, 45A,* 21–50.

Service, E., & Kohonen, V. (1995). Is the relation between phonological memory and foreign language learning accounted for by vocabulary acquisition? *Applied Psycholinguistics, 16,* 155–172.

Skehan, P. (1986). Cluster analysis and the identification of learner types. In V. Cook (Ed.), *Experimental approaches to second language acquisition* (pp. 81–94). Oxford: Pergamon.

Skehan, P. (1989). *Individual differences in second language learning.* London: Edward Arnold.

Skehan, P. (1998). *A cognitive approach to language learning.* Oxford: OUP.

Skehan, P. (2002). Theorising and updating aptitude. In P. Robinson (Ed.), *Cognition and second language instruction* (pp. 69–93). Cambridge: CUP.

Snow, R.E. (1992). Aptitude theory: Yesterday, today, and tomorrow. *Educational Psychologist, 27,* 5–32.

Snowling, M.J. (2008). Specific disorders and broader phenotypes: The case of dyslexia. *The Quarterly Journal of Experimental Psychology, 61,* 142–156.

Sparks, R.L., Ganschow, L., Fluharty, K., & Little, S. (1995). An exploratory study on the effects of Latin on the native language skills and foreign language aptitude of students with or without disabilities. *The Classical Journal, 91,* 165–184.

Sparks, R., & Ganschow, L. (1993). The impact of native language learning problems on foreign language learning: Case study illustrations of the linguistic coding deficit hypothesis. *Modern Language Journal, 77,* 58–74.

Speciale, G., Ellis, N.C., & Bywater, T. (2004). Phonological sequence learning and short-term store capacity determine second language vocabulary acquisition. *Applied Psycholinguistics, 25,* 293–321.

Spolsky, B. (1989). *Conditions for second language learning.* Oxford: OUP.

Unsworth, N., & Engle, R. (2007). The nature of individual differences in working memory capacity: Active maintenance in primary memory and controlled search from secondary memory. *Psychological Review, 114,* 104–132.

Williams, J.N. (1999). Memory, attention, and inductive learning. *Studies in Second Language Acquisition, 21,* 1–48.

Optimizing post-critical-period language learning

* – provide handout of ILR scales –

Catherine J. Doughty
University of Maryland Center for Advanced Study of Language

This chapter reports on a new language aptitude test, the High-level Language Aptitude Battery (Hi-LAB), whose development was motivated by the need for an aptitude measure for more advanced L2 speakers. Since many language learners begin as adults, critical-period constraints work against the desired outcome. All may not be lost, however, given that some individuals attain high-level, if not native, proficiency, despite a late start. We hypothesize that they possess language aptitude comprising inherent cognitive and perceptual abilities that compensate, at least in part, for the typical post-critical-period degradation in language-learning capacity. While tests currently in use were designed to predict early rate of learning in instructed settings, Hi-LAB is conceptualized to predict successful ultimate attainment. Aptitude is a measurable ceiling on language learning, holding equal all other factors. We discuss constructs and measures, reliability and validity evidence, and uses of Hi-LAB for selecting learners for language training and in aptitude-by-treatment interaction studies.

1. Introduction

Critical period[1] (CP) researchers in the fields of first and second language acquisition examine the question of whether, given a late (post-CP) start, language learners can acquire native proficiency. The cumulative empirical evidence shows conclusively that even after many years of acquisition in normal contexts, if sensitive measures are employed, post-CP learners can always be distinguished from individuals who began acquiring language at the optimal time early in the lifespan (Abrahamsson & Hyltenstam 2009; DeKeyser & Larson-Hall 2005; Long 2005, this volume). At the same time, the CP findings often reveal intriguingly that some

---

1. Recognizing that the term *sensitive periods* is often more appropriate in specific studies of first and second language acquisition, we use the over-arching term *critical period* in this chapter because all the research discussed here involves adult language learning that takes place after all the sensitive periods have closed.

late-starting learners – albeit not many – approximate native proficiency, suggesting that these individuals have exceptional language learning ability (Abrahamsson & Hyltenstam 2008; DeKeyser 2000).

Exceptional language learning ability may be conceptualized as language aptitude. In several domains of human learning and performance, aptitude is a useful construct to explain individual differences: athletes have physical aptitude, musicians have pitch aptitude, and, we hypothesize, near-native post-CP learners have language aptitude. In each of these domains, aptitude entails both potential for successful performance in the domain, and a ceiling on the ultimate level of attainment of the relevant ability. Moreover, aptitude interacts with other factors, such as context and effort; thus, certain combinations of these factors and aptitude can optimize learning and performance.

The empirical observation of the wide range of individual differences in post-CP language learning outcomes – with some exceptional individuals approximating native attainment, but most not – inspired the development of the High-level Language Aptitude Battery (Hi-LAB; Doughty et al. 2007, 2010). Hi-LAB is part of a research program that aims to solve a practical problem in instructed second language acquisition (SLA) in the United States (US): increasingly, there is a need to train learners in second and third languages to very advanced levels. The typical level of ability of an *advanced learner* – for instance, the university foreign language major – has not kept pace with workplace demands for language skills in international business and government positions. In other words, while US foreign language majors typically have functional ability in everyday language use domains, most have not yet mastered many aspects of language use. For this reason, many instructed SLA researchers in the US are now focused on the very advanced language learner.

It is at this upper range of ultimate attainment that critical-period and instructed-SLA research intersect. For instance, CP researchers employ the benchmark of native proficiency, and instructed SLA researchers set the benchmark slightly lower, operationalizing very advanced proficiency as *near-native* or *high-level*. The research methodology employed by CP researchers is informative in the domain of outcomes measures sensitive enough to detect levels of attainment by language learners, either *per se*, as in the case of instructed SLA, or in comparison with native speakers, as in CP-research. In addition, while CP research seeks mainly to explain why SLA is constrained due to the late start, instructed SLA investigates how to overcome the CP constraints, at least to the extent possible, for instance, by selecting learners with exceptional potential. While they will never be completely indistinguishable from native speakers, the level of proficiency exceptional learners can ultimately attain, given the right conditions, is much higher than is normally the case, post-critical period. Thus, given the amount of time and effort it takes to acquire a second language to very advanced levels, identifying individuals with exceptional language learning potential offers an important advantage.

In order to investigate our hypothesis that exceptional language learning outcomes are explained by aptitude, a language aptitude test was needed. A group of SLA and cognitive psychology researchers[2] was assembled at the University of Maryland Center for Advanced Study of Language (CASL) to consider whether existing and widely used aptitude batteries, such as the Modern Language Aptitude Test (MLAT) and the Defense Language Aptitude Battery (DLAB), could be employed to predict ultimate attainment. We were aware that those batteries – developed more than 50 and 40 years ago, respectively – were not originally designed to make this prediction. Rather than ultimate attainment, the focus was on early rate of language learning during the first two years, under intensive, classroom language learning conditions (Carroll 1962; Petersen & Al-Haik 1976).[3] Nonetheless, since it was possible that MLAT and DLAB could predict ultimate attainment, we drew upon SLA theory and empirical research to assess whether the constructs in MLAT and DLAB might be relevant to language learning processes known to be engaged at later stages of SLA, and whether they would be relevant to acquiring the language features that remain to be mastered at those advanced stages.

The consensus of the group was that (a) some of the constructs in the original aptitude batteries are likely relevant only to rate of learning during initial stages of acquisition; (b) some may be relevant throughout all stages of SLA; and (c) constructs were missing that could capture unique cognitive processes that characterize language learning leading to successful high-level attainment. Thus, as a first step in the high-level language research program, we undertook to develop a new aptitude battery, the High-Level Language Aptitude Battery.

2.   Defining language aptitude

In aptitude research – and language aptitude is no exception – there is a range of views on how to define aptitude. For some, aptitude is a general "readiness to learn" comprising many individual difference factors, such as motivation,

---

2.   Robert DeKeyser, Catherine Doughty, Fred Eckman, Henk Haarmann, Michael Long, Peter Robinson, and Carsten Roever.

3.   At present, DLAB is still employed primarily in this way; MLAT is now more commonly employed under less intensive learning conditions, such as at universities and in SLA research.

personality facets, previous experience, and cognitive abilities (Snow 1998). This broad definition is generally invoked in educational settings, where all of these factors can vary widely (Sternberg, Wagner & Okagaki 1993). In our Hi-LAB development discussions, we narrowed the context of learning to naturalistic and instructed SLA, focusing primarily on interpersonal communication in a second language (L2), rather than L2 literacy. In these contexts, research has shown that while lack of motivation can be a negative factor, a high degree of motivation is not a guarantee of success (for instance, Schmidt 1983). In addition, studies have found very advanced learners to be similar to their less successful counterparts with respect to personality profiles and linguistic experience, suggesting that aptitude may be the explanation for differential success above and beyond these factors (Abrahamsson & Hyltenstam 2008; DeKeyser 2000; Ioup, Boustagui, El Tigi & Moselle 1994).

Given the research findings, which indicate that very high-level success is rare, and the examples of highly motivated language learners who do not succeed beyond everyday communication, we adopted a strong cognitive definition for high-level language aptitude: all other factors being equal – motivation, personality, experience, and quality and sufficiency of language learning opportunities – we expect that cognitive (including perceptual) abilities will differentiate successful from more typical post-CP language learners, when the criterion for success is high-level language ability. Although personality and motivation likely play a role in higher-level learning, we take the view that it is primarily cognitive and perceptual abilities that constrain a learner's highest attainable proficiency level (Doughty et al. 2007).

3.   Defining high-level attainment

In instructed SLA research, defining high-level attainment is difficult, particularly since studies have only recently targeted the very advanced level. Most studies rely on proficiency scales, for example the Common European Framework of Reference (CEFR) or the Interagency Language Roundtable (ILR) Scale. In CASL's high-level language research program, we define high-level attainment in various ways, notably without the stringent requirement of being indistinguishable from native speakers (Abrahamsson & Hyltenstam 2008). For a *ballpark* criterion measure, we use US government proficiency tests (for instance, DLPT5)[4] and job performance in a single or multiple languages. Both of these outcome measures are

---

4.   Defense Language Proficiency Test.

based on the ILR scale.[5] While these measures have face validity in government settings (where the need for high-level learners is critical), they are less than ideal for research purposes, since they are global measures that do not capture language change over short periods of time. More sensitive measures are needed for that purpose. Nonetheless, the ILR Level 4 (Advanced Professional Proficiency) descriptors reveal the general high-level of proficiency and performance under investigation. The following descriptor is of ILR Level 4 Listening:

> Able to understand all forms and styles of speech pertinent to professional needs. Able to understand fully all speech with extensive and precise vocabulary, subtleties and nuances in all standard dialects on any subject relevant to professional needs within the range of his/her experience, including social conversations; all intelligible broadcasts and telephone calls; and many kinds of technical discussions and discourse. Understands language specifically tailored (including persuasion, representation, counseling and negotiating) to different audiences. Able to understand the essentials of speech in some non-standard dialects. Has difficulty in understanding extreme dialect and slang, also in understanding speech in unfavorable conditions, for example through bad loudspeakers outdoors. Can discern relationships among sophisticated listening materials in the context of broad experience. Can follow unpredictable turns of thought readily, for example, in informal and formal speeches covering editorial, conjectural and literary material in any subject matter directed to the general listener.   (http://www.govtilr.org/Skills/ILRscale3.htm#4)

4.   Hi-LAB constructs

The next phase of Hi-LAB development entailed motivating theoretical constructs that underpin the cognitive and perceptual abilities of language aptitude. Some of the original theories of language aptitude posited the importance of specific cognitive abilities for language learning success (Carroll 1981; Pimsleur 1966). Contemporary views of aptitude also include cognitive abilities in complexes that comprise language aptitude (Robinson 2002). These cognitive abilities include domain-general abilities, such as logical reasoning (Pimsleur 1966), inductive reasoning (Carroll 1981), working memory (Miyake & Friedman 1998; Robinson 2002), and associative memory (Carroll 1981). Cognitive aptitude may also include abilities specific to the verbal domain, such as auditory or phonemic coding ability (Carroll 1981; Meara 2005; Skehan 2002) and grammatical sensitivity

---

5.   Interagency Language Roundtable. Job tasks in the USG are often associated with ILR levels through ratings by experts.

(Carroll 1981; Meara 2005; Skehan 2002). As noted by Linck et al. (2012, 2013), particular cognitive control processes have been linked to specific language processing tasks. For example, better working memory has been linked to better L2 reading comprehension performance (Harrington & Sawyer 1992), and similar results have been found in the speech production domain, with better inhibitory control supporting language control when switching between languages (Linck, Schwieter & Sunderman 2012).

give as handout –

Table 1. Hi-LAB theoretical constructs

Constructs		Brief definitions and components
Memory		The capacity to process and store input with active trade-offs among these components:
Working Memory	– Short-Term Memory Capacity	The small amount of information that can be kept in an accessible state in order to be used in ongoing mental tasks: *verbal-acoustic STM; verbal-semantic STM.*
	– Executive Control	A set of processes that, collectively, regulate and direct attention and control voluntary processing: *updating, inhibition, and task-switching.*
Long-term Memory	– Rote Memory	Explicit, intentional *long-term storage* that results from rehearsal.
Primability	– Priming	The extent to which prior experience of stimuli in the input facilitates subsequent retrieval during processing: *semantic priming.*
Acuity	– Perceptual Acuity	An above-average capacity to hear or see cues in the auditory or visual input: *auditory perceptual acuity; visual perceptual acuity.*
Speed	– Processing Speed	The speed of response to stimuli: *processing speed; decision speed.*
Induction		The process of reasoning from the specific to the general, i.e. noticing similarities among several instances and drawing a generalization based on these similarities:
	– Implicit Induction	Acquiring the patterns in input without awareness of them.
	– Explicit Induction	Acquiring the patterns in input with awareness of the patterns in examples.
Pragmatic sensitivity	– In research and development	The ability to hypothesize connections between context and use: registering and tracking salient context cues; detecting miscommunication.
Fluency	– In research and development	The automaticity of planning and articulating speech.

From Doughty et al. 2010: 12.

For the Hi-LAB model, each expert proposed one or more constructs, articulating both a theoretical definition and the motivation for why a particular cognitive or perceptual ability underlies advanced language learning processes. We also determined that these abilities should be directly measureable. In other words, whereas MLAT and DLAB are multiple-choice tests, Hi-LAB was envisioned as a battery of computer-delivered tasks that engage cognitive and perceptual processes in real time. Proposed constructs, including some from the earlier aptitude tests, were discussed at length in terms of four criteria: (1) Is this a cognitive or perceptual ability? (2) Is this ability likely to be engaged during advanced stages of language learning? (3) Is this ability pertinent to language features still to be acquired at advanced stages (e.g. non-salient features or components of complex linguistic systems)? (4) Is this ability directly measurable? Constructs that could not meet all four criteria were not included in Hi-LAB development. Table 1 displays the constructs that survived this round of scrutiny – grouped by type of ability – and provides brief theoretical construct definitions.

5. Hi-LAB measures

Once the theoretical constructs were agreed upon, the next round of Hi-LAB work centered on operationalizing the constructs in cognitive and perceptual tasks that could be assembled into a battery. At first, this seemed straightforward, since one of the criteria stated that the purported aptitude could be measured directly during a cognitive or perceptual task, and several viable psycholinguistic measures were proposed. However, it turned out these measures were not immediately transferable into a practical assessment environment. The main difficulty we encountered was that measures normally administered one on one for research purposes often do not have acceptable reliability when administered to groups in aptitude-testing settings.

The process of improving the reliability of Hi-LAB through iterations of task modifications and usability studies has been described at length (Doughty et al. 2008; Mislevy et al. 2010). In brief, we devised an introduction module, which familiarized test takers with the goals of aptitude testing and with all of the response types (keyboarding, mouse clicking, and response box button pressing). We also reviewed and standardized the task directions for each component measure, such that test takers would understand the goal of each cognitive or perceptual task and would engage in sufficient practice before beginning each component measure. Finally, several small groups of participants attempted the Hi-LAB tasks and provided feedback concerning difficulty of understanding task directions, awkwardness of responses (e.g. buttons too far apart for comfort), and frustration with the apparent difficulty of the cognitive and perceptual tasks. All of the information from the usability studies fed into Hi-LAB task revisions in advance of two large-scale reliability studies. The resulting battery contains tasks that are sufficiently reliable on their own, and as a composite are highly reliable (alpha = .90) (Doughty et al. 2008; Mislevy et al. 2010).

The tests used to measure the components of high-level language aptitude in Hi-LAB are listed in Table 2. For a more detailed discussion linking each of these constructs to language aptitude, i.e. an assessment utilization argument, see Mislevy et al. (2009).

Table 2. Hi-LAB GDS constructs and measures[6]

Construct	Measure
Working Memory Executive Control	
Updating	Running Memory Span
Inhibitory Control	Antisaccade
	Stroop
Task Switching	Task Switching Numbers
Phonological Short-term Memory	Letter Span
	Non-Word Span
Associative Memory	Paired Associates
Long-term Memory Retrieval	ALTM Synonym
Auditory Perceptual Acuity	Phonemic Discrimination: Hindi, English Pseudo-Contrastive
	Phonemic Categorization: Russian
Processing Speed	Serial Reaction Time
Implicit Induction	Serial Reaction Time

Adapted from Linck et al. 2012.

---

6.   Since the Hi-LAB GDS study, an explicit induction measure has been added to Hi-LAB. Measures for pragmatic sensitivity and fluency are still under development.

6.   Validity studies

Each of the reliability studies mentioned above included a validity component that examined Hi-LAB at the theoretical-construct level (Doughty et al. 2008; Mislevy et al. 2010). Factor analyses, principal components analyses, and cluster analyses were employed to investigate whether the hypothesized Hi-LAB components emerged in empirical data, and also to probe and eliminate co-linearity. There was a practical motivation for this, since 42 measures comprised the original research version of Hi-LAB, which took 7.5 hours to administer.[7] The combined results of the construct analyses indicated that (1) the empirical factor loadings were repeatedly consistent with the hypothesized latent variables; (2) while some Hi-LAB measures are correlated, as would be expected (for example, the components of the working memory system), there is no problem of collinearity; and (3) based on cluster analysis, it does not make sense to eliminate any of the 13 measures in the current version of Hi-LAB (Doughty et al. 2008, 2010). (Many had been eliminated in the reliability study iterations).

The gold standard of aptitude testing is the prediction of outcome measures. Because we aim to predict high-level ultimate attainment, this is much more difficult to investigate than rate of early-stage language learning, obviously due to the amount of time required to reach ultimate attainment post critical period. Before undertaking the longitudinal predictive validity study of Hi-LAB, in our next analyses, we sought to obtain cross-sectional evidence – which, in a non-technical sense, simulates prediction – that Hi-LAB could distinguish very successful language learners from other individuals[8] (Linck et al. 2012, 2013). Participants could qualify for the successful, high-attainment group in three ways: (1) testing at or above an ILR Level 4 (Advanced Professional Proficiency) on the DLPT in any language, (2) working at two or more job assignments which were characterized at a difficulty level of ILR Level 4 or higher in any language, or (3) demonstrating competent multilingualism by testing at or above ILR Level 3 (General Professional Proficiency) on the DLPT in two or more languages.

Although we had planned an all-other-things-equal, extreme-groups dis-crimination design that would include both highly successful and the more normal case of moderately successful language learners, matched on the non-aptitude variables discussed above (e.g. motivation, personality, and opportunity to learn),

---

7.   Currently, Hi-LAB is about 2.5 hours in length.

8.   A total of 522 individuals participated (62% male, M_{age} = 37 years).

recruitment difficulties forced us to compare successful learners with a wider rang-ing group of individuals believed to represent a broader sample of language apti-tude, but with a similar profile to the high-attainment learners with respect to other critical variables[9] (e.g. intelligence, level of education, commitment to government service).

Although a few participants in the broader group may have had aptitude for high-level attainment, we expected this number to be quite small, due to the postulated low incidence of high-level aptitude discussed at the outset of this chapter. Participants in the two groups were matched on an individual-by-individual basis using a propensity score matching procedure, minimizing the possibility that any group differences revealed in the group discrimination analysis were due to differences along covariates (i.e. age, gender, and level of education), rather than to differences in aptitude.

After matching participants, the data were subjected to analyses to determine how well the aptitude components could distinguish the two groups.[10] Three sets of logistic regression analyses were conducted:[11]

1.   **Listening high-attainment analysis**: high-attainment group defined by listen-ing proficiency only
2.   **Reading high-attainment analysis**: high-attainment group defined by reading proficiency only
3.   **Either-skill high-attainment analysis**: high-attainment group defined by high attainment in either modality (reading and/or listening)

We used logistic regression to measure the utility of the 13 aptitude measures for discriminating between the high-attainment group and the mixed-attainment and no-exposure comparison groups. A separate analysis was carried out for three skill attainment measures – Listening, Reading, and Either-skill – for each of the two matched comparison groups. In each analysis, the models are conceptualized as predicting high attainment, and we fit a logistic regression model with the group indicator as the dependent variable and the set of Hi-LAB scores as the independent variables. (For details of these analyses, see Linck et al. 2012, 2013.)

---

9.   Experience with the L2 was a key missing variable on which these groups may differ. This potential confound, if anything, should bias results against finding any group differences.

10.   Matching produced 76, 94, and 103 matched pairs for the listening, reading, and either-skill high attainment matching procedures, respectively. Any significant group dif-ferences in age and education in the unmatched datasets were no longer significant in the matched datasets.

11.   There were no speaking outcome measures available for the participants in this study.

For the purposes of this chapter, we can examine the overall performance of the three regression models by considering their ability to classify participants with known ultimate attainment correctly. Table 3 displays the overall classification accuracy rates[12] for the three skill-attainment group indicators.

Table 3. Classification accuracy with statistical significance of likelihood ratio test, and pseudo-R^2 (averaged across imputations) associated

	Outcome		
	Listening	Reading	Any skill
Classification accuracy	70.4%	59.2%	67.2%
Pseudo-R^2	**.176	**.109	**.146

Note: Classification accuracy was computed as the percentage of participants correctly classified as members of the high-attainment group or the comparison group (mixed-attainment and no-exposure participants). ***$p < .001$. From Linck et al. 2012.

Results from these analyses indicate that Hi-LAB correctly classified high-attainment learners with up to 70% accuracy when examining listening proficiency, and nearly 60% accuracy for reading proficiency (and 67% for either-skill). The classification accuracies are statistically significantly well above chance. That is, high-attainment learners can be reliably classified based on their performance on Hi-LAB measures of cognitive and perceptual abilities.

Classification accuracy was highest for the Listening attainment indicator and lowest with the Reading attainment indicator. When interpreting the classification accuracies reported in Table 3, it is important to keep in mind that the broader group consisted of educated professionals from similar workplaces, whom we would expect to score above average with respect to the general population on any of a number of cognitive measures. Given how rare high-level foreign language proficiency is, and given the characteristics of the two comparison groups, the classification rates given in Table 3 likely underestimate the ability of Hi-LAB to classify correctly individuals who are capable of high attainment in a foreign language relative to the general population.

Overall accuracy consists of two components: correct classification of high ultimate attainers and correct classification of the broader group as not having achieved high attainment. Table 4 provides a detailed breakdown of the classification performance of the regression models for each attainment indicator;

---

12. Results are from analyses without cross-validation. The pattern of results was the same with cross-validation.

Table 4. Classification performance for each outcome, computed as the percentage of correct and incorrect classifications of high-attainment and mixed-attainment group members

| Observed | High-attainment group indicator | | | | | |
| | Listening | | Reading | | Either-skill | |
	Predicted Non-High	Predicted High	Predicted Non-High	Predicted High	Predicted Non-High	Predicted High
	Vs. Mixed-attainment					
Non-High	68.7	31.4	59.6	40.4	65.6	34.4
High	27.9	72.1	41.2	58.8	31.3	68.7
	Vs. No-exposure					
Non-High	71.2	28.8	71.8	28.2	67.8	32.2
High	23.2	76.8	28.3	71.7	33.3	66.7

From Linck et al. 2012

the broader group was divided into participants who had attempted to learn a language (mixed attainment) and those who had not (no exposure).

Results indicate that, even with propensity score-matched data, the model was biased toward classifying individuals as not being high attainers, whether or not the individuals were known to be so in reality. The model assumption was that each kind of classification error (misses and false alarms) is equally costly, or, conversely, that each kind of correct classification (hits and correct rejections) is equally valuable. This is not likely to be the case, however, in decisions made using Hi-LAB information. If, for example, an expensive and time-intensive intervention is to be given only to those predicted to be high-attainment language learners, a more conservative criterion that classifies a small number of individuals as having language aptitude would be preferred in the model, even if using such a criterion overlooks additional individuals with true high-attainment potential. The decision regarding the importance of correct and incorrect classifications is properly made with respect to each aptitude-testing context.

Since the classification accuracies from the study described above may underestimate the true ability of Hi-LAB to predict ultimate high-level attainment, we are currently undertaking a longitudinal study in which performance on these measures is assessed prior to participants achieving high attainment. Additional work is clearly needed to improve the criterion model, i.e. the measurement of high-level language learning outcomes. The classification study employed a course criterion measure, but future studies should employ a comprehensive set of more fine-grained learning outcome criterion measures. This will also allow for more specific predictions regarding the role of subcomponents of aptitude for particular outcomes. By examining a more sensitive criterion model, future studies could improve our understanding of the specific skills and abilities predicted by Hi-LAB. Such an approach has the added benefit of enhancing the diagnostic value of Hi-LAB. By connecting components of aptitude to specific learning outcomes, we can design interventions that are focused on enhancing the development of specific high-level linguistic features or skills that may be constrained by particular aptitudes. (For a detailed discussion of the uses of aptitude tests, see Doughty, to appear, 2013).

7.   Aptitude-by-treatment interactions

Aptitude-by-treatment interactions address another component of the problem that Hi-LAB was designed to solve. Predicting ultimate attainment is an important application for application for Hi-LAB; but, along the way to advanced proficiency, Hi-LAB test scores can be utilized to generate learner aptitude profiles that can inform pedagogical interventions exploiting learner strengths and circumventing or avoiding learner weaknesses.[13] This approach to instruction is known as aptitude-by-treatment interaction (ATI), where *treatment* refers to the specific pedagogical interventions (see Vatz et al. this volume).

7.1   Aptitude profiles

A first step in extracting aptitude information for ATI studies was to produce aptitude profile cards (APCs) that present and interpret the results of aptitude testing in a format that can be understood by language instructors, language managers, and even language learners themselves. Figure 1 shows the APC development cycle (from Jackson et al. 2011).

---

13.   It may also be possible to train cognitive abilities (e.g. working memory).

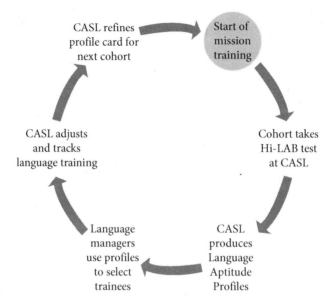

Figure 1. Process for aptitude testing and training recommendations (from Jackson et al. 2011)

A sample APC is displayed in Figures 2 and 3. Figure 2 shows the layout of the first side of the card, which provides an assessment of language learning potential. The second side, shown in Figure 3, offers more fine-grained information on specific components of language aptitude, which can be used to optimize language training for that individual.

The short paragraph at the top of side 1 of the card is a sample statement comprising a language training recommendation and a concise summary of the individual's language aptitude. Below that, the graphics present at-a-glance information about the individual's overall performance on Hi-LAB at three levels compared to: (1) a reference population of US language personnel with official test records of language skill at ILR 3 or above, (2) their own immediate cohort, and (3) the cumulatively tested population (all the cohorts). This information is intended to assist managers in making the decision of whether to assign this individual to language training, and to give an estimate of the level of language proficiency the person could be reasonably expected to achieve.

The cohort analysis is based on the number of cognitive areas in which the individual shows exceptional (greater than 90th percentile), excellent (between 75th and 90th percentile), good (between 25th and 75th percentile) and fair (less than 25th percentile) performance on the Hi-LAB. The number of person icons in the graphic indicates the number of individuals in the cohort, and the cluster

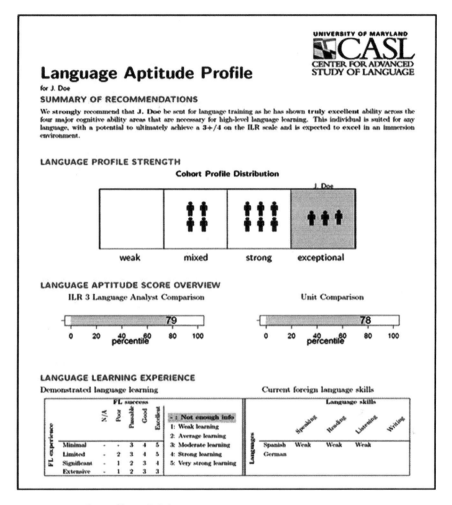

Figure 2. Aptitude profile card, Side 1

highlighted in gold is the cluster to which the individual belongs.[14] The analysis does not provide an absolute ranking, so the icons are intentionally unordered within the clusters.

Overall individual performance is also compared graphically to a population of demonstrated ILR 3 language personnel and the cumulative population (all cohorts). The lengths of the gold bars, along with the scores on the bars,

---

14.   While the segments appear against a gold background on the real cards, they are simply shaded in a light grey here.

DETAILED LANGUAGE APTITUDE PROFILE

The chart below shows scores for the abilities that were measured during aptitude testing; the percentiles are calculated in reference to a population of USG language analysts who have demonstrated ILR 3 language ability. Abilities that are above the 75th percentile are considered to be excellent, and strengths of the individual. Abilities that are in the 25th or lower percentile may indicate weaknesses for the individual. However, the reference population for the percentiles has already demonstrated good aptitude for language, and is not a "general" population in any sense. Below we comment on scores that are relative strengths or weaknesses for the individual.

This person's **strengths** include Distinguishing Foreign Speech Sounds, Focusing Attention, Inductive Reasoning, Learning Foreign Speech Sounds, Processing Speed, Rote Memory and Subconscious Meaning Association. Processing Speed represents the ability to respond to and process stimuli. This person should be able to cope with the rapid rate of information processing required in using a foreign language. Inductive Reasoning represents the ability to consciously derive patterns and rules from examples. This person is expected to do well in deriving patterns in grammar and usage if they make a conscious attempt. Learning Foreign Speech Sounds represents the ability to make use of feedback cues to improve the hearing of speech sounds. This person may be better able to overcome challenges in learning new speech sounds. Rote Memory represents the ability to memorize information. This person should do well with memorizing foreign language vocabulary and other tasks involving rote memory. Distinguishing Foreign Speech Sounds represents the ability to perceive subtle differences in non-native speech sounds. This person should be able to handle sound categories of a language very different from their native language, making listening and speaking skills easier to acquire. Subconscious Meaning Association represents the ability to build meaning associations among words in an unconscious way. This person is expected to be more efficient when associating vocabulary with related concepts. Focusing Attention represents the ability to control first impulses in language use. This person should be able to keep two or more languages separate when learning and using them.

This person's **weaknesses** include Multi-tasking and Short-Term Memory. Short-Term Memory represents the ability to hold new information in mind and actively process it. This person may not be able to cope with receiving a lot of information in real time. Multi-Tasking represents the ability to switch back and forth between two cognitive tasks. This person may need a reduction in non-language task demands in order to focus on the language aspects of a task.

DETAILED ABILITIES

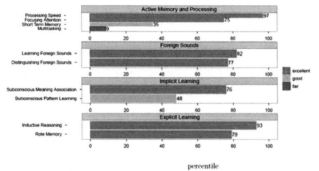

FOR MORE INFORMATION

For more information, please contact Catherine J. Doughty, PhD, University of Maryland Center for Advanced Study of Language, (301) 226-8828, cdoughty@casl.umd.edu or Scott R. Jackson, PhD, University of Maryland Center for Advanced Study of Language, (301) 226-8881, sjackson@casl.umd.edu.

Language research IN SERVICE TO THE NATION
www.casl.umd.edu | info@casl.umd.edu

Figure 3. Aptitude profile card, Side 2

indicate the percentile rank of the individual person compared to the two reference populations. To compute these percentile scores, standardized scores for each of the component Hi-LAB measures are averaged, giving a grand mean average across all the measures for the individual and for each of the two reference populations. Data on Hi-LAB test takers' language-learning experience are collected through a language history questionnaire, which is administered along with the aptitude battery. This section of the APC (at the bottom of side 1) – which reveals potential for language learning by evaluating the individual's prior achievements and experience – complements the results of the aptitude test scores. For instance, if a person has demonstrated the ability to learn a language in a short period of time, this is a likely indicator of future success.

The second side of the APC displays the complete aptitude profile of the individual, as can be seen in Figure 3. The intention is to highlight strengths and weaknesses to enable recommendations for optimizing the training of the individual, regardless of the overall aptitude assessment on the first side. This side of the card encompasses Ranked Abilities, which are derived from Hi-LAB component scores and presented as bar charts, grouped into the cognitive and perceptual abilities deemed necessary for high-level language learning (given lay-person labels to aid understanding of the profile). The paragraph preceding the Ranked Abilities chart offers written feedback and interpretation, commenting on any abilities that appear to be particular strengths or weaknesses, and what these suggest concerning the kind of training that is best suited to the individual.

Like the *ILR Potential* score from the first side of the APC, the ranked abilities percentiles are calculated with reference to a population of US language personnel who have demonstrated ILR 3 language ability. Using the percentiles, we derive an *absolute* ranking in how high an ability score is, as well as a relative ranking compared to the individual's other ability scores. The abilities that are above the 75th percentile are considered to be exceptional and noteworthy strengths of the individual. Abilities that are in the 25th or lower percentile may indicate weaknesses or problem areas for the individual. These are labeled as "Fair" rather than "Poor" because, again, the reference population for the percentiles is a population that has already demonstrated good aptitude for language, and is not a general population in any sense.[15]

The Hi-LAB component abilities are ranked from highest to lowest within a group, for that individual (i.e. the bars are always shown in descending order). Independent of whether a given ability shows up as "exceptional" compared to the ILR 3 reference population, it can be useful to know what relative strengths and weaknesses an individual possesses. It may be preferable to tailor instruction based on these, whether or not the abilities are exceptional. Therefore, in the accompanying paragraph on the APC, we comment not only on the extreme scores, but also at least the top and bottom two abilities for that person, as indicated by the relative ranking.

Next, we turn to describing the ranked abilities and how they are measured, along with a brief comment on how this ability should impact language learning

---

15. At present, these are informed, but nonetheless arbitrary, cutoffs, which may change as more data from different reference populations are collected.

and training. Scores on Hi-LAB measures of the same construct have been combined into one ability bar to reduce the amount of information presented on the APCs. Nonetheless, each of the abilities on the APC maps to a Hi-LAB theoretical construct. In addition, both the groups and the abilities have been given common names for ease of understanding by lay users of the APCs. The groups are discussed in the order shown in Figure 3, and the descriptions, like the labels, are intended for the layperson.

7.2   Active memory and processing

Focusing attention. This score is based on the Antisaccade and Stroop tasks, which measure inhibitory control. Someone with this ability is expected to be able to be better at controlling *first impulses*, such as using the native language rather than a foreign language. Someone lacking inhibitory control may have difficulty keeping two or more languages separate when learning and using them, so, for instance, languages that are more distinct may be easier for this person to keep straight than closely related languages.

Multi-tasking. This score is based on the Task Switching tasks, which require participants to allocate attention during two different cognitive tasks. Someone with strength in this ability should find it easier to manage the effort of switching between comprehending or producing a foreign language and other non-language task demands, or switching between different languages. Someone lacking in this ability may need a reduction of non-language task demands in order to focus on the language aspects of the task.

Short-term memory. This score is based on the Running Span, Letter Span, and Non-word Span tasks. This score encompasses the ability to hold pieces of information (e.g. words, numbers) in one's head for short periods of time as well as the ability to actively process that information. This is useful in many aspects of learning and operating in a foreign language. For example, when listening to a foreign language, it is often the case that some parts of a sentence or phrase are unfamiliar, and the learner may need to hold that phrase in memory during decoding. Someone with a higher score in this ability will be able to process more information in real time, which could facilitate form, meaning and function mapping.

7.3   Foreign sounds

Distinguishing foreign speech sounds. This score is based on the Phonemic Discrimination and Phonemic Categorization tasks. Someone with a good score in this ability has a good *ear* for picking out subtle differences in nonnative speech sounds. Someone poor in this ability is likely to have trouble with non-English sounds. It is natural to have difficulty hearing the sound categories of another language when they differ from one's native language; however, this must be overcome to some degree during foreign language acquisition. Note that a very high score on this task will limit the interpretability of the Learning Foreign Speech Sounds task.

Learning foreign speech sounds. This score is based on the change in success over the course of the Distinguishing Foreign Speech Sounds task. It represents the person's ability to make use of feedback cues to improve hearing of speech sounds. Someone with a good score in this ability may be able to better overcome difficulties in learning new speech sounds. This score is limited by how well individuals perform in the Distinguishing Foreign Speech Sounds task. In other words, this score is mainly informative when the Distinguishing Foreign Speech Sounds score is low or middling; a very high Distinguishing Foreign Speech Sounds score indicates that the Learning score may not be a reliable indicator, since a person good at the outset of distinguishing sounds would not have much room to improve.

7.4   Implicit learning

Subconscious meaning association. This score is based on the Available Long-term Memory task. This task taps the ability to activate semantic networks in order to make it easier to access related words. This is an indicator of how well the person builds meaning associations among words in an unconscious way. Someone with a high score in this ability is expected to do a better job with associating vocabulary with related concepts. Someone with a low score may need more help and exposure to vocabulary in context before being able to build appropriate meaning associations.

Subconscious pattern-learning. This score is based on the Serial Reaction Time tasks, and it represents the ability to pick up on patterns without needing to think about them consciously. This is especially important, since in most cases, the grammar of a foreign language cannot be acquired solely through *book learning* or explicit attention to grammatical rules. Someone especially good in this ability might be better, compared to others, at picking up subtle patterns in a language on their own. A low score in this ability may mean that more explicit attention to rules and patterns in the language would be helpful.

7.5   Explicit learning

Inductive reasoning. This score comes from the Letter Sets test, in which a set of letters that violates the pattern of the other letters sets must be identified. Someone with this ability would be good at learning patterns and rules by explicitly looking for them in language input. A low score in this ability could mean that grammar explanations would be a waste of time for this person.

Rote memory. This score is based on the Paired Associates test. Someone good at this would be expected to do well at memorizing foreign language vocabulary and other tasks involving rote memory. Someone with a low score may struggle with such memorization.

7.6   Other

Processing speed. This score is derived from the Serial Reaction Time task, and is a measure of how fast the individual is at processing and responding to stimuli. It is expected that someone who is fast at information processing should have an easier time coping with the rapid rate of information processing during listening and speaking in a foreign language.

7.7   ATI pilot studies

We are currently piloting the use of Hi-LAB aptitude profiles in small-scale ATI studies. In essence, we are attempting to develop ATI implementation procedures that are feasible. We first conduct an L2 use needs analysis to identify some aspect of new language that learners require when they are operating at General and Advanced Professional Proficiency Levels. Then, we target a pervasive language-learning problem, typically in collaboration with the instructor. Finally, we examine the aptitude profile data and develop learning materials that will engage the strong (and weak, if comparisons are made) cognitive abilities.[16] For example, we have designed task-based activities to promote both implicit (input enhancement) and explicit (rote) lexical learning in a French map task and implicit (problem-solving) approaches (in contrast with an instructor's explicit metalinguistic approach) to the teaching of Russian case information for learners who still rely on English word order. Preparing ATI materials is labor-intensive, but we expect that the pay-off will be the optimization of learning in terms of both rate and ultimate attainment. Vatz et al. (this volume) elaborate on the promise of ATIs in instructed SLA.

8.   Conclusion

In this chapter, we have put forth the hypothesis that, like rate in early stages of SLA, exceptional ultimate attainment outcomes can be predicted and explained by language aptitude. We argued that the components of high-level language

---

16.   Comparisons can be made either within individuals or between groups.

aptitude are cognitive in nature and, all other things equal, that cognitive aptitude determines the ceiling on post-CP ultimate attainment. We showed that cognitive aptitude is measured directly and reliably by Hi-LAB, and Hi-LAB correctly classifies language learners with known ultimate attainment levels. Since Hi-LAB is multi-componential, aptitude profiles are generated which can be used for diagnostic purposes. A new research program is underway to investigate the use of Hi-LAB information in intervention studies that match pedagogy to aptitude strengths as post-CP learners face the difficult problem of advancing from ILR Level 2 to Level 3 and, for exceptional learners, to Level 4. The fundamental goal is to reduce the time, effort and cost of learning languages to very advanced levels by, where possible, selecting individuals with language aptitude and optimizing the learning processes that are engaged in the later stages of SLA. Along the way to ultimate attainment, aptitude profiles offer detailed information that can guide materials development and pedagogy choices for individual learners. Taken together, the selection, diagnostic, and intervention uses of Hi-LAB will help solve the problem of getting more learners to higher levels of ultimate L2 attainment.

References

Abrahamsson, N., & Hyltenstam, K. (2008). The robustness of aptitude effects in near-native second language acquisition. *Studies in Second Language Acquisition, 30,* 481–509.

Abrahamsson, N., & Hyltenstam, K. (2009). Age of onset and nativelikeness in a second language: Listener perception versus linguistic scrutiny. *Language Learning, 59,* 249–306.

Carroll, J.B. (1962). The prediction of success in intensive foreign language training. In R. Glaser (Ed.), *Training research and education* (pp. 87–136). Pittsburgh, PA: University of Pittsburgh Press.

Carroll, J.B. (1981). Twenty-five years of research on foreign language aptitude. In K.C. Diller (Ed.), *Individual differences and universals in language learning aptitude* (pp. 83–118). Rowley, MA: Newbury House.

DeKeyser, R.M. (2000). The robustness of critical period effects in second language acquisition. *Studies in Second Language Acquisition, 22,* 499–533.

DeKeyser, R., & Larson-Hall, J. (2005). What does the Critical Period really mean? In J.F. Kroll, & A.M.B. DeGroot (Eds.), *Handbook of bilingualism: Psycholinguistic perspectives* (pp. 88–108). Oxford: OUP.

Doughty, C. (to appear, 2013). Assessing aptitude. In A. Kunnan (Ed.), *The companion to language assessment.* Oxford: Wiley-Blackwell.

Doughty, C.J., Bunting, M., Campbell, S., Bowles, A., Mislevy, M., Stimley, S., & Koeth, J. (2008). *Hi-LAB Reliability Study 1.* Technical Report: Center for Advanced Study of Language. University of Maryland, College Park.

Doughty, C.J., Campbell, S.G., Bunting, M.F., Bowles, A., & Haarmann, H. (2007). *The development of the High-Level Language Aptitude Battery.* Technical Report: Center for Advanced Study of Language. University of Maryland, College Park.

Doughty, C.J., Campbell, S., Bunting, M., Mislevy, M., Bowles, A., & Koeth, J. (2010). Predicting near-native L2 ability. In M.T. Prior, & Y. Watanabe (Eds.), *Proceedings of the 2008. Second Language Research Forum* (pp. 10–31). Somerville, MA: Cascadilla Press. Available at http://www.lingref.com/cpp/slrf/2008

Harrington, M., & Sawyer, M. (1992). L2 working memory capacity and L2 reading skill. *Studies in Second Language Acquisition, 14*, 25–38.

Ioup, G., Boustagui, E., Tigi, M., & Moselle, M. (1994). Reexamining the Critical Period Hypothesis: A case study of successful adult SLA in a naturalistic environment. *Studies in Second Language Acquisition, 16*(1), 73–98.

Jackson, S., Doughty, C.J., Tare, M., Vatz, K., & Benson, S. (2011). *Aptitude-by-treatment interaction: End of year report*. Technical Report: Center for Advanced Study of Language. University of Maryland, College Park.

Linck, J.A., Hughes, M.M., Campbell, S.G., Silbert, N.H., Tare, M., Jackson, S.R., Smith, B.K., Bunting, M.F., & Doughty, C.J. (to appear, 2013). Hi-LAB: A new measure of aptitude for high-level language proficiency. *Language Learning, 63*.

Linck, J.A., Hughes, M.M., Campbell, S.G., Silbert, N.H., Tare, M., Jackson, S.R., Smith, B.K., Wall, D.G., Meyer, J., Bunting, M.F., & Doughty, C.J. (2012). *Hi-LAB correctly classifies language learners: Results of a group discrimination study*. Technical Report: Center for Advanced Study of Language. University of Maryland, College Park.

Linck, J.A., Schwieter, J.W., & Sunderman, G. (2012). Inhibitory control predicts language switching performance in trilingual speech production. *Bilingualism: Language and Cognition, 15*, 651–662.

Long, M.H. (2005). Problems with supposed counter-evidence to the critical period hypothesis. *International Review of Applied Linguistics, 43*, 287–317.

Meara, P. (2005). *LLAMA language aptitude tests*. Swansea, UK: Lognostics.

Mislevy, M., Annis, R., Koeth, J., Campbell, S., Linck, J., Bowles, A., & Doughty, C.J. (2009). *Assessment utilization argument*. Technical Report: Center for Advanced Study of Language. University of Maryland, College Park.

Mislevy, M., Linck, J.A., Campbell, S., Jackson, S., Bowles, A., Bunting, M., Smith, B., Koeth, J., & Doughty, C.J. (2010). *Predicting high-level foreign language learning: A new aptitude battery meets reliability standards for personnel selection tests*. Technical Report: Center for Advanced Study of Language. University of Maryland, College Park.

Miyake, A., & Friedman, N.P. (1998). Individual differences in second language proficiency: Working memory as language aptitude. In A.F. Healy & L.E. Bourne (Eds.), *Foreign language learning: Psycholinguistic studies on training and retention* (pp. 339–364). Mahwah, NJ: Lawrence Erlbaum Associates.

Petersen, C.R., & Al-Haik, A.R. (1976). The development of the Defense Language Aptitude Battery (DLAB). *Educational and Psychological Measurement, 36*, 369–380.

Pimsleur, P. (1966). *The Pimsleur language aptitude battery*. New York, NY: Harcourt, Brace, Jovanovic.

Robinson, P. (2002). Effects of individual differences in intelligence, aptitude and working memory on incidental SLA. In P. Robinson (Ed.), *Individual differences and instructed language learning* (pp. 211–251). Philadelphia: John Benjamins.

Schmidt, R. (1983). Interaction, acculturation and the acquisition of communicative competence. In N. Wolfson, & E. Judd (Eds.), *Sociolinguistics and language acquisition* (pp. 137–174). Rowley, MA: Newbury House.

Snow, R.E. (1998). Abilities as aptitudes and achievements in learning situations. In J.J. McArdle, & R.W. Woodcock (Eds.), *Human cognitive abilities in theory and practice* (pp. 93–112). Mahwah, NJ: Lawrence Erlbaum Associates.

Skehan, P. (2002). Theorising and updating aptitude. In P. Robinson (Ed.), *Cognition and second language instruction* (pp. 69–93). Cambridge: CUP.

Sternberg, R.J., Wagner, R.K., & Okagaki, L. (1993). Practical intelligence: The nature and role of tacit knowledge in work and at school. In J.M. Puckett, & H.W. Reese (Eds.), *Mechanisms of everyday cognition* (pp. 205–227). Hillsdale, NJ: Lawrence Erlbaum Associates.

PART III

Age, aptitude and ultimate attainment

Reexamining the robustness of aptitude in second language acquisition

Gisela Granena
University of Maryland

Research on language aptitude has focused extensively on instructed second language (L2) learning and rate of L2 learning, but rarely on long-term L2 achievement in a naturalistic context. In addition, the few studies that have investigated the role of aptitude in morphosyntactic L2 attainment (e.g. Abrahamsson & Hyltenstam 2008; DeKeyser 2000; DeKeyser et al. 2010; Granena & Long 2013), have yielded mixed findings, in spite of having relied on the same type of outcome measure (i.e. a grammaticality judgment test; GJT). The aim of the present study was to investigate the relationship between aptitude and long-term L2 achievement as measured in two GJT modalities and sentence complexity conditions. Results showed an interaction between aptitude and GJT scores according to test modality in the L2-speaker group.

1. Research background

Language aptitude is a multidimensional construct described by Carroll (1981) as a combination of cognitive and perceptual abilities, including phonetic coding ability, grammatical sensitivity, memory capacity, and inductive language learning. Carroll (1993) further referred to this combination of abilities as "aptitudes" (p. 675) and claimed that they were innate, fairly stable traits. Although experts and laypeople alike would agree on the generic notion of aptitude as a special talent for language, there is no consensus on the abilities that contribute to such special talent. Analytical ability, memory, and phonetic sensitivity have traditionally been included in all existing language aptitude test batteries in some form or another, and thus, have come to be considered important components of aptitude.

In instructed SLA, aptitude is considered a good predictor of rate of L2 learning, with correlations that range between 0.40 and 0.60, and percentages of explained variance between 16% and 36%. The Modern Language Aptitude Test (MLAT) (Carroll & Sapon 1959), one of the most widely used aptitude tests in the second language acquisition (SLA) field, was validated as a good predictor of course grades in a foreign language learning environment, under intensive learning conditions. All other things being equal, a high-aptitude individual will learn faster and enjoy higher overall learning success. Further evidence for this claim can be found in both non-experimental and experimental research. In a survey study, Ehrman and Oxford (1995) reported a strong correlation between aptitude measures and overall learning success in a communicative language learning environment. Harley and Hart (1997) also found that aptitude was related to performance in a variety of L2 measures in an immersion learning program. Research in the laboratory yielded similar findings, suggesting that aptitude positively affects language learning under a variety of conditions of exposure. De Graaff (1997), Robinson (1997), and Williams (1999) all showed that differences in aptitude, as measured by subtests of the MLAT, resulted in learning differences in implicit and explicit learning conditions. Only incidental learning (i.e. learning of rules while processing for meaning) did not seem to draw on the abilities measured by the aptitude subtests (Robinson 1997).

In addition to research showing that aptitude predicts L2 learning in general under a variety of conditions, there is some evidence of aptitude-treatment interactions (ATI), revealing that different aptitude components may play different roles, depending on instructional treatment (e.g. Erlam 2005; Sheen 2007; Wesche 1981). Sheen (2007), for example, showed that aptitude, operationalized as analytical ability, was more strongly related to achievement with metalinguistic than direct written feedback. An important implication of ATI findings such as Sheen (2007) is that the predictive power of aptitude in SLA may have to be qualified and investigated in relation to different components and a variety of factors (e.g. different treatments, acquisition stages, language sub-domains, and target structures), as advocated by Skehan (1998, 2002) and Robinson (2002).

While aptitude determines learning rate in classroom settings, the general claim in naturalistic settings, where the L2 is largely learnt through immersion, has been that aptitude is related to variation in ultimate L2 proficiency. Skehan (1989), in fact, argued that aptitude could be even more relevant in naturalistic than instructed SLA, because of the greater amount of input that the learner has to process and the pressure to discover regularities and make generalizations merely from L2 exposure. To date, however, research on language aptitude has focused extensively on instructed settings and rate of L2 learning, but rarely on long-term L2 achievement. While the results of aptitude research in formal settings are relevant for pedagogical purposes (e.g. matching instructional treatments with learners' strengths) and can inform theories of L2 learning, they may not generalize to long-term achievement and high levels of L2 proficiency.

The few studies that have investigated aptitude and ultimate attainment have been carried out in relation to a critical period for language acquisition

(Abrahamsson & Hyltenstam 2008; DeKeyser 2000; DeKeyser et al. 2010; Granena & Long 2013; Harley & Hart 2002). Although no adult L2 learner has been shown to be entirely nativelike across language domains and tasks in a methodologically robust study (see Long 2005, for a review), there is evidence that some adult learners can reach very advanced levels of language proficiency (e.g. Abrahamsson & Hyltenstam 2009; Ioup et al. 1994; Novoa et al. 1988).

Adult L2 learners are seen as capable of compensating for the typical post-critical period degradation in language learning capacity by virtue of their language aptitude. DeKeyser (2000) hypothesized that a high degree of language aptitude is required if adult L2 learners are to reach an ultimate level of attainment in morphosyntax comparable to that of child learners. Child learners, instead, are able to attain nativelike command, regardless of their level of language aptitude. The rationale behind DeKeyser's (2000) claim is Bley-Vroman's (1988) Fundamental Difference Hypothesis, according to which there is a qualitative change in the learning mechanisms of adult L2 learners. Aptitude is supposed to relate to explicit learning, and to help compensate for the decline in capacity for implicit learning. DeKeyser (2000) argued that, while younger learners learn mostly implicitly, through domain-specific mechanisms, older learners learn mostly explicitly, through problem-solving or domain-general mechanisms, and, therefore, have to rely more on language aptitude. Individual differences in language aptitude would explain individual differences in explicit L2 learning and, eventually, in ultimate L2 attainment.

While the numerous studies of language aptitude in instructed SLA have provided converging evidence for the predictive power of aptitude in L2 learning, the few studies that have investigated the role of aptitude in immersion contexts and in relation to ultimate attainment (Abrahamsson & Hyltenstam 2008; DeKeyser 2000; DeKeyser et al. 2010; Granena & Long 2013; Harley & Hart 2002) have yielded mixed findings.

Harley and Hart's (2002) study is usually cited as evidence for the predictive validity of aptitude in naturalistic contexts, even though, due to the extremely short immersion period (three months), the results of the study can only speak to the role of aptitude in rate of L2 learning, not eventual success. The study was based on Harley and Hart's (1997) work on aptitude as a predictor of L2 outcomes in French immersion classrooms, which revealed significant positive correlations between memory and L2 outcomes for early immersion learners, and significant positive correlations between analytical ability and L2 outcomes for late immersion learners. Given that the different types of instruction early and late immersion learners are exposed to (i.e. holistic memory-based vs. language analysis) could have affected the results, Harley and Hart (2002) set out to look at the relationship between aptitude and L2 outcomes among adolescent learners after a three-month stay abroad. In addition to an aptitude (operationalized as language analytical ability) test and a memory test, they also administered a battery of language measures, out of which, after removing the effects of an outlier, only a sentence-repetition task was found to be related to aptitude. Harley and Hart concluded that their findings suggested that aptitude was a factor related to success in a naturalistic context, although not consistently so. In fact, the only two measures in the battery that were administered as pretests, and, therefore, the only measures that could provide reliable evidence of the benefits of study abroad, turned out to be unrelated to aptitude as posttests. Given this limitation of the study, and, given that participants had been learning French in a classroom context for approximately seven years before their period of study-abroad, the authors cannot discount the possibility that the significant correlations they found for the sentence-repetition task already existed before the stay abroad.

DeKeyser (2000) administered an auditory grammaticality judgment test (GJT) to 57 Hungarian speakers of L2 English on various elements of morpho-syntax. He found a significant correlation between language aptitude, defined as analytical ability, and late arrivals' GJT scores, but a non-significant correlation among early arrivals. In addition, at an individual level, those participants who were late arrivals and scored within the range of child arrivals, or came close, were all high-aptitude. On the basis of those results, DeKeyser concluded that above-average analytical abilities are required to reach near-native levels in the L2. As an alternative explanation, Long (2007) pointed out the possible role of participants' metalinguistic abilities in the results of the study. He noted that aptitude tests and GJTs have in common the fact that they allow use of metalinguistic abilities. Since, in part, they measure the same underlying abilities, "some positive association between the two sets of scores is to be expected" (p. 73). He further interpreted the lack of a correlation between aptitude and GJT scores among early arrivals as the result of the little variance within that group. Lack of variance could, in fact, have affected performance in the L2 measure, as pointed by Long, but also on the aptitude measure.[1]

One feature of DeKeyser's GJT that could have made the use of metalinguistic abilities more likely was the fact that the test did "not require participants to

---

1.   DeKeyser (2000) and DeKeyser et al. (2010) operationalized aptitude as *L1* verbal analytic ability. This entails administering language-dependent tests, which can lead to language proficiency confounds in the case of samples composed of early and late L2 acquirers. While late starters typically maintain their L1 in the L2 context, receive education in their L1, and have developed L1 literacy skills, early starters tend to be more dominant in the L2 and may have poorer L1 literacy. This may restrict early starters' range of scores on L1-based aptitude tests for reasons that are unrelated to aptitude.

perform under time pressure" (DeKeyser 2000: 515). Instead, the test was administered by having participants listen to each sentence stimulus twice. Each item was presented with a three-second interval between the two renditions. There was also a six-second interval between sentence pairs. These test administration conditions could have maximized reflection and conscious monitoring opportunities.

DeKeyser et al. (2010) provided cross-linguistic evidence for the nature of age effects in two parallel studies that looked at the acquisition of English in the U.S. and the acquisition of Hebrew in Israel by native speakers of Russian ($n = 76$ and $n = 64$, respectively). The findings for aptitude (operationalized as L1 verbal ability, closely related to language analytical ability) showed a significant correlation between ultimate attainment and language aptitude for the adult learners, but not for the early learners, thus replicating the findings in DeKeyser (2000). Specifically, significant correlations were found for the 18–40 age of acquisition range, but not for the age of acquisition < 18 group. No correlation was found for the age of acquisition > 40 group, either, which was attributed to cognitive factors. The language measure used in the study was the same as in DeKeyser's (2000); sentences were presented auditorily, but twice with a three-second interval between them.

Abrahamsson and Hyltenstam (2009) addressed previous methodological gaps in critical-period studies by using a multiple-task design covering various language sub-domains, L2 knowledge and L2 processing, and perception, as well as production. Their study with L2 speakers of Swedish included detailed linguistic scrutiny of apparent linguistic nativelikeness. The formal procedure for screening participants into the study was as stringent as the instrumentation they used, and half of the research was devoted to selecting participants who identified themselves as nativelike, but who were also perceived to be nativelike by native-speaker judges. Participants in the final sample were 31 childhood learners with ages of onset ≤ 11, and 10 adult learners with ages of onset ≥ 12. All the late learners were able to score within the native-speaker range on some of the tasks, but, unlike some early learners, none could do so across the whole range of tests employed.

When scores on the aptitude test, the Swansea LAT (Meara et al. 2003), were considered, Abrahamsson and Hyltenstam (2008) found that the 11 post-critical-period L2 learners who had passed as native speakers all had above-average aptitude. In addition, four of them were also able to score within the native-speaker range on the GJT. The correlation between GJT scores (a combination of two GJT modalities, auditory and written) and aptitude among late learners was moderately positive ($r = .53$), but not significant ($p = .094$), probably due to the small size of the group. The authors further observed that 72% of the early learners who performed within the native-speaker range also had high aptitude. In fact, there was a moderately strong and significant positive correlation between GJT scores and aptitude in the early-learner group ($r = .70$, $p < .001$). On the basis of those results, Abrahamsson and Hyltenstam (2008) concluded that language aptitude seemed to be necessary in adult near-native SLA and advantageous in child SLA.

This is a finding that runs contrary to DeKeyser's (2000) hypothesis that aptitude will not be a significant predictor among early L2 learners. It also differs from the results of DeKeyser (2000) and DeKeyser et al. (2010), which showed no relationship between proficiency and aptitude among early learners. It is, however, in line with Skehan's (1986, 1990) findings on the role of aptitude in children's L1 acquisition. As part of the Bristol Language Project (Wells 1985), Skehan reported a number of significant correlations between language aptitude at age 13 and measures of acquisition derived from the children's speech at 42 months. He suggested that aptitude was a factor in the development of language competence in native speakers. Unfortunately, the significant relationship between aptitude and the biographical variables in the study made the role of environmental factors difficult to disentangle. Specifically, factors such as family background, parents' level of education, and parents' interest in literacy were significantly and positively related to aptitude measures such as a verbal intelligence test and a grammatical sensitivity test, which, in turn, were related to linguistic indices, such as mean length of utterance and range of adjectives and determiners. Perhaps not unsurprisingly, only one of the aptitude measures, a sound discrimination test, was not related to biographical factors. This subcomponent of aptitude correlated with two of the comprehension indices in the study and with one of the vocabulary indices, suggesting a distinct dimension of aptitude in L1 acquisition.

DeKeyser (2000), DeKeyser et al. (2010), and Abrahamsson and Hyltenstam (2008) all had in common the target language domain investigated, morphosyntax, and the L2 measure employed, a GJT. The features of the GJTs, however, differed across the studies. While the GJT in DeKeyser (2000) and DeKeyser et al. (2010) was auditory, and participants listened to each test item twice, Abrahamsson and Hyltenstam (2008) combined the scores of two different GJT modalities, auditory (online) and written (offline). In addition, test items in Abrahamsson and Hyltenstam (2008) were long, syntactically complex sentences, which could have increased the computational cost involved in processing.

Also using a GJT, Granena and Long (2013) investigated the relationship between ultimate morphosyntactic attainment and language aptitude, as measured by the LAT's most recent version, the LLAMA aptitude test (Meara 2005). The results showed no relationship between aptitude and GJT performance. Participants were 65 Chinese speakers of Spanish L2 divided into three groups according to age of onset of L2 learning ($\leq$ 6, 7–15, and $\geq$ 16). Unlike the GJTs in DeKeyser (2000), DeKeyser et al. (2010), and Abrahamsson and Hyltenstam (2008), the GJT in Granena and Long (2013) included no offline features.

To summarize, in contrast to the many studies showing measures of language aptitude capable of predicting rate of classroom language learning, few have been conducted on the role of aptitude, in combination with starting age, as a partial explanation for ultimate attainment by long-term residents in a L2 environment. In addition, research to date regarding the relationship between aptitude and long-term L2 achievement has produced mixed findings. While aptitude was not related to ultimate morphosyntactic attainment among early acquirers in DeKeyser (2000) and DeKeyser et al. (2010), Abrahamsson and Hyltenstam (2008) found a relationship between aptitude and GJT performance among those participants who were first exposed to the L2 before age 12. Also, while DeKeyser (2000) and DeKeyser et al. (2010) found a relationship between aptitude and GJT performance among late acquirers, Granena and Long (2013) did not. Finally, research findings have been inconsistent when a battery of tests has been employed, as in Harley and Hart (2002).

2. Purpose of the study

The present study was designed to test the research hypothesis that the relationship between ultimate morphosyntactic attainment and language aptitude reported in previous studies may have been affected by aptitude-testing interactions. Specifically, the present study examined two features of GJTs that could have interacted with the measures of language aptitude used in previous studies of ultimate L2 attainment: Test modality (auditory vs. written) and sentence complexity (syntactically simple vs. complex).

Regarding test modality, some evidence in support of two different types of L2 tasks for assessing language competence was provided by Ellis (2005). Using an exploratory factor analytic technique, Ellis (2005) showed that an oral elicited imitation test, together with a timed GJT and a narration task, loaded strongly on the same component, whereas a metalinguistic test and an untimed GJT loaded on a separate component. Ellis (2005) interpreted these two types of measures as primarily tapping implicit and explicit L2 knowledge, respectively. Measures tapping implicit knowledge involve automatic responses according to feel, do not require metalinguistic knowledge, and are time-pressured, whereas measures tapping explicit knowledge involve responses using rules, encourage use of metalinguistic knowledge, and are not time-pressured. One of the aims of the present study was to investigate whether L2 learners' performance is differentially related to language aptitude depending on whether the L2 measure used contains features that allow participants to make more or less controlled use of L2 knowledge. If high-aptitude L2 learners with high analytical ability approach language as a puzzle-solving task (Skehan 1998), offline tests with no time constraints, or metalinguistic tasks with an error correction component, which allow controlled use of L2 knowledge, could provide them with additional opportunities to rely on their problem-solving and analytical abilities.

The second aim of the study was to investigate whether L2 learners' performance is differentially related to language aptitude depending on whether test items contain features that place additional demands on attentional resources. One feature that can make sentence processing more effortful is syntactic complexity. Complex sentences can be defined as long sentences that include subordination (Wolfe-Quintero, Inagaki, & Kim 1998). High-aptitude individuals may have strengths in the cognitive abilities on which information processing draws, such as allocating attention. As a result, they may be more able to focus on the structural properties of language when sentences are complex and involve an information burden that requires breaking down material into its constituent parts.

3.   Research questions and hypotheses

The study was guided by two research questions and five hypotheses. The first research question addressed the relationship between language aptitude scores and GJT accuracy scores according to test modality:

To what extent will adult L2 learners' ultimate morphosyntactic attainment, as measured by an auditory GJT and an untimed written GJT with a correction component, be related to language aptitude?

Hypothesis 1a.   Language aptitude will moderate adult L2 learners' performance in the untimed written GJT with a correction component.

Hypothesis 1b.   Language aptitude will not moderate adult L2 learners' performance in the auditory GJT.

Hypothesis 1c.   Language aptitude will not moderate the performance of native-speaker controls.

Hypothesis 1 predicted that aptitude would moderate L2 learners' performance in the test that was more conducive to the retrieval of explicit L2 knowledge (the untimed written GJT) because language tests that emphasize attention to linguistic code features in untimed formats and aptitude tests such as the MLAT or tests largely based on the MLAT (e.g. LLAMA) allow for the use of analytical and metalinguistic abilities to some extent. No relationship between aptitude and performance by the same participants on an auditory GJT was expected because learners perform the task online, and this modality makes it less likely, although not impossible, that they make use of controlled L2 knowledge in responding to the task. No relationship between aptitude and native speakers' performance was expected, either, because native speakers were predicted to rely on the same type of language knowledge, regardless of test modality.

The second research question addressed the relationship between language aptitude scores and GJT accuracy scores according to sentence complexity:

To what extent will adult L2 learners' ultimate morphosyntactic attainment, as measured by syntactically simple and syntactically complex sentences, be related to language aptitude?

Hypothesis 2a. Language aptitude will moderate adult L2 learners' performance in complex sentence items.
Hypothesis 2b. Language aptitude will moderate the performance of native-speaker controls on complex sentence items.

The degree of syntactic complexity of test items may increase the processing demands of a language test, such as a GJT. Hypothesis 2 predicted that when GJT items involved additional processing costs, aptitude would be related to GJT scores, keeping the effects of test modality constant. This relationship is understood as showing that performance in a test that carries an additional processing load will depend on learners' ability to cope with demanding L2 processing conditions. Unlike processing-based accounts of age effects (e.g. McDonald 2000, 2006), which argue that L2 processing deficits are the reason for poorer grammatical performance, no relationship was expected between aptitude and L2 performance when L2 knowledge was used automatically in a test where processing was not manipulated in any major way, even if the test was an online task, such as an auditory GJT. Therefore, no relationship was expected between aptitude and performance in the auditory GJT for those items that were syntactically simple. A relationship between aptitude and native speakers' performance in complex items was not ruled out in this study, since native speakers' syntactic performance under stress has been found to correlate with their cognitive abilities (McDonald 2006).

To summarize, (1) Aptitude was expected to moderate the difference score between simple and complex test scores in both the L2-learner and native-speaker group (i.e. a complexity-by-aptitude interaction), and (2) Aptitude was expected to moderate the difference score between auditory and written test scores in the L2-learner group only (i.e. a modality-by-aptitude interaction).

4. Methodology

4.1   Participants

Participants in this study were 30 L1 English-L2 Spanish bilinguals (56.7% males and 43.3% females) who were long-term residents of Barcelona (Spain). Additionally, 15 native speakers of Spanish (60% males and 40% females) were included in the study as controls. The L2 speakers were highly homogeneous in terms of their educational background. They were all professors of English language, literature, history, or international trade, or translators, recruited from universities and international academic institutions in Barcelona. Most of them had graduate degrees and were linguistically trained.

In order to take part in the study, participants had to be very advanced speakers of Spanish. Potential participants were informally screened via a telephone or face-to-face interview by a linguistically trained native speaker of Spanish. Only those participants with a slight or mild foreign accent and occasional inaccuracies with word stress or intonation were included in the study. Participants with noticeable, or strong, foreign accent and pronunciation that frequently impeded comprehensibility did not take part in the study. Some additional basic background criteria that participants had to fulfill were: be a native speaker of English, have an educational level of no less than high school, and have lived in Spain for a minimum of 10 years.[2] The length of residence requirement was included as a way of controlling its influence on participants' ultimate L2 attainment, since it has been argued that length of residence should preferably be 10 years or longer to be unrelated to ultimate morphosyntactic attainment (DeKeyser 2000).

The earliest arrival in the L2-speaker group reached Spain when she was 17. Therefore, all the L2 speakers in the study had been immersed in the L2 context for the first time as adults. According to information obtained via the biographical questionnaire, however, 12 of the participants had been exposed to the L2 prior to their arrival in Spain in an instructed language setting in their countries of origin. In all cases, formal instruction had taken place several years before arrival in the context of high-school education. Years of instruction for these participants ranged between two and four.

Native speaker controls were recruited via online advertisements. They were born in Barcelona, had a college degree or were pursuing graduate studies at the time of the study, and belonged to a similar age range as the L2 speakers.

---

2.   Two of the participants included in the study had a length of residence of seven and eight years, respectively.

Table 1. Participants' information

	Age at testing		Age of arrival		Length of residence	
	M	Range	M	Range	M	Range
L2 Speakers	49.43 (9.43)	29–67	26.97 (5.52)	17–43	22.07 (8.91)	7–31
Controls	35.80 (8.19)	25–49				

Note: Standard deviations appear between parentheses.

They were bilingual speakers of Spanish and Catalan who reported themselves as being Spanish-dominant. Table 1 summarizes the information about age at testing, age of arrival, and length of residence for the participants.

4.2   Target structures

Four target structures that are known to be particularly difficult for speakers of L2 Spanish with a non-Romance L1 were chosen for this study: (a) noun-adjective number agreement in predicative position, (b) adjective gender agreement in predicative position, (c) passives with *ser* and *estar*, and (d) verbal clitics.

4.3   Instruments and procedures

Participants were administered an auditory GJT, an untimed written GJT with an error correction component, a language aptitude test, and a biographical questionnaire. SuperLab Pro (Cedrus 2003) was used to administer the two GJTs. The order of administration of the tests was fixed. The auditory GJT was administered first, the language aptitude test was administered second, and the written GJT last. The rationale behind this order of administration was to keep the tests that allow controlled use of L2 knowledge and that encourage the highest degree of awareness last (for a similar order of administration and rationale, see Ellis 2005). Overall testing time was 90 minutes.

For the two GJTs, a total of 256 items were created and randomly assigned into conditions according to complexity and grammaticality. The reliability coefficient for internal consistency (Cronbach's α) was .947 for the auditory GJT and .937 for the written GJT. Reliability coefficients for each of the four crossed conditions ranged between .867 and .925. Each test included 128 target items, 32 for each target structure, and four practice items. Half of the 128 items were [– complex] sentences (32 grammatically correct and 32 grammatically incorrect) and half were [+ complex] sentences (32 grammatically correct and 32 grammatically incorrect). Sentences in the [– complex] condition were syntactically simple, while sentences in the [+ complex] condition were syntactically complex. Syntactically simple sentences consisted of one independent clause. Syntactically complex sentences included one independent clause and, at least one dependent clause. As a result of embedding, complex sentences were also longer than simple sentences (for sample items, see the Appendix).

In the auditory GJT, items were randomly presented once through earphones. Items were taped and spoken at normal speed by a female native speaker of Spanish. Test instructions were to indicate whether each sentence was grammatically correct or incorrect, and to press a key as soon as an error was detected, even if the sentence had not finished. Once participants pressed a key, the computer automatically moved on to the next sentence. These features were aimed at making participants process sentences online. However, he test itself was not speeded (timeout was set at 10000 milliseconds). Participants were given a break in the middle of the test. Participants' responses and response times in milliseconds were recorded. Accuracy scores were calculated by awarding one point for each correct judgment.

In the written GJT, sentences were randomly presented on a computer screen one at a time. The test was self-paced and participants were given a break in the middle. The instructions for the test were to indicate whether each sentence was grammatically correct or incorrect, either by typing in *OK* if the sentence was correct, or by typing in the correction of the error if the sentence was incorrect. Participants were told that errors would be grammatical, not lexical or orthographical, and that there would be a single error in a sentence, if any. They were also told that the test was self-paced and that they would be allowed as much time to respond as they wished. Participants' responses and response times in milliseconds were recorded. Accuracy scores were calculated by awarding one point for each correct judgment in the case of grammatical sentences and each correct error correction in the case of ungrammatical sentences.

The language aptitude test was the LLAMA (Meara 2005), the most recent version of the LAT (Meara et al. 2003). LLAMA is a computer-based test that is independent of the languages spoken by test-takers. It relies on picture stimuli and verbal materials either from artificial language systems or languages that participants are likely to be unfamiliar with (a British Columbian Indian language and a Central-American language). The LLAMA includes four subtests: Vocabulary learning, sound recognition, sound-symbol association, and grammatical inferencing (see Granena, this volume, for a detailed description of the test). It takes approximately 25 minutes. Following previous studies of ultimate attainment that have used the LLAMA or its earlier version, the LAT (Abrahamsson & Hyltenstam 2008; Bylund et al. 2010; Granena & Long 2013), and for the sake of comparability, participants' language aptitude was scored as the raw average of the four subtests.[3] The reliability coefficient for internal consistency of the test (Cronbach's α) was .76 ($k = 90$).

5.   Results

The average accuracy scores obtained by the native-speaker control group and the L2-speaker group in each of the GJT conditions are shown in Table 2. All dependent variables in each of the groups were normally distributed, according to one-sample Kolmogorov-Smirnov ($K–S$) tests ($p > .05$).

Table 2. Auditory and written GJT scores

	Controls ($n = 15$)		L2 Speakers ($n = 30$)	
	Mean	Range	Mean	Range
Simple Auditory	60.00 (2.39)	55–63	45.10 (6.23)	33–58
Complex Auditory	58.53 (3.36)	53–62	43.53 (7.03)	29–55
Simple Written	62.73 (1.44)	59–64	54.20 (6.14)	43–62
Complex Written	61.00 (2.70)	56–64	50.83 (6.80)	37–62

Note: Maximum possible score was 64 in each cell.

In terms of modality, the two groups scored higher on the written than on the auditory GJT. The average written GJT score was 123.73 ($SD = 3.88$) in the control group, and 105.03 ($SD = 12.49$) in the L2-speaker group, while the average auditory GJT score was 118.53 ($SD = 4.90$) in the control group, and 88.67 ($SD = 12.29$) in the L2-speaker group. The Pearson correlation between auditory and written GJT scores was .878 ($p < .001$) ($n = 45$).

In terms of sentence complexity, performance in [– complex] (henceforth, simple) GJT items was more accurate than performance in [+ complex] (henceforth, complex) items, but the difference was not as large as between GJT modalities, especially among L2 speakers. In the control group, the average complexity scores were 122.73 ($SD = 2.55$) for simple and 119.53 ($SD = 4.24$) for complex items, while in the L2-speaker group, the average complexity scores were 99.30 ($SD = 11.59$) for simple items and 94.37 ($SD = 12.97$) for complex items. In terms

---

3.   An equally weighted composite score was also computed by converting the raw scores in each aptitude subtest into z-scores and adding them up. The results of the study remained robust regardless of the method used to score the aptitude test.

of the four crossed GJT conditions, participants scored highest on simple written items and lowest on complex auditory items. The ranking of scores was the same in both groups: Simple written > complex written > simple auditory > complex auditory. Pearson correlations between scores on simple and complex items ranged between .822 and .912 ($p < .001$) ($n = 45$).

Table 3 shows the average response time[4] in the auditory and written GJTs in each of the groups. Response times in the auditory GJT measured the time elapsed from the onset of the auditory stimulus until the participant pressed one of the response keys. Response times in the written GJT measured the time elapsed from the visual display of the stimulus until the participant started typing in a response. The average response time was higher in the auditory than in the written GJT among control-group speakers. L2 speakers' response time, on the other hand, was higher in the written than in the auditory GJT.

Table 3. Mean response time in milliseconds in the auditory and written GJTs

	Auditory GJT		Written GJT	
	M	SD	M	SD
Controls ($n = 15$)	6466	415	5524	1453
L2 Speakers ($n = 30$)	7617	850	9777	2691

Regarding the language aptitude test, the average score in the control group ($n = 15$) was 50.67 ($SD = 11.55$), with scores ranging between 33.75 and 72.50, out of 100. The average score in the L2-speaker group ($n = 30$) was 50.65 ($SD = 15.14$), with scores ranging between 23.75 and 83.73, out of 100. The distribution of scores in each of the groups was normal, according to K–S tests ($p > .05$). The difference in mean scores between the two groups was not statistically significant ($t(43) = .003$, $p = .998$); therefore, the two groups were considered comparable in terms of language aptitude.

In order to investigate the role of aptitude in GJT scores, a $2 \times 2 \times 2$ mixed analysis of variance was conducted, with modality and complexity as within-subjects factors, each with two levels (auditory vs. written, and simple vs. complex), speaker group as a between-subjects factor (L2 speakers and controls), and aptitude as a covariate. An interaction term was added to test

---

4. Only response times belonging to correct responses were considered. Individual response times above or below 2 SDs of each participant's mean were discarded.

for possible interactions between covariate and independent factors. In the case of a significant interaction, follow-up analyses in the form of factorial ANOVAs were used by breaking down the continuous covariate into categories (i.e. aptitude groups).

Results of the $2 \times 2 \times 2$ model yielded a significant two-way interaction between test modality and group ($F(1,41) = 20.606$, $p < .001$, $\eta_p^2 = .434$), further qualified by a significant three-way interaction, with a large effect size according to partial eta squared[5] (η_p^2), between test modality, group, and aptitude as a covariate ($F(1,41) = 4.601$, $p = .013$, $\eta_p^2 = .190$). There were no significant interactions between sentence complexity, group, and aptitude ($p = .863$) or between complexity and group ($p = .340$). The significant modality $\times$ group $\times$ aptitude interaction suggested the presence of a two-way interaction between test modality and group that was further qualified by language aptitude. Figure 1 illustrates group scores on the auditory and written GJT (i.e. modality $\times$ group interaction). As can be seen, modality effects were not the same across the groups, since there was a sharper increase from auditory to written scores in the L2-speaker group than in the control group. This resulted in a larger mean difference between the two groups in the auditory than in the written modality (29.87 vs. 18.70). The interaction with language aptitude as a covariate further suggested that aptitude moderated the difference in modality scores between the groups.

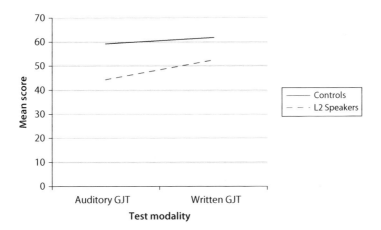

Figure 1. Two-way interaction between speaker group and GJT modality

---

5. For partial eta squared (η_p^2), a small effect size is $.01 \leq \eta_p^2 < .06$, medium is $.06 \leq \eta_p^2 < .14$, and large is $\eta_p^2 \geq .14$.

In order to investigate the interaction between modality, group, and language aptitude further, two separate 2 × 2 repeated measures ANOVAs were computed, one for the L2-speaker group and one for the control group. Each analysis included the two repeated factors (modality and complexity) and language aptitude as a covariate, as well as the interactions between the independent factors and the covariate. The results of the analysis for the control group showed a significant main effect for test modality on GJT scores, controlling for sentence complexity ($F(1,13) = 9.345$, $p = .009$, $\eta_p^2 = .418$), and a significant main effect for sentence complexity, controlling for test modality ($F(1,13) = 10.853$, $p = .006$, $\eta_p^2 = .455$). However, there were no significant interactions between test modality and language aptitude ($F(1,13) = .656$, $p = .433$, $\eta_p^2 = .048$) or between sentence complexity and language aptitude ($F(1,13) = .028$, $p = .871$, $\eta_p^2 = .002$). These results indicated that native speakers were significantly more accurate on the written than the auditory GJT, and on simple than complex GJT items. However, language aptitude did not moderate the relationship between test modality and accuracy scores or between sentence complexity and accuracy scores in this group.

Results for the L2-speaker group revealed a significant main effect for test modality ($F(1,28) = 211.218$, $p < .001$, $\eta_p^2 = .883$) on GJT scores, but this effect was qualified by a significant two-way interaction, with a large effect size, between test modality as an independent variable and language aptitude as a covariate ($F(1,28) = 9.303$, $p = .005$, $\eta_p^2 = .249$). There was also a significant main effect for sentence complexity, averaging over levels of modality ($F(1,28) = 18.015$, $p < .001$, $\eta_p^2 = .392$). This effect, unlike that of modality, was not modified by language aptitude ($F(1,28) = .226$, $p = .638$, $\eta_p^2 = .008$). These results indicated that the main effect for test modality in the L2 group was qualified by language aptitude, and that, therefore, the differences between performance in the auditory GJT and the written GJT were affected by individual differences in aptitude. In other words, aptitude level had a different impact on GJT scores, depending on whether the GJT was auditory or written. Regarding sentence complexity, L2 speakers, like native speakers, were also significantly more accurate on simple than complex GJT items. This difference was not moderated by language aptitude.

Given the presence of a significant interaction in the L2-speaker group between GJT modality and language aptitude as a covariate, L2 speakers were subdivided into three aptitude groups: high, mid, and low, according to a z-score distribution where *high aptitude* = z-scores > .5, *mid aptitude* = $-.5 < z$-scores < .5, and *low aptitude* = z-scores < $-.5$. Table 4 summarizes the scores obtained by each of the aptitude groups on the GJT according to test modality.

Table 4. GJT scores by language aptitude group in the L2-speaker group

	Auditory GJT		Written GJT	
	M	Range	M	Range
High (n = 10)	90.30 (10.13)	78–108	110.40 (7.60)	97–123
Mid (n = 11)	91.36 (11.71)	68–108	108.46 (12.31)	83–122
Low (n = 9)	83.55 (14.75)	63–110	94.89 (11.98)	80–114

Note: Maximum possible score was 128 in each cell.

Descriptively, high-aptitude participants did better than low-aptitude partici-pants in both test modalities, but the difference between the two groups was larger in the written modality. In this modality, high-aptitude participants scored 12.18% higher on average than low-aptitude participants. In the auditory modality, high-aptitude participants only scored 5.28% higher than low-aptitude participants. The range of GJT scores within each aptitude group further showed that the participant with the highest score on the auditory GJT was, in fact, a low-aptitude individual (score of 110), while the participant with the highest score on the written GJT was a high-aptitude individual (score of 123). Inferentially, univariate tests of between-subjects effects showed that the three aptitude groups only differed on their written GJT scores ($F(2,27) = 5.694$, $p = .009$, $\eta_p^2 = .297$), not on their auditory GJT scores ($F(2,27) = 1.143$, $p = .334$, $\eta_p^2 = .078$). Bonferroni-adjusted multiple comparisons further revealed that differences on the written GJT were between high-aptitude and low-aptitude individuals ($p = .013$), and between mid-aptitude and low-aptitude ($p = .029$). Specifically, high- and mid-aptitude L2 learners outperformed low-aptitude L2 learners on the ungrammatical items of the written GJT, but not on the grammatical items. A repeated measures ANOVA computed as a posthoc analysis, with modality and grammaticality as within-subjects factors and aptitude group as a fixed factor, revealed a the three-way interaction between test modality, grammaticality, and aptitude group ($F(2,27) = 10.664$, $p < .001$, $\eta_p^2 = .441$). Pairwise comparisons with Bonferroni correction confirmed that the only significant differ-ences were between high- and low-aptitude and mid- and low-aptitude participants on written ungrammatical items ($p = .008$ and $p = .033$, respectively). No differ-ences between the aptitude groups (high and low, mid and low, and high and mid) were found for either grammatical items in the written GJT ($p = .370$, $p = .413$, and $p = 1.000$), grammatical items in the auditory GJT ($p = .370$, $p = .413$, and $p = 1.000$) or ungrammatical items in the auditory GJT ($p = .150$, $p = .879$, and $p = .901$).

To summarize, the results of the follow-up analyses showed a relationship between language aptitude and test modality, keeping item complexity constant, among L2 speakers. Aptitude had an effect on written items, but not on auditory items. No evidence was found in support of a relationship between aptitude and GJT scores as a function of item complexity. This pattern of results can also be observed in the correlation matrix between language aptitude scores and GJT scores according to test modality and sentence complexity, shown in Table 5. As can be seen, in the L2-speaker group, there was a positive relationship between language aptitude and written scores. The magnitude of this relationship was moderate (r = .44 and .45) and statistically significant. In the control group, on the other hand, the relationship between aptitude and written scores was weak and non-significant.

Table 5. Pearson correlations between language aptitude scores and GJT scores

	Aptitude test scores	
	Controls (n = 15)	L2 Speakers (n = 30)
Simple Auditory	−.14 (.621)	.16 (.392)
Complex Auditory	−.12 (.663)	.17 (.360)
Simple Written	.15 (.591)	.44 (.016)
Complex Written	.17 (.540)	.45 (.013)

Note: The values in parentheses are p values.

Finally, the two speaker groups were compared on their average response times in each GJT. A repeated-measures ANOVA with average response time in each modality as a within-subjects factor and speaker group as a between-subjects factor was performed. Results revealed a significant two-way interaction between response time and group ($F(1,41)$ = .658, p < .001, η_p^2 = .342). This interaction is illustrated in Figure 2. The interaction between response time according to modality, speaker group, and aptitude as a covariate was not significant ($F(1,41)$ = .990, p = .538, η_p^2 = .010).

Follow-up independent-samples t-tests showed that controls were faster than L2 speakers in both the auditory and written GJTs ($t(43)$ = −4.776, p < .001 and $t(43)$ = −5.515, p < .001, respectively). However, at a within-subjects level, control speakers were faster in the written than in the auditory GJT (mean difference = 942 milliseconds), while L2 speakers were faster in the auditory than in the written GJT (mean difference = 2160 milliseconds). Both mean differences were statistically significant, according to paired-samples t-tests ($t(14)$ = 2.556, p = .024 and $t(29)$ = −5.030, p < .001, respectively).

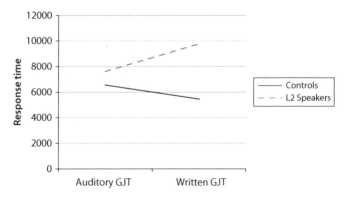

Figure 2. Two-way interaction between speaker group and response time

6.   Discussion

This study set out to investigate the effects of language aptitude on test modality and sentence complexity with a fully-crossed within-subjects design. The type of test investigated was a GJT, a widely used test in SLA research that measures morphosyntactic proficiency (e.g. Abrahamsson & Hyltenstam 2009; De Jong 2005; Montrul 2005; Toth 2006). Hypothesis 1 predicted an effect for language aptitude on test scores when the test was more conducive to the retrieval of explicit L2 knowledge. Following Ellis's (2005, 2009) construct validation studies, an auditory GJT and an untimed written GJT with a correction component were used as measures more conducive to the retrieval of implicit and explicit L2 knowledge, respectively. The adopted hypothesis was that aptitude effects would only be found for the untimed written GJT, given that participants were allowed unlimited time to analyze test sentences and monitor their performance. With unlimited time, participants were given the opportunity to make controlled use of their L2 knowledge. The need to provide a correct version of ungrammatical items further encouraged them to consciously reflect on linguistic structure and sentence correctness.

The results of a repeated-measures analysis with language aptitude as a covariate corroborated this prediction. The significant two-way interaction in the L2-speaker group between language aptitude as a covariate and test modality, holding complexity constant, showed that aptitude moderated differences in performance in the two test modalities. Follow-up analyses on the L2-speaker data further confirmed a significant correlation between aptitude and written GJT scores, as well as a significant effect of aptitude as a between-subjects factor in the written, but not in the auditory, GJT. High- and mid- aptitude L2 speakers outperformed low-aptitude L2 speakers only in the untimed modality. While language aptitude interacted with test modality in the L2-speaker group, differences between performance in the written and auditory GJT in the native-speaker group were independent of native speakers' language aptitude level.

Evidence from response-time data further indicated that, when given the opportunity to consciously reflect on language in a self-paced test, L2 speakers delayed their responses to a greater extent than native speakers (around 4 seconds on average vs. 1 second on average in the auditory GJT). Also, while native speakers were faster in the written than in the auditory GJT, the reverse pattern was observed among L2 speakers. Considering that the phonological route to meaning in L1 processing is slower than the visual route (Forster 1990; see also Murphy 1997, for empirical findings with native speakers), these results show that, when native speakers were in control of the stimulus, they were faster to react to sentence grammaticality, while L2 speakers used more time to think.

The aptitude-testing interaction found in the present study suggests that the relationship between language aptitude and variation in adult L2 learners' ultimate morphosyntactic attainment may be more complex than claimed in the SLA literature by studies where aptitude has been investigated in single-task designs (e.g. Abrahamsson & Hyltenstam 2008; DeKeyser 2000; DeKeyser et al. 2010). A relevant factor to take into account seems to be the extent to which the L2 measure allows time for participants to make controlled use of their L2 knowledge and monitor their performance. This factor was especially relevant in the case of high-aptitude individuals, whose performance improved considerably under untimed test conditions. The proposed explanation is that under those conditions, high-aptitude participants were able to use the same analytical, metalinguistic abilities that the language aptitude test measured (see Long 2007, p. 73, Footnote 9, for a similar explanation of DeKeyser's findings). Although the auditory GJT also focused participants' attention on language correctness and measured the same target language structures, the correlation between language aptitude and auditory GJT scores was weak and non-significant. In addition, there were no significant differences between high- and low-aptitude participants in this modality. This seems to be due to the fact that, unlike the written GJT, the auditory GJT administered in the present study required online processing that minimized monitoring, even if this cannot be totally discarded.

These results are consistent with those in Granena and Long (2013), and, together, provide converging evidence from two different L1 populations (English and Chinese) of the lack of a relationship between language aptitude, as measured by an omnibus test largely based on the MLAT, and ultimate morphosyntactic attainment, as measured by an auditory GJT, in adult learners. In fact, contrary to DeKeyser's (2000) prediction, the participant with the highest auditory GJT score in the present study was identified as a low-aptitude individual. She was an adult acquirer with a length of residence of 30 years who had arrived in Spain when she was 19 and who reported having started learning Spanish at university at the age of 18.

These findings also run counter to those of similar studies that have reported a relationship between aptitude and adult L2 learners' ultimate attainment in naturalistic learning settings (Abrahamsson & Hyltenstam 2008; DeKeyser 2000; DeKeyser et al. 2010). One possible explanation would be that, even though all of those studies measured ultimate attainment with a GJT, they relied on formats or conditions of test administration that allowed learners time to reflect on language correctness and make use of metalinguistic abilities. Abrahamsson and Hyltenstam (2008) combined the scores of a written and an auditory GJT, while DeKeyser (2000) and DeKeyser et al. (2010) presented test items twice in auditory format. A relevant question is what type of GJT, if any, provides a more valid measure of L2 attainment. The answer can vary depending on how linguistic competence is defined. If defined as knowledge that is available in spontaneous language use (Ellis 2005), online test conditions, where performance takes place in real time, should provide a more valid measure of L2 attainment.

Hypothesis 2 predicted a relationship between language aptitude and scores on test items that included complex sentences, holding test modality constant. This hypothesis was not borne out by the data. There was no interaction between sentence complexity and language aptitude as a covariate in either group. Complexity did not interact with test modality, either. Although no interaction was found between aptitude and sentence complexity, findings revealed a main effect for complexity in both speaker groups. Performance was significantly more accurate on simple than complex items. This was probably the result of processing-related factors, such as the greater information load of complex items or the lower salience of errors in complex sentences. While the triggering factor is unclear, the results of the study showed that the significant decrease in accuracy on complex items in the two speaker groups was unrelated to individual differences in aptitude.

Processing-related factors may also account for the main modality effect in the native-speaker group. Native speakers' scores on the auditory GJT were 5.2 lower on average than on the written GJT, a difference of roughly 4% (i.e. average accuracy was 92.60% in the auditory and 96.66% in the written). Similar results were reported by Loewen (2009) in a study investigating the effects of time pressure (timed vs. untimed) and task stimulus (grammatical vs. ungrammatical) on GJT performance. While native speakers had an average accuracy score of 96% on the untimed GJT, their average score on the timed GJT dropped to almost 80%. Loewen concluded that the speeded nature of the test seemed to decrease scores independently of participants' amount of implicit knowledge, and that this potentially irrelevant variability in the construct would need further research. The present study can further add that the nature of the test seems to decrease scores independently of participants' language aptitude level. While processing demands resulted in lower test scores on complex items and auditory items in the two groups of speakers (L2 speakers and native speakers), variability in these scores was unrelated to individual differences in language aptitude.

7.   Conclusion

The aim of the present study was to explore the relationship between language aptitude, test modality and sentence complexity in adult L2 learners' ultimate attainment. The findings demonstrated an interaction between language aptitude and test modality (auditory GJT vs. untimed written GJT) among L2 speakers, holding all other factors constant (i.e. target structure, number of items, sentence complexity), but not among native speakers. These results were interpreted as indicating a positive association between scores on language aptitude tests and language tests that allow participants time to reflect on language correctness and language structure. No evidence was found of an interaction between language aptitude and sentence complexity.

8.   Further research

The results of this study, and of any study investigating aptitude, depend on how the construct of language aptitude is operationalized and measured. They also depend on the sample of participants studied, since high-, mid-, and low-aptitude groups are sample-dependent. It is an empirical question whether other language aptitude test batteries, e.g. Hi-Lab (Doughty et al. 2007) would yield the same results found in this study. The aptitude test used here was the LLAMA (Meara 2005), which is partly based on Carroll and Sapon's (1959) operationalization of aptitude, even though it also includes new components, such as the ability to recognize sound patterns. Aptitude was operationalized as a composite of the four abilities measured by the LLAMA. Further research should address the role of different aptitude components and individual L2 aptitude profiles in naturalistic learning contexts, following the multi-faceted nature of aptitude suggested in the literature (e.g. Skehan 1998, 2002). Research on the role of aptitude for implicit language learning could be especially relevant in this respect. In addition to multiple cognitive aptitudes, further research should also consider the inclusion of multiple L2 measures to better understand how aptitude relates to variation in L2 proficiency.

Finally, the results reported in this study provide a partial picture of the role of language aptitude in ultimate morphosyntactic attainment, since the study only included adult L2 learners. Further research with both early and late acquirers is warranted.

References

Abrahamsson, N., & Hyltenstam, K. (2008). The robustness of aptitude effects in near-native second language acquisition. *Studies in Second Language Acquisition, 30*, 481–509.

Abrahamsson, N., & Hyltenstam, K. (2009). Age of onset and nativelikeness in a second language: Listener perception versus linguistic scrutiny. *Language Learning, 59*, 249–306.

Bley-Vroman, R. (1988). The fundamental character of foreign language learning. In W. Rutherford, & M. Sharwood Smith (Eds.), *Grammar and second language teaching: A book of readings* (pp. 133–159). Rowley, MA: Newbury House.

Bylund, E., Abrahamsson, N., & Hyltenstam, K. (2010). The role of language aptitude in first language attrition: The case of pre-pubescent attriters. *Applied Linguistics, 31*, 443–464.

Carroll, J.B. (1981). Twenty-five years of research in foreign language aptitude. In K. Diller (Ed.), *Individual differences and universals in language learning aptitude* (pp. 83–118). Rowley, MA: Newbury House.

Carroll, J.B. (1993). *Human cognitive abilities: A survey of factor-analytic studies.* Cambridge: CUP.

Carroll, J.B., & Sapon, S. (1959). *Modern language aptitude test: Form A.* New York, NY: Psychological Corporation.

Cedrus. (2003). *SuperLab* 3.0.7. San Pedro, CA: Author.

De Graaff, R. (1997). The Esperanto experiment: Effects of explicit instruction on second language acquisition. *Studies in Second Language Acquisition, 19*, 249–276.

De Jong, N. (2005). Can second language grammar be learned through listening? An experimental study. *Studies in Second Language Acquisition, 27*, 205–234.

DeKeyser, R.M. (2000). The robustness of critical period effects in second language acquisition. *Studies in Second Language Acquisition, 22*, 499–533.

DeKeyser, R.M., Alfi-Shabtay, I., & Ravid, D. (2010). Cross-linguistic evidence for the nature of age-effects in second language acquisition. *Applied Psycholinguistics, 31*, 413–438.

Doughty, C., Bunting, M., Campbell, S., Bowles, A., & Haarmann, H. (2007). *Development of the High-Level Language Aptitude Battery.* Technical Report: Center for Advanced Study of Language. University of Maryland, College Park.

Ehrman, M.E., & Oxford, R.L. (1995). Cognition plus: Correlates of language learning success. *Modern Language Journal, 79*, 67–89.

Ellis, R. (2005). Measuring implicit and explicit knowledge of a second language. A psychometric study. *Studies in Second Language Acquisition, 27*, 141–172.

Ellis, R. (2009). Measuring implicit and explicit knowledge of a second language. In R. Ellis, S. Loewen, C. Elder, R. Erlam, J. Philp, & H. Reinders (Eds.), *Implicit and explicit knowledge in second language learning, testing and teaching* (pp. 31–64). Bristol, UK: Multilingual Matters.

Erlam, R. (2005). Language aptitude and its relationship to instructional effectiveness in second language acquisition. *Language Teaching Research, 9*, 147–171.

Forster, K.I. (1990). Lexical processing. In D.N. Osherson, & H. Lasnik (Eds.), *An invitation to cognitive science: Language. Vol. 1* (pp. 95–131). Cambridge, MA: The MIT Press.

Granena, G. (this volume). Cognitive aptitudes for second language learning and the LLAMA Language Aptitude Test.

Granena, G., & Long, M.H. (2013). Age of onset, length of residence, language aptitude, and ultimate L2 attainment in three linguistic domains. *Second Language Research, 29*(1).

Harley, B., & Hart, D. (1997). Language aptitude and second language proficiency in classroom learners of different starting ages. *Studies in Second Language Acquisition, 19,* 379–400.

Harley, B., & Hart, D. (2002). Age, aptitude, and second language learning on a bilingual exchange. In P. Robinson (Ed.), *Individual differences and instructed language learning* (pp. 302–330). Amsterdam: John Benjamins.

Ioup, G., Boustagui, E., El Tigi, M., & Moselle, M. (1994). Reexamining the critical period hypothesis: A case study of successful adult SLA in a naturalistic environment. *Studies in Second Language Acquisition, 16,* 73–98.

Loewen, S. (2009). Grammaticality judgment tests and the measurement of implicit and explicit L2 knowledge. In R. Ellis, S. Loewen, C. Elder, R. Erlam, J. Philp, & H. Reinders (Eds.), *Implicit and explicit knowledge in second language learning, testing and teaching* (pp. 94–112). Bristol: Multilingual Matters.

Long, M.H. (2005). Problems with supposed counter-evidence to the critical period hypothesis. *IRAL, 43,* 287–317.

Long, M.H. (2007). *Problems in SLA.* Mahwah, NJ: Lawrence Erlbaum Associates.

McDonald, J.L. (2000). Grammaticality judgments in a second language: Influences of age of acquisition and native language. *Applied Psycholinguistics, 21,* 395–423.

McDonald, J.L. (2006). Beyond the critical period: Processing-based explanations for poor grammaticality judgment performance by late second language learners. *Journal of Memory and Language, 55,* 381–401.

Meara, P. (2005). *LLAMA language aptitude tests.* Swansea, UK: Lognostics.

Meara, P., Milton, J., & Lorenzo-Dus, N. (2003). *Swansea language aptitude tests (LAT) v.2.0.* Swansea, UK: Lognostics.

Montrul, S. (2005). On knowledge and development of unaccusativity in Spanish L2. *Linguistics, 43,* 1153–1190.

Murphy, V.A. (1997). The effect of modality on grammaticality judgment task. *Second Language Research, 13,* 34–65.

Novoa, L.K., Fein, D., & Obler, L. (1988). Talent in foreign languages: A case study. In L.K. Obler, & D. Fein (Eds.), *The exceptional brain: Neuropsychology of talent and special abilities* (pp. 294–302). New York, NY: Guilford Press.

Robinson, P. (1997). Individual differences and the fundamental similarity of implicit and explicit adult second language learning. *Language Learning, 47,* 45–99.

Robinson, P. (2002). Individual differences in intelligence, aptitude and working memory during adult incidental second language learning: A replication and extension of Reber, Walkenfeld, and Hernstadt (1991). In P. Robinson (Ed.), *Individual differences and instructed language learning* (pp. 211–266). Amsterdam: John Benjamins.

Sheen, Y. (2007). The effect of focused written corrective feedback and language aptitude on ESL learners' acquisition of articles. *TESOL Quarterly, 41,* 255–283.

Skehan, P. (1986). Cluster analysis and the identification of learner types. In V. Cook (Ed.), *Experimental approaches to second language acquisition* (pp. 81–94). Oxford: Pergamon.

Skehan, P. (1989). *Individual differences in second language learning.* London: Arnold.

Skehan, P. (1990). The relationship between native and foreign language learning ability: Educational and linguistic factors. In H. Dechert (Ed.), *Current trends in European second language acquisition research* (pp. 83–106). Clevedon: Multilingual Matters.

Skehan, P. (1998). *A cognitive approach to learning language.* Oxford: OUP.

Skehan, P. (2002). Theorizing and updating aptitude. In P. Robinson (Ed.), *Individual differences and instructed language learning* (pp. 69–93). Amsterdam: John Benjamins.

Toth, P. (2006). Processing instruction and a role for output in second language acquisition. *Language Learning, 56,* 319–385.

Wells, C. (1985). *Language, learning and education: Selected papers from the Bristol study, language at home and at school.* Philadelphia: Windsor.

Wesche, M.B. (1981). Language aptitude measures in streaming, matching students with methods, and diagnosis of learning problems. In K.C. Diller (Ed.), *Individual differences and universals in language learning aptitude* (pp. 119–154). Rowley, MA: Newbury House.

Williams, J.N. (1999). Memory, attention, and inductive learning. *Studies in Second Language Acquisition, 21,* 1–48.

Wolfe-Quintero, K., Inagaki, S., & Kim, H.-Y. (1998). *Second language development in writing: Measures of fluency, accuracy, and complexity.* Honolulu: Second Language Teaching and Curriculum Center, University of Hawai'i.

Appendix

Eight examples, out of 256 grammaticality judgment items, grouped by structure and sentence complexity type. Target structures are underlined, and for the ungrammatical items, the correct structure is given in brackets.

1. Noun-adjective gender agreement
   1.1. Simple
      (a) *El uso de energía en los países más pobres seguirá siendo <u>mínimo</u>.*
           "Energy use in the poorest countries will continue to be <u>minimum</u>."
   1.2. Complex
      (a) **La organización de los campeonatos de Europa de atletismo no va a ser <u>sencillo</u> [sencilla] debido a las amenazas de un atentado terrorista.*
           "The organization of the European Athletics Championships will not be <u>easy</u> due to the threats of a terrorist attack."
2. Noun-adjective number agreement
   2.1. Simple
      (a) **Los escaladores subían por la pared del pico <u>ayudado</u> [ayudados] por una cuerda.*
           "The climbers climbed up the wall of the mountain peak <u>with the help of</u> a rope."
   2.2. Complex
      (a) *Los jugadores abandonaron el terreno de juego <u>abatidos</u> por la derrota que acababan de sufrir contra el equipo de Brasil.*
           "The players left the soccer field <u>devastated</u> by the defeat they had just suffered against Brazil's team."

3. Passives with *ser* and *estar*
    3.1. Simple
          (a) *El cuadro más conocido de Velázquez <u>fue</u> pintado en el 1615.*
               "The most famous painting by Velázquez <u>was</u> painted in 1615."
    3.2. Complex
          (a) **Cada día cientos de animales abandonados <u>están</u> [son] adoptados por familias que quieren acogerlos de manera desinteresada.*
               "Everyday hundreds of abandoned animals <u>are</u> adopted by families willing to give them a home unselfishly."
4. Verbal clitics
    4.1. Simple
          (a) **La empresa <u>ha distinguido</u> [se ha distinguido] por su elevada productividad.*
               "The company <u>is characterized</u> by its high productivity."
    4.2. Complex
          (a) *La tasa del paro <u>se ha reducido</u> aproximadamente a la mitad después de que el gobierno incentivara los empleos temporales entre los inmigrantes.*
               "The unemployment rate <u>has decreased</u> approximately by half after the Government promoted temporary jobs among immigrants."

Memory-based aptitude for nativelike selection

The role of phonological short-term memory

Cylcia Bolibaugh & Pauline Foster
St. Mary's University College

Native speaker competence includes not only grammatical knowledge but also knowledge of communal and conventional word combinations, or nativelike selections. Although all speakers are idiomatic in their L1, very few, even in immersion contexts, are as successful in their L2. This chapter presents the results of a study investigating the receptive nativelike selection ability of adult onset L2 users with long residence in the target language community, and investigates the influence of exposure, phonological short term memory (pSTM) and disposition towards interaction. We suggest that L2 users do accrue information about conventional word combinations through exposure, and that individual differences in pSTM limit both rate of learning and ultimate attainment. Crucially, these influences depend both on the context of learning and age of onset of the learner.

It is generally agreed that language learning aptitude confers an advantage on some individuals which allows them to reach near-native levels of second language (L2) proficiency, despite the disadvantage of a late start. Although more recent studies of ultimate attainment have been remarkably comprehensive in their assessment of different facets of L2 ability (e.g. Abrahamsson & Hyltenstam 2008), the discussion of the relationship between aptitude and L2 attainment remains one largely framed by the concerns and constructs of the seminal study by DeKeyser (2000). In this view, high levels of verbal analytic ability are proposed to enable some learners to attain near-native command of the morphosyntax of language through conscious reflection on its structure. Relatively few critical or sensitive period studies have treated aptitude as a construct whose components differentially mediate dimensions of second language ability other than grammatical competence. One dimension which has been particularly overlooked in this regard is L2 learners' capacity to master idiomaticity, i.e. the ability to determine which combination of words are used by the L2 speech community and which are not. A small number of recent studies (Foster, Bolibaugh & Kotula in press; Granena & Long 2013; Spadaro this volume) have found that idiomaticity as indexed by various measures is subject to sensitive period effects: child learners in immersion situations have different outcomes from adult learners. While aptitude has traditionally been measured by established batteries, such as the MLAT and PLAB, and more recently LLAMA, these do not measure all cognitive abilities likely to influence language learning. In this chapter, we present the theoretically motivated proposal that phonological short term memory (pSTM) influences both the rate of learning and ultimate attainment of adult onset L2 users.

Building on our previous findings (Foster et al. in press) of a discontinuity in incidence of nativelikeness at age 12 for immersed L2 learners, and of different patterns of association for pSTM and idiomaticity depending on language learning context, the present study investigates whether long exposure in the target language community enables *adult onset* L2 users to approximate native speaker behaviour in the identification of non-nativelike combinations of words. In addition to measuring participants' ultimate attainment, we also estimate the relative contributions of amount of interaction within the target language (TL) community, pSTM, and motivation to interact with native speakers. We then present our findings in the context of our earlier work to illustrate the complex relationship between language proficiency, individual differences in cognitive abilities, context of learning and age of onset.

1. Background

1.1 Nativelike selection

As we note above, native speaker competence encompasses not only grammatical knowledge, but also knowledge of the word combinations that are communal and conventional (Altenberg 1990; Becker 1976; Erman & Warren 2000; Forsberg 2008, 2010; Foster 2001; Howarth 1998; Nattinger & deCarrico 1992; Sinclair 1991; Warren 2005; Weinert 1995). Pawley and Syder (1983) use the term 'nativelike selection' to describe these: a speech community's favoured compound nouns, verb-noun collocations, prepositional phrases, sentence stems, phrasal verbs, metaphors, sayings, quotations, exclamations, curses and the like. They range from the fully fixed locutions (*never mind, don't mention it, come to think of it, as daft as a brush*) through almost fully fixed locutions (*you/they/he/she cannot be serious, what's the matter with NP*) to simple collocations (*monumental error, low cost, far-flung*) and pre-fabricated sentence stems with embedded open-choice items (*NP be-TENSE sorry to keep-TENSE NP waiting, it's more a question of NP than of NP*). In 1976 and in contrast to the infinite novelty of expression implied by the then prevailing generative model of language, Becker depicted language production as largely a process of cobbling together such chunks inside an over-arching grammatical frame:

> We start with the information that we wish to convey and the attitude towards that information that we wish to express or evoke, and we haul out of our phrasal lexicon some patterns that can provide the major elements of this expression.....
> Then the problem is to stitch these phrases together into something roughly grammatical, to fill in the blanks with the particulars of the case at hand, to modify the phrases if need be, and if all else fails to generate phrases from scratch to smooth over the transitions or fill in any remaining conceptual holes.
>
> (1976:8)

Becker acknowledges that speakers can, whenever necessary, come up with novel combinations of words to express their meanings, but that this is a fallback position. The important point is that when they are generated, novel combinations are marked; listeners/readers recognise that they have no entry for them in memory. Of course, such novelties can be understood as deliberately and successfully creative and are thus candidates for inclusion into the communal way of expressing meaning. To take just one example, someone must once have coined the expression *on cloud nine* to express feelings of great elation. It was taken up by others, and now it is a nativelike selection in the phrasal lexicon of millions of people.

It is not possible to enumerate how many combinations of words a speaker might hold in memory but given that a vocabulary of 20,000 word families has been suggested as likely (Nation & Waring 1997) then the nativelike combinations of the various inflectional and derivational forms of these must run into the hundreds of thousands. Their pervasiveness in spoken and written language – in some estimates it makes up over 50% of use (Altenberg 1990) and perhaps even as much as 80% (Wray 2000) – is evidence of the way first languages are acquired. Children form their linguistic preferences incidentally and implicitly by dint of prolonged exposure to the linguistic choices of others around them. In the case of an L2, we would argue that it is highly unlikely an advanced command of many thousands of nativelike selections could be acquired deliberately, through conscious analysis or piece-meal memorization. Rather, it is more likely that this too is gained incidentally, and possibly implicitly, through "participatory experience [...] in social contexts" (Robinson & Ellis 2008:490).

1.2 Usage based models of language

Nativelike selections can usefully be explored through language models which attempt to account for both the productivity of the language faculty and the constraints evident in language use. Cognitive, constructivist and usage-based models (e.g. Barlow & Kemmer 2000; Bybee 1995; Goldberg 1999, 2006; Langacker 2000) share two assumptions which underpin an understanding of nativelike selections. The first is that language *knowledge* resides in a maximalist and redundant mental inventory of form-meaning pairings which vary in complexity and abstractness (Langacker 1988). The complexity continuum allows for pairings which range from morphemes up to complete utterances, while the abstractness continuum encompasses expressions which can be fully specified, fully abstract or something in between. As form-meaning pairings, nativelike selections are unremarkable inhabitants of such a 'constructicon' (Jurafsky 1996). The second shared assumption of usage-based theories is that, as we have noted above, language *learning* is exemplar based and socially situated. Communally preferred ways of describing recurrent pieces of reality arise as hearers become speakers and model what they say on what they have heard. In this view therefore, language learning is a by-product of the experience of understanding and producing language. The process is incremental and guided by general cognitive mechanisms of perception, memory and categorisation (Langacker 2000). Ellis (e.g. 1996, 2001, 2002, 2006) has been one of the strongest advocates of this type of verbal associative learning. He describes separable processes for the acquisition of word form and meaning, arguing that the largely implicit abstraction of phonological, word class and collocational properties from repeated exposure creates a robust 'label' which is then available to be linked to a given context, meaning or function (1994, 2001). He further argues that multi-word sequences undergo the same processes: "frequent collocations, phrases, and idioms […] can simply be viewed as big words – the role of WM in learning such structures is the same" (2001:46).

The bottom-up orientation of associative learning means that the first step in construction learning is the encoding of individual utterances. Working memory, and pSTM specifically, are key to this process as the 'window on the evidence' (Ellis & Schmidt 1997:159). In order for a chunk to be created, or for constituent parts of an utterance to become associated in long term memory, these must be held in mind, in phonological short term memory (pSTM). There is a large body of evidence linking pSTM, as described by the phonological loop architecture of Baddeley and colleagues' working memory model (Baddeley & Hitch 1974), to acquisition of word forms in vocabulary development. The relationship has been documented in children acquiring their L1 (e.g. Gathercole, Willis, Emslie & Baddeley 1992), in children learning an L2 (e.g. Service & Kohonen 1995), as well as in adults learning an L2 (e.g. Papagno & Vallar 1992). For recent reviews relating pSTM functioning to SLA more generally see French and O'Brien (2008), Hummel (2009), and Kormos (this volume).

PSTM has traditionally been indexed by serial recall measures, such as word and digit spans, and more recently, by non-word repetition tasks. Why do these tasks consistently predict language learning gains? Experimental evidence and connectionist modelling (e.g. Gupta 2003; Page & Norris 2009; Service, Maury & Luotoniemi 2007) suggest a mechanism which relies upon the quality of a short-term representation operating in concert with a domain-general learning mechanism, often referred to as the Hebb effect. These proposals echo Melton's early theorising that the link between initial encoding and long-term representation arises because short- and long-term memory are:

> mediated by a single type of storage mechanism. In such a continuum, frequency of repetition appears to be the important independent variable, "chunking" appears to be the important intervening variable, and the slope of the retention curve is the important dependent variable. (Melton 1963: 19)

In other words, the more often a lexical selection is encountered, the stronger its representation. Speakers have sufficient experience in most domains of their native language for the retention curve mentioned by Melton to reach asymptote and for the effects of individual differences in chunking ability to be mitigated. The question under investigation in this study is whether second language users living within the target language community accrue information about the lexical patterning of their L2 through experience in the same way as native speakers. If so, their 'retention' as gauged by an index of receptive nativelike selection knowledge, should be a function of 'frequency of repetition' as gauged by a measure of their exposure to the TL community, and individual differences in chunking ability.

Given the number of studies which have demonstrated the importance of pSTM in single word learning, and the currency of theories ascribing formulaicity to entrenchment through exposure, it is surprising that there is little direct evidence of the proposition that knowledge of nativelike selections in an L2 is limited by a combination of the two. Here, we review the evidence linking exposure and pSTM to nativelike selections in the broad sense, including collocations, idioms and other forms of conventional combinations.

1.3 Studies investigating the influence of exposure and pSTM on idiomaticity

Two studies, one experimental and one observational, have directly investigated the link between pSTM and formulaic language competence. In the first, Ellis and Sinclair (1996) investigated the ab-initio learning of Welsh in three (laboratory-based) conditions: articulatory suppression (preventing use of the phonological loop), rehearsal (repetition within the phonological loop) and control with no instruction. Learners were consistently worse in remembering the forms of Welsh words and phrases in the articulatory suppression condition, and consistently better in the forced rehearsal condition. In the second study, Skzrypek (2009) investigated the relationship between pSTM and gains in collocational knowledge made by L2 immigrants in Ireland over a six-month English language course. Measures of nonword serial recall and recognition not only predicted gains in discrete vocabulary items, but also accounted for large amounts of variance in collocational gains (30% in elementary learners, and 26% in lower intermediate learners).

Both of the above studies investigated the early stages of learning. Given evidence of declining involvement of the phonological loop in vocabulary learning at higher levels of proficiency (Gathercole 2006), an important question is whether pSTM continues to support the acquisition of a store of nativelike selections in more proficient learners. Recent studies by Granena (this volume) have found associations in advanced learners between measures of lexis and collocation and aptitude measures likely to draw on the phonological loop, including the sound recognition subtest of the LLAMA (an index of incidental phonological learning, or the Hebb effect), sound-symbol association and phonetic coding. This is suggestive of a continued effect for pSTM across proficiency levels. Only our previous study (Foster et al. discussed below) has explored pSTM's role as a possible limiter on ultimate attainment.

Higher levels of proficiency necessitate long periods of exposure. As Ellis puts it, "nativelike idiomaticity takes an awful lot of figuring out which words go together" (2002: 157). If the benefits of exposure are based on the cumulative effects of individual 'usage events', there must be evidence of the retention and recycling of individual instances. Gurevich, Johnson and Goldberg (2010) have recently demonstrated that speakers in their L1 retain detailed memory of utterances they have heard only once, in naturalistic contexts where they are not alerted to any memory tests, and tend to reuse exact clauses up to 10 days after a single exposure. Wray (2002) has argued that it is this ability to incidentally encode exact surface information about utterances which distinguishes L1 child learners from L2 learners. However, in an experimental investigation of her claim that adult L2 learners notice individual words rather than meaningful chunks, Durrant and Schmitt (2010) found that L2 learners do in fact retain information about collocations they are exposed to even a single time. This finding leads them to conclude that it is lack of exposure rather than difference in processing which is responsible for most second language learners' inadequate collocational knowledge.

There is more evidence as to the benefits of cumulative exposure on the acquisition of nativelike selection ability. In a cross-sectional developmental study, Forsberg (2008, 2010) investigated the quantity and distribution of conventional sequence use in learners of varying proficiency with differing amounts of exposure. She found that lexical sequences, that is, sequences containing at least one content word (ranging from *avoir peur*, to NP *mettre* NP *au courant*) presented the greatest challenge to learners and only underwent significant development after an extended period of residence in the L2 community. Considering conventional expressions as a pragmatic resource for study abroad learners, Bardovi-Harlig and Bastos (2011) investigated how their recognition and production related to length of stay and what they termed 'intensity' of interaction: the amount of time learners spent speaking English and watching English television. Only intensity of interaction was found to have a significant relationship with increased recognition of conventional expressions *and* rejections of unconventional ones.

Bardovi-Harlig and Bastos' finding that intensity of interaction outweighed length of stay in the recognition and production of conventional expressions highlights the fact that not all L2 users avail themselves of the contact opportunities available in the TL community, and that measures of exposure such as length of stay or length of residence mask a variety of experiences. This was illustrated in a series of studies by Schmitt and colleagues. Schmitt, Dörnyei, Adolphs and Durow (2004) investigated foreign students' acquisition of a set of formulaic sequences over the course of a two- to three-month pre-sessional course at a university in the UK. Finding no linear associations between gains and individual differences in motivation or aptitude, the authors undertook case studies of the most and least successful learners (Dörnyei, Durow & Zahran 2004). Success or failure seemed to depend on learners' determination to seek interaction outside their own language group, "that is whether they [could] break out of the 'international ghetto' they [found] themselves in" (2004: 15). Thus the exposure relationship is crucial, but more complex than it appears at first sight. Interaction with members of the TL community seems to be key, and L2 users within the TL community can be more or less willing or able to exploit those opportunities which exist.

To sum up, previous studies have found effects for pSTM on the development of phrasal and collocational knowledge at the ab-initio, elementary and lower intermediate levels in laboratory and ESOL classroom settings, while effects of exposure have been documented in advanced level use of conventional word combinations, and recognition of conventional pragmatic expressions. These findings are suggestive of an L2 learning process similar to that operational in L1. What is missing from this picture is a test of learners' ultimate attainment after many years of exposure. To our knowledge there has been only one study which has investigated the joint effects of exposure and pSTM on advanced level learners' intuitions about nativelike selections (hereafter NLS) in relation to their age of onset and context of exposure.

In a previous study (Foster et al.), we explored how exposure, memory and motivation influenced NLS ability in L2 users with differing ages of onset and contexts of learning. We recruited 80 high-level L2 users whose first language was

Polish. Half (N = 40) lived in the TL community (London) while the other half lived in Poland but still made extensive daily use of English for work or other purposes. As expected, Age of Onset (AoO) and context of learning exerted the greatest influences. L2 users in London detected significantly more non-nativelike selections in a given text than L2 users in Poland, and both groups were less successful at detecting them than native speaker controls, even after quite long mean lengths of residence or exposure. With two exceptions, only those learners who had immigrated to the TL community before age 12 were able to detect non nativelike selections to the same extent as native speakers. The two exceptions had pSTM scores 1.4 and 1.6 standard deviations above the mean. One other main finding is relevant here: patterns of association between exposure pSTM and NLS scores were quite different for L2 users within and outside the TL community. For L2 users in London, exposure as measured by Length of Residence (LoR) and pSTM explained a small to moderate amount of variance in addition to Age of Onset in the whole group. In the subset of learners who started after age 12 however, pSTM was found to be the only significant predictor of NLS ability (r = .54, p < .01). Additionally, including pSTM and LoR jointly in a regression model resulted in larger and more significant estimations of their relationship to NLS scores than considering them singly in bivariate correlations. This relationship of reciprocal suppression (Lutz 1983, Tzelgov & Henik 1991) indicates that pSTM accounts for a portion of the 'noise,' or unsystematic variance, in the relationship between exposure and NLS scores, and that the converse is also true. No evidence of such relationships was found for L2 users living outside the TL community. For L2 users in Poland, there was no association between pSTM and NLS scores in either the whole group, or in the subgroup that started after age 12, and this lack of association held when controlling for length of exposure.

These results led us to suggest that L2 users in the TL community did incidentally accrue information about nativelike selections through use, while the mechanism for learners outside the TL community was less certain. We were cautious in this interpretation however, due to the potential confound in our study with age at testing (Age). In all studies of this design, AoO, LoR and Age are linearly dependent; knowing two of the points will give you the third. This precludes their being examined concurrently in any correlational or regression type analysis (Stevens 2006). In our London group, Age was highly positively correlated with LoR and negatively associated with pSTM. Thus, another possible interpretation of our results is that controlling pSTM increases the size and significance of the relationship between LoR and NLS scores because it is controlling (life-stage or cognitive) age-related variance. Similarly, LoR could be acting as a proxy for Age in the estimation of the relationship between pSTM and NLS scores.

2.   The present study

2.1   Aims

The findings from Foster et al. suggest that pSTM is strongly implicated in adult onset NLS ability and that this association mediates gains engendered by residence in the TL community. In order to more reliably estimate the size and nature of these relationships, we repeated our investigation of the ability to detect non-nativelike selections in a second, more homogeneous group of participants living within the TL community. Through sampling criteria, we sought to minimise the influence of the variables with largest effects from our first study (AoO and context of learning) and physically control for multi-collinearity between age at testing on the one hand, and biographical and cognitive variables on the other. We also took a finer grained approach to the measurement of exposure within the TL community, wishing to document both the contact participants experienced and the value they placed on seeking such contact. Therefore, our research questions concern both the attainment of L2 users and the relative influence of predictor variables on that attainment: the richness of interaction within the TL community, the value they place on such interaction, and their pSTM. In addition to the individual influence of these predictors, we also wished to see whether the suppressing relationship between exposure and pSTM found in our earlier study is evident in the absence of the age at testing confound.

2.2   Research questions

1.   To what extent do L2 users with a minimum of 10 years' residence in the TL community converge on native speaker behaviour in identifying non-nativelike selections in text?
2.   To what extent is the ability to designate non-nativelike selections related to:
     a.   an L2 user's richness of interaction in the TL community
     b.   an L2 user's pSTM
     c.   an L2 user's valuation of the importance of interacting with native speakers (NSs)?
3.   To what extent do the predictor variables mediate or suppress variance in the relationship between the other predictors and NLS scores?

2.3   Participants

Two groups of participants were recruited (descriptive statistics are given in Table 1). The first comprised 33 Polish L1 immigrants to the UK who had arrived after age 18 and had had their earliest significant exposure to English no earlier

Table 1. Descriptive statistics for biographical variables

	Polish in UK			Native Speakers		
	M	*SD*	*N*	*M*	*SD*	*N*
Age at testing (Age)	37.15	5.65	33	37.06	12.57	30
Years of Schooling (YrsSch)	15.82	2.04	31	16.22	2.77	30
Age of Onset (AoO)	23.88	5.50	33			
Age of Arrival (AoA)	25.18	5.22	33			
Length of Residence (LoR)	12.27	3.25	33			
Years Studying English before Arrival (YrsEng)	1.12	2.01	33			
Gender	24F	9M		17F	13M	

than 13. These were found with the help of a native Polish-speaking research assistant via announcements in small ads and community centres in West London. A payment was made to each NNS participant for their time. Twenty-four of these were female and nine male. Minimum LoR for non-native speakers (NNSs) was 10 years and all participants were under 50 at time of testing. Participants were screened for hearing difficulties, reading difficulties, such as dyslexia, and exposure to Arabic (see below). All the NNSs were highly functioning, daily users of English, assessed by a linguistically trained research assistant as at minimum B2/C1 level on the Common European Framework.

The second group was made up of 30 monolingual, native speakers of the southern British variety of English. These provided a baseline for the native-like selection task, and therefore only completed this task and a biographical questionnaire. The native speaker group's age range was slightly wider than the NNS', and was more evenly distributed between male and female (17 female and 13 male). Participants were well matched for years of education, although NNS tended to be working in less professionally qualified positions than NS with equivalent YrsSch. Native speaker participants were recruited by the authors and were not paid.

2.4 Tasks

2.4.1 Nativelike selection task

Following Foster et al. (in press), knowledge of nativelike selections was measured as participants' ability to detect *non-native* selections embedded in a text. As Warren (2005) puts it, "The real stumbling blocks for the non-native speaker are expressions which are condoned by the grammar and the standard meanings of words but which nevertheless are not used by native speakers" (p. 39). There is evidence that in a speaker's L1, such (over-) generalisations are constrained by means of indirect negative evidence provided by consistently witnessing a semantically and pragmatically equivalent formulation in place of one which might be expected in a similar context (Boyd & Goldberg 2011; Brooks & Tomasello 1999; Goldberg 2006). In other words, native speakers have had repeated experience of a particular context without ever hearing a particular cotext. Thus, a grammatical, yet novel, formulation, such as *It's six less twenty*, is marked in comparison to the conventional *It's twenty to six*.

The task in this study comprised five short texts in which a speaker described a film they had recently seen. The texts were constructed from transcripts of non-native speakers responding to a set task (talking about a film or play) in the Louvain International Database of Spoken English Interlanguage (LINDSEI). The LINDSEI corpus contains transcriptions of upper-intermediate to advanced learners from 11 countries performing the same spoken tasks during informal interviews. Three speakers per national subcorpus (with the exception of the Polish subcorpus) were randomly chosen and all non-native selections manually identified. We then reduced the list to those mis-selections which differed at a single point from a clear native speaker equivalent. These were then reinserted into texts which had been corrected for grammatical errors, and whose spoken features (hesitations, filled pauses, etc.) had been removed. The final texts (see Appendix) were trialled with five native speakers, who identified 28 non-nativelike selections. Feedback from trialling also led us to further remove some spoken features remaining in the text, such as clause chaining. An example from the first text, a description of the film *In the Name of the Father*, follows with non-nativelike selections underlined: "I was really impressed by this film, which is actually a <u>realist story.</u> It's about four men who go to prison for bombing a pub in London (when really the <u>crime was performed</u> by a terrorist)."

In the actual study, participants were instructed to read the texts carefully to themselves and underline anything (words or phrases) which sounded odd or unnatural. They were assured that there were no grammatical, spelling, or punctuation mistakes. As a final criterion, they were told that if they were unsure as to the 'oddness' of a word/phrase, they should ask themselves whether they would choose those words to express that particular meaning. They were given three examples with obvious non-nativelike selections to make the nature of the task clear. NNS participants were given the instructions and examples to read in English. These were then explained again in Polish by the Polish native speaker research assistant. Native speaker participants were given the instructions to read in English, followed by an explanation in English. Following DeKeyser (2000), only incorrect items were scored: participants were given one point for each correctly identified mis-selection, with a possible total of 28. Although both the correct rejection of non-nativelike selections and the incorrect rejection of native-like selections are of interest, for the purpose of the analysis presented here, only those word combinations we had validated and piloted as non-nativelike were taken into account.

2.4.2   pSTM

A nonword repetition (NWR) task, in which participants were asked to repeat previously unfamiliar phonological forms of varying lengths, was used to measure phonological short-term memory. Given evidence that performance on short-term memory tasks is influenced by long-term lexical knowledge (Gathercole 1995; Gathercole & Baddeley 1993; Thorn & Gathercole 1999), using non-word stimulus items based on the phonotactic structure of the L2 under investigation risks turning task performance into a proxy of language familiar-ity – i.e. instead of assessing differences in phonological loop function, the task will identify those learners with better consolidated or more accurate knowledge of the L2's phonological structure. We therefore decided to base our task on an unknown L3, Arabic, following previous studies, including French and O'Brien (2008), Hummel (2002, 2009) and Mizera (2006). Although the stimulus items are real words and phrases in Arabic, they are semantically empty to participants and therefore effectively *non-words*.

With the help of a native Arabic speaker, we revised the stimulus list used by Hummel in her 2009 study to ensure consistency of items at each syllable length. The final test contained non-words which ranged from three to nine syllables with four non-words at each length. These were recorded by a native Arabic speaker and presented in pseudorandom (rather than increasing) order in Superlab. Repetitions were recorded and later double-rated by linguistically trained native speakers of Arabic and Polish. Following previous studies, accurate repetition is one in which there are no obvious phoneme replacements, omissions, or additions, although minor allowances were made for accent. A participant's NWR score was calculated as a weighted total of correctly repeated non-words (e.g. a correctly repeated non-word of syllable length five was awarded five points).

2.5   Background questionnaire

A questionnaire similar to that in Foster et al. was used to explore patterns of contact within the target language community. The questionnaire had 17 items in total that asked about participants' language learning history, English language media use, contact with native speakers prior to immigration, and attitudinal disposition toward the target culture. Three items (questions 11, 12 & 16 of the questionnaire reproduced in Foster et al.) are relevant to our investigation of the association between interaction sought and experienced with the TL community and detection of non-nativelike selections:

1. Approximately what percentage of your daily language use is English? (Circle your answer)
   i.   less than 25%
   ii. 26%–50%
   iii. about half
   iv. 76%–90%
   v.   more than 90%
2. Approximately how many of your friends and acquaintances in the UK normally speak English with you? (Circle your answer)
   i.   almost none of them
   ii. a few of them
   iii. about half
   iv. most of them
   v.   nearly all of them
3. How important is it to you to speak English in order to interact with native speakers of English? (Circle your answer)
   5 = very
   4 = quite
   3 = so-so
   2 = not very
   1 = not at all

2.6   Procedure

After an initial contact to ensure that he or she fitted the requirements of the project, non-native speaking participants were visited at a convenient place, usually their own home. The procedures were explained; it was stressed that the participant could stop at any time, and that no evaluation or judgment of the participant's English was being made. Four instruments were administered in the following order: an implicit learning artificial grammar task (not reported here), the biographical and language contact questionnaire, the non-word repetition task, NLS task, and a complex working memory task (also not reported here). All tasks were usually completed within an hour and 15 minutes.

Native-speaking participants were also initially screened to ensure that they fitted the requirements of the project. They completed the tasks either in a research office or a convenient place of their choosing. Similarly to non-native-speaking participants, procedures were explained, and it was stressed that the nativelike selection task was not an evaluation or judgement of their English. Native-speaking participants first completed a brief biographical questionnaire and then the NLS task. Both tasks were usually completed within 20 minutes.

3.   Results

Table 2 contains descriptive statistics for NLS, and all predictor variables. Native speakers ($N = 30$) detected between 20 and 28 of the total 28 non-nativelike selections in the text. The mean score was 24.27 (*SD* 2.42). L2 users detected between 0 and 23, with a mean of 11.24 (*SD* 7.01). The reliability coefficient (*KR*-20) was .90. The results show that, unsurprisingly, native speakers were significantly better than L2 users at detecting non-nativelike selections, (t (40.19) $= -10.04$, $p < .001$, equal variances not assumed). This represented a very large effect, Cohen's $d = 2.48$. Four NNS participants scored within the native speaker range, with scores of 20, 21, 22 and 23. These participants are discussed individually after correlational analyses below.

Responses to the first two questionnaire items revealed that on average, nearly half of L2 users' estimated daily language use was English. Responses ranged from *less than 25%* to *more than 90%*. On average, respondents also spoke English with slightly fewer than 50% of their friends and acquaintances (responses ranged from *almost none of them* to *nearly all of them*). Both of these items gauge L2 users' amount of interactive English use and they were averaged into a new composite variable called Richness of Interaction (hereafter, the *Richness* score) after first being converted to Z scores (with a mean of 0 and *SD* of 1).

Table 2. Descriptive statistics for NLS and predictor variables

Variable (total possible)	Polish in UK			Native Speakers		
	M	*SD*	*N*	*M*	*SD*	*N*
Nativelike selection (28)	11.24	7.01	33	24.27	2.42	30
PSTM (169)	66.76	30.37	33			
% daily use of English (5)	2.85	1.35	33			
% Friends/acquaintances English spoken (5)	2.42	1.17	33			
Importance of Interacting with native speakers (5)	4.33	.957	33			
Richness of interaction	1.12	2.01	33			

While the Richness score measures the contact *experienced* by L2 users, the third questionnaire item (Importance of interaction hereafter) indexes the importance respondents attached to seeking contact with native speakers. This item was meant to distinguish those L2 users who saw value in interacting with native speakers. This is not a given in London, as it is entirely possible for an immigrant to remain either within their own language community, or within the larger immigrant community generally. On average, respondents gauged that it was *quite important* to speak English in order to interact with native speakers. Responses ranged from *not all important* to *very important*.

Scores on the pSTM measure were normally distributed and ranged from a minimum of 15 to a maximum of 137. Inter-rater agreement was 90.49%. A random ten percent of items in addition to the disputed 9.51% were third rated by one of the authors.

3.1 Analyses

Analyses are presented as follows: we first check that our sampling has successfully controlled for possible AoO and age at testing effects, and reduced the multi-collinearity found in Foster et al. through a series of bivariate correlations. Next we describe the results from a three-step hierarchical regression exploring the associations between our predictor variables and nativelike selection ability. Comparing the models with each predictor entered sequentially allows us to estimate both the proportion of variance in nativelike selection explained by each predictor individually as well as observe the relationship between predictor variables in relation to nativelike selection. Finally we describe the four NNS participants who scored within the NS range in terms of their salient characteristics.

3.2 Correlational analyses

L2 users in this study were selected to present a more homogeneous profile than the participants in our previous study. Thus, the first analyses were conducted to check whether sampling participants with a minimum AO of 13 had successfully controlled both for the largest effect in Foster et al. (i.e. the effect of AoO), as well as the multi-collinearity between predictor variables. Neither AoO nor AoA nor YrsEng were associated with Nativelike selection ability. It appears that sampling was largely successful in avoiding critical or sensitive period effects. Similarly, neither Age nor AoO nor LoR were associated with scores on the pSTM measure. Thus, it also appears that sampling successfully controlled for age-associated decline in cognitive task performance.

Although LoR was significantly associated with Nativelike selection ability ($r = .42, p < .05$), examination of a scatterplot found this was due to leverage from

2 participants with a LoR of 1.32 *SD* and 2.07 *SD* above the mean. As our aim is to investigate the actual opportunities participants have had to interact with the TL community, it was decided to retain our more direct measure of language use, Richness of interaction, as an index of exposure. Richness was itself not associated with Age, AoO, LoR, or YrsSch.

3.3   Hierarchical regression analyses

A hierarchical (sequential) regression model was fitted with Nativelike Selection as the criterion variable, Richness entered as the first predictor, pSTM second, and Importance of Interaction last. All predictors are significantly associated with the criterion (see *bivariate correlations* in Table 3), but not with each other.

Table 3. Results of regression analysis for variables predicting NLS ($N = 33$)

	B	SE B	β	sig.	Bivariate correlations
Step 1					
Constant	11.24	1.16		.000	
Richness	2.68	1.27	.35	.043	.35*
Step 2					
Constant	1.89	2.23		.401	
Richness	3.41	1.00	.45	.002	.35*
pSTM	0.14	0.03	.61	.000	.54***
Step 3					
Constant	−7.82	3.99		.059	
Richness	2.76	0.93	.37	.006	.35*
pSTM	0.12	0.03	.51	.000	.54***
Importance of interaction	2.59	0.92	.35	.009	.55***

Note: $R^2 = .13$ for Step 1, ($p = .043$); $\Delta R^2 = .36$ for Step 2, ($p < .001$); $\Delta R^2 = .11$ for Step 3, ($p = .009$); *$p < .05$, **$p < .01$ ***$p < .001$.

The first model (Step 1) with only Richness accounts for 13% of the variance in NLS ($R^2 = .126$, $F(1, 32) = 21.49$, $p < .05$). Entering pSTM in the second step accounts for an additional 36% of the variance in NLS ($\Delta R^2 = .36$, $p < .001$). This second model (Step 2) with both predictors is significant ($F(2, 32) = 14.15$, $p < .001$) and thus accounts for a cumulative 49% of the variance in NLS. Two further interesting effects can be seen in Step 2: adding pSTM to the model has increased the size and significance of Richness' standardised regression coefficient ($\beta = .45$, $p < .01$) in comparison to Step 1, where the β equals the bivariate correlation coefficient (r = .35, p < .05); and adding pSTM to a regression model that already includes a measure of exposure has also resulted in a standardised regression coefficient for pSTM (β = .61, p < .001) larger and more significant than its bivariate correlation coefficient (r = .54, p < .01) with NLS. The increase in size and significance of both predictors' coefficients when considered together indicates that each accounts for part of the unsystematic variance or 'noise' in the relationship between the other and the criterion. Thus, pSTM accounts for a portion of the unexplained variance between NLS and Richness, and Richness explains a portion of the unexplained variance between pSTM and NLS. Lutz (1983) termed this relationship reciprocal suppression and reviews (Pandey & Elliott 2010) suggest that standardised regression coefficients are more appropriate measures of the relationships between predictor and criterion than bivariate correlation coefficients when there is evidence of suppression.

In the final model, adding Importance of Interaction accounts for an additional 11% of the variance in NLS (ΔR^2 = .111, p < .01). The model as a whole thus cumulatively accounts for 60% of the variance in NLS (R^2 = .596, $F(3, 32)$ = 14.279, p < .001). Standardized regression coefficients indicate that Importance of Interaction is moderately associated with NLS ability, as is Richness of interaction. PSTM is still the most important predictor in the model. All three predictors' standardised regression coefficients decrease relative to their bivariate coefficients when the third predictor is entered in the model, indicating that a portion of the variance between all three predictors is shared.

3.4   Individual case analyses

Four NNS participants scored within the NS range. Their pSTM, Richness and Nativelike selection scores are indicated in Table 4. Scores for pSTM and Richness are given in units of Standard Deviation from the NNS mean, while NLS scores are given in raw form with *SD* score in brackets. All four participants rated the importance of speaking English in order to interact with NS as *very important*. Beyond this observation, it can be seen that two of the participants (13 and 33) have unbalanced profiles. Participant 13 received the single highest score on the NWR task, 2.31 *SD*s above the mean, while Participant 33 received the single highest Richness score, 2.05 *SD*s above the mean. Both the other two participants (17 and 20) have NWR and Richness scores comfortably above the mean. All four participants work in English-speaking environments. The results from these participants echo what was seen in the regression analysis above: all participants recognized the importance of interacting with NS, and had at the minimum an above average degree of interactive exposure *and* pSTM, or either *extraordinary* pSTM or richness of exposure. Thus, it appears that a much better ability

Table 4. NNS scoring within NS range (pSTM and Richness scores in SD units)

Participant ID	Variable		
	pSTM	Richness	NLS
13	+2.31[a]	−.60	23 (+1.67)
17	+1.36	+1.19	21 (+1.39)
20	+.62	+.73	20 (+1.25)
33	−.39	+2.05[b]	22 (+1.54)

[a]single highest NWR score; [b]single highest richness score.

to retain short term phonological information can compensate for a *relative* lack of input (e.g. Participant 13, with below average Richness, still spends all day in an English-speaking office environment), while an environment extremely rich in interactive exposure (Participant 33, who works as a psychological counsellor, has a long term British partner, and has had minimal contact with L1 speakers for over 20 years) can compensate for a weaker than average pSTM.

3.5   Summary of results

Our first research question concerned the extent to which NNS speakers would converge on NS behaviour in the identification of non-nativelike selections after more than 10 years of exposure. An independent samples t-test revealed that native speakers detected significantly more non-nativelike selections than NNS, even after a mean of 12 years of residence for NNS in the TL community. Examination of the four individuals who scored within the NS range fitted the pattern of results described below. All participants were highly aware of the value of interacting with NS, and had either (1) above average Richness *and* pSTM; or (2) *outstanding* Richness (> 2*SD*) *or* pSTM (> 2*SD*).

Our second research question concerned the individual contribution of three predictors: richness of interaction in the TL community, pSTM, and perceived importance of interacting with NS. In order to estimate the associations between our predictor variables and NLS, we first ascertained that our sampling criteria had successfully controlled for sensitive or critical period effects, age at testing effects, and collinearity between predictors. The hierarchical regression analysis revealed that all three predictors were significantly associated with NLS ability, and together accounted for 60% of the variance in NLS. PSTM accounted for the largest portion of variance (36%), a large effect (Cohen 2003; DeKeyser & Larson-Hall 2005), while Richness of interaction (13%) and Importance of interacting (11%) each had a medium effect. In answer to our last research question, differences in standardised regression coefficients relative to bivariate correlation coefficients also revealed a pattern of reciprocal suppression between pSTM and Richness of Exposure, whereby each accounted for unsystematic variance in the other's relationship with NLS. The addition of Importance of interaction reduced the size of the standardised regression coefficients of Richness and pSTM, indicating that the three variables share common variance in their relationship to NLS.

4. Discussion

Aptitude has traditionally been understood as "degree of readiness to learn and to perform well in a particular situation or in a fixed domain" (Corno, Cronbach, Kupermintz, Lohman, Mandinach, Porteus & Talbert 2002:3), and only more recently, as a limiter on ultimate attainment. Studies which implicate aptitude as an explanatory variable in ultimate attainment have done so on the basis of associations between tests of specific cognitive ability and performance on a measure of language proficiency (e.g. DeKeyser 2000; Abrahamsson & Hyltenstam 2008; Abrahamsson 2012). In other words, these studies have inferred past learning processes from present day associations. At a minimum, any such conclusions as to the role of aptitude must be supported by evidence of the stability of the cognitive measure under consideration. A recent study found that pSTM was immune to effects of training (Holmes, Gathercole & Dunning 2009); performance on STM tasks, however, is generally sensitive to age-related declines in perceptual speed (Fisk & Warr 1996) and speech rate (Multhaup, Balota & Cowan 1996). With this study, we have replicated our earlier findings of an association between pSTM and the ability to detect non-nativelike selections, but in a sample that eliminated confounds between age at testing, LoR and pSTM. We have found this association when nativelike selections are indexed either by two-word selections or collocations (this study), or more broadly defined collocational and colligational combinations (Foster et al.). Considering these results in light of evidence for the role of the phonological loop in initial learning of phrases (Ellis & Sinclair 1996), and the influence of pSTM on the rate of learning of collocations (Skrzypek 2009), we suggest that individual differences in pSTM can be considered an aptitude for idiomaticity, which affect both the rate of learning and ultimate attainment of L2 users. This suggestion is in line with the view that specific aspects of language proficiency are mediated by differing cognitive abilities, and echoes recommendations that measures of pSTM and WM be added to aptitude batteries (e.g. DeKeyser & Koeth 2011; Dornyei & Skehan 2003; Miyake & Friedman 1998; Robinson 2005).

The findings of reciprocal suppression between pSTM and Richness of interaction in this study, and LoR in our previous study, highlight the importance of jointly considering the effects of pSTM and exposure, which in this study account for nearly 50% of the variance in NLS scores. These results confirm the previous findings in Foster et al. and provide support for a model of acquisition where an individual's ability to benefit from exposure to input depends on his/her pSTM, while the gains an individual realises from above average pSTM depend on his/her opportunities for exposure to input. However, exposure must be qualified by both the context in which it occurs, and the age of onset of the learner. In our studies, pSTM plays a significant role in the ultimate attainment of nativelike selection ability for adult onset L2 users within the target language community. We did not find any association between pSTM and NLS scores in child L2 learners within the TL community in our earlier study, although this may have been due to ceiling effects for early starters on the NLS measure. We also found no associations between pSTM and NLS scores in L2 users living outside the TL community. This suggests that the knowledge underlying their performance on the NLS test may not have been acquired incidentally through use. If the learning process were the same, but with simply less input, we would still expect to find a correlation with pSTM.

Another difference between child and adult onset learning within the TL community appears when we consider that the degree to which L2 users see value in interacting with NS (Importance of interaction) accounts for an additional 11% of the variance in NLS scores in this study. In our previous study, all child onset learners in the TL community (AoO < 12) scored within the NS range. Motivational disposition towards interacting with NS was not an issue. This may be because child onset learners are provided with a peer group through schooling which obviates the need to purposely seek out contact. The near absolute effects of AoO may also be related to maturational limits. Our findings support Dornyei et al.'s (2004) conclusion that socio-cultural integration and the determination to transcend one's own language community play an important role in adult onset naturalistic acquisition of idiomaticity. Dornyei (2010) has suggested that learner characteristics, such as motivation and aptitude, can be viewed as trait complexes, or higher order combinations that act as integrated and dynamic wholes (Robinson 2005; Snow 1992). The contribution of Importance of interaction is perhaps best understood in this light. While those individuals who come to the learning task valuing interaction with NS are more likely to seek opportunities to do so, it is equally plausible that the more an L2 user interacts in the TL community, and the greater their ability to retain the particular phrasings of that community, the more he or she will value the importance of such interaction. The mediation effects revealed by including Importance of interaction in the third step of our regression model underscore this interpretation.

This study's findings indicate that a very few well integrated L2 users with above average pSTM can identify well-formed, yet non-nativelike word combinations in a given text as well as certain native speakers. Since we only analysed their identification of those selections identified as non-native in our piloting, we cannot say whether their intuitions are the same as native speakers. Of the four participants who scored within the lower end of the native speaker range, three had substantially above average pSTM scores. The same pattern was found in our earlier study: the two adult onset participants within the TL community who scored within the lower end of the NS range had pSTM scores nearly two *SD*s above the mean. The one exception to this pattern (Participant ID 33) is intriguing; her case suggests that long years of rich interaction within the TL community might suffice to mitigate below average pSTM, in much the same way as native speakers' vast experience of interaction allows the development of nativelike selection ability.

One aim of this study was to investigate the influence of exposure, memory and motivation on receptive nativelike selection ability in a typical adult onset L2 population with long exposure to the TL community. While our findings reveal that these three variables can explain a large proportion of the variance in NLS scores, 40% remains to be explained. We believe that it is in seeking to account for this remaining variance that interesting questions lie, and that more subtle influences on learning are more likely to be detected once large known effects are accounted for. Further interesting questions concern the relationship between knowledge, processing and use. We do not know whether the four participants who scored within the NS range on the NLS task in this study would be nativelike in a measure of their use of conventional expressions, and it is likely that additional individual differences mediate productive knowledge. Indexing L2 users' patterns of exposure and pSTM should help elucidate other sources of variance in both productive and receptive knowledge.

Acknowledgements

We thank Bouran Irfaeya, Nadia Bahrani, Rana Alhussein Almbark, and Ghazi Algethami for their assistance in the refinement and scoring of the Non Word Repetition task, and Agnieszka Kotula for her help with data collection.

References

Abrahamsson, N. (2012). Age of onset and nativelike L2 ultimate attainment of morphosyntactic and phonetic intuition. *Studies in Second Language Acquisition, 34*, 187–214.

Abrahamsson, N., & Hyltenstam, K. (2008). The robustness of aptitude effects in near-native second language acquisition. *Studies in Second Language Acquisition, 30*(4), 481–509.

Altenberg, B. (1990). Speech as linear composition. In G. Caie, K. Haastruup, A.L. Jakobsen, J.E. Nielsen, J. Sevaldsen, H. Specht, & A. Zettersen (Eds.), *Proceedings from the fourth Nordic conference for English studies, 1* (pp. 133–143). Copenhagen: Department of English, University of Copenhagen.

Baddeley, A.D., & Hitch, G.J. (1974). Working memory. *The Psychology of Learning and Motivation, 8*, 47–89.

Bardovi-Harlig, K., & Bastos, M.T. (2011). Proficiency, length of stay, and intensity of interaction and the acquisition of conventional expressions in L2 pragmatics. *Intercultural Pragmatics, 8*(3), 347–384.

Barlow, M., & Kemmer, S. (Eds.). (2000). *Usage-based models of language*. Stanford: CSLI publications.

Becker, J.D. (1976). The phrasal lexicon. Report no.3081. Advanced Research Projects Agency of the Department of Defense.

Boyd, J.K., & Goldberg, A.E. (2011). Learning what NOT to say: The role of statistical preemption and categorization in A-adjective production. *Language, 85*, 55–83.

Brooks, P.J., & Tomasello, M. (1999). How children constrain their argument structure constructions. *Language, 75*, 720–738.

Bybee, J. (1995). Regular morphology and the lexicon. *Language and Cognitive Processes, 10*(5), 425–455.

Cohen, J. (2003). *Applied multiple regression/correlation analysis for the behavioral sciences*. Hillsdale, NJ: Lawrence Erlbaum Associates.

Corno, L., Cronbach, L., Kupermintz, H., Lohman, D., Mandinach, E., Porteus, A., & Talbert, J. (2002). *Remaking the concept of aptitude: Extending the legacy of Richard E. Snow*. Mahwah, NJ: Lawrence Erlbaum Associates.

DeKeyser, R.M. (2000). The robustness of critical period effects in second language acquisition. *Studies in Second Language Acquisition, 22*(4), 499–534.

DeKeyser, R.M., & Koeth, J. (2011). Cognitive aptitudes for L2 learning. In E. Hinkel (Ed.), *Handbook of research in second language teaching and learning, Volume II* (pp. 395–406). New York, NY: Routledge.

DeKeyser, R.M., & Larson-Hall, J. (2005). What does the critical period really mean. In J. Kroll, & A.M.B. de Groot (Eds.), *Handbook of bilingualism: Psycholinguistic approaches* (pp. 88–108). Oxford: OUP.

Dörnyei, Z. (2010). The relationship between language aptitude and language learning motivation: Individual differences from a dynamic systems perspective. In E. Macaro (Ed.), *Continuum companion to second language acquisition* (pp. 247–267). London: Continuum.

Dörnyei, Z., Durow, V., & Zahran, K. (2004). Individual differences and their effects on formulaic sequence acquisition. In N. Schmitt (Ed.), *Formulaic sequences: Acquisition, processing and use* (pp. 87–106). Amsterdam: John Benjamins.

Dörnyei, Z., & Skehan, P. (2003). Individual differences in second language learning. In C. Doughty, & M.H. Long (Eds.), *The handbook of second language acquisition* (pp. 589–630). Oxford: Blackwell.

Durrant, P., & Schmitt, N. (2010). Adult learners' retention of collocations from exposure. *Second Language Research, 26*(2), 163–188.

Ellis, N.C. (1994). Consciousness in second language learning: Psychological perspectives on the role of conscious processes in vocabulary acquisition. In J. Hulstijn, & R. Schmidt (Eds.), *Consciousness in second language learning, AILA Review 11*, 37–56.

Ellis, N.C. (1996). Sequencing in SLA. *Studies in Second Language Acquisition, 18*(1), 91–126.

Ellis, N.C. (2001). Memory for language. In P. Robinson (Ed.), *Cognition and second language instruction* (pp. 33–68). Cambridge: CUP.

Ellis, N.C. (2002). Reflections on frequency effects in language processing. *Studies in Second Language Acquisition, 24*(2), 297–339.

Ellis, N.C. (2006). Selective attention and transfer phenomena in L2 acquisition: Contingency, cue competition, salience, interference, overshadowing, blocking, and perceptual learning. *Applied Linguistics, 27*(2), 164–194.

Ellis, N.C., & Schmidt, R. (1997). Morphology and longer-distance dependencies: Laboratory research illuminating the A in SLA. *Studies in Second Language Acquisition, 19*, 145–171.

Ellis, N.C., & Sinclair, J. (1996). Working memory in the acquisition of vocabulary and syntax: Putting language in good order. *The Quarterly Journal of Experimental Psychology: Section A, 49*(1), 234–250.

Erman, B., & Warren, B. (2000). The idiom principle and the open-choice principle. *Text, 20*, 29–62.

Fisk, J.E., & Warr, P. (1996). Age and working memory: The role of perceptual speed, the central executive, and the phonological loop. *Psychology and Aging, 11*(2), 316–323.

Forsberg, F. (2008). *Le langage préfabriqué: Formes, fonctions et fréquences en français parlé L2 et L1.* Bern: Peter Lang.

Forsberg, F. (2010). Using conventional sequences in L2 French. *International Review of Applied Linguistics in Language Teaching, 48*(1), 25–51.

Foster, P. (2001). Rules and routines: A consideration of their role in the task-based language production of native and non-native speakers. In M. Bygate, P. Skehan, & M. Swain (Eds.), *Language tasks: Teaching, learning and testing* (pp. 75–93). London: Longman.

Foster, P., Bolibaugh, C., & Kotula, A. (in press). The influence of age, memory and social engagement on the acquisition of nativelike selections in a second language. *Studies in Second Language Acquisition.*

French, L.M., & O'Brien, I. (2008). Phonological memory and children's second language grammar learning. *Applied Psycholinguistics, 29*(3), 463–487.

Gathercole, S.E. (1995). Is nonword repetition a test of phonological memory or long-term knowledge? It all depends on the nonwords. *Memory & Cognition, 23*(1), 83–94.

Gathercole, S.E. (2006). Nonword repetition and word learning: The nature of the relationship. *Applied Psycholinguistics, 27*(4), 513–543.

Gathercole, S.E., & Baddeley, A.D. (1993). Phonological working memory: A critical building block for reading development and vocabulary acquisition? *European Journal of Psychology of Education, 8*(3), 259–272.

Gathercole, S.E., Willis, C.S., Emslie, H., & Baddeley, A.D. (1992). Phonological memory and vocabulary development during the early school years: A longitudinal study. *Developmental Psychology, 28*(5), 887–898.

Goldberg, A.E. (1999). The emergence of the semantics of argument structure constructions. In B. MacWhinney (Ed.), *The emergence of language* (pp. 197–212). Mahwah, N.J.: Lawrence Erlbaum.

Goldberg, A.E. (2006). *Constructions at work: The nature of generalization in language.* Oxford: OUP.

Granena, G., & Long, M.H. (2013). Age of onset, length of residence, language aptitude, and ultimate L2 attainment in three linguistic domains. *Second Language Research, 29*(1).

Gupta, P. (2003). Examining the relationship between word learning, nonword repetition, and immediate serial recall in adults. *The Quarterly Journal of Experimental Psychology: Section A, 56*(7), 1213–1236.

Gurevich, O., Johnson, M.A., & Goldberg, A.E. (2010). Incidental verbatim memory for language. *Language and Cognition, 2*(1), 45–78.

Holmes, J., Gathercole, S.E., & Dunning, D.L. (2009). Adaptive training leads to sustained enhancement of poor working memory in children. *Developmental Science, 12*(4), F9–F15.

Howarth, P. (1998). Phraseology and second language proficiency. *Applied Linguistics, 19*(1), 24–44.

Hummel, K.M. (2002). Second language acquisition and working memory. In F. Fabbro (Ed.), *Advances in the neurolinguistics of bilingualism: Festschrift for Michel Paradis* (pp. 95–117). Udine, Italy: Forum.

Hummel, K.M. (2009). Aptitude, phonological memory, and second language proficiency in nonnovice adult learners. *Applied Psycholinguistics, 30*(2), 225–249.

Jurafsky, D. (1996). A probabilistic model of lexical and syntactic access and disambiguation. *Cognitive Science, 20*(2), 137–194.

Kormos, J. (this volume). The role of working memory, phonological short-term memory and language aptitude in second language attainment.

Langacker, R.W. (1988). A usage-based model. *Topics in Cognitive Linguistics, 50*, 127–163.

Langacker, R.W. (2000). *A dynamic usage-based model*. Stanford, CA: CSLI.

Lutz, J.G. (1983). A method for constructing data which illustrate three types of suppressor variables. *Educational and Psychological Measurement, 43*(2), 373–377.

Melton, A.W. (1963). Implications of short-term memory for a general theory of memory. DTIC Document.

Mizera, G.J. (2006). *Working memory and L2 oral fluency*. Unpublished doctoral dissertation. University of Pittsburgh.

Miyake, A., & Friedman, N.P. (1998). Individual differences in second language proficiency: Working memory as language aptitude. In A.F. Healy, & L.E. Bourne (Eds.), *Foreign language learning: Psycholinguistic studies on training and retention* (pp. 339–364). Mahwah, NJ: Lawrence Erlbaum Associates.

Multhaup, K.S., Balota, D.A., & Cowan, N. (1996). Implications of aging, lexicality, and item length for the mechanisms underlying memory span. *Psychonomic Bulletin & Review, 3*(1), 112–120.

Nation, P., & Waring, R. (1997). Vocabulary size, text coverage and word lists. In N. Schmitt, & M. McCarthy (Eds.), *Vocabulary: Description, acquisition and pedagogy* (pp. 6–19). Cambridge: CUP.

Nattinger, J., & Decarrico, J. (1992). *Lexical phrases and language teaching*. Oxford: OUP.

Page, M., & Norris, D. (2009). A model linking immediate serial recall, the Hebb repetition effect and the learning of phonological word forms. *Philosophical Transactions of the Royal Society B: Biological Sciences, 364*(1536), 3737–3753.

Pandey, S., & Elliott, W. (2010). Suppressor variables in social work research: Ways to identify in multiple regression models. *Journal of the Society for Social Work and Research, 1*(1), 28–40.

Papagno, C., & Vallar, G. (1992). Phonological short-term memory and the learning of novel words: The effect of phonological similarity and item length. *The Quarterly Journal of Experimental Psychology, 44*(1), 47–67.

Pawley, A., & Syder, F. (1983). Two puzzles for linguistic theory: Nativelike selection and nativelike fluency. In J. Richards, & R. Schmidt (Eds.), *Language and communication* (pp. 191–226). London: Longman.

Robinson, P. (2005). Aptitude and second language acquisition. *Annual Review of Applied Linguistics, 25*, 45–73.

Robinson, P., & Ellis, N.C. (2008). Conclusion: Cognitive linguistics, second language acquisition and L2 instruction – Issues for research. In P. Robinson, & N.C. Ellis (Eds.), *The handbook of cognitive linguistics and second language acquisition* (pp. 489–545). New York, NY: Routledge.

Schmitt, N., Dörnyei, Z., Adolphs, S., & Durow, V. (2004). Knowledge and acquisition of formulaic sequences. In N. Schmitt (Ed.), *Formulaic sequences: Acquisition, processing and use* (pp. 55–86). Amsterdam: John Benjamins.

Service, E., & Kohonen, V. (1995). Is the relation between phonological memory and foreign language learning accounted for by vocabulary acquisition? *Applied Psycholinguistics, 16*(2), 155–172.

Service, E., Maury, S., & Luotoniemi, E. (2007). Individual differences in phonological learning and verbal STM span. *Memory & Cognition, 35*(5), 1122–1135.

Sinclair, J. (1991). *Corpus, concordance, collocation.* Oxford: OUP.

Skrzypek, A. (2009). Phonological Short-term Memory and L2 collocational development in adult learners. *EUROSLA Yearbook, 9*(1), 160–184.

Snow, R.E. (1992). Aptitude theory: Yesterday, today, and tomorrow. *Educational Psychologist, 27*, 5–32.

Spadaro, K. (this volume). Maturational constraints on lexical acquisition in a second language.

Stevens, G. (2006). The Age-Length-Onset problem in research on second language acquisition among immigrants. *Language Learning, 56*(4), 671–692.

Thorn, A.S.C., & Gathercole, S.E. (1999). Language-specific knowledge and short-term memory in bilingual and non-bilingual children. *The Quarterly Journal of Experimental Psychology: Section A, 52*(2), 303–324.

Tzelgov, J., & Henik, A. (1991). Suppression situations in psychological research: Definitions, implications, and applications. *Psychological Bulletin, 109*(3), 524–536.

Warren, B. (2005). A model of idiomaticity. *Nordic Journal of English Studies, 4*(1), 35–54.

Weinert, R. (1995). The role of formulaic language in second language acquisition: A review. *Applied Linguistics, 16*(2), 181–205.

Wray, A. (2000). Formulaic sequences in second language teaching: *Principle and practice. Applied Linguistics, 21*(4), 463–489.

Wray, A. (2002). *Formulaic language and the lexicon.* Cambridge: CUP.

Appendix

Nativelike Selection Task
(Non native selections are in bold.)

In the Name of the Father

I was really impressed by this film, which is actually **a realist story**. It's about four men who go to prison for bombing a pub in London (when really the **crime was performed** by a terrorist), and about their struggle to prove their innocence. It's also about the relationship between a father and his son. Before going to prison, they didn't have much of a relationship, and in the beginning the son is **disappointed upon** his father and his passivity. But later he realises that it's simply that the father has **another mentality**. It's a really good film from a political point of view, and also from a personal point of view. I won't tell you the end if you don't know it, because I don't want to **ruin your pleasure**.

Lord of the Rings

It's a complicated story about a ring which has the power to destroy all mankind, and corrupt people, and which you can use to **get invisible**. The film is also the story of a group of friends who want to destroy the ring. It's quite long, about three hours, but you are never **bored about** this film. I think the director did a good job adapting it from the book. I don't know what the author would have thought about making a film version of his novel, for example, whether it is a bad thing to depict the characters in **blunt detail**. He might have preferred that to take place in the **fantasy of the reader**. Anyway, I really like the actor who **made the role** of the king. I think he managed to **reach success** thanks to this film.

Life is Beautiful

One of the films I've **seen lastly** is set in the 1939–1944 war. It's the story of a family, a father, mother and a son who is a **single child**, imprisoned by the Germans. The father **loves his son brightly** so he tries to transform everything into a game for him. He makes the son think that if they behave in a certain way, they will win a special prize. There are a lot of funny bits: the main actor Roberto Begnini is a very **comic person**, but the terrible thing for the **watcher of the film** is that you know it is a tragedy. The end is a bit predictable, but I think the director, who was also Roberto Begnini, really managed to **pass his meaning**. It was extremely powerful.

Career Girls

This film is by the director Mike Leigh. It's a **modern time** story from the 1990s about two girls, or women, at university and the experiences they made there. They meet when they are looking for a place to live, and one girl makes fun of the other because she doesn't have a **good appearance**, but they somehow become friends and talk about their family experiences. One girl has a father who is a **heavy drunkard**, and the other one also has some problems. Then they meet again after a long time. The film is a bit depressing and the perspective is very narrow: there are only 5 or 6 actors. We only see other people once, when we see the one who is a university teacher **make some lectures**. At the end they are both successful career girls. It's a very strange film. I can't say whether it is good or bad. I can't **make the point** of it.

The Matrix

This is about a group of people who live in the future. A sort of war **broke up**, and now people are slaves and machines are the masters. They have created a virtual reality, the Matrix, that gives people the **wrong belief** that they are in the real world. But there is one man who is strong enough to fight the machines. He is living in this virtual reality, the Matrix, as a computer specialist for a **grand corporation** by day and a computer hacker by night. He earns a **big amount of money** but he keeps wondering about the Matrix. Finally he is contacted by rebels and wants to join them, but he **does a mistake** and is caught by the agents. Well, the plot is very difficult to explain but I think the message is that humanity can be killed by its own creations.

High-level proficiency in late L2 acquisition

Relationships between collocational production, language aptitude and personality

Fanny Forsberg Lundell & Maria Sandgren
Stockholm University / Södertörn University

The aim of the present exploratory study was twofold. The first was to investigate how indicators of high-level proficiency (collocations and grammaticality judgment) related to aptitude in late French L2 learners. Results showed a significant positive correlation between collocations and performance on the LLAMA D (Meara 2005). The second question concerned how personality relates to indicators of high-level L2 proficiency (collocations and grammaticality judgment). Two personality dimensions in the Multicultural Personality Questionnaire (Van der Zee & van Oudenhoven 2000) were significantly and positively correlated with scores for collocations and the LLAMA D. The preliminary findings suggest that collocations are a valid measure for high-level L2 proficiency and that it is necessary to consider both personality and social-psychological factors when predicting successful L2 learning.

1. Introduction

Researchers have shown that formulaic language, specifically collocations, pose problems at advanced levels of acquisition (e.g. Siyanova & Schmitt 2008; Bolly 2008; Durrant & Schmitt 2009; Mizrahi & Laufer 2010). In a study by Forsberg Lundell and Lindqvist (submitted), different aspects of lexical knowledge were tested in a population of very advanced L2 users of French (L1 Swedish) whose length of residence in France (LOR) ranged from five to 35 years. The participants performed in a nativelike way on a C-test and on a social routine test, but performed significantly poorer than a native speaker control group on a receptive deep knowledge test (mainly including word association) and a collocation test. It was shown that individual variation was particularly high on the collocation test. Interestingly, LOR did not explain the variation in any of the lexical dimensions investigated.

It was thus deemed relevant to go further and reflect on factors contributing to high-level proficiency among late L2 learners from an interdisciplinary point of view, namely linguistics and psychology. Two lines of thought developed. One concerned measurements that would accurately assess high-level L2 proficiency and its relationship with language aptitude. A second concerned personality characteristics that would be positively associated with high L2 proficiency among adult learners.

2.   Collocations and high-level SLA

There is increasing evidence in the literature of the specific difficulty that collocations pose for L2 learners (e.g. Mizrahi & Laufer 2010). Findings suggest that these difficulties are both psycholinguistic and cultural. It is important to situate collocations within the theoretical framework of formulaic language. As many researchers have now stated (e.g. Schmitt & Carter 2004; Eyckmans 2009; Forsberg 2010), formulaic language is subdivided into a plethora of subcategories with different forms and functions. Collocations, especially verb-noun combinations (*make a decision*) and adjective-noun combinations (*black coffee*), have been a privileged category in L2 research, probably because it constitutes a relatively well-defined category that can be measured both in spontaneous production and, perhaps more importantly, in tests.

In Wray's (2002) view, formulaic language is useful mainly for two reasons. It provides production relief for the speaker and decoding relief for the hearer (as evidenced by, e.g. Underwood, Schmitt & Galpin 2004; Conklin & Schmitt 2008), which, thus, makes it *cognitively economic* for both parties. It also implies social advantages, since ready-made sequences are community-wide in use and convey a common identity. The cultural dimension of formulaic language has also been highlighted (e.g. Skandera 2007), implying that formulaic language learning, which collocations are part of, is also part of a process of acculturation. Of particular interest for the present study is the suggestion by Dörnyei, Durow and Zahran (2004) and Adolphs and Durow (2004) that formulaic sequence learning is a socially loaded process.

However, the cultural dimension of formulaic language acquisition has generally been ignored in SLA studies, which tend to concentrate more on pure linguistic mastery of collocations. The review below will focus on findings regarding advanced/high-level learners' mastery of collocations. This concerns receptive knowledge, productive knowledge, and use in writing and speech. *Advanced* and *high-level* are subjective terms. The review is based on studies that report studying advanced or high-level learners/users.

There seems to be a common misconception that recognition of collocations at advanced levels of L2 learning is less problematic than productive knowledge and use. Both Bonk (2000) and Gyllstad (2007) found strong correlations between a vocabulary size test and a receptive collocation test, which suggests that recognizing collocations is not more problematic than recognizing single words. This suggests a less problematic role for collocations than reported elsewhere in the L2 literature. However, as already hinted, producing collocations in tests, writing and speech is more challenging for L2 learners. Several early studies found that advanced university students performed significantly worse on cloze tests involving collocations and translations tasks (Bahns & Eldaw 1993; Farghal & Obiedat 1995). Two recent studies have tested productive collocational knowledge in highly advanced L2 speakers who, according to self-identification or researcher judgment, approach near-native levels. Mizrahi and Laufer (2010) found that speakers who self-identified as near-native in L2 English and had had extensive exposure to English performed in a nativelike way on a productive vocabulary size test. Only a minority of them performed in a nativelike way on a productive collocation test. Forsberg Lundell and Lindqvist (submitted) tested highly advanced L2 French speakers on four different vocabulary aspects. Just as in Mizrahi and Laufer (2010), significant differences were found between native and non-native speakers on a similar productive collocation test.

In written and spoken production, several tendencies emerge. Some studies show that, in the quantity of collocations produced, no significant differences are found between advanced learners and native speakers (Nesselhauf 2005; Siyanova & Schmitt 2008; Forsberg 2010) (for the most advanced group of L2 users). Nonetheless, qualitative differences are often found in such areas as L1 transfer (Granger 1998; Nesselhauf 2005; Laufer & Waldman 2011), degree of restriction of the collocation (Howarth 1998; Nesselhauf 2005; Bolly 2008), frequency of collocations used (Durrant & Schmitt 2009), and type of category used (Forsberg 2010). Another trend emerges in studies by Laufer and Waldman (2011) and Mizrahi and Laufer (2011), which both conclude that advanced L2 English learners fail to produce even similar quantities of collocations. Laufer and Waldman (2011) also report persistent collocational errors in written production.

To conclude, findings as to the extent to which advanced learners are capable of producing formulaic language at nativelike levels are mixed. Some studies suggest that, at a quantitative level, nativelike attainment is possible. Others do not report nativelike attainment for either quantity or quality. One explanation could be that there is a lack of consistency in proficiency measurements, i.e. we cannot be certain that the highly advanced learners in all of these studies are really at the same level of L2 proficiency. Another possible explanation is that typological similarities between L1 and L2 will have a positive effect on L2 speakers' use of collocations. However, all studies seem to agree that non-native and native speakers differ in qualitative aspects of collocation production. Since it has been argued that collocations and formulaic language are both cognitively and culturally important, it seems plausible to turn to psychological and social factors to explain this variation in high-level L2 proficiency.

3.   Social-psychological challenges for the adult L2 learner

To attain high-level L2 proficiency, the learner has to make a major, extended effort. This constitutes a high-stakes project for the individual and may even exhaust cognitive and emotional resources. The body of literature on L2 learners inspired us to take a closer look at factors that will constitute challenges for acquiring high-level proficiency.

Judging from the reviews of findings on individual differences (e.g. Dörnyei 2005), it appears that language aptitude has been one of the most successful individual factors in predicting second language success. Lately, the role of aptitude for naturalistic high-level achievement has been highlighted (e.g. Abrahamsson & Hyltenstam 2008; Granena & Long 2013). In particular, non-traditional measures of aptitude, stemming from cognitive psychology, such as phonological short-term memory, have been linked to high-level L2 achievement and to the learning of formulaic language (Skrzypek 2009; Bolibaugh & Foster this volume). If we wish to investigate how individual factors influence the learning of collocations in late L2 acquisition, it is necessary to investigate the role of language aptitude.

However, it is believed that aptitude alone cannot explain high-level L2 proficiency. Second language acquisition is not only a cognitive challenge, but also challenges an individual's social identity. This is the case for the type of L2 users included in our study i.e. long-term residents in the TL community. While learning an L2, the individual will go through a process of re-socialisation and consistently negotiate his or her social identity and varying degrees of affiliation to different social groups. As a result, social-psychological factors such as integrativity (Gardner 2001) and ethnic group identification (Gatbonton & Trofimovich 2008) may affect the individual's development of his or her potential.

3.1   Aptitude and SLA

Language aptitude has been one of the most successful individual factors in explaining L2 research findings. Traditionally, it is defined as the "strengths individual learners have – relative to their population – in the cognitive abilities information processing draws on during L2 learning and performance in various contexts and at different stages" (Robinson 2005:46). In addition, aptitude tests have, during the past 50 years or so, conceived of aptitude in terms of the rate at which learning takes place (Carroll 1981). According to Robinson (2005), the creation of aptitude tests in the 1950s–1970's was mostly driven by an eagerness to find tests that would predict rate of individual learning for selection purposes. For a variety of these tests, the MLAT (Carroll 1981), PLAB (Pimsleur 1966) and DLAB (Peterson & Al Haik 1976), studies have yielded strong correlations between success in instructed language learning and scores on the aptitude test in question (Sawyer & Ranta 2001; Dörnyei & Skehan 2003). A newer test, based on the same theoretical foundations as the MLAT, is Meara's (2005) LLAMA test. The standard aptitude components of these tests have been phonetic coding ability, grammatical sensitivity, rote learning ability and inductive learning ability. For an overview of research on aptitude, see Granena (this volume).

The literature often stresses that these tests were not intended to predict high-level L2 use which involves pragmatic abilities that they do not measure. It has also been argued that these tests do not measure the capacity to learn a language from mere exposure, which would require more implicit learning, and that, rather, they tap into language analytic ability. Since the 1990's, new reconceptualizations of aptitude have included working memory and phonological short-term memory as relevant subcomponents of the construct (Miyake & Friedman 1998; Sawyer & Ranta 2001; see also Kormos this volume, and Bolibaugh & Foster this volume).

Convincing results have been reported concerning the effects of these components on specific aspects of language proficiency, such as a strong correlation between phonological sequence learning and vocabulary learning (Speciale, Ellis & Bywater 2004), phonological short term memory and collocation learning (Skrzypek 2009), and more general language skills, such as reading, writing, listening and speaking, and phonological short term memory in Kormos and Safár (2008). Rota and Reiterer (2009) also investigated the relationship between cognitive variables and pronunciation talent and performance. Apart from measuring working memory (which yielded significant correlations with pronunciation talent), they also included empathy as an independent variable, drawing on Guiora, Brannon and Dull's (1972) early work. Interestingly, significant correlations were observed between empathic skills (as measured by the E-scale, Leibetseder, Laireiter, Ripler & Köller 2001) and different pronunciation-related measures, including pronunciation performance ($r = 0.29$, $p = 0.013$) and phonetic coding ability as measured by the MLAT ($r = 0.20$, $p = 0.04$).

Another strand of research, which has gained more ground recently and may be linked to phonological capacities, is that of relationships between musical aptitude and language proficiency. Once considered insignificant, there is now increasing evidence of such a relationship. Gilleece (2006) found low to moderate correlations, which have been corroborated in neuroscience studies (e.g. Milovanov, Huotilainen, Välimäki, Esquef & Tervaniemi 2008). These studies have found a significant relationship between musical aptitude, English L2 pronunciation, chord discrimination ability and sound-change evoked brain activation. Nardo and Reiterer (2009) also found significant relationships between several measurements of musical ability, L2 pronunciation skills and scores on subcomponents of the MLAT.

For the present study, the most relevant findings in the L2 aptitude literature are those of DeKeyser (2000), Abrahamsson and Hyltenstam (2008) and Granena and Long (2013). All these studies found significant relationships between L2 attainment and language aptitude, especially in late learners. In DeKeyser's study, both early and late Hungarian L1 – English L2 learners completed a grammaticality judgment test (GJT). They also completed a translated version of the words-in-sentences subtest of the MLAT. The study showed that, in the group of adult arrivals, aptitude scores were significantly correlated with GJT results, but this was not the case among learners who had arrived in the L2 environment before closure of the critical period. Abrahamsson and Hyltenstam (2008), who conceived their study as a follow-up to DeKeyser's (2000), investigated the relationship between aptitude, as measured by Meara's (2005) LLAMA test, and written and auditory GJT scores in early and late Spanish L1 – Swedish L2 learners. They found strong correlations in the late group, but also trends toward significant correlations in the early group, suggesting a more important role for aptitude in child SLA than the results reported by DeKeyser (2000). Granena and Long (2013) continued this line of inquiry while adding two more linguistic domains, namely pronunciation and lexis/collocations. Participants were 65 early and late Chinese L1 – Spanish L2 learners, and 12 native speaker controls. Unlike the two preceding studies, no significant correlation was found between auditory GJT scores and aptitude, as measured by the LLAMA test, in the late group, whereas statistically significant correlations were obtained in both of the other linguistic domains in the late, but not in the early, group. Interestingly, scores on the lexis/collocation test correlated significantly with the two auditory subtests in the LLAMA: LLAMA D (sound recognition) ($r = .46$) and LLAMA E (sound-symbol correspondence) ($r = .36$). These are the two aptitude subtests where participants' phonological capacities (phonetic memory) could have played the greatest role.

3.2 Personality and SLA

The next section provides a brief review of personality characteristics, identifying cognitive styles and personality dimensions that may be favourable for engaging in learning and interacting with an unfamiliar culture, i.e. the dominant L2 community. The selection of references is diverse, as the field is rather scattered and results are mixed. Additionally, personality traits of importance for intercultural adjustment effectiveness are included. Behavioural tendencies, reflected in personality traits, influence habits that may have an impact on intercultural effectiveness. Personality traits mirror what a person *will* do, whereas cognitive styles reflect what an individual *can* do (Chamorro-Premuzic, Furnham & Moutafi 2004). Even if cognitive styles are primarily defined as innate aptitudes in psychology, they may relate to personality traits, as in the Five Factor Model (FFM; Costa & McCrae 1992). For example, openness to experience is positively related, and conscientiousness negatively related, to IQ measures.

3.3 Cognitive styles

Two cognitive styles, tolerance for ambiguity (TA) and field-dependence-independence (FDI), have been investigated for their importance for language learning and proficiency. TA and FDI represent two different modes of cognitive functioning with respect to how an individual perceives, acquires and processes information. In an early study of 'The good language learner,' Naiman, Frölich, Stern and Todesco (1978) investigated TA, defined as the tendency to perceive and interpret ambiguous stimuli as sources of threat, using a test by Budner (1962). Ambiguous situations are characterized by complexity, novelty and insoluble issues. Thus, an individual with a high level of TA would experience discomfort and anxiety when confronted with threatening stimuli, and react by avoiding or rejecting the situation. Naiman et al. (1978) found that TA was related to language proficiency.

Although L2 research has not pursued the exploration of TA, TA could be of importance in the individual's motivation to create a positive bond with the L2 community, due to its link to ethnocentrism (see Giles & Johnson 1987). More recently, researchers have drawn attention to how TA can be used to assess adjustment in cross-cultural settings (Herman, Stevens, Bird, Mendenhall & Oddou 2010). Herman et al. further developed Budner's scale and suggested four dimensions: (a) valuing diverse others, (b) coping with change, (c) dealing with unfamiliar situations, and (d) managing conflicting perspectives. It is likely that a person will adapt in a cross-cultural context if he/she has a positive attitude towards unfamiliar people, is able to cope with change and deal with strange situations (i.e. manage the unexpected), and, not least, if he/she has the ability to encompass various perspectives (i.e. understand that there are various ways to grasp what is happening).

3.4   Intuition and openness

Ehrman (2008) chose to categorize her sample as a group of "learners," and not as talents, implying that the role of language aptitude is reduced in favour of other factors influential in engagement in learning. At her disposal was a large sample of foreign service workers (n = 3,145), of whom only 2% had attained the highest proficiency level (Level 4) assessed by an Oral Proficiency Interview conducted at the Foreign Service Institute. This group was labelled "best language learners," while another group was labelled "good language learners." Using the Myers-Briggs Type Indicator (MBTI; Myers 1976), the individuals were assessed on the basis of four of Jung's personality types: extraversion-introversion, sensing-intuition, thinking-feeling and judging-perceiving, which can form a total of 16 psychological types. The MBTI is assumed to tap connections between one's personal style and professional specialization.

Results indicated that the best language learners were characterized by the combination Intuition-Thinking, although only the combination of Introversion-Intuition-Thinking-Judging was found significant. The Intuition-Thinking type is interested in mastering intellectual matters. He/she prefers analytical and strategic thinking, as shown in the drive to search for precision, especially lexical precision, including idioms. Regarding extroversion, individuals represented by the combination Extraversion-Intuition were also found in Level 4 (Ehrman 2008). In contrast, the Sensing type was most frequently found outside the best-learner-domain. These individuals rely on the concreteness of the world, i.e. observing and embracing present, physical and factual aspects.

The role of Intuition in high language achievement is underlined by Ehrman (2008). The explanation might be that intuition, as measured by the MBTI, implies a disposition to perceive patterns and relationships in information. Individuals scoring high on Intuition are inclined towards an open and tolerant attitude and prepared for constant change. They are future-oriented, seek hidden patterns, and make associations. In the case of the highly successful language learner, this would mean that "when it is necessary to adapt to unfamiliar ways of speaking or to pick up native-like ways of self-expression […], a tendency to perceive the world in intuitive ways is likely to be helpful" (2008: 6). Ehrman also pinpointed the link between Intuition and Openness to experience in the Five Factor Model. The intuitive individual has an open-minded character and shares characteristics with individuals who rate high on the scale of Openness to experience. These characteristics include curiosity, broad interest, creativity, originality and imagination. Later studies indicate that Openness correlates not only with Intuition, but also with other dimensions of the MBTI (see Furnham, Dissou, Sloan & Chamorro-Premuzic 2007).

3.5 Multicultural personality dimensions

As previously stated, research on dimensions of personality and L2 performance has focused on how individuals perceive and process information from external sources assessed by TA and MBTI. This line of research has been followed up in studies on intercultural adjustment with an important addition: indicators have been created of how individuals feel and act in a multicultural setting. There have been several attempts to identify psychological and behavioral correlates of intercultural adjustment and adaptation.

One of the more validated measures is the Multicultural Personality Questionnaire (MPQ), created by Van der Zee and van Oudenhoven (2000, 2001). They define multicultural competence in broad terms as "success in the fields of professional effectiveness, personal adjustment and intercultural interactions" (2000:293) and conclude that the Five Factor Model (FFM) was too broad to cover traits relevant for multicultural competence. The MPQ is designed for predictions of an individual's cross-cultural competencies on the basis of three criteria for successfully operating within new cultural environments: "the capacity to make things work," "a feeling of well-being in that environment," and "an interest and ability to deal with individuals from different cultural backgrounds" (2000:293). The instrument has, like the FFM, five scales, but those of the MPQ are intended to focus more narrowly on cultural empathy, open-mindedness, flexibility, social initiative and emotional stability. (For more detailed descriptions of the scales, see personality measures.)

The MPQ has demonstrated its predictive value for multicultural effectiveness among expatriates Peltokorpi 2008), business professionals (Peltokorpi & Froese 2011) and international students (Van der Zee & van Oudenhoven 2000, 2001; Leone, Van der Zee, van Oudenhoven, Perugini & Ercolani 2005). Cultural empathy, open-mindedness and flexibility are linked to the domain of intercultural interaction, whereas social initiative and emotional stability are associated with the domain of personal adjustment.

Leone et al. (2005) examined the relationship between the MPQ data and the FFM in terms of the usual five traits, and found a range of significant correlations. The strongest positive correlations were between cultural empathy and openness to experience, open-mindedness and openness to experience, and social initiative and extroversion. The strongest negative and correlations were between flexibility and conscientiousness, and emotional stability and neuroticism. The findings, nonetheless, contradict the assumed specificity of the FFM, but the predictive value of the MPQ is still superior to that of the FFM for intercultural orientation and across cultures.

All five scales are expected to be unrelated to cognitive abilities, such as intelligence. Yet Van der Zee, Zaal and Piekstra (2003) found that cultural empathy, open-mindedness and flexibility showed positive but weak associations with verbal abilities assessed as abstract-verbal-logical (analytical and logical reasoning with verbal materials), verbal fluency (vocabulary), and language comprehension and productive language skills (text completion and jumbled sentences) (GITP; Tjoa 1965). In the same study, openness to experience in the FFM was also related to verbal abilities. It seems that both open-mindedness and openness demonstrate a more intellectual orientation than mere openness to cultural phenomena. Less is known about what cultural empathy and flexibility have in common with respect to verbal abilities.

In the present study, the MPQ emerged as the first choice measure, due to its high predictive value on a range of criterion variables related to multicultural effectiveness. The chosen sample was assumed to be socially and professionally well-integrated, based on their answers to the background questionnaire. To include measures of cognitive styles appeared less appropriate, as L2 studies tend to use various criterion variables, such as learning strategies, speech production and examination grades. Consequently, most studies have yielded inconsistent outcomes. Furthermore, it is difficult to draw any conclusions regarding the influence of personality variables on L2 performance, as the linguistic variables are often too general to be affected only by individual differences, such as grades, fluency and reading comprehension.

4.   Aims of the study

Following the preceding argumentation, the present exploratory study had two major aims. The study aimed to investigate relationships among collocations, grammaticality judgments and language aptitude, as measured by the LLAMA test (Meara 2005; see also Granena, this volume) in a sample of highly proficient late L2 learners. Another aim was to investigate relationships between personality as assessed by the Multicultural Personality Questionnaire (MPQ; Van der Zee & van Oudenhoven 2000) and linguistic abilities. Further exploration of a sample of highly proficient late learners of French (see Forsberg Lundell & Lindqvist submitted) was undertaken. The individuals were contacted for an extended investigation of aptitude and personality measurements. Data on background variables, interests, informal and formal learning of foreign languages were also collected, although only demographic data are presented here.

5. The empirical study

5.1 Research questions

In view of the study's aims, the following research questions were posed:

1. How are indicators of high-level proficiency (collocations and grammaticality judgments) related to aptitude in L2 French among late learners?
2. How are personality dimensions related to indicators of high-level proficiency (collocations and grammaticality judgments) in L2 French among late learners?

6. Method

6.1 Participants

Participants were 13 late Swedish L1 – French L2 speakers, with 12 women and one man. Their average age was 38 years, ranging from 28 to 58. A majority were living with a French partner and had children at home. All of them had started learning French after the age of 12. Their average LOR in France was 14.5 years, ranging five to 35 years. The average age of arrival was at 20. Both LOR and participants' age varied significantly within the group. In Forsberg Lundell & Lindqvist (submitted), LOR did not correlate with scores on any of the linguistic tests, one of which was the collocation test. This was probably due to the fact that all participants had spent at least five years in France, and it has been suggested that the effect of LOR tends to diminish after five years in the TL community (Cummins 1981; Piske, MacKay & Flege 2001). Abrahamsson and Hyltenstam (2009) prefer the figure of 10 years, after which they suggest that an interlanguage tends to stabilize.

Most participants had studied French formally, although length and quality of instruction varied. Some had studied French as a foreign language for at least six years in school, and some had also taken language courses in France. Others had studied French in school for only a few years. All reported having mainly learnt French through language use while living in France. Some worked in bilingual settings (French/Swedish) whereas others in entirely French settings.

All of them had completed at least upper secondary education and a majority had university degrees.

In sum, this group of L2 late learners can be described as well educated, socially and professionally integrated individuals who had decided to move to France of their own free will. Most claimed they had an interest in French language and culture even before moving. For these reasons, it seems we were dealing with a group of immigrants rarely investigated in the SLA literature, i.e. highly motivated L2 users living in favourable social circumstances.

The participants were recruited mainly from lists of participants in earlier projects on high-level L2 French by one of the authors, chiefly through advertisements at the Swedish Institute and the Swedish Church in Paris. A few of them were recruited through snowballing, that is, new participants were recruited through earlier recruited participants. The linguistic tests were completed in Paris in December, 2010. The collocation test and GJT were part of a larger battery of linguistic tests, both oral and written, lasting approximately two hours. None of the individual tests was timed, but participants were told that they were to finish all of them in two hours. They were paid 20 euros for their participation. The LLAMA test and the MPQ, along with a questionnaire on background variables and language use, were administered in June and July, 2011. A French research assistant met all of the participants again for another two-hour session. The MPQ is a paper-and-pencil test, whereas the LLAMA is computerized. Participants received a gift card of 20 euros the second time around. They were informed of the overall aim of the study and assured confidentiality.

6.2   The aptitude tests

The aptitude test was the LLAMA (Meara 2005), thoroughly described in Granena (this volume) and used by Granena (this volume) and Granena and Long (2013), as well as by Abrahamsson and Hyltenstam (2008). Theoretically, it builds on the same constructs as the MLAT. The most notable difference, according to Meara, is its user-friendliness. The test is intended to measure four different components of language aptitude (to date), which also explains why the results of each subtest are accounted for individually. The four components are: LLAMA B (vocabulary learning), LLAMA D (sound recognition), LLAMA E (sound-symbol correspondence), and LLAMA F (grammatical inferencing). All the subtests are based on artificial or rare languages that are most likely unknown to the participants. The tests are downloadable and supplied by Meara and associates. It should be noted that Meara (2005) insists on the preliminary quality of the test, and that it should not be used in high-stakes situations.

6.3   Personality measurement

The intercultural personality traits were measured with a Swedish version of the MPQ (Van der Zee & van Oudenhoven 2000, 2001). The translation from English to Swedish was made by the authors of the present study. The MPQ is broadly based on Costa and McCrae's (1992) FFM, but narrowed to predict traits relevant to multicultural effectiveness. Five dimensions of multicultural orientation are assessed using 91 five-point scales, from 1 (not at all applicable) to 5 (completely applicable). Higher scores indicate increased loadings on each of the five dimensions. The scales are Cultural Empathy (18 items, high scorers have an interest in other people and are sensitive to their feelings and beliefs); Open-mindedness (18 items, high scorers have an absence of prejudice); Social Initiative (17 items, high scorers tend actively to approach social situations and take the initiative); Emotional Stability (20 items, high scorers remain calm in stressful situations); Flexibility (18 items, high scorers adapt to new situations). In a review by Ponterotto (2008), criterion-related validity was summarized. Scores succeeded in predicting variance in criterion variables, such as well-being, health, coping, job satisfaction and multicultural activity, in a range of samples, such as university students and adult professionals in various countries and continents (Europe, North America).

In addition, participants answered questions on age, gender, socioeconomic status, civil status and educational level.

6.4   The collocation test

In the present study, the overarching aim is to gauge late L2 learners' possibilities for attaining nativelikeness. It is therefore important to design the elicitation measures carefully, so as to avoid ceiling effects. It is also well-known that productive tests are more difficult than receptive tests (cf. Schmitt 2010). It was therefore decided to create a productive collocation test in French. Collocations can be conceived within a phraseological or a frequency-based framework. In the present study, as opposed to our earlier studies of free speech (Forsberg 2010; Forsberg Lundell & Lindqvist 2012), it was decided to use a frequency-based definition, since it offers a more objective identification procedure and is easily applicable to the selection of items for a test.

For the selection of items, Gyllstad's (2007) procedure was followed quite closely. With respect to the format, we were inspired by Mizrahi and Laufer (2010), since they had also designed a productive test, whereas Gyllstad designed a receptive one. There follow the different steps taken to create the collocation test.

In conformity with Gyllstad (2007), it was decided to focus on verb – noun collocates, such as *rendre justice* (Eng. "do justice"). It was also decided to work with data from written French, since the test was to be taken in the written mode:

1. 150 frequent nouns were selected randomly from Tom Cobb's frequency bands for written French. Gyllstad used words from low-frequency bands, such as 10K–14K, but since no such low-frequency bands exist for French, the 1K, 2K and 3K frequency bands from the Lexical tutor were used instead (http://www.lextutor.ca/freq/lists_download/). These frequency bands are based on the French language newspapers *Le Soir* (Belgium) and *Le Monde* (France).

2. The second step was to search for collocating verbs for these 150 nouns. This was in order to use a corpus large enough to allow strong collocational patterns to emerge. To stay within the journalistic genre, we used the database *Les Voisins de Le Monde* (http://redac.univ-tlse2.fr/voisinsdelemonde/). This database contains 200,000,000 words and is based on every edition of the newspaper *Le Monde* from 1991–2000. The database provides both frequencies and a mutual information (MI) score, which is a statistical measure used in corpus linguistics to calculate a collocation's degree of cohesiveness.

3. Several selection criteria were applied in the search for relevant test items: the MI-score threshold was set at > 3, in accordance with many other studies in the field (Ellis, Simpson-Vlach & Maynard 2008; Siyanova & Schmitt 2008). The frequency threshold was set at 200. Given the size of the database, this yields a frequency of 1/1,000,000 words. That may seem like a small number, but Ellis et al.'s study also served as a reference here, in which the frequency threshold was set at 10/1,000,000 words. Their study was concerned with lexical bundles in academic English, such as *at the end of the*, which are more frequent in the input than the content-word-based collocations in our study (see Forsberg 2010, for differences in frequency between different types of formulaic sequences). After applying these two frequency thresholds, another selection criterion was employed. As this test was supposed to target the most advanced levels, it was deemed important to eliminate overly easy items. Recent L2 collocation research has shown that collocations that are equivalent in the L1 and the L2 have, not surprisingly, been shown to convey acquisition advantages (Wolter & Gyllstad 2011). It was therefore decided to eliminate all translation equivalents, or as some would call them, *cognates*. Examples of such collocations are ***commettre un crime*** 'begå ett brott' (Eng. "commit a crime") and ***signer un accord*** 'skriva under ett avtal' (Eng. "to sign an agreement"). Having applied all the above criteria, 70 verb-noun combinations remained.

4.   Example sentences for these 70 combinations were searched for on www.google.fr.

60 items provided good sentences, which were piloted with 10 NSs of French and nine NNSs in Stockholm. The results of this pilot were used to determine the final selection of items by establishing a minimum accuracy threshold. Only if 50% or more of the NSs provided a correct answer to an item, was the item included in the final test. This procedure yielded a total of 46 items in the final test.

As stated earlier, the test format was inspired by that of Mizrahi and Laufer (2010) and looks like this:

1.   *L'ONU est fermement résolue à r_____ justice aux victimes du génocide.*
2.   *Si les petites entreprises é_____ des difficultés à embaucher, c'est aussi parce qu'elles disposent de moyens qui sont moindres.*
3.   *L'industrie porno entend m_____ un terme au piratage d'ici 2012.*

In contrast to Mizrahi and Laufer (2010), only one letter was given in the gap to avoid ceiling effects. Even though this meant that a possible alternative collocating verb was occasionally provided, it was decided, for practical reasons, only to judge as correct the answers with the most frequently collocating verbs, i.e. only one correct answer for each sentence.

6.5   The Written Grammatical Judgment test (GJT)

As already suggested, the GJT was included as a point of comparison for the collocation test and was therefore accorded a minor role in the present study. The written GJT was developed in collaboration with Inge Bartning (see Bartning 2012). The test was originally based on Bylund's (2008) GJT for Spanish. Grammatical features tested included subject-verb agreement in complex syntax, noun-phrase (NP) agreement, anaphors, verb constructions and time, mode, aspect (TMA). The test included a total of 46 items. It should be noted that both verb-phrase (VP) and NP agreement sentences include ungrammaticalities in silent morphology, which would not be audible in an auditory GJT; these probably tap into metalinguistic awareness more than any mental grammar. Here are two example sentences:

1.   *Les élèves croyaient que le sapin *avaient/avait comme origine la mythologie allemande* (The students thought that the Christmas tree *were/was of German origin).
2.   *L'inspecteur pensait que l'avion n'était plus suffisamment performant* (The inspector thought that the airplane was not able to perform sufficiently well anymore).

7. Results

The first research question involved exploration of relationships among linguistic measures, collocations, grammatical judgment and aptitude tests in highly proficient late L2 French learners. Means and standard deviations for scores on the linguistic tests are presented in Table 1.

Table 1. Means, standard deviations of linguistic tests among highly proficient adult French L2 learners ($n = 13$)

	M	SD
Collocations	29.70	8.13
Grammatical judgement	38.31	3.99
LLAMA B	54.23	24.65
LLAMA D	37.70	15.22
LLAMA E	78.46	33.63
LLAMA F	64.62	24.70

The present sample of French L2 learners can be compared on LLAMA test scores to another group of late L2 learners (Granena & Long 2013). Our sample has an age of onset of 13–17 years, and age of arrival in France of 17–21. In the Granena and Long sample, age of onset was 16–29 years, which coincided with age of arrival 16–29 years. In our sample, the participants' mean age of testing was 38 years, whereas mean age of testing was 31.8 in the Granena and Long sample. Our sample had almost the same means as the late learners in Granena and Long (2013) on LLAMA B (54.23 and 50.00, respectively). Differences between samples were greater for the other LLAMA tests. Our sample had descriptively higher means on LLAMA D (37.70 vs. 24.17), LLAMA E (78.46 vs. 62.22), and LLAMA F (64.62 vs. 45.56).

Results from correlations of linguistic test scores indicated one significant positive correlation ($r = .58$, $p < .05$) between collocations and LLAMA D scores (Table 2). Other scales were also positively correlated, but not statistically significantly so. Trends in the direction of significance were found for collocations and grammatical judgment ($r = .50$, $p = .08$), for LLAMA F and GJT scores ($r = .47$, $p = .11$), and between LLAMA B and LLAMA F ($r = .47$, $p = .10$).

The second research question concerned relationships between personality dimensions, as measured by MPQ, and linguistic measures. Means, standard deviations and Cronbach alphas for scales in the MPQ are presented in Table 3. Analyses of Cronbach alpha for the subscales were satisfactory (all above .70) and

Table 2. Pearson's correlations between collocations, grammatical judgment and aptitude tests among highly proficient adult French L2 learners ($n = 13$)

	2	3	4	5	6
1 Collocations	.50	.32	.58*	.13	.26
2 Grammaticality judgment	–	.35	.05	.10	.47
3 LLAMA B	–	–	.35	.24	.47
4 LLAMA D	–	–	–	.10	.42
5 LLAMA E					–.10
6 LLAMA F					–

Note: *$p < .05$, two-tailed.

Table 3. Means, standard deviations and Cronbach alphas for the MPQ among highly proficient adult French L2 learners ($n = 13$)

	M	SD	Cronbach's α
Cultural empathy	4.10	.31	.72
Open-mindedness	3.79	.53	.87
Social initiative	3.89	.56	.84
Emotional stability	3.15	.51	.87
Flexibility	3.05	.37	.72

comparable to those in previous studies (van Oudenhoven & van der Zee 2002; Korzilius, van Hooft, Planken & Hendrix 2011). As most individuals in the present study were professionally and socially integrated female expatriates, it was possible that their personality profiles according to the MPQ would differ from those in other samples. A comparison of MPQ subscale means indicated that this group of expatriates exhibited higher means for cultural empathy and social initiative ($M = 4.10$ and 3.79, respectively) compared to samples in the literature, e.g. exchange students ($M = 3.76$ and 3.17, respectively) (Leong 2007) and business professionals with international experience ($M = 3.78$ and 3.58, respectively) (Korzilius et al. 2011). The open-mindedness mean, as well, was higher for the expatriates ($M = 3.79$) than the means of exchange students ($M = 3.65$) and business professionals ($M = 3.58$). Means for emotional stability and flexibility were fairly similar.

Results showed significant positive correlations between two scales of the MPQ and collocation scores (Table 4). Both cultural empathy ($r = .62, p < .05$) and open-mindedness ($r = .57, p < .05$) correlated with collocation scores. Among

Table 4. Pearson's correlations between the MPQ, collocations, grammatical judgment (GJ) and the LLAMA language aptitude tests B, D, E and F (n = 13)

	Collocations	GJ	B	D	E	F
Cultural empathy	.62*	.41	.14	.67*	−.13	.27
Open-mindedness	.57*	−.11	.12	.78*	−.18	.24
Social initiative	.03	−.05	.13	.21	−.33	−.36
Emotional stability	−.06	−.13	.17	−.26	−.43	.09
Flexibility	.43	−.21	−.24	.20	−.14	−.13
MPQ	.44	−.08	.12	.46	−.41	.29

Note: *p < .05, two-tailed.

the aptitude tests, the same personality dimensions of cultural empathy (r = .67, p < .05) and open-mindedness (r = .78, p < .05) correlated positively with one of the aptitude tests, LLAMA D. The total MPQ score did not correlate with collocations, grammatical judgment or aptitude tests.

8. Discussion

The first research question concerned how indicators of high level proficiency (collocations and grammaticality judgments) relate to aptitude in L2 French among late learners. It was shown that collocations correlated positively and strongly with LLAMA D, but not with the other LLAMA sub-tests. It is interesting that collocations correlated only with the LLAMA D, since Granena and Long (2013) found a similar correlation. Some theoretical support can be found for this, as there is evidence of an association between phonological memory and the learning of vocabulary, or nativelike selection (Speciale et al. 2004; Bolibaugh & Foster this volume). The LLAMA D would also tap into such learning, since it measures phonetic memory. A more general theoretical implication of this finding would be that phonetic memory, which, according to Granena (this volume), taps into the implicit learning capacity, would be more important for high-level proficiency than grammatical inference. The latter assumption is in line with the results in the present study and shows that grammaticality judgment scores were not correlated with collocations or with the LLAMA tests.

The second research question investigated whether personality dimensions relate to indicators of high-level proficiency (collocations and grammaticality judgments) in L2 French among late learners. Findings showed that the personality dimensions of cultural empathy and open-mindedness were significantly and positively associated with both collocations and LLAMA D scores, but not with grammaticality judgment test scores. Both personality dimensions appear to involve a cognitive capacity to overcome in-group bias, usually leading to devaluation of the outer group, in this case the L2 community, as high scorers on cultural empathy and open-mindedness are disposed to adopt other people's perspective easily, to be tolerant and not prejudiced. The present sample may consist of individuals motivated to learn the L2, who had an open mind and were able to empathize with others that led to their engagement with successful learning strategies (including exposing themselves to the L2 community), in order to integrate well professionally and socially. Learning collocations may be one means of achieving these ends. All in all, these individuals can be characterized as having achieved multicultural effectiveness. From another point of view, taking the findings on associations between cultural empathy, open-mindedness and verbal abilities (Van der Zee et al. 2003) into consideration, it may be that these individuals had originally rather advanced verbal abilities and, therefore, learned collocations more effortlessly than individuals with weaker verbal abilities.

It was intriguing to find correlations between personality dimensions and LLAMA D. These correlations were not foreseen by the design and are not easily explained by the literature. We can only speculate about why the LLAMA D test, which assesses phonetic memory, was the only LLAMA sub-test that related to personality. Rota and Reiterer (2009) found an association between empathic skills (as measured by the E-scale, Leibetseder et al. 2001) and different pronunciation-related measures, including pronunciation performance and phonetic coding ability as measured by the MLAT aptitude test, which is likely similar to the LLAMA D. It is possible that the E-scale shares variance with the personality dimensions of cultural empathy and open-mindedness with respect to sensitivity and concern with emotions and cognitions. As this individual, capable of perspective-taking (cultural empathy) and showing tolerance (open-mindedness), would also understand social situations well and show empathic emotions. He/she would also be able to put him- or herself into the emotional situations of another person, as measured by the E-scale. Empathy involves investigating reactions to real-life situations and showing concern that requires cognitive analysis. The three measures appear to share a perspective-taking and empathic approach. This line of argument is speculative, and for future research it would be interesting to investigate associations between empathy and phonetic memory/pronunciation, and how those dimensions relate to levels of mastery of collocations.

Research on cognitive styles and SLA offers arguments for the importance of perspective-taking ability and tolerance for multicultural effectiveness shown in both tolerance of ambiguity (interpersonal aspects, coping with change) and field-dependence-independence (functioning rather autonomously from external sources of information, i.e. demonstrating independence).

It should be noted that it is indeed an open question if the elevated scores for cultural empathy and open-mindedness already characterized the sample at the beginning of their stay in France or if the scores were to some degree the result of successful intercultural adaptation (see Dewaele & Van Oudenhoven 2009).

Grammaticality judgement was included in the design for comparative reasons because high grammaticality judgment scores can indicate that an individual has high metalinguistic awareness. This kind of proficiency does not appear to be of importance for collocations, as there was no correlation between them in the present study, and did not relate to aptitude as measured by the LLAMA sub-tests. This confirms our belief that collocations are a particularly fruitful linguistic category to include in studies of high L2 proficiency.

We would also like to draw attention to relationships with trends towards statistical significance between MPQ scores and linguistics measures. One of the LLAMA sub-tests, namely, LLAMA E, had only negative correlations; the weakest correlation was –.13 for cultural empathy and the strongest for emotional stability $(r = -.43)$. This means that an individual with low scores on emotional stability has high scores on LLAMA E, tapping the aptitude to detect sound-symbol correspondences. Future studies are warranted to examine this link more closely; whether these rather curious findings are only relevant for LLAMA E and certain personality dimensions, or only related in samples with highly proficient adult L2 learners with similar personality profiles. Moreover, the present sample had elevated scores on social initiative. High scorers on social initiative are less likely to feel discouraged after facing obstacles and failures, whereas low scorers tend to have difficulty finding alternative solutions to problems and maintaining commitment to goals. Research shows that social initiative in the MPQ and extraversion in the FFM are strongly correlated (see van der Zee & van Oudenhoven 2000). It is interesting to note that the proactive approach of social initiative did not relate to L2 proficiency, but may have been an advantage for the present sample's successful adaption to their new country. The present result with high scores on social initiative is in line with the literature on its role for work adjustment (Peltokorpi 2008; Peltokorpi & Froese 2011) and on the extroverts' disposition to seek social contact, status and power (Wilt & Revelle 2009).

The limitations of our exploratory study need to be noted. Firstly, the sample was small ($n = 13$). Secondly, it was a convenience sample, and included socially and professionally integrated individuals. The sample was also limited in that the majority of participants were female and well-educated. Additional research with larger, more diverse samples is warranted. Despite the evident limitations, we believe that the present results add to the body of research on highly proficient late

L2 learners, due to the strong positive correlations observed between personality measures intended to assess multicultural effectiveness and measures of linguistic proficiency and aptitude.

9. Concluding remarks

The present exploratory study provides some support for the use of personality measures in L2 acquisition, as two personality dimensions in the MPQ correlated strongly with a specific linguistic measure of high-level L2 proficiency, i.e. collocations, and also with one component of language aptitude, i.e. phonetic memory/sound recognition. In particular, personality dimensions encompassing perspective-taking and an open-minded attitude appear to be more important for L2 attainment than personality dimensions emphasizing a more social and outgoing individual, when high-level L2 proficiency is concerned. Moreover, the use of measures of collocational knowledge to tap high L2 proficiency is a promising area for further investigations. Future studies are warranted to replicate the results in larger and more diverse samples, given the exploratory nature of the study and the small sample used, which could have influenced the results of the correlations. With respect to the multifaceted learning process for L2, it is suggested that both personality and social psychological factors should be taken into consideration when predicting successful L2 learning.

References

Abrahamsson, N., & Hyltenstam, K. (2008). The robustness of aptitude effects in near-native second language acquisition. *Studies in Second Language Acquisition, 30*, 481–509.

Abrahamsson, N., & Hyltenstam, K. (2009). Age of L2 acquisition and degree of nativelikeness – listener perception vs. linguistic scrutiny. *Language Learning, 58*, 249–306.

Adolphs, S., & Durow, V. (2004). Socio-cultural integration and the development of formulaic sequences. In N. Schmitt (Ed.), *Formulaic sequences: Acquisition, processing and use* (pp. 107–126). Amsterdam: John Benjamins.

Bahns, J., & Eldaw, M. (1993). Should we teach EFL students collocations? *System, 21*, 101–114.

Bartning, I. (2012). High-level proficiency in second language use: Morphosyntax and discourse. In M. Watorek, S. Benazzo, & M. Hickmann (Eds.), *Comparative perspectives on language acquisition. A tribute to Clive Perdue* (pp. 1701–1787). Bristol: Multilingual Matters.

Bolibaugh, C., & Foster, P. (this volume). Memory-based aptitude for native-like selection: The role of phonological short-term memory.

Bolly, C. (2008). Les unites phraséologiques: Un phénomène linguistique complexe? Séquences (semi-) figées avec les verbes *prendre* et *donner* en français écrit L1 et L2. Approche descriptive et acquisitionnelle. Unpublished doctoral dissertation. Université Catholique de Louvain.

Bonk, W. (2000). Testing ESL Learners' knowledge of collocation. ERIC Document Reproduction Service No. ED 442 309.

Budner, S. (1962). Intolerane of ambiguity as a personality variable. *Journal of Personality, 30,* 29–50.

Bylund, E. (2008). *Age differences in first language attrition: A maturational constraints perspective.* Unpublished doctoral dissertation. Centre for Bilingualism Research. Stockholm University.

Carroll, J.B. (1981). Twenty-five years of research on foreign language aptitude. In K.C. Diller (Ed.), *Individual differences and universals in language learning aptitude* (pp. 83–118). Rowley, MA: Newbury House.

Chamorro-Premuzic, T., Furnham, A., & Moutafi, J. (2004). The relationship between estimated and psychometric personality and intelligence scores. *Journal of Research in Personality, 37,* 319–338.

Conklin, K., & Schmitt, N. (2008). Formulaic sequences: Are they processed more quickly than nonformulaic language by native and nonnative speakers? *Applied Linguistics, 29,* 72–89.

Costa, P.T., & McCrae, R.R. (1992). *NEO PI-R professional manual.* Odessa, FL: Psychological Assessment Resources.

Cummins, J. (1981). Age on arrival and immigrant second language learning in Canada: A reassessment. *Applied Linguistics, 2,* 132–149.

DeKeyser, R.M. (2000). The robustness of critical period effects in second language acquisition. *Studies in Second Language Acquisition, 22,* 499–533.

Dewaele, J.-M., & van Oudenhoven, J.P. (2009). The effect of multilingualism/multiculturalism on personality: No gain without pain for Third Culture Kids? *International Journal of Multilingualism, 6,* 443–459.

Dörnyei, Z. (2005). *The psychology of the language learner: Individual differences in second language acquisition.* Mahwah, NJ: Lawrence Erlbaum Associates.

Dörnyei, Z., Durow, V., & Zahran, K. (2004). Individual differences and their effects on formulaic sequence acquisition. In N. Schmitt (Ed.), *Formulaic sequences: Acquisition, processing and use* (pp. 87–106). Amsterdam: John Benjamins.

Dörnyei, Z., & Skehan, P. (2003). Individual differences in second language learning. In M.H. Long, & C.J. Doughty (Eds.), *Handbook of language teaching* (pp. 589–630). Oxford: Blackwell.

Durrant, P., & Schmitt, N. (2009). To what extent do native and non-native writers make use of collocations? *International Review of Applied Linguistics in Language Learning, 47,* 157–177.

Ehrman, M. (2008). Personality and good language learners. In C. Griffiths (Ed.), *Lessons from good language learners* (pp. 61–72). Cambridge: CUP.

Ellis, N., Simpson-Vlach, C.R., & Maynard, C. (2008). Formulaic language in native and second language speakers: Psycholinguistics, corpus linguistics and TESOL. *TESOL Quarterly, 42,* 375–396.

Eyckmans, J. (2009). Towards an assessment of learners' receptive and productive syntagmatic knowledge. In A. Barfield, & H. Gyllstad (Eds.), *Researching collocations in another language. Multiple interpretations* (pp. 139–152). Basingstoke: Palgrave MacMillan.

Farghal, M., & Obiedat, H. (1995). Collocations: A neglected variable in EFL writings. *International Review of Applied Linguistics in Language Learning, 33,* 315–331.

Forsberg Lundell, F. (2010). Using conventional sequences in L2 French. *International Review of Applied Linguistics in Language Learning, 48,* 25–50.

Forsberg Lundell, F., & Lindqvist, C. (2012). Vocabulary development in advanced L2 French – do formulaic sequences and lexical richness develop at the same rate? *LIA: Language, Interaction, Acquisition, 3,* 73–92.

Forsberg Lundell, F., & Lindqvist, C. (submitted). Lexical aspects of very advanced L2 French.

Furnham, A., Dissou, G., Sloan, P., & Chamorro-Premuzic, T. (2007). Personality and intelligence in business people: A study of two personality and two intelligence measures. *Journal of Business Psychology, 22,* 99–109.

Gardner, R.C. (2001). Integrative motivation and second language acquisition. In Z. Dörnyei, & R. Schmidt (Eds.), *Motivation and second language acquisition* (pp. 1–20). Honolulu, HI: University of Hawaii Press.

Gatbonton, E., & Trofimovich, P. (2008). The ethnic group affiliation and L2 proficiency link: Empirical evidence. *Language Awareness, 17,* 229–248.

Giles, H., & Johnson, P. (1987). Ethnolinguistic identity theory: A social psychological approach to language maintenance. *International Journal of Sociology of Language, 68,* 69–100.

Gilleece, L.F. (2006). *An empirical investigation of the association between musical aptitude and foreign language aptitude.* Unpublished doctoral dissertation. University of Dublin, Trinity College.

Granena, G. (this volume). Cognitive aptitudes for second language learning and the LLAMA Language Aptitude Test.

Granena, G., & Long, M.H. (2013). Age of onset, length of residence, aptitude and ultimate attainment in three linguistic domains. *Second Language Research, 29*(1).

Granger, S. (1998). Prefabricated patterns in advanced EFL writings: Collocations and formulae'. In A.P. Cowie (Ed.), *Phraseology: Theory, analysis and applications* (pp. 145–160). Clarendon Press.

Guiora, A., Brannon, R., & Dull, C. (1972). Empathy and second language learning. *Language Learning, 1,* 111–130.

Gyllstad, H. (2007). *Testing English collocations. Developing receptive tests for use with advanced Swedish learners.* Unpublished doctoral Dissertation, Lund University.

Herman, J.L., Stevens, M.J., Bird, A., Mendenhall, M., & Oddou, G. (2010). The Tolerance for Ambiguity Scale: Towards a more refined measure for international management research. *International Journal of Intercultural Relations, 34,* 58–65.

Howarth, P. (1998). Phraseology and Second Language Proficiency. *Applied Linguistics, 19,* 24–44.

Kormos, J., & Safár, A. (2008). Phonological short-term memory, working memory and foreign language performance in intensive language learning. *Bilingualism: Language and Cognition, 11,* 261–271.

Kormos, J. (this volume). The role of working memory, phonological short-term memory and language aptitude in second language attainment.

Korzilius, H., van Hooft, A., Planken, B., & Hendrix, C. (2011). Birds of different feathers? The relationship between multicultural personality dimensions and foreign language mastery in business professionals working in a Dutch agricultural multinational. *International Journal of Intercultural Relations, 35,* 540–553.

Laufer, B., & Waldman, T. (2011). Verb-Noun collocations in Second language writing: A corpus analysis of learners' English. *Language Learning, 61,* 647–672.

Leibetseder, M., Laireiter, A.R., Riepler, A., & Köller, T. (2001). E-Skala: Fragebogen zur Erfassung von Empathie – Beschreibung und psychometrische Eigenschaften. *Zeitschrift für Differentielle und Diagnostische Psychologie, 22,* 70–85.

Leone, L., van der Zee, K., van Oudenhoven, J.-P., Perugini, M., & Ercolani, A.P. (2005). The cross-cultural generalizability and validity of the Multicultural Personality Questionnaire. *Personality and Individual Differences, 38*, 1449–1462.

Leong, C.-H. (2007). Predictive validity of the multicultural personality questionnaire: A longitudinal study on the socio-psychological adaptation of Asian undergraduates who took part in a study-abroad program. *International Journal of Intercultural Relations, 31*, 545–559.

Meara, P. (2005). *LLAMA language aptitude tests*. Swansea, UK: Lognostics.

Milovanov, R., Huotilainen, M., Välimäki, V., Esquef, P., & Tervaniemi, M. (2008). Musical aptitude and second language pronunciation skills in school-aged children: Neural and behavioral evidence. *Brain Research, 1194*, 81–89.

Miyake, A., & Friedman, N.P. (1998). Individual differences in second language proficiency: Working memory as language aptitude. In A.F. Healy & L.E. Bourne (Eds.), *Foreign language learning: Psycholinguistic studies on training and retention* (pp. 339–364). Mahwah, NJ: Lawrence Erlbaum Associates.

Mizrahi, E., & Laufer, B. (2010). Lexical competence of highly advanced L2 users: Is their collocation knowledge as good as their productive vocabulary size? Paper presented at *EUROSLA* 2010, Reggio Emilia, Italy.

Mizrahi, E., & Laufer, B. (2011). Does one need a native-like productive lexical knowledge to pass for a native writer? Paper presented at *EUROSLA* 2011, Stockholm, Sweden.

Myers, I.B. (1976). *Introduction to type*. Palo Alto, CA: Consulting Psychologist Press.

Naiman, N., Fröhlich, M., Stern, H.H., & Todesco, A. (1978). *The good language learner*. Toronto: Ontario Institute for Studies in Education.

Nardo, D., & Reiterer, S.M. (2009). Musicality and phonetic language aptitude. In G. Dogil, & S.M. Reiterer (Eds.), *Language talent and brain activity* (pp. 213–256). Berlin: Mouton de Gruyter.

Nesselhauf, N. (2005). *Collocations in a learner corpus*. Amsterdam: John Benjamins.

Peltokorpi, V. (2008). Cross-cultural adjustment of expatriates in Japan. *The International Journal of Human Resource Management, 19*, 1588–1606.

Peltokorpi, V., & Froese, F.J. (2011). The impact of expatriate personality traits on cross-cultural adjustment: A study with expatriates in Japan. *International Business Review, 21*, 734–746.

Peterson, C., & Al-Haik, A. (1976). The development of the Defence Language Aptitude Battery. *Educational and Psychological Measurement, 36*, 369–380.

Pimsleur, P. (1966). *The Pimsleur Language Aptitude Battery*. New York, NY: Harcourt, Brace, Jovanovic.

Piske, T., MacKay, I., & Flege, J.E. (2001). Factors affecting degree of foreign accent in an L2: A review. *Journal of Phonetics, 29*, 191–215.

Ponterotto, J.G. (2008). Theoretical and empirical advances in multicultural counseling and psychology. In S.D. Brown, & R.W. Lent (Eds.), *Handbook of counseling psychology* (4th ed.) (pp. 121–140). Hoboken, NJ: Wiley.

Robinson, P. (2005). Aptitude and second language acquisition. *Annual Review of Applied Linguistics, 25*, 46–73.

Rota, G., & Reiterer, S.M. (2009). Cogntive aspects of language talent. In G. Dogil, & S.M. Reiterer (Eds.), *Language talent and brain activity* (pp. 67–96). Berlin: Mouton de Gruyter.

Sawyer, M., & Ranta, L. (2001). Aptitude, individual differences and instructional design. In P. Robinson (Ed.), *Cognition and second language instruction* (pp. 319–353). Cambridge: CUP.

Schmitt, N. (2010). *Researching vocabulary: A vocabulary research manual*. Basingstoke: Palgrave Macmillan.

Schmitt, N., & R. Carter. (2004). Formulaic sequences in action: An introduction. In N. Schmitt (Ed.), *Formulaic sequences: Acquisition, processing and use* (pp. 1–22). Amsterdam: John Benjamins.

Siyanova, A., & Schmitt, N. (2008). L2 learner production and processing of collocation: A multi-study perspective. *Canadian Modern Language Review, 64*, 429–458.

Skandera, P. (Ed.). (2007). *Phraseology and culture in English*. Berlin: Mouton de Gruyter.

Skrzypek, A. (2009). Phonological Short-term Memory and L2 collocational development in adult learners. *Eurosla Yearbook, 9*, 160–184.

Speciale, G., Ellis, N.C., & Bywater, T. (2004). Phonological sequence learning and short-term store capacity determine second language vocabulary acquisition. *Applied Psycholinguistics, 25*, 293–321.

Tjoa, A. (1965). *Handleiding boekje* [Manual booklet]. International publication. Amsterdam: GITP R&D.

Underwood, G., Schmitt, N., & Galpin, A. (2004). The eyes have it: An eye-movement study into the processing of formulaic sequences. In N. Schmitt (Ed.), *Formulaic sequences: Acquisition, processing and use* (pp. 155–172). Amsterdam: John Benjamins.

van der Zee, K.I., & van Oudenhoven, J.P. (2000). The Multicultural Personality Questionnaire: A multicultural instrument of multicultural effectiveness. *European Journal Personality, 14*, 291–309.

van der Zee, K.I., & van Oudenhoven, J.P. (2001). The Multicultural Personality Questionnaire: Reliability and validity of self- and other ratings of multicultural effectiveness. *Journal of Research in Personality, 35*, 278–288.

van der Zee, Zaal, J.N., & Piekstra, J. (2003). Validation of the Multicultural Personality Questionnaire in the context of personnel selection. *European Journal of Personality, 17*, 77–100.

van Oudenhoven, J.P., & van der Zee, K.I. (2002). Predicting multicultural effectiveness of international students: The Multicultural Personality Questionnaire. *International Journal of Intercultural Relations, 26*, 679–694.

Wilt, J., & Revelle, W. (2009). Extraversion. In M. Leary, & R. Hoyle (Eds.), *Handbook of individual differences in social behavior* (pp. 27–45). New York: Guilford Press.

Wolter, B., & Gyllstad, H. (2011). Collocational links in the L2 mental lexicon and the influence of L1 intralexical knowledge. *Applied Linguistics, 32*, 430–449.

Wray, A. (2002). *Formulaic language and the Lexicon*. Cambridge: CUP.

PART IV

Implications for educational policy and language teaching

Some implications of research findings on sensitive periods in language learning for educational policy and practice

Mike Long
University of Maryland

Opinions differ as to the implications of research findings on sensitive periods in language learning – and more generally, on age effects – for educational policy and practice. This is true even among those convinced of relationships among age of beginning a foreign language, rate of development, and long-term attainment. It is argued that policy recommendations need to be determined with clear reference to the general educational context, including the importance of foreign language abilities in the society, and for the individuals, concerned. Early and more recent research findings are then reviewed, and proposals made for future work on the issues.

1. General policy considerations

The implications of research findings on sensitive periods (SPs) for educational policy and practice are not straightforward. Early French immersion programs in Canada were motivated in part by the advocacy of Penfield and others impressed by the critical period (CP) notion, and immersion programs are widely accepted as having proven very successful. *Younger is better* findings have also served as part of the rationale for educational policy decisions in countries that have lowered the age at which English is introduced in schools, e.g. from 11 to 8 in Japan, and from 11 to six in Spain (and even lower in some Spanish regions). However, a number of researchers who have examined the relative effectiveness of an early start remain unconvinced.

The skeptics include some who consider the evidence for maturational constraints to be solid, but who reason that the kind of instruction available to younger learners is inadequate to take advantage of the child's capacity for implicit learning, and/or that if available, the time it would take to do so would be time taken away from other subjects (see, e.g. DeKeyser & Larson-Hall 2005; Patkowski 1994). Rather, they say, the goal should be to adapt foreign language instruction to the age of the learners. They also include some who reject the evidence for maturational constraints, and/or think that, *in limited-input contexts*, later starters do as well as, or better than, younger starters after the same total hours of instruction (see, e.g. Muñoz 2006a, b, 2011; Muñoz & Singleton 2011). Again, they point out that a younger start will not help unless and until alternative models of instruction become available for younger children. They recommend increasing the richness of input and intensity of exposure, particularly in the early years, arguing that "younger starters have not benefitted from their younger age because of the lack of the massive exposure needed for their implicit learning mechanisms to operate in the early stages" (Muñoz 2011:128). In second language (L2) contexts, too, e.g. English-as-a-second-language (ESL) for limited English-speaking school-age children, if younger children learn more implicitly, then, instead of code-focused lessons, curricula should provide rich input and plentiful opportunities for communicative use of the language and introduce more focus on form (not forms) with increasing age (Long & Adamson 2012).

On either side of the discussion, most would agree with Hyltenstam and Abrahamsson (2001:161–164), who pointed to the differential relevance of basic and applied research in this and other contexts. Research on maturational constraints is basic research. Educational policy decisions concerning such matters as optimal timing for the introduction of foreign language teaching (FLT) or second language teaching (SLT), the relative merits of transitional and maintenance bilingual education programs, or the pros and cons of pull-out ESL, immersion and submersion for immigrant children of different ages, are issues best decided by the findings of applied research directly addressing those issues.

My own view is that the first step for policy makers is to consider societal, family and learner goals and needs, on the one hand, and societal resources, on the other. Is a native-like accent/grammar/command of L2 pragmatics, etc. unimportant, important, or necessary, and for whom – the society as a whole, the family or the individual student? Answers to such questions will vary considerably as a function of such factors as the international reach of the dominant language(s) in the country concerned, the history and power of any ethnolinguistic minorities, the availability of trained native and non-native speakers of the foreign language(s), and the human and financial resources available.

Excellent command of one or more additional languages, for example, is likely to be more important for speakers of so-called "small" languages (those spoken within countries with small populations, with limited external use, such as Dutch or Finnish), or for immigrants. If high-level proficiency is not very important, conversely, part of the rationale for an early start vanishes. Some might consider that to be outweighed, nevertheless, *if* resources are available, by the knowledge that learning a second language is easier for younger starters, due to their greater capacity for implicit learning. With respect to resources, if starting age is lowered, with a typical consequence being an increase in the total hours of language instruction required, are trained teachers and suitable materials available, or will it just be more of the same old drill and kill, made even more inappropriate for being served up to younger learners? Is kindergarten and elementary school teachers' command of the target language acceptable, or is the input their speech would provide likely to be impoverished and problematically non-native-like? 60% of Australian primary school teachers of Japanese surveyed by Nicholas et al. (1993), for example, reported that their own command of the language was not strong enough to allow them to hold even a relatively short beginners' class completely in the L2. If adequate instruction is *un*available, traditional FLT may well be better postponed, since, rightly or (I would say) wrongly, it relies so heavily on explicit teaching and learning, at which older learners are better. Moreover, an early start will not help much if the L2 is unavailable when students transition from elementary to middle school, or if only beginning and elementary classes are available at high school, resulting in younger starters being placed in classes with age peers who are complete beginners. All too often, the potential advantages of an earlier start are lost because courses in a foreign language are unavailable at a middle school or high school, or are available, but mix early starters with students just beginning the language, forcing those with some proficiency to wait while the others catch up (see, e.g. Burstall 1975, 1977; Burstall et al. 1974).

This is bad enough in cases like French as a foreign language for English school children, where students are adding another language with considerable reach to their L1, English, but there are still more serious cases. What if near-native abilities are required by as large a proportion of the population as possible, as is the situation in many so-called *small language* countries? At what age is it best to deploy whatever societal resources are available?

2. Early research findings

Earlier is better findings are from long-term studies of second language acquisition (SLA) in the target language environment, and as critics of earlier starts point out, we have insufficient knowledge of the long-term effects of earlier versus later foreign language (FL) education (typically only about three hours a week) in school settings. We do have some information, however. Beginning in the 1960s, early research on the issue showed that older children catch up with younger children fairly quickly, i.e. progress through the early stages of foreign language learning at a faster rate.

In a small-scale study comparing English-speaking children starting French in kindergarten ($n = 4$) or grade 5 ($n = 6$), Bland and Keisler (1966) found the fifth grade starters took less time (4.5 hours vs. 12.5–17.5 hours) to reach criterion on an oral production task. Vocolo (1967) found that the MLCT scores of 31 English-speaking ninth graders with four years of French in grades 5–8 were only slightly better than those of 31 tenth graders after one year. Oller and Nagato (1974) compared the cloze test scores of a group of 233 Japanese children who had studied English-as-a-foreign-language (EFL) in grades 1–6 with those of a group that had begun English in grade 7. The FLES group was better than the later starters in grade 7, but the advantage was diminishing by grade 9, and had disappeared by grade 11. Ramirez and Politzer (1978) compared the listening and speaking abilities of a group of 46 children who began ESL/bilingual education in kindergarten with a group of 21 children who began at junior high school. The junior high school group had nearly achieved grade 3 level after six months, instead of the four years it had taken the younger group. A study by Holmstrand (1980, 1982), summarized in Hyltenstam and Abrahamsson (2001: 163), found no advantage in grade 6 children for those who had started English in grade 1 over those who had started in grade 3.

The best known of the early work, a large-scale study of approximately 17,000 students of French in English state schools by Burstall (Burstall 1975), is also often reported as having found no long-term advantages for an earlier start. However, this seemed largely to have been due to the fact that most early learners were mixed in with complete beginners at age 11, meaning they had to mark time while the later starters caught up. The same problem had afflicted the Oller and Nagato study. Reviewing the Burstall et al. report at the time, Buckby (1976; see, also, Bennett 1975) noted that when both groups were tested at age 13, children who had begun foreign language learning earlier (at age 8) outperformed children who had begun later (at age 11) on listening and reading tests, and performed equally well on measures of speaking and writing, *provided* they had been able to continue their foreign language study separately from the later starters, although, except for listening comprehension, the gains had been lost by age 16. Furthermore, Buckby noted, the achievement tests used to evaluate the cohorts at age 16 were of doubtful validity on a number of grounds and did not cover pronunciation or free conversational skills, two features that had been given special attention with the early starters and for which results on age differences in *naturalistic* acquirers suggest the advantages of an earlier start would be especially important.

3. Recent studies

Globalization, easier mobility for citizens of different countries for educational and occupational purposes, and greater economic and political integration across national borders in Europe and elsewhere have led to increased public recognition of the importance of foreign language learning. This, in turn, has triggered a resurgence of interest in the optimal timing issue and a second wave of empirical studies.

In general, the more recent comparisons of earlier and later starters of English as a third language in Catalunya (Muñoz 2003, 2006a, b) and the Basque Country (e.g. Cenoz 2002, 2003; García Mayo & García Lecumberri 2003) have reported no advantages for an earlier start, either (for review, see Muñoz 2008a, b; Muñoz & Singleton 2011). Such results have to be treated cautiously, however. When tested, students had received a total of 600 hours of classes (two or three hours of English a week) in the Basque studies, equivalent to approximately just 10 weeks of eight-hour days, and exposure, no doubt, to input less rich and more non-native-like than that commonly available to learners in the target language environment. The BAF (Barcelona Age Factor) project (Muñoz 2006a) involved some 2,000 students who had started English at age 8, 11, or 14. When tested, they had received 726, 416 or 200 hours of classroom instruction, respectively, equivalent to approximately just 13, 8, or 4 weeks of eight-hour days of naturalistic exposure, so Muñoz recognized that the results speak only to a short-term rate advantage. The older starters were usually also older when tested, which could itself be expected to convey a cognitive advantage. Muñoz (2006b, 2008a, b, 2011: 116) pointed out that advantages for older starters were larger when the ages at which students were tested were more significant in terms of general cognitive development, e.g. ages 10 and 12, than when less so, e.g. in the late teens. In both cross-sectional studies and at 18+, after secondary education was complete, older starters outperformed younger starters on more academically-oriented grammar measures. The groups were comparable on listening comprehension and sound discrimination tasks.

The question is whether any *long-term* advantages accrue to younger starters. To answer that question, it is necessary to test students after they have been exposed to far longer periods of input and opportunities to use the language. Three recent studies have attempted to do just that.

Working with 200 Japanese students of EFL, Larson-Hall (2008), found some modest evidence of long-term advantages for an earlier start, although once again, total L2 exposure was still not enough. Larson-Hall began by examining the relationship between age of onset (AO) and performance on DeKeyser's (2000) adaptation of Newport and Johnson's (relatively easy) grammaticality judgment test (GJT) of a group of 61 Japanese students who had begin English as a foreign language between the ages of 3 and 12 (mean 8.3), all tested when they were college students (mean age 19.4). Controlling statistically for aptitude, measured using a Japanese version of the MLAT, and amount of input, Larson-Hall found a statistically significant advantage for earlier AO *within* the earlier starting group on a GJT ($r = -.38$) once students reached a range of 1600–2200 hours of input, i.e. about 30–40 weeks, but not on a phonemic discrimination (r/l/w, e.g. read, lead, weed) task ($r = .03$). The advantages on the GJT disappeared, however, when input levels became higher. Also, *within* the group of younger starters, while numbers were too small for significance testing, there was a suggestive trend in the data for those who had started before age 6 *and* had had a native speaker (NS) teacher to do better on the sound discrimination task than those who had started before age 6 and had *not* had a NS teacher. The issue of when to deploy whatever native input is available is an obvious research focus for the future.

Larson-Hall further compared the younger starters' scores with those of a second group of 139 students, also tested at college age, who had begun EFL later, at 12 or 13 (mean 12.5) in junior high school. The mean age at testing (AT), again, was 19.4. The focus was on the learners' abilities after much longer exposure to the typical 2–4 hours of English input a week, and often, to additional hours of private classes outside school. In *between-group* comparisons, the earlier starters outperformed the later starters statistically significantly on the phonemic, but not on the morpho-syntactic, measure, even when amount of input was controlled for.

Thus, with the caveat that the n-size was small, the tests very limited, and the amount of exposure still only equivalent to about 43 weeks, Larson-Hall identified modest advantages for an earlier start in both domains. The key seems to have been to wait long enough for the advantage to show itself. After 800 hours, the later starters scored higher on the GJT than the early starters, paralleling results in the Spanish studies when students were tested after about 600 hours of instruction. As more input accrued, however, the younger starters began to show their stuff. The sound discrimination advantage for an earlier start appeared after 1200–2200 hours of input (equivalent to approximately 20–40 weeks). Motto: Do not test too early (or if you prefer, never drink a good wine before its time). In fact, Larson-Hall notes that one might reasonably expect the advantage of an early start to be strongest in phonology. The fact that it was not as obvious as that for grammar *within* the younger group may simply have been due to the fact that most students had experienced a majority of non-native pronunciation, with some having experienced no native input at all.

No advantages for earlier AO were found by Al-Thubaiti (2010) in a study of 132 college-age, female EFL students in Saudi Arabia. The research compared the abilities of a group of 50 who had begun English in elementary school between the ages of 3 and 11, with those of 82 who had started in middle school at ages 12 or 13, and both groups' scores with those of 11 native English-speaker controls. Using a cloze test, acceptability judgment, aspectual interpretation, and gap-filling tasks, Al-Thubaiti focused on five grammatical and semantic properties of English: vP ellipsis, resumptive pronouns, and adverb placement, and semantic differences between progressive and habitual forms and between preterite and present perfect forms. All four tests were unspeeded, off-line measures, each involving reading and writing; pronunciation and listening and speaking abilities were not assessed. vP ellipsis, resumptive pronouns and the difference in meaning between preterite and present perfect forms proved the most problematic for both groups. No statistically significant differences were found between the abilities of the earlier and later starters.

A rather different conclusion from Larson-Hall's – that in a typical limited input setting, an earlier start does not produce superior long-term results, whereas amount of input does – was reached by Muñoz (2011) on the basis of the third study. This involved 162 undergraduate Spanish-Catalan bilingual students of EFL, tested at university age (mean of 21.3). The average starting age for EFL was 7.8 (range 2–15.5). Mean total amount of exposure (English classes, plus periods of study abroad) during the intervening average 14-year period was 2,400 hours, i.e. the equivalent of about 43 weeks in a naturalistic setting. There was no statistically significant effect for AO on any of the three computer-delivered measures: a general proficiency test, a receptive vocabulary test, and a test of categorical perception of vowel contrasts, even controlling for amount of instruction. When subjects were divided into two groups, earlier starters ($n = 130$, AO = 2–11) and later starters ($n = 16$, AO = 11–15.5), controlling for amount of input, there were, again, no statistically significant differences between groups on any of the three measures. In contrast, controlling for AO, statistically significant positive correlations were found between global proficiency and vocabulary test scores and measures of exposure, especially recent exposure, including exposure in university courses, during study abroad, and frequency of current contact with English outside the classroom. Also, sound discrimination ability correlated significantly with current contact with English outside the classroom. With reference to typical limited-input settings, Muñoz concludes as follows:

> "In sum, the findings of this study confirm that in the long term input does not cease to have a significant effect on foreign language outcomes, and clearly indicate a prevalence of these effects over the effects of starting age in the long term." (Muñoz 2011: 129)

4.   An alternative interpretation

Note that if Muñoz and others are correct, the results for learning a foreign language in a classroom setting are, on their face, sharply different from those repeatedly observed in naturalistic SLA:

1. In naturalistic SLA, controlling for length of residence (LOR), AO is negatively related to ultimate attainment. In instructed FLL, controlling for LOR, AO is unrelated to ultimate attainment.
2. In naturalistic SLA, controlling for AO, LOR is unrelated to ultimate attainment. In instructed FLL, controlling for AO, LOR is positively related to ultimate attainment.

One can be forgiven for suspecting something is wrong. I believe several things are.

To begin with, findings on naturalistic SLA have suggested that LOR, a rough measure of total amount of exposure, *is* related to ultimate attainment, although seemingly for different periods, depending on learner age and linguistic domain (for review, see Krashen et al. 1979; Long 1990) – perhaps for somewhere between one and three years (Fathman 1975) or as much as five years for grammar (Johnson & Newport 1989; Munnich & Landau 2010; Oyama 1978; Patkowski 1980), and potentially indefinitely for lexis and collocations (Granena & Long 2013). Ten years of meaningful opportunity to acquire has become the minimum accepted standard for assessing both ultimate L2 attainment and (so-called) fossilization. Studies show, however, that the effects for LOR are relatively minor compared with those of AO. After an extensive review of research findings, Flege (2009) concluded that LOR accounts for only about 5–10% of variance in L2 speaking ability once age of arrival (AoA) is controlled for, and that access to input from NSs was the crucial factor, as shown by Flege and Liu (2001) and as suggested by some findings in both the Larson-Hall (2008) and Muñoz (2011) studies.[1] Where amount of exposure in the Barcelona study is concerned, while Muñoz writes (2011: 121) that "participants' mean length of exposure to English since the beginning of instruction was 13.9 years," what the data really showed is that *LOR up to a maximum of 43 weeks **during** the 13.9 years* – a period well within

---

1.   Flege also suggested, *en passant*, that few, if any, studies to date have measured input of any kind satisfactorily. He proposes the Experience Sampling Method (ESM) (Csikzentmihalyi & Larson 1987) as a more valid approach, because time-sampled logs, in which people report on their current L2 use, are more likely to be accurate than reports after the fact, which must be filtered through their memory.

the 2–5-year estimate – is related to ultimate attainment. This is a useful finding, but one that is utterly consistent with results in naturalistic settings.

Second, regarding starting age, in naturalistic SLA, AO and/or AoA have consistently been shown to be inversely related to ultimate attainment within a sample of learners whose AO ranged from 0 to 20 or higher. For perfectly understandable reasons, the sample in Muñoz's study is heavily concentrated in the far narrower range of eight to eleven, with a few outliers who began EFL either before or after that four-year period. The lack of effect for AO is most likely an artifact of the low variability in AO represented in the sample, making correlations between AO and anything else difficult, coupled with the fact that when the original 162 learners were split into two groups (those who had begun English before or after 11), there were 146 in the younger group, and just 16 in the older group, rendering average scores in the older group vulnerable to outliers.

Third, and perhaps most important, *all* 162 learners had begun EFL comfortably within the projected SP for morphology and syntax, meaning that one would expect their scores not to differ greatly after 43 weeks, or indeed, after the minimum desirable period for assessing ultimate attainment, 10 years of full-time exposure. Where scores might well have differed – with an advantage for the younger starters – was in pronunciation, but as in several studies to date, no doubt for valid logistical reasons, pronunciation and speaking skills were not assessed.

5. Needed research

Comparative assessments of the value of an early start to FLL face all manner of difficulties, such as the labor-intensive nature of measurement of listening and speaking skills in large samples, the scarcity in many countries of sufficient numbers of trained NSs of the target language, especially for young children, and finding valid measures usable with children of different ages. In addition, FL instruction in most countries, especially in school settings, still tends to focus on language as object, or code, not as medium of communication. That kind of instruction favors older starters, who can use rules, structured input, and conscious noticing better than younger children, and it simultaneously bypasses the advantage that younger starters' capacity for implicit learning could produce if they were exposed to rich, natural input in early FLES programs. Tests in these studies, moreover, tend to focus on *language-like* abilities, using off-line tasks, where declarative knowledge and metalinguistic awareness can be brought to bear by older starters, and often ignore pronunciation and speaking skills, where the benefits of a younger start would be most likely to show up. As Muñoz has noted, to get a fix on any true long-term benefits of an early start, studies cannot wait 245 years, which would be roughly the time required for students receiving 2–4 hours of FL classes a week to accumulate the equivalent of about 10 years of natural exposure. How, then, can the research question be answered?

I suggest that cases be sought out where a younger start, probably in pre-K or K, is utilized to expose children aged four or five to rich input and plentiful opportunities for interaction with NSs. Were NSs unavailable on a regular basis, children would be exposed to as much native input as possible, e.g. through the use of class visitors (especially age peers) and the use of technology. Essentially, teachers would strive to make lessons reflect situations like those that occur spontaneously when young children are engaged in play and age-appropriate problem-solving with a NS adult and/or NS age peers. Pre-K and K classes offering part-time or full-time FL immersion education would be ideal and are increasingly available in private schools in several countries in the Arab world, East-Asia, and elsewhere. After either one or two years of such exposure, as students migrated to regular elementary schools, instead of 2–4 hours a week of drill and kill, made worse by the early starters being mixed with beginners, the children would be allowed to continue as part of a group of similarly proficient children – and as anyone who has observed their own children given such opportunities can attest – after one or two years of quasi-naturalistic exposure, would be well on the way to substantial communicative ability in the FL. Compared with those of children who started the FL later, the testable hypothesis would be that both their off-line and, especially, on-line, abilities would be far superior to those of children starting regular FLES at, e.g. age 8 or 11. That alone should be enough to make societies where either near-native or native-like ultimate attainment is considered desirable reconsider where and when best to target their resources.

Such comparisons would, of course, confound AO with time on task, or total hours of exposure, meaning that additional comparisons would be desirable of groups offered one or two years of immersion-like opportunities later, during equivalent total amounts of exposure. But the issue facing many countries today is how best to raise foreign or second language proficiency in large segments of their citizenry, even if the new curriculum would involve more hours, earlier. Fortunately, the research on French immersion education in Canada shows fairly convincingly that learning some subjects, such as mathematics or social studies, through the medium of a foreign or second language does not entail lower standards in the content areas, *provided* the teacher has adequate command of both subject matter and the language concerned, and students are of comparable L2 proficiency. With the caveat that comparison groups have sometimes been less than perfectly comparable, research has also shown that bilingual children develop several transferable cognitive advantages over their monolingual age peers, including some that bestow benefits across the lifespan (see, e.g. Bialystok 2008; Bialystok, Craik, Green & Gollan 2009).

Given the critical importance of the timing of foreign language education or some variety of foreign language immersion in so many societies, it is obviously a priority for attention and serious research funding. I would look forward to the day when age-appropriate delivery of at least half of children's first two years of schooling through the medium of a foreign language was the norm, whereupon I am confident the long-term advantages of an early start, particularly, but not only, in pronunciation and listening and speaking skills, would be obvious to all.

References

Al-Thubaiti, K.A. (2010). Age effects in a minimal input setting on the acquisition of English morpho-syntactic and semantic properties by L1 speakers of Arabic. Unpublished doctoral dissertation. Wivenhoe, Essex: University of Essex, Department of Language and Linguistics.

Bennett, S.N. (1975). Weighing the evidence: A review of 'Primary French in the Balance.' *British Journal of Educational Psychology, 45,* 337–340.

Bialystok, E. (2008). Cognitive effects of bilingualism across the lifespan. In H. Chan, H. Jacob, & E. Kapia (Eds.), *BUCLD 32: Proceedings of the 32nd annual Boston University Conference on Language Development* (pp. 1–15). Boston, MA: Cascadilla Press.

Bialystok, E., Craik, F.I.M., Green, D.W., & Gollan, T.H. (2009). Bilingual minds. *Psychological Science in the Public Interest, 10*(3), 89–129.

Bland, M., & Keisler, E. (1966). A self-controlled audiolingual program for children. *French Review, 40,* 266–276.

Buckby, M. (1976). Is primary French really in the balance? *Modern Language Journal, 60,* 340–346.

Burstall, C. (1975). Primary French in the balance. *Foreign Language Annals, 10*(3), 245–262.

Burstall, C. (1977). Primary French in the balance. *Foreign Language Annals, 10,* 245–254.

Burstall, C., Jamieson, M., Cohen, S., & Hargreaves, M. (1974). *Primary French in the balance.* Windsor: NFER Publishing Company.

Cenoz, J. (2002). Age differences in foreign language learning. *I.T.L. Review of Applied Linguistics, 135–136,* 125–142.

Cenoz, J. (2003). The influence of age on the acquisition of English. In M.P. García Mayo, & M.L. García Lecumberri (Eds.), *Age and the acquisition of English as a foreign language* (pp. 77–93). Clevedon: Multilingual Matters.

Csikzentmihalyi, M., & Larson, R. (1987). Validity and reliability of the experience-sampling method. *Journal of Nervous Mental Disorders, 175*(9), 526–536.

De Keyser, R. (2000). The robustness of critical period effects in second language acquisition. *Studies in Second Language Acquisition, 22*(4), 499–533.

DeKeyser, R., & Larson-Hall, J. (2005). What does the critical period really mean? In J. Kroll, & A.M.B. de Groot (Eds.), *Handbook of bilingualism: Psycholinguistic approaches* (pp. 88–108). Oxford: OUP.

Fathman, A. (1975). The relationship between age and second language productive ability. *Language Learning, 25*(2), 245–266.

Flege, J.E. (2009). Give input a chance! In T. Piske, & M. Young-Sholton (Eds.), *Input matters in SLA* (pp. 175–190). Clevedon: Multilingual Matters.

Flege, J.E., & Liu, S. (2001). The effect of experience on adults' acquisition of a second language. *Studies in Second Language Acquisition, 23,* 527–552.

García Mayo, M.P., & García Lecumberri, M.L. (Eds.). (2003). *Age and the acquisition of English as a foreign language: Theoretical issues and fieldwork.* Clevedon: Multilingual Matters.

Granena, G., & Long, M.H. (2013). Age of onset, length of residence, language aptitude, and ultimate L2 attainment in three linguistic domains. *Second Language Research, 29*(1).

Holmstrand, L.S.E. (1980). *Effekterna pa kunskaper, firdigheter och attityder av tidigt på-boirad undervisning I engelska.* En delstudie inom EPAL-projektet [Early English teaching: Effects on knowledge, proficiency, and attitudes] (Pedagogisk forkning i Uppsala 18). Uppsala, Sweden: Uppsala universitet, Pedagogiska institutionen.

Holmstrand, L.S.E. (1982). *English in the elementary school.* Stockholm/Uppsala: Almqvist & Wiksell International.

Hyltenstam, K., & Abrahamsson, N. (2001). Age and L2 learning: The hazards of matching practical "implications" with theoretical "facts." *TESOL Quarterly, 35,* 151–170.

Johnson, J.S., & Newport, E.L. (1989). Critical period effects in second language learning: The influence of maturational state on the acquisition of English as a second language. *Cognitive Psychology, 21,* 60–99.

Krashen, S.D., Long, M.H., & Scarcella, R.C. (1979). Age, rate and eventual attainment in second language learning. *TESOL Quarterly, 13*(4), 573–582. Reprinted in S.D. Krashen, R.C. Scarcella, & M.H. Long (Eds.), *Child-adult differences in second language acquisition* (pp. 161–172). Rowley, MA: Newbury House, 1982.

Larson-Hall, J. (2008). Weighing the benefits of studying a foreign language at a younger starting age in a minimal input situation. *Second Language Research, 24*(1), 35–63.

Long, M.H. (1990). Maturational constraints on language development. *Studies in Second Language Acquisition, 12*(3), 251–285.

Long, M.H., & Adamson, H.D. (2012). SLA research and Arizona's structured English immersion policies. In M.B. Arias, & C. Faltis (Eds.), *Implementing educational language policy in Arizona. Legal, historical and current practices in SEI* (pp. 39–55). Bristol: Multilingual Matters.

Munnich, E., & Landau, B. (2010). Developmental decline in the acquisition of spatial language. *Language Learning and Development, 6*(1), 32–59.

Muñoz, C. (2003). Variation in oral skills development and age of onset. In M.P. García Mayo, & M.L. García Lecumberri (Eds.), *Age and the acquisition of English as a foreign language: Theoretical issues and fieldwork* (pp. 101–181). Clevedon: Multilingual Matters.

Muñoz, C. (2006a). The effects of age on foreign language learning. In C. Muñoz (Ed.), *Age and the rate of foreign language learning* (pp. 1–40). Clevedon, UK: Multilingual Matters.

Muñoz, C. (Ed.). (2006b). *Age and the rate of foreign language learning.* Clevedon, UK: Multilingual Matters.

Muñoz, C. (2008a). Age-related differences in foreign language learning. Revisiting the empirical evidence. *International Review of Applied Linguistics in Language Teaching, 46*(3), 197–220.

Muñoz, C. (2008b). Symmetries and asymmetries of age effects in naturalistic and instructed L2 learning. *Applied Linguistics, 29*(4), 578–596.

Muñoz, C. (2011). Input in foreign language learning: More significant than starting age? *International Review of Applied Linguistics in Language Teaching, 49*(2), 113–133.

Muñoz, C., & Singleton, D. (2011). A critical review of age-related research on L2 ultimate attainment. *Language Teaching, 44*(1), 1–35.

Nicholas, H., Moore, H., Clyne, M., & Pauwels, A. (1993). *Languages at the crossroads. A guide to the report of the national enquiry into the employment and supply of teachers of languages other than English.* East Melbourne, Victoria: The National Languages and Literacy Institute of Australia Limited.

Oller, J., & Nagato, N. (1974). The long-term effects of FLES: An experiment. *Modern Language Journal, 58*(1–2), 15–19.

Oyama, S. (1978). The sensitive period and comprehension of speech. *Working Papers on Bilingualism, 16*, 1–17.

Patkowski, M.S. (1980). The sensitive period for the acquisition of syntax in a second language. *Language Learning, 30*(2), 449–472.

Patkowski, M.S. (1994). The critical age hypothesis and interlanguage phonology. In M. Yavas (Ed.), *First and second language phonology* (pp. 209–221). San Diego, CA: Singular.

Ramirez, A.G., & Politzer, R.L. (1978). Comprehension and production in English as a second language by elementary school children and adolescents. In E.M. Hatch (Ed.), *Second language acquisition: A book of readings* (pp. 312–332). Rowley, MA: Newbury House.

Vocolo, J.M. (1967). The effects of foreign language study in the elementary school upon achievement in the same foreign language in the high school. *The Modern Language Journal, 51*, 463–469.

Aptitude-treatment interaction studies in second language acquisition
Findings and methodology

Karen Vatz, Medha Tare, Scott R. Jackson &
Catherine J. Doughty
University of Maryland Center for Advanced Study of Language

Research in second language acquisition has long posited that learners' individual differences affect ultimate attainment. This chapter reviews studies that examine how learners with differing cognitive aptitudes respond to instructional treatments. Most of these studies showed significant aptitude-by-treatment interactions (ATI), which suggest that the effectiveness of a particular type of instruction depends on stable, cognitive abilities, such as language analysis or working memory. From our review of this literature, we conclude that, although some interactions have been shown, there is still limited work using a rigorous ATI matched/mis-matched design. We therefore assess the strengths and weaknesses of existing ATI studies, as well as their practical implications, as it is our hope that future research will incorporate the necessary design elements to probe how tailoring instruction to individual cognitive aptitudes affects second language learning.

1. Introduction

Building on the premise that "people look as different on the inside of their heads as they do on the outside…" (Diller 1976: 342), researchers have long considered individual differences in learners, such as motivational states and personality traits, to be possible sources of variability in the effectiveness of instruction. Learners may also differ in their cognitive abilities, which are relatively stable characteristics that may affect how they benefit from particular learning situations (Snow 1998). Some examples of cognitive abilities include processing speed, perceptual acuity, and executive function. Much research, primarily in the field of psychology, has investigated how various characteristics relate to the effectiveness of instruction, and findings show that students with different characteristics can respond differently to particular instructional techniques, resulting in more or less learning.

In this chapter, we present a comprehensive review of research examining how learners' differences in aptitude interact with the type of instruction they receive during second language acquisition (SLA). Our two primary goals are (1) to assemble a comprehensive body of research that addresses the interaction between cognitive aptitudes and instructional treatments in the field of SLA and systematically review those findings, and (2) to identify the strengths and weaknesses in research design and methodology, in order to promote successful aptitude-treatment interaction (ATI) research in the field of SLA. To this end, the studies included in this review, although not necessarily originally conceptualized as ATI studies, all include an interaction component between cognitive aptitudes and instructional treatment. Crucially, they all provide some evidence of the extent to which the effectiveness of a particular type of SLA instruction depends on cognitive abilities. Further, all of the research reviewed offers some insight into how to study these effects empirically.

Because the notions central to ATI research are complex, the next section defines terminology that will be used throughout the review. We then present a straightforward example of a state-of-the-art aptitude-treatment interaction study from the field of education psychology, in order to provide an illustrative example of the terminology and concepts. With this background information in mind, we move on to describe the ATI research design and review ATI studies in the field of SLA. Finally, we discuss strengths and weaknesses of ATI research designs employed in the studies reviewed, and propose a set of elements necessary to conduct a successful instructed SLA study incorporating an ATI focus.

2.   Terminology

To begin, we clarify the terminology encountered in the studies reviewed. *Individual characteristics* is a broad term used for dimensions along which learners may differ, including personality, motivation, and experience, some of which are not necessarily stable characteristics, and, thus, may change over the course of a semester or lifespan. In this chapter, we focus more specifically on *aptitudes*,[1] which we define here as a constrained category of stable[2] cognitive abilities, that

---

1.   See Kormos (this volume) for an extensive discussion of aptitude.

2.   We do not intend to take a hard stance on the notion of stability. Some abilities conceived as aptitudes may be trainable, or may be impacted by experience. Additionally, many abilities may be influenced by temporary circumstances, such as sleep deprivation. The relevant notion here is *relative* stability, contrasted with qualities that are more inherently dynamic.

differ among people, and may allow a person to excel in a specific learning area under particular learning conditions. The studies we describe examine specific learning conditions, or *treatments*, which are defined as different instructional approaches. The treatment that is proposed to enhance learning for a subset of learners with a particular characteristic is often designated the *matched* treatment, whereas the treatment that is not expected to be as beneficial is the *mis-matched* treatment. Treatments that are neither may be referred to as *unmatched*. Differences in the effectiveness of a treatment (potentially due to aptitude) are examined in the study's *outcome* variables, which are often measures of proficiency gains.

3. Cognitive aptitude and instructed SLA treatment interactions

Researchers have long hypothesized that some learners have an aptitude for language learning, or an "ability to learn a new language quickly and to a high degree of proficiency" (Wesche 1981:119). More recently, they have aimed to investigate the important role of aptitude, particularly in post-critical-period learning (see Abrahamsson & Hyltenstam 2008; DeKeyser 2000; Granena & Long 2013) and to produce cognitive aptitude measures that predict who, among a group of students, has the capacity to attain the highest success in language learning, and who is less likely to progress beyond an average skill level (see chapters by Doughty (this volume), Granena (this volume), Kormos (this volume) for discussions of aptitude measures). The question remains as to how researchers have used aptitude measures to study the optimization of second language learning.

In the following sections, we describe the research design of ATI studies and review these types of studies in the field of SLA, which are still relatively scarce. This review provides the basis for our discussion evaluating the strengths and weaknesses of the SLA ATI literature, in order to highlight the elements necessary for a rigorous research design.

3.1 Aptitude-treatment interaction research design

As noted above, the purpose of the ATI research design is to take advantage of findings on individual differences in cognitive aptitude, in order to propose and test optimized training which may yield better learning outcomes for learners with differing abilities. In some cases, the ATI design is a method for studying the effects of what may already be occurring in classrooms when teachers individualize instruction. Intentionally matching and mis-matching the students' measured aptitudes with their instructional treatment variables, researchers can investigate the success of matching aptitudes to treatments by looking at whether an interaction of effects occurs, namely, whether the students who are matched outperform the students who are mis-matched. Figure 1, below, depicts one type of ATI study design for matching aptitude and treatments, as well as hypothesized outcomes.

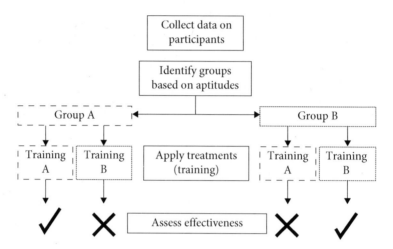

Figure 1. Example of an ATI research design

In addition, while some studies have followed the design in Figure 1, in which distinct groups are formed and then assigned to particular treatments, more have been exploratory and have treated aptitude measures as continuous variables (as opposed to grouping variables) to determine whether different relationships exist between participants' aptitudes and outcome measures based on the treatment condition. Nonetheless, the studies have in common the aim of determining which kinds of individual differences yield better learning in specific circumstances.

Figure 2 illustrates a hypothesized aptitude-treatment interaction effect, with two aptitude groups on the x-axis, achievement on the y-axis, and the two instructional methods represented as intersecting regression lines. This sample graph shows that the degree to which the instructional methods are effective differs by aptitude group, and indicates that, for students with mid-range aptitude, the type of treatment they receive does not matter.

Following Pashler et al. (2009), strong evidence for an interaction between treatment and aptitude would require a cross-over interaction, such that, for example, treatment A optimizes achievement for the low aptitude group, but not the high aptitude group, *and* that treatment B optimizes achievement for the high aptitude group, but not the low aptitude group. Conversely, a finding that both the low and high aptitude groups have similar outcomes under treatment A, but only the high aptitude group shows improved achievement under treatment B

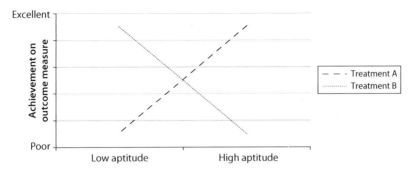

Figure 2. Example of an aptitude-treatment interaction

is *not* evidence of a strong aptitude-treatment interaction. In other words, the two treatments must differentially optimize achievement for the two aptitude groups, providing evidence that the aptitude groups represent distinct student profiles. This is not to say that studies using other designs do not offer useful evidence regarding how aptitude information can be used to optimize students' instruction, a point we address in the discussion.

3.2 Aptitude-treatment interaction studies in SLA

Many instructional SLA studies that include an ATI component are not explicitly labeled as such because the ATI finding was not the primary focus or because the participants in the study were not systematically matched to a treatment for the purpose of examining this interaction. However, such studies can, nevertheless, inform our understanding of ATIs in SLA; thus, we cover these findings in our review of ATI research. To this end, we included studies with (1) a measure of cognitive aptitude, (2) second language instructional treatment(s), and (3) an interaction between learners' aptitude and instructional treatment(s), as measured by language proficiency gains.

One of the earliest studies that sought to match students' training to their language aptitude reports data from an investigation of the language training program of the Public Service Commission of Canada (Wesche 1981). In this program, language learning aptitude, as well as attitudinal, physiological, and academic background data, were used to predict students' learning styles and to match students to the most appropriate method of instruction, in this case defined as audio-visual, analytic, or functional.

The measures used to assess language learning aptitude were the Modern Language Aptitude Test (MLAT, Carroll 1962) and Pimsleur Language Aptitude Battery (PLAB, Pimsleur 1966). Scores on those tests, in addition to information drawn from questionnaires and interviews regarding students' backgrounds and attitudes towards learning, were used to characterize students' aptitude and place students into one of three methods of instruction: most students were placed into (1) audio-visual classrooms, and others into (2) adapted analytical, or (3) functional classrooms. Wesche's (1981) study examined the efficacy of this process by taking a group of students whose aptitude profiles suited the analytical approach (based on various MLAT subtest scores), and placing half of them into the adapted analytical classroom (matched) and half in the audio-visual classroom (mis-matched). Analysis of the matched versus mis-matched groups showed that matched students had significantly lower scores on French class anxiety and higher scores on the following variables: interest in foreign languages, initiative to learn French beyond course requirements, general attitude toward the instructional method, and achievement tests for listening comprehension and oral expression. Wesche (1981) concluded that aptitude tests, along with other types of data can be used to improve the effectiveness of a language training program.

Another very early study to examine the relationship between language aptitude and instructional method is Hauptman (1971), although students in this case were not intentionally matched to a treatment condition based on their aptitude. The participants were children in third to sixth grades, who were taught Japanese for a short amount of time each day for three weeks. The aptitude measures were the MLAT – Elementary Form and the Stanford-Binet I.Q. test. The children were exposed to two instructional methods, structural and situational. The structural material was sequenced in order of increasing difficulty of grammar and vocabulary and involved drilling patterns and orally practicing single utterances. In contrast, the situational materials were age-relevant dialogues, which were introduced irrespective of their relative difficulty and involved orally practicing related utterances. All children took both the structurally and situationally oriented oral outcome tests. There were different patterns of results for children of higher and lower aptitude. Students in the situational group who had higher language aptitude and I.Q. scores performed better on the situational outcome test than the children in the structural group, whereas there were no differences for students with lower aptitude and I.Q. scores in the situational group or the structural group. Thus, even this short intervention showed that students' aptitudes interact with different instructional methods. In this case, Hauptman argues that the students with higher aptitudes might have benefited from the situational method because they were better able to abstract the grammatical principles.

The benefits of high aptitude can also be seen in a study by Sheen (2007), who probed the interaction between aptitude and type of error correction. She tested the relationship between English as a Second Language (ESL) students' scores on a language analytic ability test and their learning of definite and indefinite articles in two different treatment groups. The difference between the two instructional methods was the type of error correction the students received on an L2 writing task, which consisted of re-writing a story they had read and heard. The traditional group received feedback on the location of their errors and the corrected form, whereas the metalinguistic group received this feedback, as well as metalinguistic comments explaining the corrected form. Three different repeated-measure outcomes were employed to test students' knowledge of the definite and indefinite articles in a pre-test, post-test and delayed post-test design: (1) a speeded dictation task, (2) a story-writing task that used sequential pictures as prompts, and (3) an error-correction task, where students had to correct statements using *a* and *the* appropriately. Both treatment groups outperformed a control group on the error-correction test administered immediately after students received their feedback; however, the group that received metalinguistic feedback performed better on all three measures in the delayed post-test. Students' gain scores were positively correlated with their aptitude for language analysis, and this relationship was strongest for students in the metalinguistic feedback condition, suggesting an interaction in which students with high language analysis aptitude were able to take greater advantage of the metalinguistic feedback.

Like Sheen (2007), Robinson (1997) found that the relationship between treatment and outcomes differed by students' aptitude. The study examined the efficacy of four different learning conditions (which varied primarily in their degree of explicitness) on ESL learners' acquisition of simple versus complex rules. The aptitude measures consisted of the paired associates and grammatical sensitivity tasks of the MLAT; the outcome measure was a grammaticality judgment task administered after training on two syntactic rules. Aptitude for grammatical sensitivity was correlated with scores on the outcome judgment task in all but the incidental training condition. Further, aptitude and outcome scores had the strongest relationship in the implicit learning condition, in which students were asked to memorize sentences containing examples of the target structures, suggesting an interaction in which students with high grammatical sensitivity performed better in the implicit training condition.

The effects of training were found to interact with language analytic ability and working memory in a study by Erlam (2005), who looked at various components of language-learning aptitude and how they related to L2 proficiency. High school students in New Zealand learning French were tested on sound discrimination (PLAB), language analytic ability (MLAT Words in Sentences subtest), and working memory; however, the aptitude tests were administered after students had been through the instructional treatments. Thus, the instructional settings that students experienced – deductive, inductive, or structured input – were not matched to their particular aptitude profiles prior to learning. Their training focused on direct object pronouns in French, and they took pre- and post-tests, as well as a delayed post-test six months later, measuring their listening and reading comprehension and written and oral production. On all measures, the deductive training group performed best, followed by the structured input group, and finally the inductive training group.

Regarding interactions between aptitudes and instruction, better performance on the language analysis task predicted better outcomes in the inductive instructional condition. Additionally, the language analysis and working memory tasks predicted outcomes for students in the structured input condition, with learners with higher language analysis aptitude and working memory benefitting more in their written production, on the delayed post-test. These results suggest that students with greater processing ability during learning could maintain long-term representations of linguistic structures. There were no effects of language aptitude for the students in the deductive instruction condition. The interpretation proposed by Erlam (2005) was that the explicit rule explanation and language production activities in the deductive training benefitted all students, therefore having an equalizing effect.

Language analytic ability, however, was not found to interact with instructional method in Ranta (2002), which examined the relationship between language analytic ability and a communicative teaching environment. Ranta discusses language aptitude in the context of Canadian government policies that select learners based on their language aptitude scores. A government employee was found to have been discriminated against after she was excluded from language training because of poor performance on a language aptitude test. This situation brings up several interesting questions regarding how aptitude relates to proficiency and whether the type of instruction a student receives might mitigate the limitations of lower aptitude. Ranta examined the nature of the relationship between learners' language analytic ability and L2 proficiency measures when all students were engaged in communicative language instruction, in which functional language use, particularly speaking, is emphasized. To ensure fidelity to this teaching style, teachers were observed, formally and informally, and they completed questionnaires regarding their teaching practices.

The participants in Ranta's (2002) study were 150 French-speaking, grade-six students in a year-long ESL program. The students' language analytic ability was assessed through a metalinguistic task involving error detection and correction in their L1. The students' English proficiency, including aural vocabulary recognition and listening comprehension, was tested at the beginning and end of the five-month language intensive portion of the program, wherein the full school day was conducted in English, and again five months after the intensive training had ended. The clearest answer to the question of whether aptitude related to learning outcomes emerged from a hierarchical cluster analysis, which showed profiles of participants' scores on the metalinguistic task and L2 proficiency tasks. Two of the clusters showed an association between language analytic ability and L2 proficiency: The strongest students on the metalinguistic task had the strongest L2 scores, and the weakest students on the task had the weakest L2 scores. Therefore, the results did not support the hypothesis that communicative instruction would offset the effects of learner aptitude.

Two measures of working memory storage capacity – non-word repetition and reading span – were utilized in Payne and Whitney's (2002) study testing their hypothesis that individual differences in working memory would relate to L2 learning. Specifically, Payne and Whitney examined the possible interaction between participants' working memory skills and how they practiced L2 conversations and its effect on their L2 speaking proficiency. The treatment conditions involved students engaging either in traditional classroom-based conversational practice or in online *chat room* conversation with their classmates. The chat room situation was hypothesized to place fewer demands on students' working memory because previous conversational elements would stay up on the screen and everyone would type slower than they would normally speak. More students were expected to benefit from this treatment because of the reduced demands of the task. The researchers designed a proficiency measure for the study that would be sensitive to changes in a student's ability over the short period of the semester. Participants were asked to speak in the L2 on a set of topics for a period of five minutes. Their speaking was rated on comprehensibility, fluency, vocabulary usage, grammar, and pronunciation by examiners who were asked to consider a very fluent, but non-native speaker as the highest score.

There was a strong main effect for using a chat room conversational environment, with the students in that condition performing better on the oral proficiency outcome measure than students engaging in traditional practice. There was also evidence of an interaction effect, supporting the idea that working memory load was lessened in the chat room condition. The correlation between working memory and the oral proficiency outcome measure was higher for those students in the traditional classroom condition than those in the chat room condition, suggesting that working memory ability played less of a role in students' ability to engage in chat room conversational practice.

Working memory has also been shown to affect L2 learners' noticing of feedback. Goo (2012) examined the role of working memory capacity in Korean students' learning of the English *that*-trace filter construction (e.g. "Who does John think is reading the newspaper?"), in two different feedback conditions, recasts and metalinguistic comments. Participants were university students who took part in four sessions. In the first session, learners completed two working memory tests: reading span and operation span. In the second, learners took two pre-tests, a grammaticality judgment task and a written production test, both designed to assess their knowledge of the *that*-trace filter construction. The third involved an information-gap activity that elicited questions with a *that*-trace filter. Learners worked with a native speaker instructor to complete the activity and received different types of feedback in response to incorrectly formed questions. Learners either heard a recast, which is a reformulated version of the sentence that corrects the error, or received metalinguistic feedback, which is explicit linguistic information about how well formed the learner's utterance was. The last session involved participating in the information-gap activity again, and then completing the post-test grammaticality judgment and written production tests. The control group only took the pre- and post-tests. The analysis focused on which type of feedback was associated with the greatest gain in correct understanding of the construction and whether working memory predicted gains differentially for students receiving the two types of feedback.

The results showed that gains in the recast and metalinguistic conditions were not different from each other, and that both groups performed better than the control group on the posttest. Interestingly, working memory capacity was predictive of gains in the recast condition but not in the metalinguistic feedback condition. Goo argues that working memory is more necessary for success in the recast condition because the feedback is implicit in nature and, thus, more difficult to notice than the more explicit metalinguistic feedback. The recast feedback also required learners to keep their original utterance in mind while processing the corrections in the recast, which would require more working memory capacity. Thus, there was an interaction between learners' aptitudes and how well they were able to take advantage of this particular type of instructional feedback.

In a carefully designed study, O'Brien, Segalowitz, Freed, and Collentine (2007) investigated the role of phonological memory in L2 oral fluency development in two learning contexts, study abroad and at-home classroom. University students, who had taken at least two semesters of Spanish and who were enrolled in L2 Spanish classes either at their home university or in a study abroad immersion program in Spain, were assessed on their ability to retain phonological elements in serial order in the short term with a Serial Non-Word Recognition (SNWR) task. Phonological memory, the aptitude variable, is considered necessary for development of L2 oral fluency. Participants' oral proficiency was evaluated at the beginning and end of the semester based on four-minute excerpts of an Oral Proficiency Interview. Oral fluency comprised (1) overall oral ability, assessed by the total number of words spoken in the extract and the number of words in the longest turn, and (2) fluidity, assessed by the following four measures: speech rate in words per minute, absence of hesitations, absence of filled pauses, and longest fluent run. Oral proficiency gains were computed using a residualized change score for each of the six measures. O'Brien et al. expected to predict oral proficiency gains based on the phonological memory score, separate from the effect of the at-home versus immersion learning context.

Results revealed that learning context accounted for a significant amount of variance for all six oral proficiency measures: Study abroad students made greater oral proficiency gains than did at-home students. However, after controlling for the effect of learning context, SNWR scores also accounted for a significant amount of variance in five of the oral proficiency gains. That is, beyond the proficiency gains attributed to learning context, students with greater phonological memory made greater gains in proficiency than students with lower phonological memory in both contexts.

In addition to the findings of the main effects of learning context and phonological memory on developing oral proficiency, an interaction was found for two of the oral proficiency measures: amount of speech produced and absence of filled pauses. For these two measures, SNWR scores explained a significant amount of variance for the study-abroad students, but not for at-home students. The investigators do not offer an explanation for this interaction; however, it may be attributed to the fact that the study-abroad students had more opportunities in the immersion context to exploit their aptitude. An additional consideration is the difference in starting proficiency scores between the two groups, with the study-abroad students scoring significantly higher on two of the pre-tests (the absence of filled pauses and longest fluent run measures) than the at-home students. Their higher starting proficiency may have interacted with the role of aptitude, thus influencing the study's findings. In any case, the results point to the value of using an ATI study design to further investigate the relationship between phonological memory and oral fluency gains in the two learning contexts.

In a study explicitly designed to test an aptitude-treatment interaction, Brooks, Kempe and Sionov (2006) examined the role of participants' executive functioning abilities as a cognitive aptitude when varying the size of the training vocabulary they were given in their learning of Russian noun gender. The cognitive tests included Cattell's Culture-Fair Nonverbal Intelligence Test, which has been shown to be a good measure of executive functioning, as well as language-learning aptitude (Duncan et al. 1996; Grigorenko et al. 2000). The measures also included non-word retention to test phonological memory and reading span to test verbal working memory. The treatment variable was the amount of *type variation* of the nouns in the input that students heard when learning the correct gender declensions, during six separate training sessions. In this study, type variation was represented by the number of different words presented in the training input. All participants heard the same number of examples (24), but were pseudo-randomly assigned to three conditions where they (1) heard 24 different words once each,

(2) heard 12 different words repeated twice, or (3) heard six different words repeated four times.

The question of interest was the extent to which individual differences in the cognitive assessments could explain how learners are able to make use of the type variation in the learning materials when learning Russian inflectional morphology, as measured by their production of accurately inflected new nouns in the testing session. The greater type variation condition did not lead to more learning across all learners; only the participants above the median executive functioning score could effectively utilize the extra vocabulary types to learn the grammar rules. This significant aptitude-by-treatment interaction suggests that greater executive functioning, specifically attention allocation, allowed participants to take advantage of increased variation in the learning materials when learning Russian morphology.

In another input variation study, Perrachione, Lee, Ha, and Wong (2011) investigated the interaction between learners' perceptual ability and training in non-native phonological contrasts. The design of this study is especially noteworthy, in that the cognitive variable and training conditions were theoretically motivated, based on previous research, and were implemented in a pure match-mismatch ATI research design. Sixty-four English NSs completed a test assessing their basic perceptual abilities for pitch (as measured by a Pitch Contour Perception Test [PCPT]), which is hypothesized to predict success in learning lexical tones. Participants were divided into high ($n = 31$) and low ($n = 33$) aptitude groups based on their PCPT scores.

The two treatment conditions were low-variability and high-variability versions of the training input, in which participants listened to 18 pseudowords, composed of six different syllables produced with a level, rising, and falling pitch contour (that is, each of the six syllables represented three words minimally distinguishable by pitch contrast). Each pseudoword was associated with a common object, (e.g. bus, table) during the training. In the low-variability condition, participants heard the pseudowords produced by one speaker, and in the high-variability group participants heard the pseudowords produced by four speakers. Both groups heard each pseudoword four times, resulting in 72 trials during each of the eight training sessions. Learning was assessed after each training session; and learning achievement was assessed after the final training session by asking participants to match the spoken pseudowords to the correct object.

Generally, a high-variability training environment is considered superior to a low-variability training environment, in that learners are exposed to different exemplars of the feature they are learning, which should support generalizations. However, the researchers also point out that lack of consistency or predictability in phonetic features across input trials increases processing costs, which may impair some learners' ability to benefit from this type of training. To investigate the effectiveness of the variability in training conditions based on perceptual aptitude, half of the low, and half of the high, aptitude learners were each assigned to the low-variability and high-variability conditions.

Perrachione et al. (2011) assessed learning on three levels: learning *progress* during the training, learning *achievement* after training, and ability to *generalize* learning to novel speakers. The results for learning progress showed that the high aptitude group learned significantly faster than the low aptitude group, regardless of training condition, and both the high and low aptitude groups learned significantly faster in the low variability condition than the learners in the high-variability condition, although this was especially the case for the low aptitude learners. The results for ultimate learning achievement also revealed that the high aptitude learners outperformed the low aptitude learners in both training conditions. However, a significant interaction was found between aptitude group and training condition. The high aptitude group demonstrated significantly greater final learning outcomes in the high-variability condition than in the low-variability condition, whereas the low aptitude group demonstrated significantly less learning in the high-variability condition than in the low-variability condition. In other words, the high aptitude learners benefitted from the high-variability training, whereas the low aptitude learners were impaired by it. Despite this impairment, both high and low aptitude learners in the high-variability group were better able to generalize their ability to novel speakers than high and low aptitude learners in the low-variability group.

Overall, Perrachione et al. (2011) conclude that, while the high-variability training resulted in better generalization ability for all learners experiencing that treatment, the high aptitude learners benefited even more from high- than low-variability training, although not without cost, given their slower learning rate, and the low aptitude learners not only benefited more from the low-variability training, but were acutely impaired by the high-variability training.

In sum, the studies we have reviewed demonstrate that, within the field of SLA, aptitude-instruction interactions are often complex. However, the majority of instructed SLA studies that examine aptitude-treatment interactions do produce significant findings, indicating that more research on the effects of tailoring instruction to cognitive aptitudes is warranted in order to support greater learning.

4. Discussion

Our review of ATI studies began with the goal of examining research design and drawing conclusions pertaining to the role of cognitive aptitudes in instructed SLA. The key conclusion from the research findings is that cognitive aptitudes can interact with instructional treatments to yield differential outcomes for language learners with lower versus higher, or qualitatively different, aptitude. Furthermore, the review of these studies reveals that, in addition to the shortage of ATI studies in SLA, especially research explicitly designed to examine ATI, the aptitude variables and types of instruction vary drastically across studies, making it impossible, at this time, to conduct a meta-analysis of the research findings. Moreover, while many of the studies show that a particular aptitude is, indeed, relevant to the success of a certain type of instruction, there is not enough research on matching a treatment *a priori* to fit a student's aptitude profile to warrant any conclusion that the ATI instructional strategy would maximize learning.

Only one of the studies reviewed (Perrachione et al. 2011) employed a fully crossed ATI design, in which students were systematically matched and mismatched to an instructional treatment based on their aptitude. Despite this state of affairs, many of the studies reviewed include valuable research techniques that add validity to their findings. Next, we highlight strengths and identify weaknesses in these ATI investigations, in order to help guide future ATI research in the field of SLA.

4.1   Strengths of research design

As evidenced by Brooks et al. (2006) and Perrachione et al. (2011), a well-designed study can yield interesting and potentially useful results regarding how individual differences affect language learning. A common strength of these two studies is that the cognitive aptitude variables used by the researchers were well-motivated, based on prior research in the field, and chosen because they were hypothesized to relate to how learners would fare using specific instructional materials. Brooks et al. expected that a greater ability to use attentional resources would allow learners to make use of more word-type variation in the input, which is indeed what they found. Perrachione et al. matched a domain-specific aptitude, perceptual ability for pitch, to a training regimen hypothesized to benefit those with high aptitude and impair those with low aptitude. They placed participants into distinct aptitude groups based on a clear conceptualization and operationalization of aptitude that is hypothesized to interact with a certain type of instruction.

Another strength of the study by Brooks et al. (2006) is that the researchers attempted to control for learners' individual characteristics that were not being tested directly. For example, the participants had varying prior experience with foreign languages, so, in order to ensure that learning differences among the conditions were not due to language background, the researchers matched participants on this measure across the vocabulary size conditions.

Well-designed treatment conditions are also required, so that any lack of learning cannot be attributed to either poor quality of training or poor fidelity to the training regimen. For example, Payne and Whitney (2002) took careful measures in implementing their treatment conditions of online chat room versus classroom-based discussion groups; their two instructors each taught an experimental and control condition class, so that any differences found between the conversational practice methods could not be attributed to differences between the instructors.

In addition to mitigating the effect of different instructors, careful observation of fidelity to treatment can ensure that the training conditions are carried out as planned. Studies in educational psychology, such as Connor et al. (2009), have implemented extensive observations, where instruction was videotaped, and detailed field notes were written simultaneously, to capture what was not interpretable from the video alone (i.e. times children entered and left the classroom, explanations of events/activities that took place outside the camera's view, and descriptions of worksheets/activities). The level of detail of the observations allowed the researchers to document differences in instructional treatment qualitatively and quantitatively. Ranta (2002) also used an observation instrument and teacher questionnaire to ensure that teachers were employing the necessary characteristics of communicative teaching.

Finally, the outcome measure should reflect a skill that generalizes beyond the laboratory to real-world tasks. Examples of relevant outcomes are found in the study by O'Brien, Segalowitz, Freed and Collentine (2007), who developed a range of measures of participants' speaking fluency, so that specific effects of aptitudes and treatment conditions could be detected. The ATI outcome measure should also be designed to capture subtle differences in proficiency gains, in order to avoid failing to find a difference when there actually is one. Payne and Whitney (2002) designed their own outcome measure of fluency, rather than relying on the standard ACTFL measures, which are typically not sensitive enough to show students' improvement over one semester or to reveal differences between the treatment and control conditions. Additionally, potential interactions between aptitude and the outcome task should be kept in mind, as those with higher aptitude may show advantages on particular types of tasks (Kormos & Trebits 2012).

4.2 Weaknesses of research design

Several weaknesses are also apparent from the studies we examined. A common challenge in ATI studies is selecting grouping criteria that result in distinct aptitude groups. Wesche (1981) aimed to match students' aptitude profiles to their instruction, but she also used other information, such as interview data, in addition to the standard aptitude measures, to create those profiles. Therefore, it is hard to know how those other, more subjective, data affected students' placement. Of equal importance to creating groups that exemplify particular aptitudes is to ensure that the groups do not differ on other important dimensions that may confound the findings. O'Brien et al. (2007) did not control for students' starting proficiency in the two groups of study abroad and at-home learners. This confound makes their findings difficult to interpret, because the differences in starting proficiency may have interacted with the students' aptitude or learning context.

Weaknesses were also apparent in the implementation of some of the treatments. In examining how aptitudes interact with instructional methods, Erlam (2005) tested students' aptitude after they had gone through the treatment. In this case, there was no opportunity to tailor instruction to individual students' profiles or strengths, so it is unclear whether students' learning could have been optimized. Another weakness in the Wesche (1981) study is that, in addition to students' division into the two instructional types, other classroom adjustments were made to accommodate individual differences in, for example, students' hearing, memory ability, or job requirements. Therefore, it is difficult to draw conclusions about the success of matching to instructional types when the treatment was tailored to such an extent. While, eventually, using all possible information to optimize instruction makes sense, to advance our understanding of ATI, future studies should be more systematic with respect to aptitude placement criteria and consistent in keeping treatment conditions distinct.

4.3 Interaction patterns and implications for instruction

While Figure 2 illustrates a *classic* type of cross-over interaction sought in ATI studies, very few of the results reviewed here fit this pattern. Pashler et al. (2009) argue that showing this type of interaction is the only way to confirm theories of the effects of learning styles. These theories typically predict that learning styles are mutually exclusive, such that a treatment matched to one style should be detrimental to another. While related, ATI studies address a wider range of theoretical possibilities for learning; thus, many patterns of interactions other than the signature cross-over in Figure 2 may be informative. We briefly examine the general patterns observed in the studies reviewed here, and discuss how these different kinds of interactions may have very different practical implications for language learners and instructors.

First, three of the studies have results in line with the classic cross-over. Brooks et al. (2006) show that higher-aptitude learners benefitted from the higher variability conditions, while lower-aptitude learners benefitted from conditions with lower variability. Perrachione et al. (2011) found a parallel result in the domain of phonological learning, such that greater variability was beneficial for high-aptitude learners but detrimental for low-aptitude learners. While not precisely depicted by an X-shaped cross-over, these studies have the same implications as the classic cross-over interaction, namely, that the choice of instruction has an impact on both high- and low-aptitude learners. Wesche's (1981) results may be consistent with this pattern; however, it is not clear, because Wesche only examined the effects of instruction on one aptitude group (the *analytical* group). Nonetheless, she reported that the overall government tailored training program resulted in similar achievement for both analytical and audio-visual instruction types, which suggests that the cross-over type of interaction was occurring.

The other studies examined here all fall into a class of possible interaction patterns, whereby there was at least one treatment type for which aptitude did not appear to affect outcomes (or the effect of aptitude was reduced). However, the practical implications of such results vary greatly, depending on the relative success of the different treatments. One example is a pattern that identifies a treatment that *levels the playing field*; that is, one treatment produces superior results for all aptitudes, and moreover, leads to similar outcomes for different aptitude groups. Payne and Whitney (2002) showed this kind of effect, such that their chat room intervention appeared to result in improved outcomes for all aptitudes, and the relationship between aptitude and outcomes was attenuated for this intervention. The results of Erlam (2005) also showed this pattern, suggesting that the deductive instructional condition produced the best outcomes for all aptitudes, and, in this condition, aptitude did not seem to predict outcomes very well. Assuming that the interventions produced the best effects for all learners and displayed attenuated effects of aptitude, these studies are examples of the leveling effect of instruction, such that there is a single instruction type that benefits all learners and allows all learners to succeed at a high level, regardless of aptitude. The implications for both aptitude testing and instruction are that aptitude testing is virtually irrelevant, and the choice of instruction is very clear.

The converse pattern is one in which a treatment produces overall superior results for all aptitudes, but aptitude still plays a role within the treatment. In other words, the superior treatment *does not level the playing field*. From the studies reviewed here, Hauptman (1971), Sheen (2007), Robinson (1997), and O'Brien et al. (2007) may fit this pattern, although it is difficult to be certain, given the results reported. Remember that these studies are often not designed to examine an ATI. In studies by Hautpman (1971) and Robinson (1997), there appeared to be an instruction type that produced overall better (or at least not worse) outcomes across aptitudes, with the high-aptitude groups benefitting more. The pattern of results in the study by Sheen (2007) appears to show that the direct metalinguistic treatment produced better outcomes for all groups, but also that aptitude effects were shown in that condition. In the investigation by O'Brien et al. (2007), the general pattern of results suggests that study abroad was the better intervention, although higher aptitude learners were expected to benefit more from it. The implications of this type of pattern across these three studies is that the same instruction type might be chosen for all aptitudes, but that aptitude still plays a large role in outcomes. This means that some learners will benefit from a type of instruction more than others, due to aptitude, but a given instructional type is still as good, or better than other options, even for the lower-aptitude learners. This may have great practical importance, depending on how expensive (in terms of time or money) the superior treatment is. To illustrate, even if study abroad is the best option for all learners, if resources for this type of treatment are limited, then learners with greater aptitude could be prioritized, since they are expected to benefit more from the experience.

Finally, there is a third pattern, in which two treatments show similar outcome results in the aggregate, but one treatment's effectiveness varies by aptitude. Goo (2012) shows this pattern, because the metalinguistic and recast conditions appear to have similar overall outcome results, but the effectiveness of recasts is mediated by working memory. This means that learners with high working memory benefit from recasts, but learners with low working memory are hurt by recasts. Compared to the classic cross-over pattern, this pattern has slightly different practical implications, depending on policy decisions and the availability of aptitude testing. If aptitude testing is available, then selecting a treatment which matches aptitude level would be expected to benefit all learners. However, if aptitude is unknown, and it is more important for all learners to achieve similar outcomes than for one sub-group to benefit at the expense of another, then the treatment that does not benefit one aptitude group over another might be preferred.

In summary, ATI studies not only contribute to a theoretical understanding of language learning, but can also inform practical decisions related to the need for aptitude testing, the selection of instructional techniques, and the selection of learners to receive specially designed treatments. Even this review of a small number of ATI studies demonstrates that there is a wide range of implications, depending on the precise pattern of results. Merely identifying an interaction between aptitude and treatment is not sufficient. We, therefore, encourage future ATI research to report results with the implications for decision-making in mind. One way to frame this discussion would be to consider the following: (1) for a given individual and their aptitude scores, does one treatment produce better results than another, and (2) for each treatment, how does the performance of one aptitude group compare to another? Presentation of results in a manner that addresses these questions would allow instructors and learners to draw useful conclusions from a wide variety of ATI results, not exclusively the signature X-shaped cross-over.

5. Conclusion

It is clear from the studies reviewed that cognitive aptitude interacts with instructional treatment in second language learning; however, findings are often complex and difficult to interpret, thereby limiting applicability. Nonetheless, the different data patterns do provide some information about how student strengths and weaknesses might be leveraged, as well as valuable theoretical insights into the role of individual differences in language acquisition. This review serves as a call for more rigorous research design and methodology in SLA ATI studies. Meeting this challenge will result in a better understanding of language aptitudes, effectiveness of instruction, and, perhaps most importantly, how to tailor language instruction to individual differences in order optimize learning.

References

Abrahamsson, N., & Hyltenstam, K. (2008). The robustness of aptitude effects in near-native second language acquisition. *Studies in Second Language Acquisition, 30*(4), 481–509.

Brooks, P.J., Kempe, V., & Sionov, A. (2006). The role of learner and input variables in learning inflectional morphology. *Applied Psycholinguistics, 27*(2), 185–209.

Carroll, J.B. (1962). The prediction of success in intensive foreign language training. In R. Glaser (Ed.), *Training research and education* (pp. 87–136). Pittsburgh, PA: University of Pittsburgh Press.

Connor, C.M., Piasta, S.B., Glasney, S., Schatschneider, C., Crow, E., Underwood, P., Fishman, B., & Morrison, F. (2009). Individualizing student instruction precisely: Effects of child x instruction interactions on first graders' literacy development. *Child Development, 80,* 77–100.

DeKeyser, R. (2000). The robustness of critical period effects in second language acquisition. *Studies in Second Language Acquisition, 22*(4), 499–533.

Diller, L. (1976). A model for cognitive retraining in rehabilitation. *The Clinical Psychologist, 26,* 13–15.

Doughty, C. (this volume). Optimizing post-critical-period language learning.

Duncan, J., Emslie, H., Williams, P., Johnson, R., & Freer, C. (1996). Intelligence and the frontal lobe: The organization of goal-directed behavior. *Cognitive Psychology, 30,* 257–303.

Erlam, R. (2005). Language aptitude and its relationship to instructional effectiveness in second language acquisition. *Language Teaching Research, 9*(2), 147–171.

Goo, J. (2012). Corrective feedback and working memory capacity in interaction-driven L2 learning. *Studies in Second Language Acquisition, 34*(3), 445–474.

Granena, G. (this volume). Cognitive aptitudes for second language learning and the LLAMA Language Aptitude Test.

Granena, G., & Long, M.H. (2013). Age of onset, length of residence, language aptitude, and ultimate L2 attainment in three linguistic domains. *Second Language Research, 29*(1).

Grigorenko, E.L., Sternberg, R.J., & Ehrman, M.E. (2000). A theory based approach to the measurement of foreign language learning ability: The Canal-F theory and test. *The Modern Language Journal, 84*, 390–405.

Hauptman, P.C. (1971). A structural approach versus a situational approach to foreign-language teaching. *Language Learning, 21*, 235–244.

Kormos, J. (this volume). The role of working memory, phonological short-term memory and language aptitude in second language attainment.

Kormos, J., & Trebits, A. (2012). The role of task complexity, modality and aptitude in narrative task performance. *Language Learning, 62*(2), 239–472.

O'Brien, I., Segalowitz, N., Freed, B., & Collentine, J. (2007). Phonological memory predicts second language oral fluency gains in adults. *Studies in Second Language Acquisition, 29*, 557–582.

Pashler, H., McDaniel, M., Rohrer, D., & Bjork, R. (2009). Learning styles: Concepts and evidence. *Psychological Science in the Public Interest, 9*, 105–119.

Payne, J.S., & Whitney, P.J. (2002). Developing L2 oral proficiency through synchronous CMC: Output, working memory, and interlanguage development. *CALICO Journal, 20*, 7–32.

Perrachione, T.K., Lee, J., Ha, L.Y.Y., & Wong, P.C.M. (2011). Learning a novel phonological contrast depends on interactions between individual differences and training paradigm design. *Journal of the Acoustical Society of America, 130*, 461–472.

Pimsleur, P. (1966). *Language aptitude battery and manual, Form S*. New York, NY: Harcourt, Brace and World.

Ranta, L. (2002). The role of learners' language analytic ability in the communicative classroom. In P. Robinson (Ed.), *Individual differences and instructed language learning* (pp. 159–179). Amsterdam: John Benjamins.

Robinson, P. (1997). Individual differences and the fundamental similarity of implicit and explicit adult second language learning. *Language Learning, 47*, 45–99.

Sheen, Y. (2007). The effect of focused written corrective feedback and language aptitude on ESL learners' acquisition of articles. *TESOL Quarterly, 41*, 255–283.

Snow, R.E. (1998). Abilities as aptitudes and achievements in learning situations. In J.J. McArdle, & R.W. Woodcock (Eds.), *Human cognitive abilities in theory and practice* (pp. 93–112). Mahwah, NJ: Lawrence Erlbaum Associates.

Wesche, M. (1981). Language aptitude measures in streaming, matching students with methods, and diagnosis of learning problems. In K.C. Diller (Ed.), *Individual differences and universals in language learning aptitude* (pp. 119–154). Rowley, MA: Newbury House.

Subject index